BO
CAM

THEY DON'T MAKE THEM LIKE HIM
ANY MORE

Paul Firth

Paul Firth, Liverpool, United Kingdom.
paulfirth@blueyonder.co.uk

Page Layout by Highlight Type Bureau Ltd, Bradford
Printed by Hart & Clough Ltd, Cleckheaton

ISBN 978 0 9566984 2 1

A bantamspast publication.
P.O. Box 307, Shipley, BD18 9BT
www.bantamspast.co.uk
email: glorious 1911@paraders.co.uk

CONTENTS

ACKNOWLEDGEMENTS

This book could not have been written without the help of a number of people and organisations. I would like to take this opportunity to place on record my sincere thanks for all the assistance I have received.

Let me begin with the photographs. While I have borrowed many from Bobby's personal collection, a number of organisations have been kind enough to give me permission to use their photographs. In strictly alphabetical order, my thanks for allowing me the use of their pictures goes to the Bantamspast museum; Bradford City; Wigan Athletic FC; The Wigan Evening Post; and Yorkshire Post Newspapers. Dave Pendleton, the curator at Bantamspast, and Laura Brett, the archivist at Aston Villa F.C., have both been more than helpful in my search for photographs. The cover photograph of Bobby playing for Northern Ireland against Scotland at Windsor Park, Belfast on 28th April 1982 is reproduced by kind permission of Victor Patterson.

Most of the statistical research (and any mistake that goes with it) is mine, relying on the combined results of a number of sources. There is, however, one piece of that particular jigsaw that I thought was lost forever, namely Bobby's full playing record in his one season with Brisbane City. I am especially grateful to Mark Fowler of the website Antipodean Bantams, who came up with a game by game record of that spell.

So far as concerns the text, it will be obvious that several former team mates gave me information that has added considerably to the verbal picture of Bobby that the book seeks to present. I am grateful for the time that each of them took and for the stories they were able to provide.

Lastly, none of this would have been possible without the encouragement and support of one man. I have taken hours of his time, borrowed his photographs, drunk his coffee (and other beverages) and been privileged to share his great good humour.

Thanks, Bob. I hope you think it was worth it.

PREFACE

*'For those who never saw him play, Bobby Campbell is
more legend than fact.'*
(Michael Wood – www.boyfrombrazil.co.uk)

I had watched him play, so I had seen him score quite a
few goals before I had my first close encounter with Bobby
Campbell. It was a dark night and we were in an even
darker setting. The back few rows of that ancient Valley
Parade stand, with its dim lighting, was a gloomy place at
the best of times. Watching Bradford City not playing
especially well was a long way from 'the best of times'. But
I had long become accustomed to this way of life, having
been a Bantams regular for almost twenty years before
Campbell joined.

On this particular evening – and I can't remember who
we were playing – I had had my choice of seats in the
stand. In those days you didn't get a ticket with a seat
number and there was no queue when you turned up a
few minutes before kick-off. The only skill was in picking
a seat in the dry, so many were the leaks in that asphalt
roof. I was two or three rows from the back and toward
the Bradford End. There were very few people
sitting around me, but, until I had cause to look behind, I
couldn't have told you if there was anyone at all on the
back row.

What made me look round was the shouted – no, the
screamed – exhortations to the team. Not only were they
loud, but they appeared to be at the same time
strangulated and knowledgeable. It was as if they had
come from a fully qualified coach who happened to have
a sore throat. As I looked round, there were only two men
in the vicinity. I did not recognise one of them, but the
other was plainly Campbell, sitting just behind me in the
stand because on this rare occasion he was not fit enough
to play. I immediately concluded that the unidentified
man sitting next to him must be the coach with the sore
throat. It just shows we all make mistakes. Others, much

more famous than I, had been there before.

Although I was to watch him score many more goals, I was never to get that close to him again until Campbell was well into his retirement from professional football.

Anyone meeting Bobby Campbell for the first time needs to know nothing beyond the fact that they are looking for a personality. As soon as you walk into his current place of work, the personality comes up to meet you. You just hope it doesn't come up and hit you. Even now, more than twenty years since he stopped clattering centre halves, you wouldn't want him hitting you. He looks well over six feet tall, although he insists he was never more than six feet and half an inch. It was, he says, the big arms that always deceived the opposition into thinking he was taller.

In his playing days, he will tell you, he liked to weigh in at around 13 stone 10. If he got up to 14 stone, he would take remedial action. Back then he knew that any injury that prevented him from training had to be addressed by curtailing his lifestyle. Reduced intake of food and alcohol was required. In the years since he gave up putting his body through such rigours Campbell has put on a stone or three. Golf is his sport these days. And when your job is selling alcohol, it's hard not to have the occasional glass. What he takes in, be it food or drink, is these days more likely to be determined by a recent diagnosis of diabetes.

Being welcomed by Bobby Campbell inevitably entails being offered a drink. Once you've got a glass of whatever you fancy, he'll sit you down and talk to you. Some of his features may have altered over the years, but the unique, 'sore throat', voice was unchanged as he told me story after story, often with a chuckle, sometimes with a raucous laugh, occasionally with a touch of sadness. That voice and the still strong Belfast accent might mean you have to listen carefully for a few minutes until you attune yourself to how he speaks, but it is well worth the effort. In no time at all he's off on some sort of reminiscence. It might be about a football match or a night out. It might be about some coach's odd training methods or how one of his old team mates has carved out a new career. But it's always entertaining, always worth listening to and usually has a twist in the tail. He's a natural story teller and you really can't do better than just sit back, sip your drink and listen.

Football, the old heads will tell you, has lost all its characters. While I'm not so sure that some of the modern day players would entirely agree with that, there certainly aren't many around today like Bobby Campbell. There couldn't be. Their managers and their agents wouldn't allow them to be like Bobby, because the publicity they would attract would soon rebound on both the player and his club. The inevitable result would be either that the character would be 'reformed' or sacked. It took a lot of years and a few sackings for the Bobby Campbell character to be reformed and it had a lot of reforming to do. But it certainly was worth the wait, especially for those of us who saw Campbell play game after game and score goal after goal.

He has plenty to say about goals, as befits the man who holds Bradford City's all time goal scoring record. His tally of 137 goals is almost 50% more than his nearest rival. It is true to say that the previous record, held by Frank O'Rourke, includes some of those goals scored in Bradford City's most successful season, when the F A Cup was won and the team finished fifth in the First Division. But in the current era, where players move between clubs with almost the same regularity that the younger Campbell himself followed, the risk of his total being exceeded seems remote.

Campbell also has a few things to say about modern day football. His world seems completely alien to the vastly wealthy Premiership players of the 21st century. He himself says that he never made much money out of football, although he's very quick to say that he was given one or two other gifts of far greater value to him. His story bears many of the hallmarks of the players of the 1970s and 1980s, but it also has some quite remarkable features, not least the insight which he now has into his own behaviour.

While football and Bradford City play a central part in the story, this book is primarily about Campbell the character. Anyone who has ever come across Bobby Campbell will tell you that the word 'character' was invented for him. There are plenty of ways you can describe the Campbell character, not all of them especially complimentary. But, as others tell some unexpected tales about their former team mate on subjects he does not even mention, it slowly becomes evident that there are so many sides to his character, on and off the football pitch.

This, then, is the story of a man who has now had the same job for over twenty years, in sharp contrast with one spell of just over six years, in which he managed to play for seven different clubs (two of them twice each) on three different continents. It is also the story of a one-time very bad lad who now maybe regrets a few of the things he did in his impetuous youth, including jumping just a little too quickly when he accepted an offer from one particularly famous club. Most of all it is the story of a good old fashioned centre forward, who came back from a career-threatening injury at 19 and part-time football at 22 to the World Cup finals by the age of 25, even though he had been banned for life from international football.

I need to return to the subject of his voice one more time. A more detailed account of how the permanent state of the Campbell voice was graphically explained to the young Stuart McCall can be found later in this book. For the moment the only advice is to those who want to put it down to his smoking or to some blow to the throat. They are best advised to say nothing. The only opinion he's ever had that counts came from a consultant, who told him it wasn't a sign of something far worse. That voice and his way of telling a story are, however, so much a part of Campbell's personality that much of what he says deserves to be repeated verbatim. With that in mind, in the chapters that follow some passages are printed in italics. Each of these passages tells part of the story in Bobby's own words. I was fortunate enough to hear them first hand and I pass them on to the reader unaltered, so that others might be able to get some sort of picture of the 'legendary' Bobby Campbell sorting through the facts.

Chapter 1
BABY CAMPBELL

Any mother of a new born child will be naturally anxious to make sure that her older children, who will inevitably want to cradle the newcomer, know the correct way of holding a small baby. Picture the scene, then, sometime in late 1956 as Mrs Campbell is heard to emphasise to her twins, by then two years old, how important it is to support the head of their baby brother. Babies' necks, she explains, are not strong enough to sustain the weight of the head and extra support is essential.

Twenty or thirty years later, if you had asked about the weakness of his neck, anyone who had ever seen that particular baby Campbell earn his living would have given you nothing but disbelieving looks. By then Robert McFaul Campbell, Belfast baby, had become rather better known as Bobby Campbell, professional footballer and a man with neck muscles that could hold up the deck of one of those ships that he might have helped to build at Harland and Wolff's.

Mr Campbell senior was brought up just outside Belfast's Crumlin Road prison. In the 1940's and 50's those who lived in that area would make tea and coffee for people waiting to hear about the latest execution within the prison walls. Given where his younger son was eventually to enjoy by far the most successful part of his football career, Mr Campbell might have quite enjoyed telling stories about his roots in Bradford Street, Belfast. His roots may have been in Belfast, but he didn't feel the need to work in the city. It was through his life in the merchant navy that he was to meet the future Mrs Campbell, who was herself a nurse on the cruise liners which went to South Africa.

Bobby's mum was in her late thirties when he was born on 13th September 1956. By then she had enjoyed quite a career at sea. Although her parents were still alive in 1956 and running a small shop in Whitehouse, just north of the city, Bobby recalls that he was very young when his maternal grandparents died. His father's parents were already dead when Bobby was born, so the most familiar figure for him from that generation was his Auntie Annie. She was strictly has great-aunt, being his grandmother's sister, and Bobby clearly has fond memories of her.

She was an old spinster and she spoiled us rotten. She had her own little house, but she came to live with us once. She came for Christmas dinner and she never went back! She stayed until she died.

Among the younger members of the family there was a story about Auntie Annie's funeral, which Bobby admits may not be entirely accurate. She was quite a short lady, but was described as 'stumpy'. The story goes that the grave diggers had not been forewarned of the rather unusual shape of the deceased and that the coffin and the grave were of different proportions, necessitating a certain amount of last minute widening of her final resting place to permit the coffin to be lowered into the ground. In his more mature years Bobby concedes that, humorous as the story might sound now, '*you don't laugh when these things are happening*'.

Although little Bobby was the youngest in the family, it comes as no great shock when he says '*As it happens, I grew a lot quicker than my brother. They used to take me for the twin.*' The twins and their own families still live in Northern Ireland. They live in a place called Rathcoole, just to the north of Belfast, the area where Bobby himself grew up. Rathcoole was at the time the biggest housing estate in Europe, described as 'massive'. Houses on the estate were, however, much more modern than those Bobby was to encounter in the mid-1970's. The houses in 1960's Rathcoole had bathrooms, indoor toilets and gardens to the front and rear. When the 18 year old Campbell first came to Huddersfield, he couldn't believe it when he came across houses with outside toilets, something that had largely disappeared in Northern Ireland in the late sixties.

With three small children to care for, Mrs Campbell's career at sea came to an end. Her husband, however, remained in the Merchant Navy for some years.

When I was about 14, my mum made him stay at home because I was a bit of handful round the housing estates and she was finding it hard to keep us all in.

Bobby Campbell, a bit of a handful? Well, who would have thought that? And just who would have dared say so, except the man himself, of course? It also becomes clear that Bobby didn't see all that much of his father. Mr Campbell senior didn't end his sea-going career and finally come home to stay until Bobby was 14. Bobby was to leave his Belfast home before his sixteenth birthday, never to live there again. Mr Campbell, then, had very limited opportunities to give his son the paternal guidance that, later on in his life, Bobby clearly sought after.

But however much of a 'handful' young Campbell may have been for his mother, there was always one place she could expect to find him. If he wasn't actually on a football pitch, he would be practising out by the coal shed at the back of the Campbell home. From his earliest years Campbell and football just went together.

When I was a kid, we had a coal shed at the back of our house. I'd stand there and head a ball against the wall. I'd head it with one side, head with a full head and head it with the other side. Even when I was a young kid – and anyone who knew me from when I was a twelve year old would tell you – I could head a ball.

Those who during the 1970's and 80's were eye witnesses to Campbell's heading ability might go a little further than saying merely that he 'could head a ball.' Former team mates queue up to say how good he was in that aspect of a sport that is unique in using the head so frequently as means of propelling the ball. It is hard to find another player of his generation who could head one better. As a result, it is impossible to do anything but respect his opinions about strikers who can or can't head a football. Take, for example, this assessment of a twenty first century striker.

Peter Crouch can't jump and he can't head a ball. All he can do is touch it, touch it, touch it. I don't think the guy's got any neck muscles. They want to sit him down and put a weight round his neck. Or throw the ball up against the wall and say head that, move those muscles. That's how I developed when I was a kid.

When he wasn't practising his heading or using weights to build up his neck muscles, young Bobby was out on the field of play.

I played for school teams and a youth club. We used to play Saturday mornings or a Saturday afternoon. We played during the week as well, in the school weeks. There were times when we could change and have a shower by having a pull on the nearest tap. There were a lot of places we went to play where there were no changing rooms. You'd just put your kit on, take it off, wipe yourself down with a towel and put your clothes back on. There'd be a couple of kit bags where you'd put your clothes in while you were playing the match. You used to have to make sure there was somebody there watching the bags or you could be going home with just your shorts and your football boots. That's happened a few times with teams.

One of those school games should go down as a quiz question. The true football anorak reckons he knows who scored six goals in a game and ended up on the losing side. The non-anoraks should look at a 1961 F A Cup game between Manchester City and Luton Town for the answer. (To be absolutely accurate, Denis Law scored a total of seven goals in the tie, over one and a bit games, and still ended up on the losing side.) But there's another answer involving one game where young Campbell also achieved the same feat, although by a rather different method. Two of his Northern Ireland contemporaries were Jimmy Nicholl and David McCreery, both of whom went on to play for Manchester United. The tale begins with the simple fact that Bobby went to a different school to the other two. However, the story is then best taken up by the main player.

I actually played for David McCreery's school once. They came to play us one Saturday and were short. My old school team always laughed at me. They used to take the Mickey, because I always used to say 'You're nothing without me.' So I actually started on their team, because they were short and we had plenty of players. I scored four against our team, my own school, before they put me back in our team. I said 'It looks like you need me for the second half, lads.' I was talking to David McCreery about that and I was the talk of their school. He said 'We'd been hoping for you.' We were the top team then. He was telling everybody 'Campbell played for us in the first half.' This was one school team against another. You never played in a league. It was just a friendly Saturday game and then you played in the knock-out competition. We had a real team from first year to last year. I was just surprised that out of that team I was one of only two players who went on to make a career in football. And I scored four against my own school. I got two for my team in the second half. When I turned round it was 5-1 and I'd scored four. When I came back on in the second half, I ended up scoring two for my own team and we ended up losing 5-3 or 5-4 and I got six in that match, a double hat trick.

Bobby is generous both to the schoolmaster who was in charge of the team that day and about the reasons why the school had such a good team.

I don't think many schools would do that these days. I'll give our old teacher his due. There were a lot of games where we'd start the game and then he'd take us off. We'd maybe a bigger selection to pick from. Our housing estate was the biggest housing estate in Europe at the time. There were another two estates coming to our school, because our school was that big. The estate was called Rathcoole. Then there was Monkstown at the top and they were coming from Greenisland. So we had a pretty good nucleus of players. You started first year, so by the time you're in the fourth year everybody knows everybody.

It is the second of those comments, about the area in which he grew up, which inevitably leads to questions about what life was like for a Belfast lad in the late 1960's and early 1970's. During Bobby Campbell's teenage years the chance to earn decent money by becoming a professional footballer was not the only incentive to train and develop his skills. With a meaning which Bill Shankly surely never intended, football for Bobby and his contemporaries really was a matter of life and death.

In the years when Bobby was growing up on the Rathcoole estate, the majority of his neighbours were Protestants. However, as he himself explains, this simple fact did nothing more than reflect the overall balance in the province. As he reached his mid-teens, however, significant changes were on the horizon, changes which would permit even a loving mother to rejoice at her young son's desire to leave home. Sectarianism and The Troubles were taking over young lives, some of which were to come to a violent and premature end.

I was lucky. I got out in 1972 before it really kicked off, before it got widespread from the towns. It wasn't in the suburban areas then. It was more or less concentrated in the towns, the Shankill, the Falls, the Crumlin, the Ardoyne. You didn't ask your neighbours what their religion was when you wanted a favour. Nobody had anything, but whatever they had they used to share out. By the time I left and came back a couple of years later, the estate was all Protestant.

The note of sadness in his voice as he witnessed such a dramatic change in so short a time is explained by some of his own recollections of his youth. Even the very first professional football match that he attended illustrates the extent of the changes from the way things were when Bobby was growing up.

The first football match I went to watch was Linfield against Crusaders. I don't know why I picked Linfield. I suppose they were the best Protestant team at the time. Peter McCloughlin was a couple of years older than me, but we lived in the same street. He took me to my first match. My mum wouldn't let me go by myself. The funny thing was that Peter was a Catholic. That shows you what it was like, how we got on together.

When I was playing for the Northern Irish youth team, we had Catholic players there. No one questioned your religion there. I remember when I went to Villa, it was funny because we had about five players came over on trial from this one club from the Falls Road. I had a right laugh with them. I was a right Mickey-taker. Then on the Sunday I had to take them to the local chapel because they didn't know where it was. So there's me, had to sit all through a service while these five Catholics crossed themselves and I didn't know what to do. They came over to Birmingham for trials and I had to pick them a chapel!

I had lots of Catholic friends and lots of Protestant friends. In fact I used to go to a Catholic disco at a Catholic school on the corner of our estate. I had as many Catholic friends as I had Protestant friends. I've got on with everybody, if anybody remembers me from my Belfast days.It was a friendly place when I was growing up. You could go anywhere you wanted.

There was a family called the Monaghans, they had

boys called Sean and Bobby, who got assassinated. I used to help Mr Monaghan with his milk round for the Co-op for a pint of milk or two when I was a young lad. They were a lovely family. Their uncle was Rinty Monaghan, the boxer.

(For those not too good on their boxing history, John Joseph Monaghan, always known as Rinty, was the undisputed World flyweight champion from 1948 to 1950. He was forced to give up his title after contracting chronic bronchitis.)

Andy Monaghan had a bar called Monaghan's in Belfast, which my brother used to go to a lot. Andy used to ask about me. He actually said it was a non-sectarian pub. Everybody was welcome in that pub.

Then there were the McLauchlins. We used to have the fire at the back of their house. We used to have a party at their house and all the adults would get together. Back then it was just a party thing; it was something that happened three hundred years ago that we used to laugh about. How it got so serious I'll never know. If any Irishman thinks back to the start of The Troubles, they had as many Catholic friends as they had Protestant. The Troubles just divided everybody down the middle.

As Bobby talks about the Belfast friends he left behind when he came to England to pursue a football career, the tone of his voice reveals his great sadness over the tragedy of those wasted years. The words in print may seem somewhat prosaic. If they do, then they fail to reflect the obvious sorrow in which he remembers those young people who never grew old.

I had a few friends who were assassinated, one just for courting a Catholic girl. That was after I'd left. The captain of our school team, Brian Smyth, could have been a fair player. I was surprised he never got in the Northern Ireland team – he ended up getting stabbed to death on his own estate. He would only be about 19 at the time. He could have had a football career. There was a bloke called Noaky

Shaw, who was a hard man for Summerdale. He ended up getting murdered on stage – pistol whipped and then shot, because he was a young lad. He was only about 17, but he was a hard man for his age. Because he stood up against these older men, they tried to make an example of him. That just shows you how that place went.

When Bobby talks about Noaky, the surprising thing is that he describes the football field as though it were some sort of sanctuary, a place immune from whatever conflicts were growing in the streets.

Me and Noaky used to have a lot of battles when he played for Summerdale. Although Noaky was from the town, from the Shankill, and I was from Rathcoole, that was just a sporting vendetta when we played against them – nothing was carried on afterwards.

Remember that in Bobby's own words Noaky was 'a hard man' and you can only imagine what sort of 'battles' they must have had on the field of play.And then, in the midst of the same conversation about his one-time football opponent, Bobby's train of thought takes a sudden and serious turn toward the wider world in which he grew up. Noel 'Noaky' Shaw's body was found on 30th November 1975. He was 19 at the time of his death, a brutal killing, part of a feud within the Ulster Volunteer Force and attributed to a gang known as the Shankill Butchers.

What happened to him would have happened to me.If I hadn't got out of Ireland, I could easily have gone down the same street as him.The good thing about it was that I got out of that place before it got serious. Life was very cheap in Northern Ireland at that time. They'd knee-cap you for nothing. You were easily dragged in because it was easier for your protection and easier for you just to get on with your life. You didn't have to do anything, but you did have to show support. It would come to that point where they'd say 'If you're not with us, you're against us.' A lot of the time you weren't allowed to sit on the fence.

You had to take a side.

Although Bobby's mind is still very much on those old friends he played football with or against, he can no longer take his thoughts off the wider issues facing all those of his generation in Northern Ireland. When he begins to recall another of his old footballing mates, for a short time he is back on the pitch. But very soon The Troubles take over again. This is Bobby talking about a team mate from his school football days starting in 1968. In a team that seems to have won every competition it entered, Campbell is recorded as having scored 31 goals that season. Another 24 goals were scored by a lad called Robert Skillen. Campbell's story concerns an incident about five years later.

He could have been a good footballer. He hit the old wine even at that age. At that age you used to get a bottle of cheap wine, got to a youth club and try to dance all night and pull a bird. Or a quick bottle of Harp or Carlsberg Special to get hammered. On a street corner you'd get these people coming up and more or less putting their own curfew on. One of them told Skillen it was time he was off home and he said, more or less, 'sod off.' Skillen was only 16 or 17, but he could handle himself. Anyway, they tried to manhandle him. He battered a couple of them, thought nothing of it and went home. A couple of hours later there were five of them at the door. 'We're coming to take you to Romper Room.' Romper Room was a place they used to take them away and do their own little things. It was actually a little showbiz programme in Belfast at the time that the kids used to watch. The kids used to want to play. This was how it got its nickname, their version of Romper Room.

Anyway, Skillen knew they were going to come in for him, so he opened the door, smacked one and ran. He lived down the glen for a couple of days or stayed out of the way for a couple of days, until his brother-in-law, one of the Nicholls, who were a handy family and well involved, sorted it out, saying 'Leave him alone. He's my family.' If Skillen hadn't got that family, they could still have gone looking for him.

Another resident of the Rathcoole estate was Bobby Sands. He was two years older than Campbell and, at almost exactly the same time as the apprentice footballer was leaving Rathcoole for Birmingham, Bobby Sands and his family were moving to another estate in west Belfast. In 1981 Sands was elected to Parliament while serving a 14 year sentence for a firearms offence. By the time of his election he was already on hunger strike and, within weeks of becoming a Member of Parliament, he was to die in prison. But, in typical Campbell fashion, Sands is remembered first and foremost by reference to the football team that he played for, The Star of the Sea.

That team was made up of at least five Protestants from Rathcoole. But Bobby Sands was kicked out of Rathcoole. You feel sorry for all of those people. They've had thirty years wasted.

Having lived away from his native city for so many years and with the maturity that comes with having seen many other cities throughout the world, Bobby Campbell can now make a very stark historical comparison, perhaps one that many from Northern Ireland have made over the years.

It goes back too far. Nobody hates the Germans any more, yet we were at war with them twice. Yet there's Catholics and Protestants hating each other for 300 years. The atrocities that the Germans did to the European people, it goes way higher than what the Protestants and Catholics have done to each other in the last umpteen years. I just hope now that it becomes a nice place to live again. The Antrim coast, nothing better.

And anyone who has travelled along the Antrim coast will have no difficulty in agreeing with that last sentiment.

This brief account of the fate of some of his footballing contemporaries and rivals brings Bobby to the turning point in his life, indeed to what he would say was the moment which probably saved his life. But it was a turning point that was not as inevitable as it might appear with the benefit of hindsight.

I didn't always know I was going to be a professional footballer. I'd set my mind on being an engineer, carpentry, the army, even the navy. I think whatever I'd done, I'd have moved away. My dad was in the navy, my mum preferred the navy. I just thought everybody likes to see the world, don't they? I'd probably have got my qualifications and cleared off. If you can get them while you're doing it, well even better. So I was thinking about the army.

We all joined the army cadets when we were kids. I think that was to keep you off the street. There was a big hall. There was a gym there. You could mess about. You got a free pair of army boots, which saved your mother a tenner. It wasn't that disciplined. It was more like a youth club. I think it was easier than trying to rope you in and then, when you signed up, then you did the marching. There were Catholics and Protestants. At that time before I left Ireland there wasn't the sectarianism. On my estate there was Catholic and Protestant. Everybody got on. Within the space of three years everybody didn't get on. That was after I left. I had a lot of good friends from both sides. I like to think that if I bumped into them nowadays they would still say Hello, that they wouldn't be calling me. I was always one that was easy going. I got out when I planned to get out.

It was embarrassing about my qualifications. My last two years at school I never did one exam. I was either playing football, hockey or basketball. I remember going to Harland & Wolff shipyard. You had to take your four years' exams. I went for my interview for engineering. I was asked where my exams for the third and fourth year were and I said I was playing football for school and representing Northern Ireland. 'Oh yes, you're young

Campbell. *Off you go.'* All my uncles worked in the shipyard. In those days if your uncle worked in a local factory, you could get a job there. I think if I'd joined the army, they wouldn't have been looking for my qualifications either. They would have been looking for my sports. I was always told that if you did sports well, the army was a good life.

But neither Harland & Wolff nor the army was to benefit from having Bobby Campbell in their ranks.

Chapter 2
FROM BELFAST TO BIRMINGHAM

During his schooldays Bobby Campbell, by his own admission, spent a huge amount of time on the football field, at the risk of his more formal education. Despite the prospect of getting an apprenticeship, all his eggs were very firmly in the one basket, aiming for life as a professional footballer. He was well aware that the vast majority of the young lads who were given the opportunity even to take the first few steps along that road were destined never to make a living from their skills. But Bobby admits that he was one of the lucky ones, who did indeed make a career out football. In the end he didn't need the paper qualifications that would have been required to get him a more conventional job.

I actually started at full back. I played left back for my school in my first year. Then I played inside right, midfield, because I had a good engine. I was 13 then. Then I was an out and out striker from 13 or 14. I was going to be a goalkeeper or a centre half, but because I was a big bugger they said 'Get him up front and score some goals.' That has always been me. Never a change from then on. I always fancied myself as a centre half. I never thought of doing it later on because I'd lost that bit of pace and my old leg played me up. Although you don't do a lot of running, you've got to be quick on the turn. I wasn't that quick on the turn. I was quick at turning when I had to turn, but not turning to chase somebody.

From those school games where he washed under a tap

and needed someone to keep an eye on the kit bags Bobby's progress was rapid.

I played in trials and in a schools league on a Saturday. There were always scouts knocking about. I played for the international team as a schoolboy - the Northern Irish Schoolboys. I scored against England. We went to England and we drew one apiece. I scored against Scotland. I had a decent game against Wales. We won 3-0 there. In fact I think we'd have won the championship that year if we hadn't had to go to Scotland.

It wasn't, in Bobby's opinion, the fact that the Scottish Schoolboys were so much better than the Northern Irish lads. It was the fact that the game was away from home that caused the problems.

For the Scotland match we were up in the morning from 6.00. We went over on the 7.30 ferry from Larne to Stranraer; we played the match at dinner time; we were back on the ferry for about 4.30 and we were back in Northern Ireland for 7.30. I was lucky because I'd been a few times. The last school I went to, the Scots would come over one year and we went over there the next. So I'd been over a couple of times and I knew what it was like. But some of our lads were just as sick as a dog. It's where the Irish Sea meets the Atlantic Ocean. It may be only a three hour crossing, but it can be a nasty crossing. We didn't have a nice flat day that day and the young lads were sick.

We were 15 year olds and the most they'd been was out on a row boat on the Belfast Lough. When we got there, everybody was knackered. A lot of them didn't want to eat anything because their stomachs were turned. You could see them. It was a struggle. We lost 2-1. If they'd had to come to Belfast, we'd have beaten them. That was after going to England. We were lucky when we went to England. I think the English FA paid for us to go over because they refused to come to Ireland because of The Troubles. I think what they did was they put us up in hotels in England. I don't think Northern Ireland could have afforded it.

That trip to England with the Northern Ireland Schoolboys team brings back some personal memories for Bobby of the lads he played with and against.

Jimmy Nichol from Man United was in that team. Butch Wilkins was in the England side. John Trewick was in the England side.

For the benefit of those who do not wish to be classified as 'football anoraks', John Trewick played over 300 league games for West Bromwich Albion, Newcastle United, Oxford United (in their better days) and Birmingham City, before going into management with Hereford United. He is also famous for making the comment, which he insists was a joke, during a West Brom trip to China, that 'once you've seen one wall, you've seen them all.'

While some of those schoolboys went on to much greater things in their footballing careers, one other member of the English team may not have reached the same heights, but became a friend and, in some ways, an inspiration for Bobby.

A guy called Frank Pimblett, he became a very good pal of mine when we signed for Aston Villa. He was from Huyton, a right Scouse scallywag. I always felt sorry for Frank. He was a bit like me. In his early days he let himself go a bit. Although Ray was already signed up for Chelsea, every club wanted Frank. He chose Villa. Thinking back, maybe he'd have been better choosing Liverpool or Everton, because that's where he came from. Maybe his family wanted him out of Liverpool, just like they wanted me out of Belfast. Sometimes maybe it's better to have some family there just to hold you back when you go off the beaten road. I think that's what happened to me and Frank in our early days.

Bobby's reflections on those early days of his career at Aston Villa alongside the young Frank Pimblett give the first hint of regret about the lack of a mentor. Just as Campbell had played as a schoolboy alongside future Northern Ireland internationals, so Pimblett had been part of the same Huyton boys team as Peter Reid, who went on to win 13 England caps. But by the time Bobby met up again with Frank, they had both slipped a long way down the professional ladder. Campbell had to reach his 23rd birthday before greater maturity was to bring about a true turning point in his football career and, indeed, in his entire life.

Frank ended up in Australia in part-time football. I ended up in Australia for a bit in part-time football, but I came back and had a go at Bradford. I said to Frank 'I'm not accepting this. I'm going to have another go.' I managed to make a little bit of a come-back, but not to the standard I should have done.

Those who watched Bobby Campbell as he made his 'little bit of a come-back' must wonder what sort of standard he might have achieved if he had done what he 'should have done'. Fans and managers alike can now only wonder and imagine where the Northern Irish Schoolboy might have ended up, if he had had the right supervision and attitude off the pitch during his early career.

All the chief scouts went to the schoolboy international matches. They were from numerous clubs, including Arsenal. They actually wanted me to team up with Frank Stapleton. I played against Frank in a friendly against the Republic. I think he actually scored and they beat us 1-0. He's the same age as me. He had an excellent career with Arsenal. He was a very fit lad. If you're dedicated, you get the rewards at the end of the day. Of course he didn't get the injuries I got as a younger lad.

Scouts would go see your school teacher or whoever was coaching you. If he knows he's legit, he'll give him all the details. Usually they knew each other from years gone by. I had Wolves, Everton, Man United, Man City and Villa and a couple of other teams interested in me. I went to

17

Derby on trial. I never kicked a ball in a match. I couldn't understand that.I was a week at Derby and never played a competitive match. All I did was muck in with the apprentices and play two-touch football, which I'd never played before in my life. For a young kid that's just come in, to play two-touch football is very hard, especially when you're a forward and you want a few touches to take a player on and have a shot. I was only 15.

Eleven years later the same Derby County were to pay a transfer fee to acquire the services of the full international that Bobby Campbell had by then become. While his second stay at the Baseball Ground lasted a little longer than a week, it would be fair to say that neither was exactly a resounding success. Even the complaint about two-touch football was to be repeated.

I went to Villa and had a look round. I rushed in at Villa. I could have gone to Man United. They came knocking at the door. Jimmy Nichol came in. I said 'No, I'm going to go to Villa.' It was one of my main regrets, because at least at Man United they let you come home on a lot more regular basis to keep with your family.

While there may be plenty of professional footballers who may think they should have gone to Manchester United, there can't be too many who actually had the opportunity to do so and turned it down in favour of a club who were one division lower. There are not that many things in his life that Bobby Campbell would change, even with the benefit of considerable hindsight. A decision he made as a fifteen year old is certainly one thing he would change. But another decision he made at the same age is one he certainly has no cause to regret.

I was offered the chance to play in the Irish League, but I turned it down. Once you signed, you were stuck there. Then they started on about wanting transfer fees or wanting this or wanting that. A lot of Irish League clubs wanted me to sign on their junior books, but at that time if you signed on junior or school books, even with Man

United or anywhere like that, you were tied to them. I always wanted to keep my options open.

We all know the old saying about those who rush in where angels fear to tread. Nobody would ever describe Bobby Campbell as an angel, but perhaps his self-confessed 'rushing in' at Aston Villa might best be attributed to his youthful exuberance rather than to any foolishness. In any event, there was never any serious prospect of young Bobby staying put in Belfast.

If Villa hadn't come along, I would have got out anyway, probably joined the army or the navy. Villa came in and that was it. I got out at 15. My mum did an Irish jig when I left Ireland because she knew I was getting out. My mum could see what was coming.Even though I was leaving home at 15, she was glad.

Still short of his sixteenth birthday, Bobby Campbell's footballing dreams were on the verge of being fulfilled. Every sports-mad boy of his age would have thought that life could not offer more than being taken on as an apprentice by one of the most famous football clubs in England, even if Aston Villa were going through one of the less successful periods in their long history. It didn't take long, however, before the young Campbell wasn't quite as pleased as his mother to be leaving his native Northern Ireland.

It doesn't really hit you until you start at the other places and you can't do the normal things you do at home. You throw your dishes down and you throw your clothes down. All of a sudden you're in like a youth hostel and you have to be responsible for your own room. It was like being in junior boot camp. I was in that hostel for two years. That was the problem. Apart from the local lads, who went home, bickering developed and a few fights. A few lads moved out and couldn't hack it. They didn't like being wrapped up all day long. I came from Ireland and liked to stay out all night down the glen at weekends. When I did sign pro, all of a sudden it was as if I'd done three years in the nick. I was off out playing. My only problem was, when I did get out, I should have had a probation officer to keep hold of me, somebody to say 'You've had your little blow-out. Get home now.'

We didn't have to do our own washing or cleaning. That was one good thing. You were just tied up. You felt as if you were in prison the whole time.

Mrs Campbell had obviously looked after her son extremely well, despite his being a handful. While she and her husband were mightily relieved that their son was escaping from the violence that she foresaw, they themselves had no intention of leaving Belfast. Bobby makes the comparison with one of his future team mates, Jimmy Nichol. As a schoolboy Jimmy joined Manchester United. The club found a job for his father and a whole new life for his family. But Bobby does not believe that his parents, his brother or his sister would have made the same move, even if it had been available to them.

He describes himself as a big lad for his age. But the Bobby Campbell who arrived at Villa Park in the summer of 1974 was still only fifteen years old and had a lot of growing up to do. He was going to embark on this important stage of his personal development in a strange environment, away from all his family and friends, without the guiding hand that he needed (although he himself may not have realised at the time just how great that need was) and in a profession where the vast majority of his contemporaries would fail within their first two years as full-time football players.

His parents' wish to get him away from Northern Ireland and his own obvious desire to play professional football were always going to be too strong a combination to allow for such fine judgements as which English club he should join. The decision was made and Bobby went straight from school to an apprenticeship - not at Harland & Wolff, but at Villa Park.

Chapter 3

THE APPRENTICE

When the fifteen year old Bobby Campbell arrived at Aston Villa for the start of the 1972-3 season, he was not only 'a big lad', but, as he himself says, he was 'a cocky lad'. He had already come to the conclusion that having a touch of arrogance was the only way to get on in the highly competitive world where he hoped to make a name for himself.

You needed that little bit of confidence in yourself. There were a lot of guys that did come who were so quiet that they ended up getting overlooked. You've got to be forceful. Some players have been quiet all their lives, wouldn't say boo to a goose, but they're not the ones that are going to be waking up a game. To me young lads have got to be seen to be doing something. If you want to get on, you've got to be seen to be doing something, whether it's talking, shouting or even kicking somebody. We had to get through to the coach, who would always tell us to get stuck in. Everybody wanted the effort first and the skill afterwards. Once you were seen putting the effort in, you were half-way there.

In the summer of 1972 Aston Villa were just coming out of something of a low point in their long and illustrious history. They had just had their first taste of life in the Third Division. Campbell had gone along to Villa Park during the 1971-72 season and had seen for himself the start of Villa's rise back up the Football League.

When I joined Villa they were actually a third division

club. You could see they were definitely going to win promotion. They were averaging crowds of over 40,000 when they were in the third division. Bruce Rioch could hit the ball. We used to have a goalkeeper called Jim Cumbes, one of the funniest guys. He was so witty, it wasn't true. He played for Worcester. He was the keeper at Villa for a couple of seasons when I was there. Chico Hamilton came through that year and Andy Lochhead, who never forgave me for stealing his boots.

During that promotion season Rioch had proved just how well he could hit a ball. He had scored a goal at Villa Park in the 3-0 win over a team with which Campbell would eventually spend the most successful part of his career, Bradford City. The shot had been hit so hard that the unfortunate City keeper, Pat Liney, couldn't even catch the rebound as the ball sped past him in the opposite direction, having hit the stanchion in the back of the net.

Cumbes, a Mancunian by birth, had played cricket for Lancashire and Surrey before joining Worcestershire in 1972. Although it was still possible to play cricket in the summer and football in the winter, Cumbes concentrated on his goalkeeping, playing for Tranmere Rovers and West Bromwich Albion, before signing for Aston Villa in 1971. He would, however,eventually carve out a career for himself at Old Trafford. Jim Cumbes might never appear for Manchester United, but he would eventually return home in 1998 as Lancashire County Cricket Club's Chief Executive.

At the age of 31, Andy Lochhead was very much the senior striker at Villa when young Campbell arrived. He had scored over 100 goals for Burnley and had appeared in two cup finals. As for Andy Lochhead's boots, therein lies a story that spreads over many years, from Bobby Campbell's days as an apprentice to his last season as a professional player.

One Christmas I was going home and my brother was the same size and Andy had a spare pair of boots he never used. I thought I'd just slip them in my bag. Just my luck, his boots split while I was away and he was looking for his spare pair. There's nothing worse than breaking in a new pair of boots. I came home for Christmas, gave them to my brother, who's as happy as hell with a pair of adidas 2000, which was an expensive boot at that time, about a week's wages. The first thing I know Andy's got me by the throat. 'Where are my boots?' I lied and lied and kept a straight face. I was 16.

Years later I saw him at Haydock races. We were on a day out with Wigan Athletic. Andy was over from Bolton with a few of his pals. I saw him in the paddock. I'd had few drinks. I said 'Do you remember those boots?' He said 'I know you pinched them.' So I said 'I hold my hands up.' We had a laugh about it.

As so often happens with Campbell, as soon as he recounts one story about a former team mate, he has another to tell – and usually with a smile on his face.

At Bradford City, we once got a video on the bus. Gary Watson had taped this programme called 'Ripping Yarns' and said we had to watch it. It was about a Yorkshire football team called Barnstoneworth United. There was a bloke called Neville Davitt, a head like a stainless steel bullet. That was Andy Lochhead. He once scored with the back of his head from 22 yards against Barnsley reserves. I remember Andy heading one on to the cross bar. He must have headed it from the edge of the box, bang, and it went out for a throw-in.

Perhaps, then, there is a centre forwards' union, such is Bobby's admiration for the heading abilities of one of the senior players at Villa Park. But the cocky Campbell still had to learn the hard facts of the apprentice's life.

You've got to remember that you're a 15 or 16 year old, you're the cock of your team. You have been for probably four years, since you came through from 12 years old or maybe even seven years old. All of a sudden you arrive somewhere, you're maybe 16, but you're bottom of the class. You don't know that you're bottom of the class. You think you're higher than what you are. You're more or less told 'Look, this is where you stand, kid.'

I remember the first thing they gave me, when I was an apprentice, was a brush.

'What's that for?'

'The changing rooms, to clean the changing rooms.'

My first tools as a footballer were not a pair of boots or a tracksuit, but a shovel and a brush. I had a paint brush at the end of the season as well. All you were was cheap labour. How many apprentices became painters and decorators? That's what I would love to know, because that's all we did when we were apprentices.

In no time at all, the young Campbell became familiar not only with a sweeping brush and a paint brush, but with another sort of cleaning implement.

I had three players to look after – Bruce Rioch, Andy Lochhead and George Curtis. I didn't know anything about cleaning boots, apart from cleaning my own. The best story was George Curtis. He once strung me up by the neck because I wouldn't clean his boots. He just picked me up and, as the colour drained out of my cheeks, I asked if he'd like some dubbin on them.

'Yes', said George, 'That would be nice.'

For the benefit of those who never saw Mr Curtis in his playing days, he could best be described as a man who took no prisoners. He had played for most of his career as a centre-half with Coventry City, where he was known, with good reason, as 'The Ironman'. Many a player older and wiser than the apprentice Campbell would have avoided a confrontation with him. It seems that even the 'cocky' young Campbell quickly appreciated his position in the footballing hierarchy. If this was a lesson well learned, it was also a teaching method equally well remembered. Bobby Campbell would later be the one 'stringing someone up by the neck', even if his young victim was doing his very best to please the older player and was someone destined to become a great admirer.

During his apprenticeship at Villa Park Bobby lived in a hostel alongside a number of other young trainee footballers, who came from all over the country. He remembers particularly a Scottish lad called John Pelosi, who seems to have suffered just about all of the worst possible fates.

He couldn't handle it and went home a couple of times. When they actually came and said 'We don't want you now', he cried his eyes out. He'd wasted two years of his life down here or maybe he just thought 'I've tried so hard to make it down here. I've come back umpteen times from being homesick and now they're kicking me out.'

The disciplined routine of the hostel and the necessity of cleaning other players' boots may well have irked young Campbell, but he knew that the reality was that he had to keep doing what he was told – well, most of the time. The apprentices were not in charge of their own destiny and life could be very miserable, especially if home visits were not allowed.

Your apprenticeship can take you through until you're 18, if they want. For every one that signed pro, there were ten that got shown the door. They might give some of them an extra year, but they were hit and miss. The ones that got the extra year, many of them didn't do it.

Bobby Campbell's apprenticeship was that one in ten. It turned into a full-time professional contract.

I played in the youth team to start with. That was a very good youth team. To break into that youth team was a very good thing in itself, because they'd won the Youth Cup the year before and they'd only lost a couple of players. They still had apprentices who were 17 or 16 and who were there the year before me. I broke straight into the youth team, so that was a good thing in itself. For a first year apprentice to hold his place in the youth team is a remarkable achievement. Usually you're just a sub or whatever.

The season before, when they won the Youth Cup, they played Birmingham in a two-legged semi-final. There were 22,000 at one game and 20,000 at the other – for a youth game! Francis was playing for Birmingham. They played Liverpool in the final. I felt sorry for a guy called Bobby McDonald. He played left back. Bobby got sent off and they held back his winner's medal. For a young lad, that's terrible.

It didn't take long before the press had their first picture of Campbell scoring with a header. The official newspaper of Aston Villa F.C., the Villa Times, may not have had the same circulation as the nationals, but it sold at 6 pence a copy to plenty of Villa fans. And its edition of August 30 1972 shows the fifteen year old striker scoring with a header for the only goal of the match against local rivals Birmingham City.

By the October 25 edition, a headed goal against Oxford produces the first recorded instance of the headline 'A Bobby Dazzler!' The match report for that game gives a pen-picture of each of the players. The writer, who sounds as if he may have had some inside knowledge, has this to say about the centre forward: - 'This lad's a real character, on and off the park. He just doesn't know what the word 'quit' means and he's as brave as they come. He's sharp, hits the ball with both feet and, as his goal proved, is a good header.'

Another match report, from a Youth Cup tie in early December 1972 describes how 'Bobby Campbell delighted the 1,000 crowd with a superb goal. He took a short pass from Dave Smith, ran on, switched feet, and thundered a great shot low past the keeper.' The accompanying photograph shows the strike was left-footed. The first year apprentice, now 16 years old, was certainly making his mark in the youth team.

I played for the reserves when I was 16. I was playing with the pros. Everybody else was getting home leave, but I was playing in the reserves and still having to do all the work of the apprentices. I wasn't getting any home leave. 'You're playing in the reserves, so you can't go home.' It was like a sweetener to keep you from going back to Belfast. I'd lived at home all the time up to the age of 15.

If missing out on trips back to Belfast was painful, the reasons behind the restrictions, namely Campbell's remarkable progress in the Youth and Reserve team systems, were more than enough compensation. He was playing against much more experienced opponents and learning the professional game very quickly indeed. It was fortunate that, even at the age of 16, he was physically well able to look after himself on the football field. Had he been a slight figure, it is quite probable that he would not have been given those opportunities.

At 16 I was about 13 stone 2 and six foot. That Central League was a bloody hard league. You'd be playing against Liverpool and they'd have a team of internationals in their reserves. Play against Leeds United and they'd have a team of internationals. The Central League was all the northern sides. Reserve football now is just made up of maybe seven or eight of the fringe players. It's not the standard it used to be. Over the years I saw some good players coming through and some players hanging on to their last legs.

It wasn't long after my 17th birthday that I signed pro. They started me on £25 a week at 17, only a starting wage. Then I got a rise when I was 18 to £40. I was 17 and a half when I first played for the first team. Villa were in the second division in those days. I've got myself in the first team and I'm doing well. I've knocked a few goals in.

According to Villa's official records, that first team debut was on April 20th 1974. Bobby Campbell came on as a half-time substitute for Alun Evans in the second division match against Sunderland. Four days later he was again a substitute, this time coming on as soon as the 16th minute, against Nottingham Forest. This match was memorable for the very good reason that it was the occasion of his first goal in league football. His thirtieth minute goal is described in the club records as an '18 yard volley'. Sadly only 12,439 were there to see Campbell make his impact. Three days later, on the penultimate weekend of the season, in a 2-0 defeat away to Carlisle United, young Bobby made his full debut.

But even as he was making such rapid progress on the field, there was another, rebellious side to Bobby that he couldn't subdue. He was still a teenager, away from home and without proper guidance away from the training ground. These circumstances combined to produce a feeling of inevitability that bore remarkable resemblances to that other Belfast lad who had come to England ten years earlier.

Going to Birmingham at that age was the worst decision I ever made. They stuck us in a hostel with guys from London, guys from Scotland, guys from Liverpool, all young footballers. Apart from a table tennis table in the place and curfews, it wasn't the best. OK, you know that they're safe when they're there, but everybody was under everybody's feet. There was always bickering. There was always something. If somebody wanted to watch something, there was only one TV. Now everybody would have a portable TV in their own room, but in those days there was just one TV room.

I was so used to being out. Even with The Troubles in Northern Ireland, at 15 I was used to camping out on a night down my own local glen. My mum didn't worry about me. You have to get on with your life, haven't you? The problem in Birmingham was that you had to be in by 10.00 on a Saturday night. I suffered it for a couple of years and then I signed pro. Then the rebel in me took over. I just turned round and said 'I'm going to go out now and make up for all those two years', instead of maybe saying to myself 'Here just take it easy.' But there again, you've no family there, have you? I was 17 and out hitting the nightclubs in Birmingham.

It was to be some years before anyone came along and instilled that note of caution into the Campbell brain. In the meantime, those visits to nightclubs were to become a central and recurring part of his reputation.

Whatever may have been happening off the field, Bobby continued to make an impact in the Villa first team in the 1974-5 season. Long before the days when Arsène Wenger would regularly put out almost an entire youth team in the League Cup, Campbell recalls being picked for the Villa team that travelled to Goodison Park in the days when the League Cup still had room for a second round replay.

The best match I ever had for Villa was when I was 18. They drew 1-1 at home to Everton when Everton were top of the league. They had Bob Latchford and all these top players playing for Everton at the time. He was the most expensive player in the country at the time. Brian Little got injured, so I got the call up and played up front alongside Sammy Morgan, a big old Irish centre forward with absolutely no touch at all, but a heart of gold. He'd get stuck in. I had one of the best games of my life that night. I didn't score, but we won 3-0 and I had a hand in all three goals. That day everything that was whacked up to me just stuck like glue and I brought everybody into the game.

I put the keeper in a rest home for three months! Johnny Gidman, who was a free transfer player from Liverpool, he had a real career at Villa and at Man United. He cut in and let one go. The keeper palmed it out. It was a greasy night. Then I came in. Most keepers try to put their head over the ball to drag the ball back into them. I came in and just took the lot. The ball went sideways and Sammy Morgan just put it in the net. It wasn't a nasty challenge. It was there to hit, but he threw his body over across me and I caught him on the side of the neck. Before they realised how bad he was, we'd scored again. They tried to get a sub, another goalkeeper. They were looking for a late consolation, but we got another goal towards the end, when they were pushing forward. That was a hell of a night.

Campbell and opposition goalkeepers were never best friends. Just ask Dave Beasant about his 1984 trip to Valley Parade when he was in goal for Wimbledon and, after a brief encounter with the home team's striker, struggled to extricate his studs from the netting! So phrases like 'it wasn't a nasty challenge' and 'it was there to hit' have to be put into the context of that relationship and of the era in which this game was played. Breathing on goalkeepers did not always bring a free kick back in those days. Even allowing for how that first goal might have been scored, it was still a remarkable achievement for a second division team, albeit one about to win promotion to the first division, to win away to one of the most successful teams in England at the time. (Everton were to finish the season in fourth place, three points behind the champions, Derby County.) Bobby is obviously pleased to remember his part in the victory as one of the best nights of his early professional life.

Unfortunately there was to be a limit as to how far his team's continued run in the League Cup would produce a financial return for Bobby.

I played the hardest game in that round and then I played the quarter-final and got dropped for the semi-final, when all the big bonuses were coming out. I think I got fifty quid for that win. My mate played in the semi-final and he got five hundred. I was pig sick!

Bobby is certainly right about the second round tie against Everton being Villa's hardest game on the road to winning the League Cup that season. After beating Everton, Villa's remaining ties were against Crewe, Hartlepool, Colchester and a two-legged semi-final against Chester, before they beat Norwich 1-0 at Wembley on 1st March 1975. By the time of that League Cup Final, however, Bobby Campbell had played his last game for Aston Villa.

I had a couple of runs in the team, but I didn't score enough goals in the first team. Maybe I was trying to do too much instead of concentrating on what I was supposed to do, stay in the box, round the box, don't be going wide. But when I was a young player I used to do too much of that, trying to get involved. When you're a young player and playing against lesser opposition, you can get away with that and still score goals because you can cut inside. With the better defences you can't. You're best saving your energy for in the box.

Bobby played under two managers at Aston Villa, Vic Crowe and Ron Saunders. Saunders took over in the summer of 1974, just after Campbell's first-team debut. In his first season as manager at Villa he was to oversee both the League Cup Final victory and promotion to the First Division, a feat which saw him named Manager of the Year. In 1977 Villa won the League Cup again, but Saunders' greatest achievement came when Villa won the League Championship in 1981. Saunders had something of a reputation for being a disciplinarian. Bobby has a slightly different choice of words.

Old Ron was a nasty bugger. But I'll give him his due, he was fair. He gave me a decent run in the team, but when it came to the point when me or Frank [Pimblett] had to go, because together we were a bad influence on each other, and when Ron and the scouts got together, I think he had the vote. I said 'You're making a mistake because I'm not the bad lad.' Twelve months later Frank was out the door, so he couldn't blame me for Frank after that.

It isn't difficult to see how a manager who placed so much emphasis on discipline might decide that the young Campbell, nightclubs and all, was best 'being a bad influence' somewhere else. As Campbell himself concedes, the natural talent had not produced enough goals. It could even be argued that there was a lack of discipline on the pitch, 'trying to do too much'. For a combination of reasons, the manager of a team about to regain its First

Division status decided that Bobby Campbell was no longer required at Villa Park.

Campbell's last first team game for Villa came on 26th December 1974 in a 1-0 Second Division win over Bristol Rovers. He was to finish the 1974-5 season far away from the triumphs that by then surrounded Villa Park. In the latter part of that season he played 15 games for a team who could hardly even dream of Wembley success, promotion to the top flight of English football and European glory. Ron Saunders loaned out his wayward young striker to Halifax Town. Although Bobby's stay in the West Midlands was coming to an end, his links with West Yorkshire were only just beginning. And they were destined to be much stronger and lasting ties.

Chapter 4
TWO YORKSHIRE FIELDS

At the end of the 1974-5 season Halifax Town avoided relegation from the Third Division by four places and five points. Bobby Campbell could hardly claim to have made the biggest contribution to their cause, since his 15 game loan spell produced no goals. He would doubtless say that he made a few! Unsurprisingly, with that goal scoring record, Johnny Quinn, the Halifax manager, saw no reason to convert Campbell's loan into a permanent deal as his time at Aston Villa came to an end. Less successful than Halifax, finishing bottom of the same division, were Huddersfield Town. But it was for the relegated club on the other side of the M62 that Campbell, still short of his 19th birthday, was to sign.

His moves between nine more clubs and three continents in the remainder of his football career might suggest that Bobby enjoyed a nomadic lifestyle. While that might have been true – and occasionally necessary - on the pitch, in a domestic context nothing could be further from the truth. The day that he first went into Yorkshire digs in 1975 was also the day that he found somewhere to settle for years to come. He may have played football all over the world, but, despite some unpromising first impressions, his home has been in Huddersfield ever since that fateful day.

When Bobby first came to West Yorkshire, he met another footballer called Alan Jones, who was also to spend time as a Bradford City player in 1979 and 1980. At the time of their first meeting Jones was playing for Chesterfield. He was, according to Campbell, 'a Barnsley lad'– born in Grimethorpe, actually – and would accordingly greet his drinking partner with 'Are thee alright, Bob?' Now Campbell thought the Northern Irish accent perfectly normal and he must by this time have come to grips with the West Midlands tones. But he had never before come across anyone from the heart of South Yorkshire and for a time he was misled into believing that perhaps he had met not so much a new drinking partner as 'a Bible thumper, until somebody told me that's the way they talk'.As it turned out, Bobby soon discovered that he need have no fears about his new friend's sociability.

Bobby hadn't been long in Huddersfield when he met an old colleague from his Aston Villa days. Trevor Hockey was born in Keighley and had started his professional football career at Bradford City as an apprentice back in 1958. Bobby had known him as 'a seasoned pro at Villa when I was coming through the ranks'. During his time at Villa Park and for some years previously Trevor had worn a long piratical beard and had required the services of a head band to keep his hair under control during matches. Only some old photographs Bobby had seen gave away the fact that in his early days at Valley Parade the young Trevor had sported a completely different hairstyle, something not much more than a crew cut.

Hair cuts apart, there were some striking similarities between Bobby and Trevor. By the summer of 1974, when he left Aston Villa and rejoined his boyhood club, Trevor Hockey had played for no fewer than seven different teams, albeit over a period of time rather longer than it took Campbell to achieve the same feat. Campbell would eventually play for three of those seven teams – Aston Villa, Sheffield United and Bradford City. With a considerably larger gap between appearances, Hockey was also to pre-empt Campbell's return to Valley Parade after a previous successful spell. Sadly Trevor Hockey, as

Bobby recalls only too well, was to die at the age of just 43 on 2nd April 1987, after just finishing a five-a-side game in his home town.

When I came to Huddersfield we were playing Bradford in a West Riding cup game and he was playing for Bradford. We played pre-season. It was one of my first matches for Huddersfield Town. I talked to Trevor afterwards and he said 'All right, young Bob. What do you think of Yorkshire?' I said 'It's a crap hole.' He replied 'Listen, son, when you've been here a couple of months, you'll love it.' I said 'Fair enough' in a doubtful tone. I'm still here, so I must have fallen in love with it.

Bobby's landlady back in 1975 was someone who clearly made a lasting and positive impression on him. Her name was Edith Hargreaves.

I can't say enough about her. She was a mad Huddersfield Town fan. Every time she went to Bradford she never had to get a ticket, because I would make sure she got a ticket. Her husband died on a Saturday night. He went to watch Huddersfield Town with her. She was making his tea, he sat down and died. She got a trophy made. They stopped calling it the player of the year and started calling it the Hargreaves trophy in memory of her husband.

To this day the Huddersfield Town player of the year receives the Hargreaves trophy.

Apart from Mrs Hargreaves, Bobby was very much on his own in those early days with Huddersfield Town. He still recalls how 'she was a great old cook and she looked after me', but he has one very special reason for remembering her care.

For the rest of his life Bobby will have a constant, very visible and permanently painful reminder of one of his earliest games for Huddersfield Town. There is a photograph that hangs above his head where he works, but he doesn't really need that picture to bring back the memories of a game against Newport County in October

1975. The photograph shows Bobby and a few other Huddersfield players, including Terry Dolan, who was soon to turn out as a player for Bradford City and would later return to Valley Parade as manager. The players in the photograph are being presented before the kick-off to Huddersfield's most famous son, the Prime Minister of the day, Harold Wilson. Not for the last time in Bobby's career, a presentation before a match was to be followed by tragedy during the game.

One of Bobby's team mates that day was a player called Martin Fowler, who had joined Huddersfield as an apprentice in 1973. He played 73 games for the Leeds Road side, scoring 2 goals, before leaving for Blackburn Rovers in 1978. But Bobby has his own particular recollections of his team mate.

Martin Fowler, he was in the fourth division with Huddersfield Town and Manchester United offered twenty five grand, not bad for a fourth division reserve. Martin was a half decent player, but he wasn't over the top, as his career showed later on. If Tom had let him go for twenty five grand it might have been better for him. Tom Johnston (the Huddersfield manager at the time) *said he was worth a hundred thousand and put him in the first team.*

As the match was going on, he was trying to put on too much of a show. I was inside him, calling for the ball. By the time he passed it, I slipped inside and the defender came straight through me. It was what you call a hospital pass and the centre half obliged. The people that were there heard the crack all the way round the ground. And I had shin pads on, so I think the shin pads saved it from being a compound fracture.

Campbell's shin bone was broken in the tackle and surgery was needed as a matter of urgency. But in the 1970's fourth division players were not treated quite as well or as swiftly as their modern day counterparts. Bobby's travails were only just beginning.

I had to wait until the Wednesday for the first operation. I was dosed up on morphine until the Wednesday, that was the first time they could squeeze me in – and I was private! They put a plate in it and either five or seven screws. Then I got an infection in my leg, so I had to go back again. At Christmas my leg was hanging off. I always remember they operated on me on New Year's Eve in the Royal Infirmary, Huddersfield. By Christmas, when it hadn't knitted, that's when they did the bone graft and the bigger plate. They took some bone from my hip for the graft.

First time I was in for two weeks, second time I was in for three weeks. I'd no family, I'd only just moved to Huddersfield, so I didn't know many people in Huddersfield. I was still on my own apart from my new landlady, old Edith Hargreaves. She looked after me, especially at the bad time I had with my leg.

A brief word of explanation is needed about Bobby's use of the word 'old', particularly when he talks about 'old Edith Hargreaves'. Mrs Hargreaves was far from being an old lady in 1975, unless you take the view that to a 19 year old everyone over the age of 30 is old. Bobby clearly holds her in great affection for all she did for him at that time and during the months that followed. His tone makes it clear that he uses 'old' in this context very much as a term of endearment.

When that second operation involved a bone graft, it was vital for Bobby's career that the surgery was successful. In particular, it was important that the site of the graft should heal properly. When he talks about the risks of that operation, he is remarkably calm and matter-of-fact.

If it hadn't have healed, it would have been the old saw job.

Bobby Campbell faced the prospect of joining players like Derek Dooley and Brian Clough, who had already had the misfortune to suffer injuries that in more recent times would not end a professional football career. While Bobby Campbell may not have been the first 19 year-old to lose half a leg and certainly would not have been the first lad of that age to have a very promising career ended so early, football would have lost forever one of its true characters if that New Year's Eve surgery had not been a success.

At the time it could hardly have seemed much like a success to Bobby.

I could get around with the crutches. I was on the crutches overall for 15 months. By the time it came to give my crutches back I had arms and shoulders on me like Arnold Schwarzenegger. I'd take on anybody at arm wrestling. I wasn't like present day footballers. I couldn't afford to retire. There was no insurance then. So I had to soldier on and what pace I did have I lost when I broke my leg. I was just 19 and they said 'you'll have some rheumatism in that.' But as a young lad you laugh at it, don't you?

Well, yes, perhaps as a young lad Bobby Campbell found it easy to laugh at the distant prospect of suffering from rheumatism. After all, it was a prospect far preferable to some of the alternatives he had already faced. But it turned out not to be quite as distant as he might have hoped. At the peak of his playing career, aged 28, the prognosis became reality and from then on Bobby would have to learn to live with rheumatism. But that was not the only lasting effect of the fractured leg.

My leg was never the same. The muscle was never the same. I was always prone to knee strains.

Most remarkable of all, though, given that Bobby over many years was famous for leaping to head goals, is the statement that he couldn't jump off that broken right leg.

I couldn't jump off that leg as much after it had been broken when I was 19. I more or less adapted my game. When a cross was coming in from the left, I used to try to get across the defender, because I knew I wasn't going to be able to jump too well off that foot. So if a cross came from the left, I used to try to get to the near post. If the cross was from the right, I could hang more at the far post because I could spring better off my left leg. I could still hang at the far post, but for the majority of crosses from the left, I always attacked the box. That was my football brain. Coming from the right I had two options. Coming from the left, if I wanted to be more effective, I was better with the one option, going across the player.

Sometimes you can get up as high, but you have to really time it right. Sometimes you just have a little hop, skip and a jump. No problem with the left foot. But with the right foot, it's maybe two hops and a skip to try and get up there. Sometimes I used to try to jump off of two feet, which is hard to do on the run.

That was my handicap, from being 19. I never got the muscle back. Sometimes in my mind I knew. Sometimes the ball would come over and I knew I couldn't get up. It would go over my head. I would think 'What the hell's happened to Campbell?' I don't think the opposition would have known that. He would just think it was bad timing or something. I'd try to make a run forward and whoever was coming in behind me would be coming in for a free header.

There will inevitably be people who read Bobby's descriptions of his own aerial abilities and who never saw him in action. But there are plenty who did see the Campbell he depicts, mainly in the years after the broken leg. To put his own comments into some context, it is worth listening to what some other players say about him.

Bobby himself says that 'the best compliment' he ever received was from Ian Mellor. Mellor was an unusual left winger, not least because he was very tall, perhaps an inch or two taller than Campbell, albeit with a rather less robust frame. He played alongside Campbell for Bradford City for just a season and a half between 1982 and 1984. But, as Bobby remembers, Ian Mellor admitted on his arrival at Valley Parade as a 32 year old that he had 'been around a bit'. One of the players for whom Mellor had put in lots of crosses was Joe Royle, a classic centre forward of his era who scored plenty of headed goals for Everton and England. But Ian once voiced an opinion to Campbell that 'Even he wasn't as good as you in the air.' Mellor went further than that and was prepared to say 'I've never seen a better header of a ball than you.' Bobby reckons that such a judgement is 'not bad'. And who is going to argue?

But for later generations of fans, those unfortunate enough not to have seen Campbell in his prime, perhaps the opinion they most respect comes from another who played and trained alongside Bobby for a number of seasons, one of those who had the doubtful privilege of staying behind after training to put in one cross after another for a 'traditional centre forward'. That description of Campbell comes from Stuart McCall.

'We used to spend hours and hours after training. When training had finished, he always wanted balls he could head in. I've played with Graeme Sharp at Everton, who was an old traditional centre forward, and Mark Hateley at Rangers, again a good, powerful centre forward. And I played with Bobby. I would put Bobby on a par with big Hateley, who was brilliant for Rangers, and Graeme Sharp who played for Scotland and was brilliant for Everton. I'd put Bobby, as a header of the ball on a par if not better. He never mis-headed one. He always had the big mud spot right there. We used to be petrified if a cross wasn't right on his head.'

And while McCall might have been putting in those crosses after training from the right wing, the crosses from the left were being sent over by Mark Ellis, who had joined Bradford City as an 18 year old and who broke into the first team in the 1981-2 season. Mega, as he was christened (by Les Chapman, one of Bobby's big mates from his Bradford City days), also recalls 'Campbell was so good in the air. I was naturally right-footed, but played on the left wing. I had a tendency to cut in on my right foot

and cross, but that was not such a good angle for Bob.'
Perhaps now we know why.

The timing of the injury and the long period over which
the healing process took place could hardly have been
worse for a young player seeking to establish himself at a
new club. In the two months he had been at Huddersfield
before his leg was broken, Bobby had been a first team
regular and had scored just the first few of what he and
his manager must have hoped would be the many goals
he might have expected to produce.

I started one season (1975-6) *and finished the next. . I
played the last five matches of the following season* (1976-
7). *The only reason I got in was because I knocked in three
goals in the reserves. I was still struggling with the leg.*

In those two very truncated seasons, Bobby played a
total of 31 games for Huddersfield Town, scoring nine
goals. The game he remembers most vividly, apart from
that life-changing October day, was a League Cup tie
pitching Fourth Division Town against a team which had
just been crowned as the Champions of England for the
second time in four years and could boast among its ranks
a number of England internationals, one of whom was
later to feature more than once in Bobby's career.
Huddersfield were drawn away to Derby County and
Bobby's marker would be the regular choice at centre back
for England, Roy McFarland.

*I missed a sitter against Derby when we lost 2-1 down
at Derby. I had a good game against McFarland. I had an
easy header by my standards and, instead of just banging
it into the net, I tried to tap it into the corner. The keeper
was coming across the goal. I learned from that. We were
in the fourth division and we gave them a run for their
money. Charlie George was playing for them then. They
were a top side. McFarland was playing for England at
that time. They were in the first division. I think at that
time they were under Mackay when Cloughie had gone.*

Dave Mackay had taken over as manager following

Brian Clough's controversial departure from The Baseball Ground in October 1973. Mackay was to have three very successful seasons, with his team finishing third, first and fourth in the First Division. Derby were, indeed, 'a top side' in 1975.

While his injury kept him from making his own contribution to the remainder of Huddersfield's season, it wasn't even as though Bobby could watch his team mates' success on the field with any financial security. Although Huddersfield were to finish the 1975-6 season just one place away from promotion, Bobby was not to receive his promised share of the regular win bonuses his team mates earned.

You were supposed to get the bonuses until you were fit again. I was supposed to get the bonuses when I broke my leg, but I only got them for four weeks.

Whatever the financial reward may have been and no matter how much he was still struggling with his leg, once he had a few more games under his belt Bobby was determined to carry on and to progress as a professional footballer.

I trained more or less all the summer. I came back for pre-season. That was the beginning of the 77-78 season. They'd signed a few players. The Chief Scout who'd signed me from Aston Villa had moved on. He came and asked me if I wanted to go to Sheffield United. So I went to Sheffield on loan, scored a few goals in the pre-season, got my fitness up and they bought me for £10,000 from Huddersfield. I think they wanted rid of me.

If it is true that 'they' wanted to get rid of Bobby Campbell, the most likely 'they' in question would have been one of the three Huddersfield Town managers Campbell played for, a Scotsman by the name of Tom Johnston. When Campbell had first signed for Huddersfield, the first team manager had been Bobby Collins. Soon after Campbell's injury Collins had lost his job and had been replaced by Johnston. Johnston had been general manager for a time, having previously served as manager in the mid-sixties. It is fair to say that Campbell and Johnston were not best friends.

The story, as related by Stuart McCall, goes that one day the Huddersfield squad were taking part in a game of follow-my-leader. After various instructions such as 'touch your toes' the time came for the 'leader' to be Bobby Campbell. Johnston's car was parked in the club car park and Campbell's instructions to the other players were simply to follow him in a jog round the car park. Except that 'round the car park' involved every player going into the manager's car by one door and out by another, leaving a trail of mud behind them. It would be no surprise if Tom Johnston wanted to 'get rid' to Sheffield United, even if, strictly speaking, the first team manager when Campbell left was John Haselden, destined to survive in his post for just 18 matches before Johnston began a third spell as manager.

For those whose geography is not all it might be, perhaps it should be briefly mentioned that Sheffield is not very far from Huddersfield. The journey, either by car or even by public transport, does not take much time. In short, although Campbell was about to play for his fourth club, including his loan spell at Halifax, there was no need for him to move home. He probably lived nearer to Bramall Lane than many of his new team mates.

It should also be pointed out that, even if it was true that Huddersfield 'wanted rid' of him, Sheffield United must have seen something in the 20 year-old Campbell. Not only were they willing to pay a fee for him, but Bobby was moving up two divisions. The Blades were a club still adjusting to life outside the top flight of English football, having been relegated from the First Division at the end of the 1975-6 season. Campbell was about to become an automatic first team choice at that higher level, but yet again he played under three different managers in one season, changes which would do nothing toward establishing any stability in his career.

Jimmy Sirrell was the manager when I signed. He went to Notts County. He was a gentleman of the old school, Jimmy. He could see through everybody. He knew I was a bit of a rogue, but that I wouldn't let him down on the pitch. I put 100% in every time.

Jimmy Sirrell, to be absolutely accurate, went back to Notts County in 1978. He had managed them previously, with quite remarkable success. In 1969 Sirrell had joined the oldest established club in the Football League at a time when they were playing in the Fourth Division. During three spells with Sirrell as manager, Notts County were not only promoted to the First Division, but they retained that status for three seasons. It is little wonder that a stand at Meadow Lane is named after him. It is also no surprise that such a shrewd judge of character should see both sides, the roguery and the reliability, in his new striker.

They sacked poor Jimmy midway through, towards the end of the season. The assistant (Cec Coldwell) *took over for a few weeks, but they didn't give it to him. They gave it to Harry Haslam.*

It was the second season after I broke my leg that I went to Sheffield United and played 30-odd games, which was not bad. I was joint top goalscorer with Simon Stainrod and Keith Edwards. I think we all got 12 apiece. Keith Edwards could score for fun and Simon Stainrod had a good career at QPR. We finished half way in the second division with Sheffield United.

As usual, the Campbell memory is not far out. He actually started 35 league games out of the 42 Sheffield United played that season and came on as a substitute in 2 others. His 'not bad' is something of an understatement and his appearances show just how hard he had worked to regain his fitness and how well he was playing. He scored 11 goals in those Second Division games, but perhaps the three others he scored in the pre-season games were the goals to persuade Jimmy Sirrell that here was a young striker worth taking on.

As is often the case, the arrival of a new manager brings about a chain of other changes in personnel. Harry Haslam was hardly likely to leave the Sheffield United squad untouched.

He was like a Delboy. He knew everybody. He signed Steve Finnieston from Chelsea for ninety-odd grand.

Finnieston had been an apprentice at Chelsea and had enjoyed one particularly good season, making 39 appearances and scoring 24 goals in the 1976-7 season, when Chelsea had won promotion to the First Division. Perhaps the First Division proved a step too far for him. In the following season his 20 league appearances brought just three goals and in June 1978 he left for Bramall Lane. Finnieston was not to prove quite as durable as the man with the damaged leg. He made only 23 first team starts for Harry Haslam's team before being forced to retire through injury in 1980. But the change of coaching staff and the arrival of Steve Finnieston spelt the end of Campbell's time with Sheffield United. The changes in personnel did nothing for The Blades' progress. Having finished the 1977-78 season in mid-table, 1978-79 saw them relegated to the Third Division. And within another two seasons Sheffield United would find themselves in the Fourth Division. By way of a sharp contrast, Bobby Campbell took full advantage of the opportunity to cement a move, albeit a temporary one, to somewhere far away from the football fields of West and South Yorkshire.

Chapter 5
THREE CONTINENTS

I always said that I wanted to go to the States.

Despite finishing the 1977-78 season as Sheffield United's joint top scorer, a second change of manager and the signing of a new striker were to grant Bobby Campbell his wish. Although much of the football he was to play in the summer of 1978 was indeed played in the USA, the club that he was playing for were based north of the border. Bobby joined the Vancouver Whitecaps in the North American Soccer League.

I played up front with some of the best players I've ever seen in my life. They were towards the end of their careers, but they were still bloody good players. Alan Hinton could cross a ball on a sixpence. There was Alan Hinton, Kevin Hector and me up front.

Kevin Hector had made his initial impact as a striker with Bradford Park Avenue. He had made his name, however, in those Derby County sides, managed first by Brian Clough and then by Dave Mackay, that won the English Football League Championship. Hector left Derby when Tommy Docherty took over, although he did return there after his spell in Vancouver. To be able to play alongside Hinton and Hector was the best footballing education the young Campbell ever received.

I used to try too hard in the first team at Villa. That's when my goals dried up. I was trying to do too much donkey work. I was running wide, running in, running back. I put that down to bad coaching. It was the same when I went to Huddersfield. When I broke my leg, I sat down and watched a lot of football. I realised that I needed to ask what I was doing out on that wing. When I twigged on was when I was playing for Vancouver. Alan Hinton said to me 'You stay in the box. Kevin Hector does all this stuff. Kevin Hector can do this stuff and still score goals.' He was a hell of a player, Kevin. He could get involved outside the box and be in the box. He'd say to me 'Bob, as soon as you get the ball, give it to a midfield player and get your arse into the box.' When I started doing that, my pitch used to be the box size of the pitch. That's where I used to stay. When I started staying there, that's when I started scoring goals – alright, with the assists.

I took Possee's position because they wanted a bit more strength up front and they signed me from Sheffield United.

Derek Possee played most of his football for London clubs, most notably featuring in over 200 games for Millwall. He was some ten years older than Campbell and arguably somewhat on the short side for an out-and-out striker. Although Campbell took his place as a striker for Vancouver in 1978, Possee was still with the club when for the only time in their history they won the Soccer Bowl the following year, making a total of 53 appearances for the Whitecaps and scoring 17 goals.

It was Alan Hinton who said to me 'Bob, I don't want you out on the wing. I want you in there. Kevin'll do all this work and the midfield players will do all this stuff. You stop in there and we'll cross the ball to you. You make yourself nasty in there. We'll get you goals and you'll make goals for us.'

I played at Vancouver and scored 11 goals in 16 games. I thought that wasn't a bad ratio. I remember Hinton saying to me, 'Campbell, if I'd got hold of you while you were a young lad, I could have made you a superstar.' You'd make the run and he'd put the ball in front of you.

It was there.

Quite apart from the quality of his crossing, a skill that Campbell always admired in a winger, there was one particular memory Bobby retained of his time playing alongside Alan Hinton.

We shared our stadium with the American football team. The soccer pitch is wider than the American football pitch. The soccer pitch was in red, the football pitch was in white. Alan Hinton used to dribble down the white line, take the defender on, put it over the white line and at the white line the defender automatically puts his hand up 'Ball out', without realising it's the red line he's playing to. By the time they'd twigged on Alan Hinton could have got two or three crosses in. He'd do it on one wing and then go straight over and do it again on the other wing. You'd be surprised how many times we got a quick goal from that.

Again, for those who don't remember him, Alan Hinton played in the 1960's and 1970's for Wolverhampton Wanderers, Nottingham Forest and, with the greatest success, Derby County. He was perhaps most famous in those days for being one of the very few players to wear white boots. He was the living proof of the famous saying that 'anyone wearing boots like that has to be good.' Brian Clough certainly thought he was good enough to play for Derby County and, since the team in which Hinton played won the Second Division title in his second season and were twice champions of the Football League, perhaps Mr Clough was right – again.

There were plenty of old-timers. I felt a right young kid with them. I was just 21. There was Jon Sammels from Arsenal and Leicester in midfield. There was Phil Parkes, the goalkeeper from the West Midlands. There was Derek Possee from Millwall. Later there was Stevie Kember, known as Gippo. He was from Palace and Chelsea; all these top players hanging on for another couple of years. Terry Yorath came two seasons after, when Johnny Giles was manager. He got all Leeds players out there. Tony Waiters was manager in my time. He played for England.

The Phil Parkes who kept goal for the Whitecaps in 1978 was a one-club man in England, playing over 300 games for Wolverhampton Wanderers, which may explain why Bobby remembers him as being from the West Midlands. He is not to be confused with another goalkeeper of the same name who played over 300 games for each of Queens Park Rangers and West Ham United, even though he was born in Staffordshire and began his professional career with Walsall. Tony Waiters did indeed win five England caps as a goalkeeper in 1964. He played most of his football with Blackpool and Burnley. He had been manager at Plymouth Argyle before taking over at Vancouver. Canada and Tony Waiters must have grown to like each other; he went on to manage the Canadian national team in both the 1984 Olympics and the 1986 World Cup.

When Vancouver Whitecaps played against Detroit Express, one of Campbell's opponents was a centre back who had also just finished playing for Sheffield United. Eddie Colquhoun played almost 400 games in ten years for The Blades, winning nine Scottish caps in the process. There was one particular incident in that game, when Bobby remembers taking advantage of an unusual offside rule, to the discomfort of his old team mate. The North American Soccer League drew two additional lines across the pitch, each one 35 yards from the dead ball line, leaving an area between those lines and the half-way line where the usual offside rule did not apply.

Eddie was a big centre half, a big Scottish bloke. He was playing for Detroit. He used to love playing the offside. The only thing was that he forgot there was a 35 yard rule. What they did was make a rule that you could only be offside 35 yards out of goal. I remember I was making a run just over the half way line and Eddie stepped up to put me offside. I went through and scored and came back and said 'That's the line!' He totally forgot.

The Whitecaps finished top of the North American Soccer League National Conference, Western Division in that 1978 season. They then entered a play-off system to decide who would win the Soccer Bowl. They beat Toronto in the first round of the play-offs and this put them into the semi-finals, where they were drawn against Portland.

Their season ran in our summer. I played 16 games and scored 11 goals. We got to the play-offs. We'd beaten Portland earlier in the season. We played them away and they beat us 3-0. That was it.

So far as Bobby Campbell and Vancouver Whitecaps were concerned, that play-off defeat was indeed terminal. Contrary to his personal wishes and despite his excellent goals-to-games ratio, he was never to play for them again.

It was a good experience, to see so many cities in America that you dream about. We played our home games on a Wednesday night, we played our away games on a Saturday night, and so every Saturday was a night out. So it was always good! For a 21 year old even then I had to carry my own passport, because they were that keen on age I had to pull my passport out. They put John Craven to look after me because he was the captain, but he was worse than me.

There is only Campbell's word that John Craven was worse than him. Craven cannot answer for himself, having died suddenly at the age of just 49 in 1996. He was almost ten years older than Campbell, having made his name with his local team, Blackpool,   between 1965 and 1971. He had also played for Crystal Palace, Coventry City and Plymouth Argyle before playing the first of his 70 games for Vancouver in 1978. Whether or not the choice was entirely suitable, someone perceived the need to give Campbell a mentor. Others were to follow the same path with varying degrees of success.

It was full-time football. I actually thought it was going to take off. I was going to go there. I love Vancouver, one of the most beautiful cities in the world. And I've been to a few. I was gutted. When the season finished the club said to me 'Just go back, relax, take it easy, mess about and we'll sort out your contract for next year.' But other people said 'Get it sorted out before you leave, Bob.'

There were changes everywhere. I came back with the wrong attitude. I thought I'd made it in the States. 11 goals in 16 games wasn't a bad return. I came back to Huddersfield, spoke to Paula, my wife who was my girlfriend at the time, and said 'Look, we're going out.' Paula came out for three weeks and loved it. I said 'We're going back next season. I'm going to get a new contract. We can sort ourselves out.'

But Vancouver Whitecaps played only in the summer months and Bobby Campbell, still only 21 years old and striving to make a more permanent mark in professional football, needed to be playing full-time. In the autumn of 1978 he was back in England and without a club.

They always say 'Don't go back', especially to a club you've had bad times with before. I left Huddersfield on bad terms before. But Huddersfield wanted me to sign for them and Sheffield United agreed. I came back! I came back to Huddersfield with the wrong attitude, still with a chip on my shoulder. I don't know why I signed for them. I should have gone to Sheffield Wednesday with Jack Charlton. With the big long ball, the ball into the box, I would have suited Jack's style anyway. Anyway that didn't work out.

Behind all of these changes of clubs lurk two very relevant facts. The first is that, except for his brief footballing forays to the far corners of the earth, Bobby never left the Huddersfield he had by now come to regard as his home. The second, even more important, fact is that Bobby Campbell, as he himself quite willingly says, has never been an angel.

Everybody knows what I'm like. I still live in Huddersfield. You can't go out for a pint anywhere. I used to like to go down the pub for a game of dominoes and a pint, even on a Friday night. I couldn't see the harm in that. When we used to play away matches, they let me have a pint at the bar. Everybody could see that I wasn't getting drunk. I was just sitting there relaxing. If anything, I'd have two pints. I'd rather have just two pints of lager than drink pop and eat crisps all night, which I used to see them all doing when we played away, feeding themselves on pints of pop and crisps.

It was, as Bobby soon realised, a mistake to ignore the old advice about not going back, especially when he had gone back to West Yorkshire with personal regrets and to a club he had left with some ill feeling. Although Bobby was to start the 1978-9 season very successfully at Leeds Road (he scored three goals in the seven games he played up to October), he was to spend most of it yet again back on the northern side of the M62 at The Shay, playing for a Halifax Town side destined to finish the season next to bottom of the Fourth Division.

Jimmy Lawson, who was manager of Halifax, said they'd take over my contract. I thought, 'Well, I don't have to move then. I can go down to Halifax.' If I'd realised Jimmy Lawson was going to get the sack in three matches I would never, ever have gone to Halifax.

Like most professional footballers over the course of their careers, Bobby Campbell was becoming attuned to the idea that the manager who signed him might not be a permanent fixture and that the new manager might be a different character altogether. His second spell at Halifax Town was probably the most obvious example of both of those phenomena. Halifax had no fewer than seven managers in the 1970's, including George Kirby for two separate spells, one of which began soon after Campbell's return to The Shay.

They brought back 'Colonel' George Kirby, the worst manager I've ever played under in my life. He just didn't have a clue. What harmony there was in that Halifax team he just destroyed. He brought his own regime in with him. He wasn't living round here. We had to train on a Monday afternoon just to suit him, because he was travelling up on a Monday morning. If he was taking his job seriously, he should have been up on a Monday morning.

Whatever the more widespread problems might have been as a result of the new regime, there was one particular issue that rankled with Campbell.

He'd take us all running. I still hadn't recovered from my broken leg. I still found it hard on hard grounds. I did all my career. At that time you didn't have the footwear. I had to take the pounding on my leg. You'd complain and he'd just laugh at you. We just fell out. He did everything he could to sack me. He got a few things. I could have fought the case. I was well within my rights, the things he did to me, but I just wanted to get away.

Not being wanted by Halifax Town might have been enough to bring an end to some professional careers. Having your contract terminated for misconduct was even more damaging. It was never going to be the best line to put on your footballing CV. Worse still, at least in Campbell's eyes, was the fact that the goals had almost dried up. He scored just three times in 22 appearances for Halifax. In the space of just one season he had fallen from being an automatic choice and joint leading goal scorer with Sheffield United, who had finished mid-table in the Second Division, to being sacked by a club having to apply for re-election to the Football League.

The knowledge that Vancouver Whitecaps had, without telling him, signed someone else was a further blow to Bobby's hopes. Alan Hinton had stayed with the NASL and moved into management at Tulsa, but there was no call from him to the striker whom he had told he could have made into a superstar. But Bobby Campbell was still only 22 years old and made of sterner stuff than many. He was determined to start afresh, no matter where his football might take him.

One of those friendships that footballers make in the game, especially those who have played for a few different clubs, was to come good. Bobby was contacted by one of his old mates to tell him that there was an Australian club manager in the UK looking for players. Arrangements were made for the manager to meet the unemployed Campbell. Bobby wasn't out of work for very much longer. In fact, in next to no time he had two jobs at once and was off to the other side of the world again.

So off I go to Brisbane, part-time footballer, part-time steel erector. I had to have the steel erector job, because they trained three nights a week, every day was free and we played on Sundays.

The big centre half was a fellow called Pete De Kuyser, the most gentle man you'll ever meet in your life. A typical Aussie of German descent, big, blond sportsman, he had it all. Built like a brick shit house, Big Pete. He and a few of the lads had their own business. With it being an Italian run club, they had all the contracts, which was good for Pete, because he had all the contracts for laying down the steel. So there was plenty of cash in hand. I used to do that for 50 dollars a day. I was on 200 dollars a week with the football. You could live comfortably on 200 dollars a week and I was getting 50 dollars a day on the steel fixing. I never felt as fit and strong. You'd be pulling out in the morning and it would be freezing. By 10.00 in the morning the steel was too hot to pick up. I had a real good time. If they'd have given me the money to stay, I would have stayed.

Two other players in the Brisbane squad provided a link with the Campbell past and the Campbell future. Bobby had been a bad influence on Frank Pimblett in their days as apprentices at Villa Park – or was it the other way around? Frank had made his Aston Villa first team debut just nine days after Campbell played his last game for the club, but he was to play just nine games in total for Villa before moving on loan to Newport County during the

1975-76 season, at the end of which he joined Stockport County. By the time of Campbell's arrival in Queensland, Pimblett was virtually a fixture in the Brisbane team and some years later, although the team was by then called Brisbane United, he was awarded a testimonial and effectively declared a local hero by the time of his retirement.

Another member of the same squad who was also to stay in Australia, eventually taking Australian citizenship and winning 21 international caps for his adopted country, was Dave Ratcliffe. Described by Campbell as 'a big, smart, dark-haired lad, looked like Donny Osmond', Ratcliffe had played 30 games as a centre half for Bradford City before joining Brisbane in June 1978. At the end of that Australian season Campbell and Ratcliffe discussed their futures. Ratcliffe wanted to stay in Australia and, as well as winning international honours, he played for and coached a number of club teams, including the splendidly named Wollongong Wolves.

He stayed on. I think he did a decent enough job. When I told him I was going back home, he said 'What are you doing?' When I told him 'I think I'm going to Bradford City for a trial', he told me all about it and said he knew most of them from playing with them. When I came to City, Gary Watson and Ces Podd knew him. So when I went there, I said 'Dave Ratcliffe sends his regards' and that broke the ice.

Brisbane City were not a bad side. In the 1979 season, which was again played largely during the English summer, they finished fourth in Australia's National Soccer League Championship. That meant that they qualified for the end of season play-offs. These had a rather unusual format, where the top four teams at the end of the regular season played each other once in a mini-league, the top two teams in that mini-league qualifying for a Grand Final over two legs. In the mini-league Campbell scored in every game and Brisbane reached the Grand

Final against Sydney City. Campbell had scored both goals in the 2-0 mini-league win against Sydney and everything was set for an evenly matched final. Sydney won the first leg at home 1-0. The second leg was played on 4th November 1979 and a 1-1 draw saw Sydney ending up winners by the narrow margin of 2-1.

So, with another continent providing a good life style and goals going in, why didn't Bobby Campbell stay on as a part-time footballer in Brisbane? Long after his retirement, he still toys with the idea that 'I could have ended up an Australian international, if I'd stayed.' But the answer comes back to one simple thought Bobby Campbell still couldn't get out of his mind.

At the same time I still fancied having another go.

Chapter 6
TROUBLE

Bobby Campbell may very well have 'fancied' having another attempt at establishing himself as a full-time professional footballer in England. But persuading yet another club to offer him a full-time contract was never going to be quite as easy as that for the 23 year old with a disreputable past. Everybody knows, so the folk lore has it, that Campbell had always been a bad lad. He was nothing but trouble even as a schoolboy. He was always getting himself arrested by the police. Throughout his career as a so-called professional footballer he had done nothing but smoke, drink and get into fights. He was always coming into training with a hangover. He was always out of condition.

Even the page devoted to Campbell on a website devoted to all things Bradford City, where unwavering support for the club legend might be expected, allows itself to say that he 'played when sober and, if reports are to be believed, a few times when he was not'. The same website, while emphasising that they do not want 'to suggest that there is any truth in any of the following' (that way they hope they will not get an unexpected visit from an irate ex-striker), can't resist repeating a few of the stories that 'have been told and retold around the pubs of Bradford'.

Occasionally the folk lore also has it that, even in an age when the professional game permitted rather more by way of physical contact than could be dreamed of in its modern day version, he was forever being sent off and was lucky that any club ever kept him for more than two minutes, given his overall disciplinary record.

Well, that's a summary of the story. Now let's have a look at the evidence to back it up. As will become clear in a later chapter, the young Bobby Campbell did indeed come to the adverse attention of the police, even if, rather unusually, the policemen in question were Swiss. This particular run in with the law was to have serious consequences for his professional career that would continue to his detriment for a very long time indeed. But, while his mother may have found it increasingly difficult to keep him under her control back in Belfast, he had never got into mischief serious enough to involve the Northern Ireland police. But once he was away from home, either for a short time in Switzerland or a much longer stay in West Yorkshire, matters took a distinct turn for the worse.

It seems ironic that almost all of Bobby's problems off the field have occurred in and around Huddersfield, the very place he was to make his home after leaving Birmingham. His conviction for drink-driving was, he accepts, entirely his own fault – and, some might say, equally predictable. However, more than one of his other brushes with the law reflect the attitude that some of the residents of Huddersfield adopted to having a professional footballer in their midst. Sportsmen with 'tough' reputations are often seen as fair game by young men who also want to impress as being macho.

I hold my hands up. I went down town early doors and had a couple of brawls in town with a few people in Huddersfield. They picked fights with me when I was in Huddersfield. I stopped going down town.

Some of those incidents brought him to the adverse attention of his employers. In September 1976 Campbell was still recovering from his broken leg, was not able to train properly and was some months away from being fit to resume his career. Without the regular discipline of training and playing, the worst of his habits took over. Eventually he received a letter from the Huddersfield Town Secretary telling him that 'the Directors discussed at some length reports on your recent conduct and they are most disturbed.' He was warned that 'unless you behave yourself in future, your contract will be cancelled.' History says that the contract was not cancelled and that at the end of the season Huddersfield made a profit from the sale of Campbell to Sheffield United.

I did get done for assault at one time. It was while I was playing for Sheffield United, but it happened in Huddersfield. I stopped going out in Huddersfield at that time. It's such a small town, everybody was picking on me.

But the one guaranteed method of aggravating Bobby Campbell was to start any violence in front of the lady who would eventually become Mrs Paula Campbell.

There was another time at a club. I was at the top of the stairs and I went to meet the wife. There was trouble starting in this bar. There were a lot of Huddersfield Town fans I knew from my young days in Huddersfield. I said to the bouncer 'I want out. I just want to get out of here.' When he opened the door to go down these steps, he tried to push me and Paula down the steps. When you went down the steps, you went half-way. He came at me, him and another bouncer. At that time I was 13-10, 14 stone, big muscles and strong as a bull. I just got hold of this guy all the way down the steps. As we went down the steps, I hit him on the head. They dragged me all the way down the stairs. The bouncers kicked me out. I opened the door and it was like something out of the Wild West.

The police came in and I said, pointing at this guy who was flat out, 'Arrest him. He's just assaulted me.' But I got locked up as well. I got bail. I went to make my statement and the bloke said to me 'I'm going to charge you with assault'. I said 'He tried to pull me downstairs. There were three bouncers attacking me. I was just trying to defend myself. It's not my fault he got the worst of it coming down the steps.'

The police said to me 'We've had numerous reports that they've thrown people downstairs and they say they've fallen and then it's just one word against them. They more or less said upstairs that he's got his comeuppance. There's nothing we can do about it, because it's your word against his. It puts him on the line as well. If you keep your nose clean, nothing will happen.'

Huddersfield being a small enough place, it was inevitable that this would not be the end of the matter. Sooner rather than later, the bouncer and the striker were bound to bump into each other again.

I saw him a few times in town. One time it was in a pub. There were three of his mates and I had just one mate with me. He walked over and said 'Get out of this pub.' I said 'Are there any steps? Are you going to throw me out? You couldn't do it last time. You needn't think you can do it now. Piss off.' He walked away and left me alone.

Even with a four to two advantage, walking away from a fit and angry Bobby Campbell must come high up the list of good ideas!

One particular involvement with the West Yorkshire police did, however, have a rather different and more positive outcome, although the start of the episode did not exactly foretell the brighter ending.

I was arguing with this taxi driver and the taxi rank started kicking off. The police came in and these two taxi drivers started attacking a copper. I jumped in and pulled these guys off. Next thing you know the police have come in, cuffed me, taken me to the cells and want to beat me up. I knew I'd done nothing wrong and this guy was poking me. I said 'I haven't assaulted a copper. I gave him a hand'. He said he saw it and I said 'You saw it wrong.' He was going to give me a slap and I had these plastic cuffs on. So I was getting ready to give him a head butt and pulling myself up off the chair, when this guy comes in and

says 'Let him go. He was helping.' 'Oh, sorry, Mr Campbell.'
Next thing they wanted a statement.

Just in time the prisoner, possible victim and potential defendant had turned into a witness for the police. Indeed, the quite dramatic change of status was not yet complete. But you can't be Bobby Campbell and just accept even the most remarkable and possibly advantageous turnaround.

I got a letter from the chief of police thanking me for helping a bobby in his hour of need. I should have kept that letter for future reference, if I was owed a favour. Anyway, I threw it in the bin in disgust.

Some of the time, of course, it can be hard to distinguish between what amounts to criminal behaviour and something that is nothing more than a bit of fun.

I got on great with Trevor and with Yorath. I can remember only once he pulled me in one Monday morning. Sunday night used to be a good night round here. We were all having a laugh. I climbed up a drain pipe and was banging on the windows. Trevor took me to one side and said 'Someone's rung up to say you were drunk and disorderly in Lindley on Sunday.' I said 'What about Saturday? Didn't they tell you the same about Saturday? It was my weekend. I was having a laugh with the lads. It was a bit rowdy, but that was it.'

In the current era Campbell would almost certainly have faced a club fine for that sort of behaviour, if only to protect the good name of his employers. Then again, maybe Trevor Cherry recognised that within fairly wide limits he had to take the whole or nothing of the Campbell character. Didn't Matt Busby adopt a similar approach with another Northern Irish player ten years earlier? Now, if Campbell had fallen off that drainpipe and injured himself, who knows what his manager would have said? But, whatever went on in that office on that Monday morning, Bobby's opinion of Cherry and Yorath was in way diminished by the stance they took.

I would put Yorath and Cherry on a par with George Mulhall.

And Campbell has no greater compliment to pay to a manager than to liken him to the man who, as Bobby is the first to acknowledge, rescued his career. He is ready to make it plain that some of the managers he has worked with are not held in the same high regard.

But even Bobby Campbell was 'not guilty' occasionally, although there were times when it seemed that for the self-confessed rogue it was always a case of 'guilty until conclusively proved innocent'. He recalls one lucky, if wholly deserved, escape from the wrath of one manager earlier in his career.

It was the same at Huddersfield. I couldn't do anything at Huddersfield, but the phone was ringing. I could be sat in a pub playing dominoes and the phone would go and someone would say 'Campbell's pissed up. Campbell was pissed up in a pub last night.'

I remember once I was sat with the commercial manager. A bloke asked for the manager, so they put him through to the commercial manager, thinking it was Tom Johnston. He said 'Bobby Campbell's in town pissed up.' 'Is he? Hang on a minute.' And I went 'Hello, this is Bobby Campbell. Who's this?' The phone went down!

If pushing and shoving while Paula was around was guaranteed to risk Bobby's wrath, there is no doubt in his mind that she herself had exactly the opposite effect on him.

I quietened down a hell of a lot because of her. I wasn't going down town. I stopped all that. I kept a low profile. I stayed out of town. I thought I don't need the hassle. If I went out in Bradford, everybody knew me, but there was nobody jealous of me because I was playing for Bradford. If I went to Huddersfield, there were people jealous of me because I was playing for Huddersfield. There was a different thing about that. There was always somebody wanting to have a dig at you. In Bradford there was never anybody. I used to go to pubs, clubs, everywhere. I used to go into Working Men's full of Paddies – Catholic Paddies as well. There would be a big Celtic flag and I'd get called a Protestant bastard. I got treated better in Huddersfield when I was a Bradford City player than when I'd been a Huddersfield player, because they used to take the piss and we used to have a little bit of banter. Maybe it's one of the better things I never went to live in Bradford. We used to socialise a lot in Bradford, but used to get out before it was late. It would be maybe afternoon or teatime.

If living out of Bradford kept Bobby away from those who liked having a 'dig' at him, he still found at least one place in Bradford that proved invaluable to him.

I remember trying to get a pair of black pants once. I couldn't get a pair to save my life. I just happened to be at the bar talking to this lad. 'What's that, Bobby, you want a pair of black pants?' I had big legs and a slim waist then. I could get 36, but they were a bit bulky. He looked at me like a tailor looking at me. He came back about 15 minutes later and said 'Here you are, Campbell, what about them? Black pants – just go try them on.' So I went to the toilet to try them on. Perfect fit! It was the only time I paid the asking price, I was that shocked. They fitted me that well I paid the asking price. I think he wanted a tenner for them. I still can't get a pair and I think to myself that the next time I want to go shopping I'll go see him! That was Bradford for you. If they haven't got it, they'll get it!

Bobby Campbell would never seek to deny that he likes a drink. His definition of what amounts to 'a few drinks' might differ from others', but he was never quite the regular frequenter of police cells that the stories might suggest. And, once Paula was firmly on the scene, there was a marked improvement with more sensible behaviour, even if 'sensible' also has to be judged by Campbell standards.

So, back to the commonly held belief that Campbell

was just as much of a bad lad on the field as he was off it. During his career with seven different English league clubs Bobby Campbell played a total of 476 games. You would think that such a bad lad would have picked up any number of suspensions during those games, even allowing for the more robust approach that the professional game permitted in the 1970's and 1980's. The reality is that he was sent off on just three occasions – and he remembers each one of those dismissals in some detail, with the occasional regret and the inevitable little smile.

His first sending off was while he was playing for Sheffield United. He remembers the occasion for a typical Campbell reason – it gave him the opportunity to sample the match sponsors' alcohol a little earlier than he had anticipated – and that particular tale is told on another page.

During his 274 games in a Bradford City shirt, Campbell was sent off just once and he tells the story blow by blow, so to speak.

Bradford City and Mansfield Town must have got to know each other rather well by the autumn of 1982. They had already been drawn against each other in the 1981-2 League Cup, in the days when the early rounds were played over two legs. They had also met in Fourth Division league games against each other, including on the last day of the season, when Bradford City's 2-0 win at Field Mill was to be their last game in that division for a quarter of a century. As the two clubs prepared for life in different divisions, they could have been forgiven for thinking that they had seen the last of each other for a while.

But before the 1982-3 season started the draw for the first round of the League Cup paired them once again over two legs. Bradford City won both games, Campbell scoring each time, along with an away goal from a certain Mark Ellis, known to one and all as Mega. As if that had not been bad enough for Mansfield, the two teams were then drawn against each other in the second round of the F A

Hopefield school, champions of East Antrim and Belfast, 1968-69. Campbell back row, centre. Skillen front row, second from left.

Northern Ireland Schoolboys. Campbell back row centre – head and shoulders above the rest of the team.

65

*Aston Villa Youth Team 1972-73. Campbell back row, left –
younger, but taller, than most of the team.*

*Campbell and Frank Pimblett, team mates from the Aston Villa
Youth Team. Two rogues with their hands on three trophies.*

A BOBBY DAZZLER!

CUS

the

uths

en You can't beat

T Embassy

● LEFT—BOBBY CAMPBELL, after a fine cross by BARRETT, rises above the Oxfo
defence to head home.

● ABOVE—CAMPBELL again in the thick of the action as he and DAVE SMITH w
to pounce on any slip-up by defender FLAY and 'keeper BAKER.

ll header dashes
's cup hopes

Villa Times claims the first use of a much repeated headline.

youths are "halfway" to victory as Bobby Campbell, after a superb
run, grabs the second goal.

*Villa Times again, showing that Campbell could certainly shoot
with his left foot.*

October 1975. Terry Dolan introduces Campbell to the Prime Minister before kick-off at the Huddersfield Town v Newport County match.

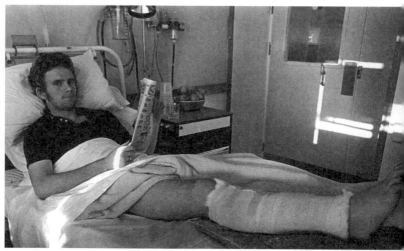

Three days after that Newport game, 19 year old Campbell looks suitably glum about his future prospects.

A formal picture of Campbell, the young striker Huddersfield Town hope will become a star for them.

1977-78. A typical diving header for Sheffield United from the striker who would finish as their joint leading scorer for the season.

1977-78 again. Sheffield United's number 8 rises above the Hull City defence, as Billy Bremner can only stand and admire.

70

The summer of 1978. The pitch, with all kinds of markings, may not be grass, but Campbell scores one of his 9 goals for Vancouver Whitecaps.

27th August 1980. It's all a blur as Ray Clemence and Alan Hansen can't stop Campbell scoring against the mighty Liverpool at a packed Valley Parade.

1981-82. The official Bradford City team photo, showing Campbell (back row, centre) and the new player/manager, Roy McFarland.

Summer 1982. The Northern Ireland World Cup squad in Spain, with Campbell second from the left in the next row to the back.

Cup, a game to be played on December 11th. One player who must have become truly sick of the sight of the number nine and the young winger with the flowing blonde locks was the Mansfield centre half, Billy Ayre.

Bobby Campbell has fond memories of Billy Ayre, although it may not be obvious from the initial description.

Big rough centre half, he played at Hartlepool, Halifax and Mansfield.

Centre halves do not have a monopoly on being described in uncomplimentary phrases. Some centre forwards have, in their time, been described as both big and rough, among other epithets. Even so, no one should believe that this was a mutual respect society. But Bobby had other reasons for enjoying playing against Billy, including the very best reason he ever had for playing against anyone.

I always used to score against him. He was one of these people where you think you'll always get a chance against him.

It is that second round F A Cup tie from December 1982 that Bobby remembers so clearly.

Billy Ayre, he was kicking Mega all over the place. He'd been kicking Mega and then the ball was in my area. He was coming through and I just put my studs there. I didn't connect with him too much. A typical centre half. They want to hand it out, but they don't want to take it. He goes down like a sack of spuds. The referee sends me off. Just before I walked off the pitch, he's getting up smiling. I said 'Wipe that smile off your face. This game isn't over. I'll see you in the replay.' We drew down there.

The game did indeed end up as a 1-1 draw and for once Campbell didn't stay on the pitch long enough to score, Bradford City's goal coming from Terry Gray. And in the days before police leave and health and safety requirements pushed cup replays back ten days or further, the two teams were to meet again just four days later to decide who would make it into the potentially lucrative third round.

This was also an era when suspensions, even those accrued for a straight red card, did not kick in immediately. Bobby Campbell was available for the replay. He was to miss the next two games after the cup tie, one of the very rare occasions he was absent from the Bradford City team. Bad weather meant that those games were not played until December 27th and 28th. Bradford City drew both of those Christmas matches, away to Preston and at home to Wrexham, but, as it turned out, didn't manage a goal in either. It is not even worth the passing thought that Bobby was just executing a cunning plan to get his Christmas off when his studs went through on Billy Ayre's leg. He couldn't be that devious.

So it was that on December 15th Bobby Campbell was there to greet Billy Ayre on the Valley Parade pitch.

As soon as he looked at me before the start of the second game, he knew he didn't want the battles. I said 'The decisions will go my way tonight.'

Whether or not the referee's decisions had any influence on the outcome of the game, it was indeed Bradford City's night. In their 3-2 win the goals came from Lester, McNiven and, inevitably, Campbell, setting up a third round Yorkshire derby with Barnsley that was to bring in a crowd of over 11,000 – and, sadly, a 1-0 defeat.

Bobby was not the only Bradford City player to come into the close proximity of Billy Ayre. He remembers another occasion, again at Valley Parade, but this time involving Ayre and Joe Cooke. Anyone who knew Joe from either of his spells at Bradford City would be unlikely to put him into the 'shrinking violet' category. Joe was always able to add to his footballing skills by being big and strong. It must also be remembered that Joe, Ces Podd and the few other black players of their generation were unlikely to be judged solely on their ability, especially by opposing fans and players. Society was very different and professional footballers back then could adopt stances that today would not be tolerated by their own profession, let alone by the law of the land.

One of the tried and tested methods of gaining an advantage over an opponent was to make a comment liable to distract him from his game. If the subject of that comment by the time of the 2006 World Cup final had become an opponent's family members, back in the 1980's there would certainly have been less reluctance to refer to the colour of his skin. According to the story, this was Billy Ayre's method of attempting to distract Joe Cooke.

He'd called Cookie a black bastard or something like that. Then he said to Cookie 'I'll see you after the match.' Cookie said 'You'll see me now.' Bang, in the tunnel at half-time. Neither got found out.

Many, many things in professional football have changed for the better since those dark days. Structurally Bradford City's ground is almost unrecognisable. But one of the smaller features at Valley Parade that has remained virtually untouched is the players' tunnel. Even as late as the 1999-2000 season, Bradford City's first in the Premier League, all sorts of unsavoury incidents took place in that confined area when teams were alongside each other. Just ask Stuart McCall. Bobby Campbell can probably recall more than one exchange of words and worse.

There were a lot of things happened in that old tunnel. You go back up the steps. There have been more injuries in that tunnel than on the pitch!

Battles on and off the pitch with Billy Ayre are, however, put to one side in Bobby Campbell's reminiscences, when he gets to the point that really matters. The combative tone that describes the blows on the field and in the tunnel changes dramatically when Bobby reaches his final thoughts on that 'big, rough centre half'.

He's dead now, Billy, God rest him

After retiring as a player, Billy Ayre went into

management. In 1995 he was first diagnosed with lymph node cancer, but seemed to have battled through it. However, while he was assistant manager at Bury in 2001 the cancer returned and, despite apparently successful treatment, he died in April 2002, just short of his fiftieth birthday. Many football players and managers are fondly remembered after their deaths by the fans who supported them. A few also bring a smile when remembered by their old opponents, but perhaps that type of soft spot requires the mellowing qualities that come with being long retired.

In case anyone should think that Bobby Campbell began to display those mellowing qualities in his later years as a player, the tale of his third and final sending off will instantly dispel that thought.

I remember a game at Bournemouth when I got sent off for Wigan. Our player went through, put the ball past the keeper, the keeper arcing him up in the air. The decision's a penalty or a goal kick. He gave us a corner. I pulled all the lads away and said to the referee 'You made a total mistake there. It's gone now, so let it go.' As that game went on and on, he didn't give us jack shit. We ended up losing the game.

I cracked a player almost. This player was kicking at everybody and he wasn't giving us free kicks. That's where you say you'll take the law into your own hands and I thought 'I'll catch the bugger.' I was sent off because I elbowed the guy. He was niggling me. That was just frustration. We'd lost the game and this guy was still wanting to go through people. I didn't connect with him, but he went down like a sack of spuds.

His biggest regret of all, though, is not the fact that he allowed himself to be niggled by an opponent or even that he was sent off at a stage when the game was effectively over.

What makes it worse is when you get sent off and you haven't caught the bastard! It's a waste of a two match ban!

By way of a brief postscript to the Campbell on-field misdemeanours, it should be added that the suspensions for those three dismissals were the only ones he ever faced. He never accrued enough bookings in a season to be suspended. There must be a strong case for arguing that he would never get away with many of his unpunished actions in the modern game and thus would have picked up many more cards and suspensions. Then again, maybe he would have simply worked out different ways to impose himself on defenders that would have fitted in with the twenty first century stance on foul play. Watching a modern centre half trying to hold back Bobby Campbell at a corner kick by pulling on his shirt might prove amusing!

Campbell has no reservations and a limited number of regrets about describing himself as a rogue. He sees even less wrong in his drinking habits, seeking merely to quash the more extreme stories about him. He would not even bother to deny that some training days, especially Mondays, might involve a little less heading practice than later in the week. But what he would fervently maintain is that none of this made him either less fit or less effective as a player. While many observers might beg to differ with that appraisal, only Campbell himself can say whether he is being 100% open in his self-assessment. The broken leg undoubtedly took its toll. The constant change of managers, not always because of anything Campbell did, was another problem. But there are times when even he hints that, especially in his early career, with greater discipline he could have achieved much more than he did.

Chapter 7
A ROGUE ON TRIAL

When Bobby Campbell played for Brisbane City in the second leg of the Grand Final of Australia's National Soccer League play-offs, he was six weeks past his 23rd birthday. The date was 4th November 1979 and his Australian playing days were at an end. In his still short career he had played on three continents for eight clubs - two of them twice. In a period of a little over 18 months with five different clubs, he had gone from being a regular choice and leading goal scorer for a club in the English Second Division to a part-timer in Australia. He had been dubbed 'a rogue' or 'a bad lad' or 'a trouble maker' by a number of different managers. He had failed to recover fully from a broken leg, even though the injury was by now four years old. And he had had more than one brush with the authorities, both the football variety and the police, as a result of one of which, as we shall come to see later, he had been banned for life from playing international football.

With this less than glorious history he came back to West Yorkshire, still determined to give professional football 'another go'. The plus side for him was that he had recovered significantly from the broken leg, that he had regained as much of his fitness as he was ever likely to regain, that he had learned a lot on his travels about how to be a more effective striker and that, as a result, at virtually every club he had played for he had scored goals in abundance.

There was another, less tangible side effect of the itinerant Campbell career. Whether it had come from his sociability, his football ability or a combination of the two, no one can tell. But one certainty is that Bobby Campbell had made plenty of friends and admirers in the football world. He was never going to be without a reference, albeit one that might have attached to it a bit of a health warning. That was precisely how matters turned out on his return to West Yorkshire in late 1979.

By the start of the 1979-80 season George Mulhall was manager at Bradford City and Bryan Edwards was his first team coach. Mulhall had taken over at Valley Parade part way through the previous season and his team had finished 15th in the Fourth Division. But this season they had got off to the sort of start every manager dreams of. They had won seven and drawn one of their first eight league games. They had even managed to produce no fewer than six different goalscorers in one game. But their form had dipped somewhat after the clocks had gone back and their big centre forward and joint leading scorer, Dave Staniforth, had scored only two goals in twelve league matches by the time they came to play Peterborough United on January 12th 1980.

During his time as reserve team manager at Huddersfield Town, Bryan Edwards had seen plenty of Bobby Campbell on the training ground. George Mulhall had also come across the young Campbell in the days when he had been assistant manager to Ian Greaves at Bolton Wanderers. Two seasons previously Bolton had played home and away against a Sheffield United team with Campbell up front. Bolton had, in fact, won the Second Division title in the season Bobby played for Sheffield United, so it might have taken something special for an opponent to make much of an impression on the assistant manager. But neither George Mulhall nor Bryan Edwards had forgotten this particular striker.

Bryan Edwards knew I could still play a bit.

If you want an example of the way Bobby Campbell saw his own career up to that point, that short phrase gives you all you need to know. Bobby himself had always believed he could play rather more than just 'a bit'. All young professionals need that self-confidence or they will not make a career out of football. But Bobby never over-estimated his ability when judged against his achievements. He never saw himself as the greatest centre forward who ever lived. He always thought he could and should have done better; in particular, that he should have scored more goals.

I'd played for the Villa first team, but didn't score as many as I wanted.

He knew he was better than a part-time player in a limited league on the other side of the world, but he also knew that he had to prove himself all over again, both to George Mulhall, Bryan Edwards and, most importantly, to Bobby Campbell.

During that dip in Bradford City's early season form Campbell had been 'on trial' in the reserves. This was a rather different sort of trial to that faced by many players – and for once in Campbell's life it had nothing to do with the sort of trial that involves lawyers. The Valley Parade trial was very little to do with what Bobby did on the training ground or in reserve team games. It had everything to do with how he behaved the rest of the time and whether he continued to behave as he had done with some of his other West Yorkshire clubs.

I know, I know, I didn't make the most of it. I realised I'd lost my way. I just needed guidance. They guided me back to Bradford. George was of the old school. He thought 'If he can play in the second division, he must have something.' From there on he sat me down and said, 'Bob, I know you're a rogue. One step out of line and you're out. Bryan's recommended you. I know you're all right.'

Bobby clearly has a great deal of affection and respect for George Mulhall. He is the first to recognise that being given the opportunity to resurrect his professional career at Bradford City was just about a last chance and certainly a turning point in his life.

George gets the respect because of the man he is. George was a man's man. He'd seen both sides of it. George stuck his neck out for me. I think he knew that I wasn't a bad lad. I just wanted steering in the right direction. George gave me a lot of rope, but I didn't hang myself. I did more or less what I did before. He used to think there was nothing wrong with a guy having a beer on the night before a match. There was nothing wrong with that. Everything in moderation. I wasn't as bad as everybody used to think.

The 'rogue' was given his chance to impress by playing in three reserve team games. He only ever played those three games for the reserves. His fourth game for Bradford City was that first team match against Peterborough United. He would start another 308 first team games for Bradford City after that one. In that first game he was allocated the number 11 shirt, playing alongside Dave Staniforth and David McNiven, City's joint leading scorers at that stage in the season. After that game and except for one odd game in the next season, when he came on in a number twelve shirt while recovering from injury, Bradford City's number nine shirt was made only in Campbell's size. The occasions when anyone else would need to wear it were to be very few and far between.

I scored on my debut. I scored in my last match. In between there's about eight seasons to talk about.

And Bobby Campbell has a lot more than the little matter of 137 goals to talk about.

I came back from Brisbane. I joined City more or less straightaway. That's why I came back. I came back because they said they'd give me a trial. Give me a month. Bryan Edwards contacted me on behalf of George. They said 'Come over and let us know when you're back and we'll arrange something.' So I came back and played in a couple of reserve matches and more or less they took me on. Brisbane wouldn't give me the money to stay and I thought I'd give it another go. It was half and half whether I was coming back. I really enjoyed the lifestyle over there, but it wasn't full time. You still miss the full time job. So I came back. It wasn't worth a trial. It was to see if I was a reformed character. It was more to see what my behaviour was going to be like. That's my behaviour off the pitch. My behaviour was OK, so they took me on.

I played a couple of reserve team games and then I was in the first team. I got my first goal on my debut against Peterborough. One apiece. That was the start of a good run. We just missed out on promotion from the fourth division that year.

The squad that Bobby Campbell joined in January 1980 included one or two players who were to become part of the fabric at Valley Parade. No fewer than eight of them would go on to make more than 200 appearances each for the club, including the one Bobby calls 'the man himself', Ces Podd, who holds one very special Bradford City record, hardly likely to be broken these days, of 566 appearances. Ces and Bobby form an unlikely pair and yet the hard-living Irishman became great friends with and still has enormous respect for the mild mannered Kittitian.

Old Ces was The Preacher. We used to wind him up every morning. He was a lad when he was young, Ces. I just knew him to play against in the old days. By the time I came to City he was already the reformed character. Ces would have a laugh; he was a Mickey-taker.

Right back, up and down that line, but he was another one who couldn't really cross a ball, Ces. But what a great defender. Nobody could take him for speed. Nobody really got the beating of Ces. He might have been bony, but he could tackle. He wasn't one of these that would tackle head on. He would tackle from the side. He would get his leg round you like a snake. He could pinch the ball as well. He used to come inside and try to swing his left leg. He might as well have tried to swing his left arm because he would have made better contact!

But then not wishing to belittle his old friend, who did in fact score four goals in those 566 games for Bradford City, Bobby has an afterthought.

I remember Ces scoring a hell of a goal against Huddersfield Town with a diving header.

This was in a Third Division game at Leeds Road on 1st January 1983. Huddersfield won 6-3, with City's other two goals coming from Mark Ellis and, inevitably, Bobby Campbell. It is impossible to avoid the thought that Campbell remembers this rare Ces Podd goal largely because even the great header of a football would have been proud to have scored that one.

Another regular member of that 1979-80 team, David McNiven, is given enormous credit by Campbell. McNiven was another of those who made over 200 appearances for Bradford City, scoring 66 goals. But what Campbell recalls is the number of goals he scored following 'assists' from the man known as 'Daisy' or 'Frank Cannon' (a bit cruel, this one, since it is from the name of the overweight star of an American detective series). McNiven would, in effect, be doing much of the running, wide and deep, that Campbell had by then learned to take out of his game.

When I went to Bradford I nearly steered away from staying in the box. It was great because the first thing when I went there McNiven says exactly the same to me as I wanted to hear. 'You stay in the box. I'll go out there and do it all.' Daisy used to go out there, do a little shuffle and cross the ball for me. He was fast enough to spin, put the ball across, I'd knock it down and he'd put the ball in the net. When I started staying in that area, that's when I started scoring goals. It's not standing still. You've got 10 yards that way and 10 yards that way. I used to stay in the middle of the box and I'd turn round and walk toward the edge of the box. I may even walk four steps, but I'd turn and I'd sprint and I was back into that place where I was just stood a minute ago. I'd hope I'd got the centre back just off key a bit.

He makes this goal-scoring business sound so very simple, doesn't he?

To come back to the early days when George had the team, there were a lot of old pros then. I was classed as one of the young lads then. I'd just gone past 23.

Of those who played a significant number of games that season, only two, Steve Smith and Peter Jackson, were younger than the much-travelled Campbell. By way of contrast, there were indeed a good few members of the squad who were 30 or over.

Big Pete was a good goalkeeper, a very good goalkeeper. I didn't know he'd played in the final for Swindon, in the League Cup Final, against Arsenal.

Peter Downsborough never actually played in the first team that season and retired in the summer of 1980. But by then he had played 252 games for Bradford City and is clearly well thought of by Bobby. Downsborough had, indeed, been in goal for Third Division Swindon Town in the 1968-9 final of the League Cup, when they had won 3-1 against Arsenal, perennial members of the old First Division.

Don Hutchins, of whom more in a moment, was 31. Mick Bates was 32. Lammy Robertson was also 32. Bobby remembers him as 'an experienced player. He was a good player to have in midfield.' Soon after Campbell's arrival Les Chapman signed at the age of 31, another player Bobby is prepared to call 'a star'. Bobby has another nickname for Chapman, one which at first sight might suggest a rival to Campbell's own ability in the air, but which turns out to be rather more prosaic in its origins.

Then there was Les Chapman, the young salmon. He used to get into the bath and fly out like a young salmon.

And as soon as Bobby brings Les Chapman to mind, he also recalls one of his 'good stories'.

I remember a good story when I got sent off for

Sheffield United. Grouse whiskey were sponsoring the match. At half time I said 'Am I all right for a drink after the match?' to the sponsors. The sponsors' little room was just as you were walking out. He said, 'Yes, come in after the match.' When I got sent off ten minutes into the second half, I said 'Can I come in a bit earlier?' I got changed and before the match had finished I'd drunk nearly half a bottle of scotch. Chappy and I thought I was getting a lift home to Huddersfield and my mate thought I was coming back on the bus. So when they'd all pushed off. I came out and there was just me, big Vic Halom, who used to play for Sunderland, and Chappy. Chappy said 'I live in Delph, but big Vic lives in Stalybridge. He'll drop you off and you can get a train straight through to Huddersfield.' Big Vic dropped me off and I jumped on a train and they just kicked me off at a platform. I didn't know where I was!

I got sent off because it was me and another Northern Irish lad, an international. He had a dig at me and I gave him a little touch with the shoulder and he swung one at me. I only palmed him off. He lifted his hand. It was only handbags. We both got sent off, so it wasn't too bad. And the team won, so I didn't get much of a bollocking after the match.

Campbell's disciplinary record, the extent of which will have surprised many people, has already been discussed, although on this occasion 'a little touch on the shoulder' might not necessarily seem quite as innocuous as it sounds. But one of the interesting asides, arising from the fact that Campbell wasn't driving at the time, is that his two friends and potential chauffeurs from the game, Les Chapman and Vic Halom, were not playing for Sheffield United. They had both been playing against Campbell for Oldham Athletic.

Stuart McCall also has good reason to remember the friendship between Bobby and Les Chapman. 'Bob used to be always with Chappy. They used to come over from Huddersfield. He used to get into Chappy's car. They both of them had hearts of gold. We used to train at Apperley Bridge. We (Stuart and Mark Ellis shared a car) always used to set off before them on the way back. No matter which way we went or how we got back, they always used to be in the car park before us. All the time! There was a time he actually drove his car over a grass roundabout, rather than going round it. We were going round the roundabout thinking we were well in and then the next minute…'

But Campbell and Chapman had more than one way of defeating the young McCall and Ellis. Another tactic still brings a smile to Stuart's face. 'I remember once coming back from Apperley Bridge. We got to the bottom of Midland Road, waiting to turn left. Bob and Chappy were about ten cars behind us. We've only got to go round the corner when the lights change, up Midland Road into the car park and for the first time ever we've got back before them. It was a warm day and Chappy was shouting down to us. Next minute we turned round and Bob's crawled along the road where the cars are, put his hand through the window, taken the keys out and thrown them across the other side of the road. All the other cars overtook us and we were stuck there. For weeks after that on the way back from training Mark and I used to look for little short cuts you could take. But I remember that. Bob's crawled up one side on his hands and knees while Chappy's been taking our attention at the other side.'

At the end of Campbell's first season at Bradford City they finished one place short of promotion. Only their better goal difference saw Portsmouth get into Division Three. Starting with that Peterborough game, Campbell played in all their 21 league matches to the end of the season and scored 8 goals. Bradford City lost just three of those 21 games, securing 28 out of a possible 42 points in the process. Taken over the season as a whole that points-to-games ratio, in the days of two points for a win, would have been more than enough to secure promotion. The trial had proved a success for all concerned.

Chapter 8
MANAGERS, TRAINING AND FITNESS

For Bobby Campbell the 1980-81 season was the time he became firmly established in the Bradford City first team. He played in 42 of the team's 46 league games, including his one and only substitute appearance for the team, scoring 19 goals. He also played in City's only FA Cup game and in all four of their League Cup games, adding another 3 goals to his tally.

In that League Cup run he scored one of the more famous goals ever seen at Valley Parade, when City beat Liverpool, the League Champions, 1-0 in the first leg of the second round. He may have been the England goalkeeper, but Ray Clemence never stood a chance! The second leg didn't go quite so well. This was the first of four seasons when the League Cup was to become Liverpool's personal property. They won 4-0 at Anfield on their way to beating West Ham in a replay at Villa Park to win the competition. But back at Valley Parade a little piece of history had been made, although the next time Bradford City were to beat Liverpool 1-0, almost twenty years later, would quite certainly be seen as an even more historic occasion.

George Mulhall, the man who had taken the risk with the rogue striker, left Valley Parade and returned to Burnden Park as assistant manager in March 1981, although he was to take over as manager from Stan Anderson within three months. After a less successful season, Bradford City had finished 14th in Division Four. They could hardly have been more mid-table, eleven points behind the fourth promoted club, Wimbledon, and eleven points ahead of the bottom team, York City.

Then George went to Bolton and then McFarland came and that was a trail of disaster.

Roy McFarland came to Bradford City from Derby County as player/manager at the end of the season. This was his first managerial post. Bobby Campbell and Roy McFarland were to cross paths and swords more than once during the Campbell career and Campbell's opinion of McFarland the manager contrasts sharply with his views on McFarland the player.

He was still a good player at a good level. When McFarland came, he gave us that bit extra at the back. Even when he went back to Derby he played a few games.

McFarland played 31 games for Bradford City in his only full season as player/manager, making 47 appearances in total before returning to the Baseball Ground in November 1982, where he was to make a further 8 appearances in the Derby County first team.

McFarland and Campbell had first met, perhaps at something of a distance, when the Belfast schoolboy had been on trial at Derby. Back then McFarland was just beginning to establish himself as first choice centre back for England and he would go on to win 28 caps for his country. The young Campbell spent a week at the Baseball Ground, 'mucking in with the apprentices and playing two-touch football', neither of which he enjoyed. Even as a schoolboy, Campbell knew where his particular skills were to be found and he wondered to himself 'how can they see how I can play?' He was to be reminded of those training methods in the 1981-2 season.

When McFarland came to Bradford I couldn't believe he was doing the same thing as I'd done as a 14 year old trialist at Derby years before. Two touch, in little areas and with goals the size of a table. It was just crap. There was no real incentive for you and it doesn't bear much relation to Saturday afternoon. It's nice to see a team play two touch and spraying the ball about. But I'd sooner see a header or a shot go into a big net, not a couple of cones a yard and a half apart where there's no goalkeeper.

The contrast between training methods of different managers and coaches is obviously a factor to stick firmly in Campbell's memory. Alan Hinton's comments from Bobby's days in Vancouver clearly produced a significant and very productive change in his style of play. Back in England and under the management of George Mulhall, coaching again concentrated on getting Bobby into the penalty box and then on getting the ball in to him. George Mulhall had been a professional player for many years. He had played over 250 games as a left winger at Sunderland in the days when just about the only task for the rest of the team was to get the ball into the middle to that man Clough. But even as a manager, George couldn't resist returning to his old skills.

George Mulhall used to go out to the wing and do crossing with me. George was an old winger, he'd be knocking in crosses and I'd be heading them. 'Hutchy this is all Campbell wants on a Saturday.' He'd make Hutchy stand there for five minutes just watching him cross, when Hutchy wanted to get off to do his job.

'Hutchy' was Don Hutchins, who wore the number 11 shirt for Bradford City for seven seasons until his retirement in 1982. Like several of those who followed him on to either the left or the right wing of the Bradford City team in the next few seasons, he would suffer at the hands of the centre forward. Wingers never gave him the right service, so he would be constantly reminding them. It is to be hoped that none of them took the criticism too seriously, especially when Bobby is quick to say 'I liked Hutchy, a nice lad.'

Bobby Campbell has strong views about many aspects of professional football and it is no surprise that he also has clear memories of the different training regimes during his time at Valley Parade.

Training with George Mulhall was good. We went to

Apperley Bridge on a Monday, five-a-sides, bit of running, finish. Tuesday bit of running, depending on where we were, might just train on the car park, do some running round the track. Have Wednesday off. If you had a game Tuesday or Wednesday, you would just have a game of five-a side or whatever. Thursday you'd come in, you'd be all more or less ball work and shooting. On a Friday it would just be a light morning, make sure everybody was fit. And then back to the game on Saturday. This was after all the pre-season training; because of the pitches, you couldn't train too hard or your legs would be too lethargic. At that time even Valley Parade was a bog. Some Mondays we hardly trained at all, maybe with little strains and niggling things. So Monday was always an easy day. Two and a half hours. Never more than two and a half. You'd be surprised at what you can put in those two and a half hours.

Managers and their training methods may have come and gone, but some things in the Bradford City set up remained unchanged for over thirty years after Campbell's arrival.

We played at Apperley Bridge. Come winter time, if you trained at Apperley Bridge twice a week, it was too heavy to run round.

Matters on the training ground changed markedly with the arrival of the new player/manager in the summer of 1981.

McFarland had played at the highest level, but I'd no respect for him at all as a coach. It doesn't prove anything. I thought his coaching methods were absolutely terrible. Training with McFarland was shit, because all you did was stand around in a big circle and he'd have you there for an hour and a half doing piggy in the middle. You used to get bored. You'd have a little five a side with two touch and a little goal. It was absolute crap. The best thing that ever happened was when they brought in the bigger goals. You'd have thought that as an ex-international his training would have been better. We'd hardly any crossing, hardly any shooting. We'd stand about in a circle.

I'd put him on a par with George Kirby.

George Kirby was Campbell's manager for most of the time during his ill-fated spell as a player at Halifax Town. It can safely be assumed that any comparison between McFarland and Kirby is not meant to be a compliment to either manager.

After the end of the McFarland regime, when Trevor Cherry and Terry Yorath were the management pairing at Bradford City, Campbell's views on training change back again, even though some of the training routines remained the same.

We used to do it in a circle with Yorath and Cherry, but they didn't bleed it dry – 20 minutes and that was it. We used to get the touch; that's good. But doing it for an hour and a half was just monotonous. We used to do a lot of cone work with Yorath, which meant a lot of running. But you were running with the ball, so you didn't actually realise that you were doing the running. We were dribbling round the cones, chipping it back, so it was all ball skills plus running. With the training with Terry and Trevor it was absolutely top drawer. Coachwise, he (Yorath) knew his coaching. There wasn't a lot of coaching in terms of tactics and the like. It was more or less keep the ball, pass it, get it in the box. If you could dribble and you could pass and do all that, you wouldn't be playing in that league. It was play to the team's strengths, which was Bob in the air, Daisy down the wing, give the ball to Mega. Mega would run all day. It was just play to your strengths.

And then comes half a confession about the Campbell attitude to training. It is only half a confession because the extensive mitigation comes with it.

I was one of the worst trainers. I wasn't lazy. I just didn't like running. I don't mean tracking and the like. Once I'd done my leg, I just didn't like the running, especially the running on the roads. It was only towards the end of my career that these kinds of pumps came out with a cushion on them. It used to jar me too much. There are plenty of lazy trainers. I liked to save it for a Saturday.

While road running may not have been top of Bobby's list of training routines, his favourites should come as no surprise.

If it was crossing and shooting, I'd do twice as much as any of them. You'd get Ces Podd and the defenders and they'd have a shooting practice session. As soon as I shot, I'd go to the front of the queue. I'd say 'Come Saturday, how many chances are you going to get to shoot? Maybe once in every six months you're going to have a shot. I'm going to be shooting every week, so I get to practise more than you.' It was the same with a new signing. The lads would say 'It's Bob's turn'. He'd say 'Bob's just gone', but they'd say 'It's Bob's turn again.' It was the same with the heading. Somebody would be crossing and I'd just walk out in front. They used to say 'It's Bob's session. We're not allowed to have a go.' I'd say 'You're allowed a go when I've had a go.' I'd have two goes to their one!

As if his praise for the training methods of Trevor Cherry and Terry Yorath were not enough, there is one other coach who comes in for special mention, his training being described as 'absolutely fantastic'. This particular coach, who strictly speaking never managed Bobby Campbell, was an old team mate from that 1979-80 season, a player Bobby always refers to as Doley, but who is properly speaking Terry Dolan. Dolan was another member of that squad who played over 200 games for Bradford City. He also returned to the club as manager in the 1986-7 season, not long after Campbell himself had moved to Wigan Athletic. It was while Bobby was a Wigan player that he came across the Dolan training methods.

Sometimes I couldn't get to Wigan and I'd go down to Bradford training. Dolan used to make me welcome and Dolan's training methods were absolutely fantastic. He'd have small games, but big goals, which was great. So you'd get chips and headers in the big goals all the time. You'd play six or seven a side, with a proper size goal, but maybe a half sized pitch. There'd be shots coming in from everywhere. So you had to close down quicker, because a guy could shoot from thirty yards. He's not going to shoot from thirty yards if you're playing two touch and you're playing with a goal the size of a table. He's just going to pass it, so you don't have to shut him down. It spoils it because on a match day you're going to have to shut him down because he's going to shoot. To me all that did was breed bad habits.

And just in case there might be a question mark over the fitness of 'one of the worst trainers', Bobby even has a strong opinion there.

The games keep you fit, as long as you haven't picked a niggling injury up. Then you're having to play and rest, play and rest. That's the hard part. The few times that happened to me, that's when you've really got to watch it with your lifestyle. Whereas you go out during the week maybe you might eat that bit more, that week you don't. You say that, because I'm not burning it off in training, I've got to keep it down all week. You're better going swimming or something like that.

Once the season started, you were off and running. It was all more or less keeping toned up. When we got promotion, both years, I think I missed one game in three seasons. There were a couple of times I played with injuries. There was one time I played when I couldn't kick a ball with my left foot. It was all strapped up. I went over on my ankle. Someone said 'Can you jump?' I said yes and he said 'As long as you can head a ball, get out there'.

In the two seasons Bradford City were promoted with Campbell in the side he played 45 out of the 46 league games in 1981-2 and all seven of the cup ties that season. In the 1984-5 promotion season he played in all 46 league games and again in all seven of the cup ties.

I had a dodgy ankle for about two seasons. Sometimes if I went over on it, I had to come off. Yet the next day it would be back to normal. It would just click back in. It was coming towards I was going to have that operation at the end of the season, but it seemed to release itself. It fixed itself. I always used to have that strapped up. Same with my wrist. I broke my wrist when I was young. I had to have a bone chipped off, it would always go numb. The majority of things were all slight hamstring strains the lads would get or little calf knocks. I could play with injuries, not major ones, but niggling ones I could get through.

In those days the level of football was more or less as long as you could make yourself big and head a ball, more or less get in the box, you could carry little injuries. You couldn't do it in the first division, now the Premiership, because you had to do more twisting and running, and it was so fast passingwise, whereas in that lower league there was more or less three of us in the box. Let's get it in the box and find out what we can do.

While it is tempting to challenge the extent to which Campbell underestimates the abilities of himself and those who played with him, for those who saw him in his heyday it is impossible to ignore something else he says.

When I was at Bradford City, I had the best two feet in the club. I'd take anybody on at shooting, right foot or left foot, pass with my right foot, pass with my left foot. I'd beat them hands down. As a forward I could shoot with both feet, I could control a ball with both feet. I was the best header of a ball in the team.

There might be a few of his old team mates who would argue with some of what he says, but there can surely be no one who would want to challenge that last remark. Indeed, it could be extended far and away above 'the best header of a ball in the team'. Campbell was surely one of the best headers of a ball in his generation.

We should also remember that this player who suffered a broken leg at the age of 19, an injury of which he bears the scars to this day, rarely missed a game for any reason over a number of seasons. There was no such thing as rotation or being rested in those days. In all sorts of ways, good and bad, Bobby Campbell really was from a world long gone.

Chapter 9

PROMOTION

When George Mulhall left Valley Parade to return to Bolton Wanderers in March 1981, Bradford City began to tread water for the rest of the season. Despite Bobby Campbell's 19 goals in 42 league appearances and the historic League Cup game against Liverpool, they finished in 14th place in Division Four, a severe disappointment after so nearly gaining promotion the previous season. By the end of that 1980-81 season, however, expectation was high following the announcement of the new player/manager, Roy McFarland. Bobby Campbell's opinions on McFarland as a coach need little repetition. Mick Jones went to Valley Parade as assistant manager to Roy McFarland, the pair having been team mates for a time following McFarland's arrival at Derby in 1967.

Jonesy was more or less in the same mould as McFarland. They were nice enough blokes, don't get me wrong.

Stuart McCall, still to make his first team debut at this stage, recalls the same Mick Jones telling a story about Bobby, which reveals everything about Campbell's desire to play football at any price. 'He has a plate in his shin. Mick Jones tells a story about that. He'd looked at him one Saturday morning and said "You're not playing." It was sticking through the shin and you could feel it. Campbell's response was "I'll get it all strapped up. I'm playing." He didn't like missing games. That sums Bob up, really. He's very pale, white legs, but that protruding shin, with hardly a hair there because that's where his plate protrudes.'

But training wasn't up to standard. To me for my personal training that I wanted, they didn't do enough of it. They didn't do enough shooting and crossing. They knew I didn't like the long running. But running in and out, crossing, I'd do that all day. I'd do that twice, three times longer than any other player because I knew there was an end product. I'd pick myself up and run back and do it again, because there might be that one time in the match when you're knackered and you just think to yourself 'I've got to make the effort to get into that box. If the ball comes in, at least I'm going to be there for it.' That's why I used to love that. But when they turned round and said run to that cone and back, I'd say – Well, you can probably work out for yourself exactly what Campbell would have said.

There was, however, another side to McFarland's managerial style that clearly had a much greater appeal to Campbell.

I'll give McFarland his due - apart from that I didn't like his training. He made all the lads come down for a drink after the match. He said 'I don't give a shit if you have Coke, lemonade or whatever. We're all going for a drink and then you can all go home.' The only thing was I used to stay there all bloody night!

Going out with team mates after a match might have been just the sort of social event Campbell would have enjoyed. But organised nights out, at least those organised by Roy McFarland, were another matter altogether.

With McFarland everybody went to a do one night and he said to me 'Everybody has to come in their new club suits.' I said 'I'm not going.' I said 'You told me you were going to look after me. You haven't looked after me. You offered me another twenty quid a week. That's not looking after me. You can fine me if you want. At the end of the season I'm going back to Australia. I may even go back now, because my contract's up. I'm too old to listen to your shit. You aren't talking to some school kid you can frighten.' He left two weeks later, so it didn't matter!

In those two weeks there was no fine for the troublesome striker, there was no return to Australia and there was nothing to suggest that, had he stayed at Bradford City, Roy McFarland would have done anything to deprive the club of the man upon whose goals much of their (and McFarland's) success depended. Bobby Campbell was certainly not bigger than Bradford City, but, as was to be demonstrated all too quickly, he was the club's biggest single asset.

Campbell might not have thought much of the training methods, but he did respect the playing abilities of his manager, who, after all, had been winning international caps only four years before coming to Valley Parade. Indeed, what you achieved on the field of play was just about the only way of gaining respect in Bobby's eyes. And, since goal-scoring was what his own game was all about, it was goal-scoring that he thought should earn him his manager's respect. But there was one occasion, during an early season game, when it didn't quite work out that way.

McFarland was moaning at half-time 'We're not doing enough', giving me stick. At the start of the season all games are hard. You just don't turn it on. It's like training a racehorse to get out there and win the first race. They break them in. It's hard. The idea with those games is to get your fitness. Then Barry Gallagher crossed it. I might have been on the edge of the D and the box. I belted it into the top corner. I turned to McFarland and said 'What about that?' He threatened to fire me!

Whatever Campbell may have thought about McFarland's training methods, whether it was because of them or perhaps despite them, there is no disputing that his only full season in charge at Valley Parade was one of the more memorable and successful in Bradford City's history. 1981-82 saw the introduction into the Football

League of three points for a win. The new system was brought in to make draws less attractive and thus to give teams more incentive to go for a winning goal. In truth it made little difference, especially to the teams who became used to winning, no matter how many points a win brought for them.

Bradford City's season got off to a slow start with a 3-3 draw at home to Wigan and a 2-1 defeat at Hull. Campbell's personal season got off to a much better start, since he scored three of those four goals. But starting with the next game, at home to York City, things took off for both the team and the number nine. That game produced a 6-2 victory, with a Campbell hat trick that included a rare penalty. It was also the first of nine consecutive victories, a club record at the time, albeit one that was not to last for very much longer.

Although that sequence of victories was brought to an end by two successive defeats, including a home loss against the eventual league winners, Sheffield United, the pattern was already set by that nine game winning run. There were to be only seven defeats all season and, after losing 1-0 at Blackpool on March 3rd, the remainder of the season would see just one more defeat in the final seventeen games as the team maintained their position in the top four.

I remember scoring an equaliser against Bournemouth with the last kick of the game when we got promotion. It was two apiece. It was Cookey who'd flicked the ball on for me. There's no way David McNiven would have flicked that ball on for me. With my electric pace I managed to get past the centre back and whack it in from the edge of the box.

This is one of those occasions when it is not a description of the Campbell voice that is needed, but a word or two about his Bobby's facial expression. The reader, quite simply, has to imagine the huge grin as he utters the words 'my electric pace'. He would never claim that pace, electric or otherwise, was his greatest asset, but he was always blessed with a wicked sense of humour.

Joe Cooke had been brought back to Valley Parade midway through that season. He had come up through the City ranks, initially as a schoolboy, and had made his first team debut as a substitute as far back as September 1971. In his first three seasons he played mainly as a central defender, but during the 1974-75 season Bryan Edwards would switch Joe from defence to attack at regular intervals, depending on who else was available to play. From then on he became the regular first choice striker, scoring 24 goals in 1975-76 and another 18 the following season. In January 1979, having already scored 10 goals in his 21 appearances, he was transferred to Peterborough United. From there he had spells at Oxford United and Exeter City before returning to Valley Parade in January 1982, once more as a central defender.

Not that there was much likelihood of Joe returning as a striker. In that promotion season Messrs Campbell and McNiven played together in all but one of City's league matches, scoring 43 goals in the process. McFarland and Peter Jackson had been the regular centre back pairing, with Jacko having firmly established himself in George Mulhall's final season as City manager. But the new manager had a decision to make.

He left Jacko out of the team toward the end of that season. Jacko lost his place. There was McFarland and Cookey at the back. Cookey gave us that bit of nastiness at the back that we needed.Cookey not only gave us a bit more, but he could play at the front as well as the back.

And then, as though changing his mind after a moment's thought, Bobby has a slightly different opinion of where 'nastiness' starts and ends.

I thought I was a bit nasty, but Cookey wasn't nasty at all. He was just a big cumbersome bugger. He would run through a guy rather than run round him. He'd have made a real quarter back, running back in America.

Despite continuing to wear the number five shirt for the rest of the season, Cooke was still given the chance to show his versatility when the need arose. His occasional presence up front was much appreciated by the regular striker.

We had so many injured, Cookey probably came up alongside me. I think the last couple of games of the season Cookey actually came and played up front with me. A lot of players used to like playing off me. But I liked to play off a big lad myself just as much as they liked to play off me.

However the combination of Campbell, McNiven, Staniforth, Gallagher and occasionally Cooke may have fitted together in attack, there can be no doubting that they produced results. Dave Staniforth, whom Campbell had effectively replaced as centre forward two seasons earlier, played in 34 of the league games, scoring 7 goals from more of a midfield position. Barry Gallagher, another player to have come through the Bradford City apprentice system, made more than his fair contribution, playing in 42 league games and scoring 16 goals. For once Campbell's memory is rather less than generous about his former team mate's goal tally on this occasion. Gallagher was very much the dead ball expert in the team. He scored 6 of those goals from the penalty spot and he was always at the front of the queue for free kicks outside the penalty area. More important, or so Bobby would tell you, was the fact that he could also cross a very decent ball.

Young Barry Gallagher - he'd run all day, but just hadn't got that turn of speed for a winger. He could score quite a few goals from free kicks and stuff. I would say for the lower leagues he was the best dead ball kicker in the league. He scored masses of free kicks. He used to bend the ball all over the place. He was very good.

If you keep yourself in there with a chance, especially against a team that's better than you, and pray that you're going to get a couple of corners or a free kick outside the box and your star man might just come up with the goods. Like Barry Gallagher. There was many a result we scraped out. I used to play for them. I'd be backing in and he'd be climbing all over me and I'd fall down, because I knew I'd get a free kick. You never got a penalty for them, but you always got a free kick outside the box. And Gallagher used to punish them like nobody's business. That season we got promotion, Barry got about 12 goals. I'd say about 8 of them were free kicks outside the box. We used to have a little free kick we worked out. Barry would just stand on the ball on the corners of the edge of the 18 yard box, maybe 20 yards out. He'd just look at me and I'd make a run. He'd put that ball there and I'd put my arm out to make sure I got across the centre half. I'd head that in. I bet I got 8 goals that season as well from just that one move.

The defence almost picked itself that season. Steve Smith started the season in goal, remembered by Bobby as a craftsman 'who used to make as much money in the afternoons from painting and decorating', such was the pay of a fourth division goalkeeper. Neil Ramsbottom took over part way through the season, following a pattern that had begun the previous season and was to repeat itself the following season, the only difference being that in 1982-3 Ramsbottom would take over from Eric McManus. The centre backs were almost always two out of the three of Jackson, McFarland and Cooke, with Mick Wood getting just eight starts there and another five at left back. The full back shirts were very rarely vacant. It almost goes without saying that Ces Podd played all 46 games at right back with Garry Watson, another product of Bradford City's youth system, playing 40 games at left back.

We used to nickname him Neville Davitt after the Ripping Yarns story. It was the best programme I'd ever seen in my life.

Now, if you want to get Campbell laughing – and the

Campbell laugh is quite something, especially when you put it into the context of the Campbell voice – then get him talking about a television series called Ripping Yarns. The programmes featured Michael Palin in spoofs of schoolboy stories from the inter-war years. Just one of them is about a football club, based in Yorkshire and with the wonderful name of Barnstoneworth United. Just how or why Garry Watson was named after their left winger, who famously 'scored two in t'last minute' on a regular basis, is a mystery best left to Campbell and his team mates.

The season did not finish until May 15th, bad weather having caused the postponement of a number of games from the middle of November until the end of January. These postponements resulted in some odd fixtures, including City playing both of their matches against Crewe during an unbeaten last six games of the season. The away game brought a 1-0 win, courtesy of a Campbell goal, and the home game a 4-1 win, with all four goals coming from David McNiven. A home draw against Bournemouth finally made promotion to the third division a mathematical certainty. The two goals that Campbell scored that day brought his total for the season to 27.

The last game of the season, a 2-0 win at Mansfield, confirmed that Bradford City would finish as runners-up, five points behind Sheffield United, but nine points clear of fifth placed Peterborough United. The club was to go through very many ups and downs in the next twenty five years, during which time even relegation could be put into a context where it was no longer seen as quite such a disastrous event. But Bradford City were not to return to that fourth division for the rest of the twentieth century.

Chapter 10

IN A GREEN SHIRT

Bradford City's 1981-2 season may have reached its finale with a win against Mansfield Town on May 15th, but Bobby Campbell's own season still had several more weeks to run. This was not another Campbell expedition to Canada or Australia, however, but a rather more serious trip to Spain. In an era when it was practically unheard of for a current Bradford City player to win an international cap, especially when the club was striving to escape from the fourth division, Campbell found himself in the wings at the world's greatest football stage. But nothing was ever that simple in the Campbell career and this particular episode has to be put in the context of his youthful activities on and off the pitch.

We have already come across some of Bobby's exploits with the Northern Ireland team at schoolboy level. By the age of 15 he had played alongside Jimmy Nicholl, John McLelland and David McCreery. Nicholl was to go on to play over 200 games for Manchester United and win 73 caps for Northern Ireland, even though he was born in Canada. Belfast born McClelland was to play league football for a number of clubs in both England and Scotland, winning 53 international caps. McCreery, who played 67 times for Northern Ireland, won an F A Cup winners medal in the same 1977 Manchester United team that included Jimmy Nicholl and was part of the Newcastle United team that won promotion to the first division in 1984.

From an early age Campbell had been used to playing in talented sides. He was certainly good enough to continue playing for his country beyond schoolboy level, while pursuing his professional career with Aston Villa. He had already made his debut for the Villa first team when, as an 18 year old, he went with the Northern Ireland youth team to Switzerland to play in the European Championships. With the Campbell of those days there was always a very thin line between the next giant leap forward and the nearest disaster. He was expert at crossing that line.

We'd just played one game, drawn 0-0. We were supposed to be playing England on the Saturday. We'd been more or less tied up for the last ten days getting prepared and we were just letting off steam. What happened was they'd let us have a few beers. Everybody thinks I can drink. We'd maybe had only half a dozen and maybe not even that. I took one of the barmen's Volkswagen for a little joy ride round the car park and I smashed it up – still in the car park. There were better ways of letting off steam. The coach was Tommy Casey, the manager of Grimsby, a nice bloke. I felt really embarrassed, really bad about letting him down.

One of the lads went to hospital because he went through the windscreen. Two of the lads were in the back and just went back to bed. They locked me up and I denied everything. They said to me that if you say you did it, we'll pay the damages and you'll be out to play for the England game. I said this and the next thing I knew I was out and on a plane home.

I was only 18 years old and they put me on a plane to London. Didn't they know I lived in Birmingham? I had to walk through London by myself at 12 o'clock at night to get a bus from Heathrow to Euston station to get a train to Birmingham. Just as well I was streetwise.

Bobby's upbringing in Belfast may have made him 'streetwise' in many ways, but he had a lot to learn about dealing with the authorities, especially when it came to motor cars, drink and the available penalties. Although the Swiss incident brought lasting repercussions for him, it was not quite enough to keep him out of further similar difficulties a few years later. Meanwhile, the footballing authorities were ready to make an example of him.

They banned me for life. I thought I could live with that. I said to myself 'I'm too old to play for the youth team now.' I didn't realise that the ban meant the whole lot.

So at the age of just 18, Bobby Campbell was banned from international football by the Irish Football Association and the ban wasn't just, as he had briefly imagined, from playing for the youth team again, but really was meant as a life time ban. He was banned from playing international football at all levels. But that particular obstacle was far from the end of Bobby's involvement with the Northern Ireland team.

I remember when I was at Sheffield United, way back, Jimmy Sirrel, God rest his soul, a very, very clever gentleman and with a lovely wife; they had a youth hostel and I stayed a couple of nights there. It was like a hotel. That hostel was run a lot better than the one they had at Villa. Most of the lads used to go home on a weekend as well. Coming from Northern Ireland, I couldn't go.

Danny Blanchflower was manager of Northern Ireland. I suppose Jimmy knew him from his playing days in the sixties. Jimmy got him to come and have a look at me. We played Sunderland at home and I had a stinker. The referee gave us nothing. There was one occasion when I jumped up. It's always been my biggest beef with referees that you jump up on the half-way line and the centre half goes over the top of you, you get a free kick, but if he does it in the penalty box, you never get a penalty. This was so blatant, that he'd come over the top of me, and the referee didn't give a penalty. I ended up getting booked for dissent.

I was mouthing it at the ref and trying too hard and got myself booked for dissent. After that game Danny Blanchflower said 'You haven't had a good game because you got yourself involved.' I sat there and listened to a bloke like that telling me that and I never got booked for dissent ever again. Never once.

I didn't realise at the time that Danny Blanchflower was such a sportsman that he accepted results. I was trying to impress so much because Jimmy had told me he was coming to watch me. I was running round like a headless chicken. The more I tried the worse it got. I might have been better not knowing he was there.

Neither Jimmy Sirrel nor Danny Blanchflower seemed to know that they were wasting their time looking at this young centre forward and assessing his chances of making it into the Northern Ireland under 21 squad or even the senior squad. Bobby may have hoped that someone back at the Irish F A had made a mistake and that the ban really was over. But his hopes were unfounded. His booking for dissent had, in any case, ruined any chance he might have had with the national team manager. There was no need for any further enquiry with the Irish Football Association into Campbell's precise status as a potential international player.

Jimmy Sirrel was soon to leave Sheffield United for his beloved Notts County and Bobby Campbell was to begin his intercontinental wanderings as a professional footballer. Eventually those wanderings brought him to Bradford City and the goal scoring that had so impressed Jimmy Sirrel, a man whom Campbell clearly admired and respected, began to impress Roy McFarland, his manager at Valley Parade, even if Campbell had rather less respect for McFarland's own managerial abilities. By the middle of October 1981 Campbell had scored 14 goals in the first 15 league and cup games of Roy McFarland's managerial career.

I was knocking the goals in under McFarland and Roy

rang up Billy Bingham and said 'You'd better come and have a look at him.' I was playing well that year. I never struggled to score goals. I've played against top centre halves, like Butcher and McFarland, during my career and I've held my own. I think that given a chance I would have held my own at international level as well, even with the bad leg.

This time the Irish manager liked what he saw. Perhaps Campbell didn't get booked! More likely is that he scored a goal or two. Billy Bingham was sufficiently impressed by the striker to join the Bradford City directors and manager in appealing to the Irish F A to lift the life ban which by then had been in place for seven years.

The ban was lifted. I'll give the people of Northern Ireland their due. Once you've done enough time, they're always willing to forgive. There was enough time left in the bag.

So now all that remained for the fourth division striker to do was convince the national team manager that the way he had seen him play in the claret and amber could be reproduced in the green and white. Of course, if the manager was ever going to be convinced by the Campbell case, Bobby would need to be given the chance to play in the national side. Billy Bingham gave him that chance on 28th April 1982, when Northern Ireland played Scotland in what was then called the Home International Championships.

Neither Northern Ireland nor Bradford City could usually be counted as being among the big boys in their respective competitions, although both were about to improve their standings. The timing of these improvements could not have had greater importance for a player determined to prove himself at the highest level. Bobby Campbell was once again at a make or break stage in his professional career. No matter what was expected of him, by club or by country, he could not start complaining about being tired from playing too many matches in a short period. Throughout his career, Bobby Campbell was hardly likely to complain about playing too much football. In this instance he was to turn out in four games over a period of just a week. Each of those games was clearly going to be of great importance both for Bobby's own career and for the future prospects of both of the teams he was representing. There were no easy rides to be taken in this hectic programme.

On Saturday April 24th 1982 Campbell scored the only goal in a 1-0 win at home to Blackpool, a victory which took Bradford City that bit nearer promotion to the Third Division with five more league games left to play. On Monday April 26th he again scored the only goal in another Bradford City win, this time at Crewe, and on Saturday May 1st he was to play in a 1-1 draw at Rochdale. By the middle of May he had played no fewer than 52 games that season for his club. But the Windsor Park game against Scotland was Bobby's biggest (and, for all he knew, only) chance to show the international manager just what he could do. It just had to be fitted in to this schedule on the Wednesday, even if it was his third game in five days.

'The big ginger-haired lad from Aberdeen' who was marking Northern Ireland's 'big centre forward' was Alex McLeish, then playing under Alex Ferguson in the days when Aberdeen rarely went a season without winning a major trophy. McLeish, in fact, did not stay on for the whole 90 minutes. Perhaps Jock Stein just wanted to see how a different centre half would deal with Campbell when he decided to give the last 15 minutes to Alan Hansen. It is rather more likely that Stein wanted to try out an alternative defensive pairing, just in case the McLeish-Miller partnership that had been so dominant for Aberdeen and Scotland should not be available to him in the World Cup finals that were only weeks away.

I remember John Wark playing for them. I think Asa Hartford was playing. I can't remember who was up front for Scotland.

Well, the Scottish number nine shirt was worn by somebody called Dalglish, who was a different sort of front man to Campbell, but did OK for himself. And out on the left wing for the opposition was John Robertson, who was to become a team mate of Campbell's for a short period in the 1983-4 season. For the record, Bobby didn't score in the 1-1 draw, but this was the game which brought Northern Ireland their only point in that season's Home Internationals.

In the Northern Ireland team was Sammy McIlroy. I played up front with a guy called Healy, who I ended up rooming with. I played up front with him because they wanted to see how we got along. We did alright. I think Sammy scored the equaliser. I had a hand in it along the way. Jimmy Nicholl played. That night they played the reserve goalkeeper, used to play for Middlesbrough, Jim Platt. There was Mal Donaghy and John McClelland who I went to school with. They were a good bunch of lads. A lot of them I knew from schoolboy football, as well as playing against them through youth team and first team matches.

That is quite a list of names, rattled off instantly. Some may be better known than others. The Campbell memory is accurate once again – Sammy McIlroy did indeed score in the 52nd minute. Given the precision of his memory, perhaps Campbell's recollection of an 'assist' can also be relied upon. In 1982 McIlroy was at the end of a 400 game career with Manchester United. He won 88 international caps and went on to manage his national side for three years.

Felix Healy, like Campbell, was making his international debut. He was playing for Coleraine at the time. He was actually from Derry, but his local team, Derry City, had withdrawn from league football in Northern Ireland in 1972, at the start of what would have been a second season of being forced to play their home games in Coleraine. The civil unrest in Northern Ireland led to their home ground being declared unsafe. In 1987 Healy was to begin a six year career as a player for Derry City, by then playing in the top division of football in the Republic of Ireland. He was also to manage them in the second half of the 1990's.

Campbell's recollection that Jim Platt was in goal means that this was one of the very few Northern Ireland games in these years not to feature Pat Jennings. Although Platt won 23 caps, Jennings' 119 international appearances stretched from 1964 to 1986, by which time he was able to claim the record for the oldest player then to have appeared in the final stages of the World Cup.

At the time of Campbell's full international debut Mal Donaghy was in the midst of the 400 games he was to play for Luton Town, who were on the verge of winning the second division title. He was later to play for Manchester United and Chelsea and to win 91 Northern Irish caps. John McClelland was playing for Rangers at the time, but was about to spend four seasons in the English First Division as a Watford player. There were plenty in that Northern Ireland team who had very successful careers, some of whom were on the verge of becoming very famous indeed in a green shirt.

The Home Internationals were spread out over the latter months of the season. Northern Ireland had been beaten 4-0 at Wembley in February and their remaining game, against Wales, was not to be played until May 27th, some two weeks after the end of Bradford City's season. But Bobby had every possible reason for wanting to play in that game and to impress Billy Bingham. Back in November 1981 a 1-0 win at home to Israel had secured Northern Ireland's place in the World Cup Finals, bringing automatic qualification with a second place finish in their group behind Scotland and ahead of Sweden and Portugal. Despite Northern Ireland's position in the Home Internationals table, the game against Wales would be the last chance for the manager to decide which of the fringe players would be given World Cup shirts.

Bobby Campbell didn't start the game at Wrexham. Northern Ireland's established strikers were Gerry Armstrong and Billy Hamilton.

I scored more goals than Billy Hamilton, who was the centre forward for Northern Ireland. I would have scored three against his one. He was playing at Burnley. I played against them, so they were in the second or third division.

Hamilton played for Burnley from 1979 to 1984. Burnley did indeed play in the third division in 1981-2, winning the title. Sadly, they were relegated the following season and played in the same division as Bradford City from 1983-4. In the 1981-2 season Hamilton scored 11 goals in 44 league games. His most prolific season for Burnley was 1983-4, when his total of 21 goals included 18 in 46 league matches. In total he scored 58 goals in 200 league games for Burnley. His 41 games for Northern Ireland produced 5 goals.

As usual, Bobby's opinion of a player centres on their abilities on the pitch. When he discusses strikers, the first and last consideration is the number of goals scored. His own goal scoring record can be found elsewhere in this book. Comparisons with Billy Hamilton's are unavoidable, although it must be borne in mind that Hamilton played some of his games one division higher than Campbell.

At the end of the day, as a centre forward they don't look at 'Campbell, 40 games, 28 man of the matches.' They straight away look at 'Campbell, centre forward, 40 games, how many goals?' At the end of the season that's what it boils down to. You're there to score goals.

And at first it sounds as though his opinion of Gerry Armstrong is also limited to that single facet of his personality.

Gerry Armstrong was the first choice centre forward. I don't know why, because he couldn't score a goal to save his life.

But immediately Bobby adds an extra dimension to his

opinion of this particular striker.

Gerry is a lovely man. I won't hear a bad word said about him.

So Gerry Armstrong clearly has something about him. It takes a lot for Campbell to admire a striker who 'couldn't score a goal to save his life.' While it is true that Armstrong was a long way short of Campbell's goals to games ratio, it has to be accepted that he played for much of his career at the highest levels and had just helped Watford gain promotion to the first division for the 1982-3 season. By the time he had scored Watford's first goal in the top division, he had already made his name with a 'goal he's lived on ever since'.

And so, for that late May game against Wales, Campbell had to settle for a place on the bench. He came on as a substitute, but too late to do anything about the inglorious 3-0 defeat Northern Ireland suffered that night. However, whether it had been through his performances for Bradford City or in his two appearances in a green shirt, he had persuaded Billy Bingham that he was good enough to be included in the squad to play in the World Cup Finals in Spain.

Two and a half years earlier, Bobby Campbell had been a part-time footballer and a part-time scaffolder. He had gained a reputation as a hell-raiser and had left lower league clubs in inauspicious circumstances. He had known that he was banned for life from playing for his country. And yet, in the summer of 1982, the same Bobby Campbell was part of the greatest international competition the game of football has to offer. Almost inevitably, things were not to go smoothly for him.

I played all year, never missed a game. I always had this dodgy ankle. We went to Brighton and the bloody thing pinged, didn't it? The ankle went. I struggled a bit in training. By the time I got fit, the team was picking itself.

Campbell did, in fact, miss just one game for Bradford City, at home to Torquay United in March. But he played in 52 games in addition to the two international appearances, scoring 27 goals. Immediately before the World Cup finals the Northern Irish training camp was set up in Brighton, although the story goes that it was better preparation for the Spanish conditions than being in Barcelona, temperatures on the south coast of England at the time being somewhat higher.

Billy Bingham was not necessarily Bobby Campbell's favourite manager, despite being the man who gave him his international caps after helping to have the life time ban lifted. Bobby Campbell, as it turns out, may also not necessarily have been Billy Bingham's favourite player eventually. But Bobby knows fair play when he sees it.

I'll give Billy his due; he asked if I was fit for the last game. I think he was going to make me sub. I tweaked my groin on the morning during training. I couldn't believe it. All season I was fit and playing. At international level you can't carry injuries.

That last game, when Campbell was not fit enough to be included even as a substitute, was against France. 24 countries had qualified for the 1982 World Cup Finals and, in the first round, they had been divided into six groups. The top two teams from each group would go into a second round, consisting of four groups of three. The winners of each of those four groups would go into the semi-finals. In the first round Northern Ireland had been drawn in the same groups as Yugoslavia, the outsiders from Honduras and the clear favourites to progress, the host nation Spain.

Draws in the first two games against Yugoslavia and Honduras and a win the previous day for Yugoslavia against Honduras had left Northern Ireland with the certain knowledge that defeat in Valencia against Spain would send them home early. Gerry Armstrong had scored Northern Ireland's only goal to date in the 1-1 draw with Honduras. Gerry Armstrong's next goal, the most famous goal in his country's history and the one that he was to live on forever thereafter, would provide the shock of the competition. Spain were beaten 1-0 and Northern Ireland topped their first round group. In the second round they were up against France and Austria.

Billy Hamilton then scored both goals in a 2-2 draw with Austria, who had already lost to France in the second round group. With only the winner of the group to go through to the semi-finals, Northern Ireland needed to beat France to reach the last four. The French 'were a good team'. Among others they included Platini, Giresse and Tigana, so Bobby's description is certainly no exaggeration. Because he knew he wasn't even fit enough to be on the bench, Campbell had rather more freedom than he might have expected. And that freedom explains why 'I had one of my best afternoons out that day.'

The game was to be played at the Vicente Calderon in Madrid and was a 5.15 kick off. The Northern Ireland squad arrived at the ground some two and a half hours before the game was due to start.

We were pulling up outside Athletico Madrid's ground. There must have been thirty French fans chanting 'Bobby, Bobby Campbell'. They were wearing the blue and white of France. I just said 'It's my French fan club. The Bordeaux fan club.' They weren't even Northern Ireland fans. All this comes from one guy who lived in Huddersfield and went to live in Bordeaux. This lad who lived in France used to come home to Huddersfield every Christmas and summer, Stevie Fallon. He went on a bit of a holiday and settled down and met people. These lads used to come over and I used to give them things as souvenirs to take back. We used to socialise with them when they came over.

On this particular occasion, however, it was Bobby who was on his travels, even if the French supporters were also some little distance from home. But whether it is Huddersfield or Madrid, Bobby Campbell is always prepared to socialise.

I wasn't sub and all you're going to do is kill time. Nobody likes to see you hang around the dressing room. I thought I'd come with him for a drink. There was no trouble at all. There was a good atmosphere. I said to Stevie 'Where are you going?' I went into the changing room, took off my tracksuit top. I've got the green tracksuit bottoms and a white polo shirt. I had plenty of money, flashed my pass that gets me anywhere in the ground. I went across the road to the pub. They couldn't believe it when I went for a drink with them. Can you imagine that? A World Cup player going for a drink with them before a match? That is one time I could drink before a match. I definitely knew I wasn't playing. They're the opposition fans and they were cheering me. Marvellous!

It was full of French fans, all these lads from Bordeaux. I said the drinks were on me. I must have been there about two hours. He said 'We've got to go to the game now.' I'd had a few wines and a few beers. Where we were going in, I had to walk all the way round. I thought I'd go through with them and walk round when we got into the ground. I flashed the pass, went through this gate.

And so it turned out that the Northern Ireland reserve striker, albeit ruled out even as a substitute earlier in the day, ended up watching the first half of his team's World Cup match from a spot in among the opposition fans. It was near to kick off when Bobby discovered that, although his pass worked in most situations, it didn't allow him to change ends inside the ground. He had to wait until half time to leave his new found fans, go back outside the ground and make his way in through an entrance at the other end to rejoin the rest of the squad. Sadly the second half that he watched was to be his team's last action in the competition. France won 4-1 and Bobby was as good as on his way back home. But he had one quite extraordinary memory of a competition where he hadn't even kicked a ball in anger.

There's a Bobby Campbell fan club in Bordeaux. The Bobby Campbell fan club. I never forget it.

Bobby, being the man he is, prefers to remember those happy and sociable moments, even when he has to finish the story of his World Cup on a less jovial note.

I was always disappointed that Bingham and I must have fallen out somewhere along the line, because he never picked me again. I don't know what happened there with Billy Bingham. But I never gave him any cause to be disciplined and I was never out of order. I came back and Billy Bingham came round all the lads saying 'We'll see you guys. We'll be watching you. Have a nice time.' I had my best season for Bradford the next season. I scored thirty-odd goals for Bradford in the third division and I wasn't picked again. I just put it down to a clash of personalities. Maybe I should have picked the phone up or let the manager pick the phone up and find out why they wouldn't pick me. If it was something that I'd done, we could sort it out. He never picked me again.

The Spanish press had run stories of disagreements between the Northern Ireland players, one or two allegedly even reaching the stage where blows were exchanged. But Campbell does not believe there was any disciplinary issue that might have affected his future chances.

I know we had a couple of does, but I wasn't involved in them. I had a little dig at Billy because he had a dig at me. When we came home on the plane, Jimmy Nicholl and I were the last on the plane. We had our load of duty free. What you have to remember is that I was getting married two weeks later. I had all the family coming over from Ireland. You have to offer them a drink. It's only hospitality. I've got loads and loads of pesetas to spend, so I've bought all these. And he's turned round and said 'Where the hell are you?' I said 'Look Billy, what's up with you? It's all over now. You can't send me home now.' I don't know what happened, but he never picked me again. I had a real season, that season after the World Cup. I scored 30-odd goals. Billy Hamilton didn't even get 20 goals for Burnley. I never got a sniff. That was the only reason I went to Derby.

Campbell did indeed score 30 goals in 49 games for Bradford City in the Third Division. But something had clearly gone awry between him and the Northern Ireland manager. His track record with managers and his hint of regret at not contacting Bingham suggest that even Campbell acknowledges that there might have been some fault on his part. His stay at Derby County was to be especially short, even by the standards of a player once famous for moving between clubs at regular intervals. At least that was one poor decision that could be easily remedied. Much more importantly, his international career was at an end after just two caps and a trip to Spain – hardly a fitting return for a player of his undoubted abilities. But at least it took him to the biggest international tournament in the world and brought him into contact with one of the more unlikely fans clubs!

Chapter 11

NUMBER NINE MEETS NUMBER FOUR

The summer of 1982 had hardly given Bobby Campbell a free moment. His call up to the Northern Ireland training camp before the start of the World Cup finals had cut short his own participation in Bradford City's promotion celebrations. Then the Northern Ireland team had confounded the pundits by staying in the competition for longer than most had dared to forecast, even if Campbell's role was restricted to training and keeping his French fan club entertained. And he came back to Huddersfield to enjoy the biggest celebration of the lot, his marriage to Paula. It must have seemed no time at all, then, before he was re-joining Roy McFarland and the rest of the Bradford City squad to set about tackling the greater challenges of the third division after The Bantams had spent four seasons in the Football League's basement. In the first game of the new season there are always some fresh faces and, as City beat Reading 3-2 with Campbell scoring the first goal of the new campaign, one particular face was just about as fresh as they come.

While the new goalkeeper, Eric McManus, had all the experience in the world, only the legendary Pat Jennings having prevented him getting international honours, the new right back, making his debut in the absence of the injured Ces Podd, was a small, baby faced eighteen year old who would have struggled to persuade the most generous barman that he was old enough to buy his own drinks. McManus was destined to build on an already excellent reputation among the faithful during the course of over 100 games for City. The newcomer in the number two shirt, however, was to become a true legend, albeit to be forever associated with a different number on his back. But we need to go back a little in time to witness this newcomer's first encounter with Bobby Campbell.

Although the first league game of the 1980-1 season wasn't to be played until 16th August, George Mulhall had the players back for pre-season training in early July. On the first day back the few new faces were all trying to get to know those who had just missed out on promotion. Especially keen to get involved and to make a good impression were the new apprentices, meeting their heroes for the first time. It was one of these apprentices, only days past his sixteenth birthday and, in his own words 'three foot one and just in awe of everyone that's coming in', who caught the attention of Bryan Edwards. Bryan told the new lad to go to the chemists and fetch some strapping and some tape. It was, after all, one of the jobs of the apprentices to make sure that the first team players had all the necessary kit.

Before he left the dressing room on the way to the chemists, the new apprentice, keen to get in the good books not only of Bryan Edwards, but also of the first team players, spotted an opportunity to win early brownie points. The Bradford City players weren't exactly household names, but at least one of them was known to anyone who had even a passing interest in the club, even if, like the young apprentice, the only time they'd ever seen the team play was in the end-of-season testimonial game for the club's retiring goalkeeper Peter Downsborough.

The face and the physique of Bobby Campbell were unmistakable. It was, however, very clear to the sixteen year old that the star striker had a problem with his voice. Thus it was that he thought he'd take his chance to win even more points by offering to help out. 'Excuse me, Bob, can I get you something for your throat?' asked the young lad. The reply was swift, severe and never to be forgotten. The apprentice may have recognised the star striker, but that did not mean the recognition worked both ways. He immediately found himself being lifted off his feet by the Irishman and faced with both a question and an explanation. 'Who are you, little lad? I always speak like this.' There may well have been a few other words used as well, but the apprentice was so terrified by his first introduction to Bobby Campbell that he can't recall whether he was able to give a proper answer to the striker's question by declaring himself to be Stuart McCall.

But that wasn't quite the end of their first meeting. Stuart went off to the chemists on his errand, wondering whether he might risk bringing back some mints to help disguise the smell of alcohol on his new colleague's breath. (He decided against it, by the way – probably a wise decision in all the circumstances.) When he came back, Bobby had obviously had a moment to reflect on their earlier encounter and greeted the errand boy with the much more placatory 'You all right, wee man?'

It was to be the start of a lasting friendship, summed up by one small incident never forgotten by Stuart McCall. 'I watched him one day with a pint. It just went straight down like a drain. At 18 I thought of him as a great header of the ball and a man who didn't have a gullet. What a memory!' And, so long as the two halves of that memory are kept together, Campbell himself would hardly object to the 18 year old's imagery.

The young McCall didn't make his first team debut for another two years after that initial and 'up-lifting' encounter with the man in possession of the number nine shirt. At the start of the 1982-3 season Ces Podd, who had played every game in the promotion season, was suffering from an eye injury. A replacement right back was required for the first three league games. The number two shirt went to Stuart McCall for those three matches. Once Ces was fit again, the 18 year old found himself almost inevitably out of the first team for a while. He made an appearance on 13th November as a substitute for Ian Mellor and in the next match for the first time wore the number four shirt that is for ever associated with him by all at Valley Parade. His first game as Bradford City's number four was a League Cup 3rd round replay at Old Trafford. Bryan Edwards, by then the acting manager at Valley Parade, decided it was essential that the Manchester United midfield should not have the freedom of the park. With this tactic in mind, he gave McCall the simple task of man-marking the England captain, Bryan Robson.

Despite losing that replay 4-1, with Campbell scoring again, Stuart McCall has every cause to remember that first outing in central midfield. But it was the 'wee man's' first league match in the number four shirt that both he and Bobby remember. That game was away to Bournemouth on 27th November, just three days after the defeat against Manchester United. The squad had travelled down to Bournemouth on the Friday and were staying in what Campbell describes as 'a nice hotel'. The evening was spoiled only by a blanket of fog. The local knowledge was to the effect that the fog would not lift over the next 24 hours and that the game would almost certainly be called off. After dinner the players went out for a walk. There may be a little confusion about who consumed what sort of liquid refreshment during that walk, with one or two insisting that they confined themselves to orange juice, while others were perhaps just a little more relaxed. No one drank very much of anything, however, because the entire squad was back in the hotel by 9.30 on that Friday evening.

Sure enough, when they awoke next morning, the players and their hotel were still engulfed by the fog. They made their way to the old Dean Court ground in the certain knowledge that they would soon be going back home, only to be greeted by the referee, who promptly told them that, since he could see both goals from the half-way line, the match would be going ahead.

At some stage in the game the ball was in the hands of the Bournemouth goalkeeper. Young McCall decided to chance his arm and head the ball out of the keeper's hands. Having done precisely that, he promptly stuck it into the net for his first Bradford 'goal'. The City fans knew little or nothing of this, since they were standing behind the goal at other end of the ground and clearly did not share the referee's powers of X ray vision. As it happened, the referee's vision, perhaps a fraction less than perfect, did extend to seeing the ball in the net and for a brief moment McCall thought he'd 'got away with it'. The linesman's eyesight was, however, keener than that of the man in the middle. The raised flag proved decisive. The 'goal' was chalked off and McCall would have to wait until 15th January for his first real goal.

Although some sort of justice had been done by the referee, there were others who were still intent on extracting their own brand of summary judgment. The Bournemouth centre half was called John Impey. McCall remembers him as an archetypal eighties centre half, 'a big bruising bloke with no teeth'. It was Impey's arm that McCall felt round his throat as he attempted to run back into his midfield position. The difference in their respective builds made this a telling intervention on Impey's part. Stuart might even have suffered a flashback to another arm around his throat. In this state of alarm, McCall managed to pick out only a few words from the brief conversation, but he understood that Mr Impey was suggesting that young Stuart was a cheat. More words might have been exchanged, but for the intervention of the Wee Man's knight in shining claret and amber. Enter Campbell from out of the mist, with all the tact and diplomacy for which he was ever famous.

McCall's recollection is that Campbell stepped into the

middle of the confrontation, which then came to a very rapid end. That is to say that it came to an end as far as McCall was concerned. It seems that Impey was one of those centre halves it paid not to annoy – and Bob, by sticking up for his wee friend, had just caused considerable annoyance to his opponent. 'I skipped back into the middle of the park with my head down', Stuart recalls, 'while those two had an almighty bang-bang for the rest of the ninety minutes.'

After the game had finished, Campbell showed all the signs of battle. The back of his legs, especially his calves, had been frequently kicked and he'd been scraped down his Achilles. Worse still was the fact that, despite a 2-2 draw, neither of the City goals was Campbell's. He didn't have time to finish the sentence that began 'You, you little so-and-so, if I ever have to fight your battles again,…'. Stuart quickly nipped in with a 'Thanks, Bob, thanks.' His conclusion that Campbell was 'none too pleased' at having found himself so frequently on the wrong end of John Impey's studs was almost certainly correct.

Those two games against Manchester United and Bournemouth came during a week of turmoil at Valley Parade – although Campbell himself may not have seen the events quite in that light. On Saturday November 20th Bradford City had won 1-0 away to Port Vale in the first round of the F A Cup, Campbell scoring the winning goal. The team and their manager knew that they had the League Cup replay to face in midweek. What the players didn't know was that the game at Vale Park was to be the last match for Roy McFarland as Bradford City's player/manager.

Earlier that month McFarland's old club Derby County, for whom he had played well over 400 games, had found themselves bottom of the second division and a change of manager had been inevitable. Following the much publicised departure of Brian Clough, John Newman had been Derby's fifth manager in less than nine years. His team had won just six out of 35 games during his managerial reign and his dismissal cannot have surprised even Newman himself. The new manager at the Baseball Ground was Peter Taylor, who had retired at the end of the previous season as Brian Clough's right hand man at Nottingham Forest. It was something of an open secret that Taylor was an admirer of McFarland from their time together at Derby, but it still came as a shock, not least in Bradford, when McFarland and Mick Jones both resigned from their Valley Parade jobs just a few days before the Manchester United game in order to join Taylor's managerial team. Derby were subsequently punished by the football authorities and ordered to pay Bradford City compensation for their part in 'poaching' the pair, but that was some distance away. For the immediate future Bradford City were in sudden need of a new manager.

The man who had been partly responsible for bringing Campbell to Valley Parade, Bryan Edwards, took over as caretaker manager until the chairman, Bob Martin, agreed a £10,000 fee with Leeds United to bring in another player/manager and former England international defender, Trevor Cherry. Cherry was also to recruit another favourite from Elland Road, by now playing for the same Vancouver Whitecaps club which had once employed Bobby Campbell. The new player/assistant manager was Terry Yorath and, for Campbell at least, a new and much improved coaching era was about to begin.

It was Cherry's first management job. They came as a team. They were playing a bit and we did alright. We didn't have a particularly good season that season, but we held our own. I had a very good season. I scored 30 goals.

Terry Yorath was, in fact to play in just three games that season, but Trevor Cherry took part in each of the 28 games played after his appointment. Bradford City eventually finished in 12th place in the third division in their first season after promotion, a feat which many, given the mid-season upheaval, might consider to be rather more of an achievement than merely 'holding our own'. While such an individual goal-scoring tally would be seen as exceptional by most strikers, those 30 goals came in that rarity for Bobby Campbell, namely a season reduced by injury.

Yorath and Cherry knew me better. They looked at it and said that's the way to work Bob. They'd put me at the side of that lad. He's a midfielder. We want him up and down like a yo-yo, let's get him running. Bob, let's get him doing in and out crossing and shooting, because we'll get his fitness that way. That's the way I used to be, in and out, in and out. I'd sweat more doing that than I would doing these long runs. I was never any good at a long run and I hold my hands up to it. I wasn't there to win a race. I'd maybe win a five yard race in the box and that's what I concentrated on. That was why I had to work my own way out. Get in that box. That was my area.

When I got into the first team at Villa, I used to be all over the pitch. I did too much donkey work. After I broke my leg and I sat and watched and studied it more, I thought to myself 'Why would I be doing that running out there?' When I came back, he (Tom Johnston, the Huddersfield Town manager at the time of Bobby's return from his broken leg) *would say 'Come on out here, Bob.' I'd say 'No, get a midfield player out there. If I go out there and lay the ball off, the midfield player's going to run into the box. He can't head a ball. Get him to run out there and I'll get into the box to head the ball.'*

When I started not doing my own thing, but doing the things that I thought were beneficial for the team, that's when I started scoring regular goals and I was more effective. If I didn't score, I was making a lot more goals. If I didn't get a clean header, I made sure the centre half didn't get a clean header. Or if the goalkeeper was there, I made sure he never got a clean catch. There was someone there to tap in or pick the pieces up. But if I'm out on the wing, laying the ball off for somebody to cross, to me I might as well be in the bloody stand.

It is important to put those earlier comments into their context. Bobby Campbell was just returning to action from a broken leg he had suffered as a 19 year old. His manager, Tom Johnston, had almost twenty years' experience as a coach and was in his late fifties. But it was the young unproven striker who was telling the manager how he should be playing. Can it be any wonder that Campbell and his managers didn't always see eye to eye? In those circumstances it has always been the case that the manager wins and the young player either gives way or goes away. In Campbell's case, he went away – and on more than one occasion.

Stability came only when he had found a coach, George Mulhall, who saw things the same way as Campbell and was prepared to take him on, warts and all. Roy McFarland's eighteen month stay at Bradford City and the coaching methods Campbell disliked so much briefly threatened that stability. It was only with the arrival of Trevor Cherry and Terry Yorath, coaches who had ideas about how Campbell should play that matched his own views, that he settled down again to enjoying his football.

Bobby Campbell hardly ever missed a first team game for Bradford City. But in that 1982-3 season he missed six league games, including two almost as soon as the new management team had taken over.

Then Cherry and Yorath came and I got an injury. I busted a rib and if you touched me on that bone I'd go down like a sack of spuds. I played on with it. It was probably a knee, maybe from a keeper as I was coming down. I felt it at the time, just another knock. I played for a month with it and Terry Yorath saw me and said 'Ah, it's nothing, Bob'. I said 'Terry, I can't do any sit-ups.' I couldn't do sit-ups for a month, but then it healed over.

I actually played for a month and I never got hit in that area. I'd have got up OK, but it was just like a bullet hitting you. And the exact same injury happened to Terry

Yorath three months later. And I said to Terry 'You've got the Celtic Curse on you.' And I was touching him and he was shouting 'Give up, Bobby.' I said 'Now you know what I was like.' When he got the same injury three months later, I was trying to poke him all the time.

But the rib injury wasn't the only one that would cause Campbell to miss games before the season was finished.

I remember towards the end of the season I missed a few games. I broke my scaphoid (a bone in the wrist near to the base of the thumb). *They used to say 'Shut the full back down. Shut the full back down'. One way to shut the fullback down was to make yourself big. This guy from Bournemouth – a big Irish lad called Tommy Heffernan – he whacked the ball and the pain just shot up my arm. I played with a plaster on for a few weeks. I didn't play the last game of the season against Huddersfield Town, but we were safe. I played a couple of games and then we were safe.*

Bobby suffered this injury in the home game against Bournemouth on April 30th. Despite scoring in that game, he finished on the losing side. The next match, away to Gillingham, must have caused the kit man a bit of a problem. Bobby didn't play and his number nine shirt was given to no less than his young friend Mega – Mark Ellis, who might have been about half Campbell's shirt size, whatever measurement you took! There is a good indication of the difference in sizes in a story Mark Ellis tells, where his own slight build actually proved useful against a Campbell onslaught.

'He used to love letting off the fire extinguishers at the training ground,' recalls Mega with feeling. 'They could be painful, such was the force of the jet. He got me once. I was only skinny and I had no clothes on, so it was really painful. But I was that thin I managed to get out through the little window at the top.' Campbell may have climbed drainpipes in his time, but escaping through small windows was never an option for him. And Mega also remembers that Bobby was as likely to resort to a pair of scissors for his entertainment. 'He once cut off my fringe.' Who would ever have thought that Bobby Campbell might have a career as a hairdresser?

Campbell returned, still with the injury, for the following game, scoring in the 1-1 draw with Walsall, a point which finally ended any fear of relegation. But he missed the next game, which was played, quite amazingly, on the very next day, Sunday May 8th. Bradford City beat Sheffield United 2-0 and on May 14th beat Huddersfield Town 3-1, with the 18 year old David Hill making his only two league starts in that number nine shirt in Bobby's absence. The Walsall draw brought mathematical safety and those last two wins left City eight points clear of relegation.

Although Bradford City's 1982-3 league season had finished with comparative safety, so far as matters on the pitch were concerned, a much greater danger was lurking behind the scenes. Bobby Campbell was to become a somewhat unlikely pawn in a serious game of keeping Bradford City Football Club alive and kicking. Except, of course, being Bobby Campbell, he turned out to be more of a king than a pawn.

Chapter 12

A REPOSSESSED TV

Football club chairmen and their bank managers must dread the summer months. Those clubs in the lower leagues have most cause for alarm. Staff have to be paid, bills still come in and work needs to be done on the stadium or, at the very least, on the pitch. But little or no money comes in after that last home game of the season, unless the club can find other uses for the ground during the light nights or has some smart business plan about early payments from sponsors or deferred instalments from transfer deals done months earlier. Only in more recent years has there also been a significant change in the ratio of season ticket holders to those who just pay on a match by match basis. With more season tickets being sold at lower prices before the start of the new season, advance sales have increased and brought in some important finance during the summer months.

Income streams have extended beyond match days in more modern times, with many clubs, even smaller ones, having facilities that bring in earnings all year round. But back in the 1980's, when lower league grounds were designed (and not particularly well designed, at that) only for watching football, that time until the few season tickets were bought could be very difficult indeed.

The summer of 1983 proved to be one of the most difficult on record for Bradford City, although other summers in later years were to create new records in the difficulty stakes. City had finished 12th in the Third Division with average gates below 5,000, despite the fact that the last home game, against Huddersfield Town, had attracted a crowd of over 10,000. Back in November the club had received a little windfall, when Manchester United were the visitors in a third round League Cup tie. Better still, a 0-0 draw at Valley Parade had meant that City were ultimately to receive a share of gate receipts over two games watched by a total of almost 40,000 fans. The manner in which the board were running the club meant that that little windfall hadn't survived long beyond the autumn, although the little red-haired lad who had pulled on a number four claret and amber shirt for the first time in the Old Trafford game was to survive considerably longer than the chairman.

The chairman was a man called Bob Martin, a name perhaps best known as a brand of dog health product. But Bradford City's Bob Martin was nothing to do with this health product or, it seemed, anything remotely connected with the well-being of a football club. Bradford City (1908) Limited was, not to put too fine a point on it, broke. With the club facing debts of £400,000, of which much was owed to the Inland Revenue and National Insurance, Peter Flescher, a local accountant, was brought in as receiver. While £400,000 is undoubtedly a hefty sum to be owed, to an organisation as large as the Revenue it was proportionally much less than the amount the club owed to one particular individual.

The first chairman when I went to Bradford was a guy called Bob Martin. He ended up owing me a lot of money when I signed my contract. He disappeared owing me my signing-on fee. He owed me about five grand. When I signed a new contract when Cherry came, I did everything they wanted and my contract was more or less up. I said give me another. They gave me a bit up front and then they gave me a contract for £270 a week, which made up for my lost earnings. It was thoroughly deserved, I think. I was supposed to get £5000 at the end of the year, but then the club went into administration.

Campbell even kept hold of two cheques, each for £1,000, which were intended to be part of his end of season bonus. The cheques have a number of stamps endorsed on them by the bank, each one saying either 'refer to drawer' or 'represent'. It soon became clear that neither of these courses of action would produce the desired result.

Fund raising received more and more publicity and, as those who were around at the time remember only too well, Bradford City (1983) Limited was created largely due to the cash given by thousands of fans and the efforts of Stafford Heginbotham, Jack Tordoff and that very same Peter Flescher. Eventually Peter Flescher became a member of the new board, but in the summer of 1983 his name was mud, at least for a while, among the regulars on The Kop.

As receiver, Peter Flescher had to do what he could to keep the business afloat. If this involved realising the company's assets to go towards paying off its liabilities, then he was charged with realising what few assets the company had. But Bradford City had one obvious and very valuable asset. They had a man who had just scored 30 goals in the 1982-3 season, including the best goal of the match in that Old Trafford replay, making him valuable to a number of other football clubs. That man, of course, was Bobby Campbell.

In those pre-Bosman days, footballers were little more than chattels, to be bought and sold by different companies, masquerading as 'clubs', in accordance with contracts that meant rather more than some might do today. English professional football had got rid of the serfdom that was the 'retain and transfer' system only some twenty years earlier, thanks largely to George Eastham, who had successfully sued Newcastle United and won a ruling that allowed players more say in their futures when their contracts expired. It certainly wasn't ready for 'freedom of movement' in 1983. So Campbell it was who was sold to Derby County that summer for £70,000, whether he particularly wanted to leave or not. His Bradford City career – 87 goals in 179 games over three and a half seasons, including one promotion season – was surely at an end.

Bobby's own account of what might have happened that summer and how Bradford City might never have been the same again, for better or for worse, makes an interesting little story in its own right.

I had the choice to go to Derby or Sheffield United. I went to Derby first and had talks there. That's when you need an agent. I was supposed to have words with Sheffield United as well, but I turned round and said I'd settle for that. I should have gone to Sheffield United. I'd been to Sheffield United and I knew what a good league club it was. Porterfield wanted me just as a centre forward.

Ian Porterfield, best known for scoring the winning goal for Sunderland against Leeds United in the 1973 Cup Final, was the Sheffield United manager at the time. His first season at Bramall Lane had been 1981-2, when Bradford City had been promoted from the Fourth Division as runners up to Porterfield's team. He must have had a fair idea of Campbell's strengths and weaknesses from that campaign, although there were one or two people on the coaching staff at Derby County who could rightly claim to know Campbell's game in much greater detail.

But there was more to this transfer than just being sold off as Bradford's only asset. Bobby had his own, more positive reason for the move. While Sheffield United started the season in the same division as Bradford City, Derby County were in the Second Division, somewhere Bradford City hadn't been since 1937. And City hardly looked likely to get back there in the near future with the club's finances as they were in 1983. Derby had been relegated to the Second Division only in 1980. In 1972, with centre backs called McFarland and Todd, and again in 1975 they had been the Champions of England. They were a club to be reckoned with and the opportunity to play at the highest level open to him gave Bobby another reason for joining them. Little could he have known that in not much more than a year's time it would be Derby County who would be soundly beaten by Bradford City, including a goal from Campbell himself, in a Third Division match following Derby's relegation and during City's progress towards the second tier of English football.

The reason I went to Derby was that I thought I could get back in the Ireland team. But I don't know what happened with me and Billy Bingham when we went to the World Cup, but he never picked me again. That was the only reason I went to Derby, thinking that these players – but I didn't realise that they were in the twilight of their career, that they were playing five-a-side football in Division Two.

What Bobby found when he arrived for pre-season training with his new Derby team mates is described in typically plain-speaking style and reveals much about the man himself and the way he played his football.

I got to bloody Derby and I'm back playing five-a-side again. Everything's to feet. Robertson's at the end of his career. Gemmill's at the end of his career. They've got Watson at the end of his career, ex-international. Everybody's at the end of their career! At that time I think Derby was a graveyard for top players.

There could be no doubting that Derby County had some 'top players'. John Robertson had made the goal for Trevor Francis that won the 1979 European Cup for Nottingham Forest and then scored the goal that won the same competition in 1980 for Brian Clough's team. Archie Gemmill, another Scotland international, had also been part of the 1979 team managed by Clough and Peter Taylor. Dave Watson had played for Sunderland in that

1973 Cup Final and had gone on to win 65 England caps. But Campbell found a problem with having so many of these players who had already achieved so much.

They were well the wrong side of thirty. Don't get me wrong, they were fit enough, but they didn't have that thing. It's all right carrying a couple of them, but they had seven or eight of them. That was the problem. They had no harmony.

Peter Taylor was in charge at Derby, but McFarland was his assistant. I said to Peter 'He knew my strengths. I came on his recommendation. It isn't going to work.'

Bobby Davison was up front. He was a greedy bastard. He was a greedy goalscorer. Another - Keith Edwards - horrible to play with. When he got in the box, he was so selfish. I suppose that's the way of a striker. But me, I scored my fair share of goals, but I still had the balls to turn round and say 'Here, tap it into an empty net.'

I'm not getting any service. I said to them 'Why have you bought me? You know what my strengths are. My strengths aren't my feet. I'm no Tony Woodcock. This is not my style.'

Roy McFarland had been Campbell's manager at Bradford City for the best part of seventy matches in the previous two seasons. He was surely in a position to advise Peter Taylor that Campbell and Tony Woodcock, yet another member of that Nottingham Forest team of 1979, were very different players.

Anyway, we came to an agreement that they'd made a mistake and I'd made a mistake. I left on a good note.

The only thing was I should have gone to Sheffield United. But, having said that, if I'd gone to Sheffield United and stayed there, I wouldn't have gone back to Bradford, Bradford might not have won any promotion; there might not have been any fire. You don't know, do you? It's a big word for two letters – 'if'.

For a short time this is a very different Bobby Campbell. Once he starts talking about his football career, he can be as single minded as he was on the pitch. It is unusual for him to digress. But not only does he touch on the future here, he does so in an unexpected tone. From the familiar belligerence that accompanies his blunt statement that he was not a striker of the Davison and Edwards type, he expresses his genuine regrets at not going to Sheffield United and then almost immediately touches on an event that goes far deeper than simply wishing he could have made a different footballing decision.

It is rare to hear Campbell hesitate between his words. As soon as he warms to his task, he usually tells his stories at breakneck speed. When it comes to discussing his return to Bradford, his thoughts could so easily go straight to his goal scoring exploits. But instead his mind leaps forward straight to the events of May 1985. He is more thoughtful, to the point of being philosophical. There are short silences, especially after he says *'there might not have been any fire'*. All of this is entirely out of character, but illustrates how those events still hit home with even this strong willed personality.

But he is soon back on familiar territory. Although Campbell didn't go to Sheffield United, he didn't stay much longer at Derby County, either.

I was at Derby for three months top whack. I went for a month of pre-season training and played 7 or 8 games. I scored five goals for them. Then they said Bradford want you back on loan. Bradford couldn't afford me at the time, so I went to Bradford for a month.

The only fly in the ointment at the beginning was that, despite his status as a loan player, Bradford City wanted him to play in a first round FA Cup tie against Wigan. Campbell, unsure how long he would remain at Bradford and still perhaps hoping that another club, like Sheffield United, might want to sign him on a permanent basis, was unwilling to be cup-tied and didn't play in the game at home to Wigan. But when *everything was sorted out*, he played in the replay, only for City to lose 4-2.

Just how things were 'sorted out' was a typical piece of Campbell's life style. He knew that Bradford couldn't pay a transfer fee, but he also found out that Derby hadn't paid all the £70,000 up front.

I think Derby owed £25,000, so I was more like a repossessed TV. They said I could go back. They wrote it off. I took a pay cut, which I shouldn't have done. I should have said 'If you want me back, you're taking my contract over.' I should have stuck to my guns. That was £100 a week. I'd only had the extra money for a couple of months. I just wanted out. Really I should have hung on for a bit. I knew there would have been more offers in the pipeline.

So this was no returning hero, at least not in his own eyes. The man destined to become Bradford City's all time record goal scorer regarded himself as 'a repossessed TV'. He knew he should have stuck out for more money, but Bobby Campbell was never one capable of resisting an impulsive action for too long. Instead he returned once more to the permanent fold at Valley Parade and a new era for him and the club began almost at once.

Bobby's first game back, while he was still on loan, was City's 16th game of the season. In their previous 15 they had secured just one win and five draws. That first game back proved no more successful, a 4-1 defeat making the journey back from Wimbledon's Plough Lane seem interminable. The result may not have suggested that Campbell's return would have much of a dramatic impact. But what happened on that homeward journey, an event that Bobby himself keeps quiet about, showed the rest of the City squad that, whether it was on or off the pitch, Campbell was going to lead from the front.

The Wimbledon game was played on 5th November 1983. The inevitable Bonfire Night smoke combined with the intermittent fog to make the coach trip back up the M1 something of a stop-start journey. At the back of the coach, as would often be the case on such long trips, a

1982-83. The traditional pre-season photo, as the newly promoted Bradford City striker prepares for life in Division Three.

Still Summer 1982. 'A Big Difference.' Bobby marries Paula, with his old mate Les Chapman as Best Man.

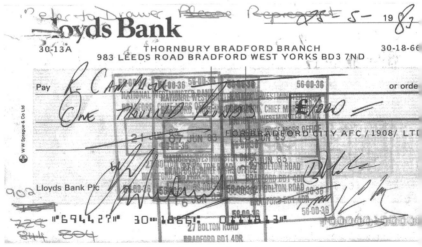

May 1983. One of the cheques that shows how Campbell never did receive his end of season bonus, as Bradford City's liquidator realised the club's best asset.

1984-85. Bradford City's official team photo, with Campbell (fourth from left, back row) apparently in pain. The old stand forms the background for the last time.

16th February 1985. A Billy Whitehurst challenge accounted for Eric McManus' multiple injuries. Tony Clegg had the privilege of causing the Campbell cut.

Summer 1985. Two genuine smiles and a Championship trophy. One of Campbell's many visits to the burns victims.

1985-86. A new season starts for a nomadic Bradford City, which explains why the photo is taken at the training ground. Campbell, as ever, gets among the goalkeepers.

1986-87. Campbell, socks down by his ankles, scores for Wigan Athletic. Paul Jewell waits for the rebound that never came.

1986-87. A full Springfield Park watches another classic headed goal from The Latics' leading scorer against Rotherham United.

1987-88. Very smart in the club blazer, Campbell shows his Man of the Match award after the Port Vale game.

An England XI re-open Valley Parade. The "guest player" in the number nine shirt is front row, second left.

27th March 1997. Reigning on our Parade. A hero at Bradford City, a damp Campbell waits with Stuart McCall while H.M. speaks to another Bobby.

A sketch, perhaps from 1985-86, by an unknown artist. The unmistakable Campbell smile.

card school had started up. One of those playing was the young Stuart McCall. He remembers being aware of the coach braking from time to time, but most particularly he recalls the unmistakable noise of the coach hitting the back of another vehicle. With the motorway shrouded in darkness and fog, from his seat at the back of the coach about as much as McCall could make out at first was that the coach driver was 'absolutely distraught'.

Campbell, however, was no longer on board the coach. The vehicle that the coach had run into was a family car, carrying two young children in the back. What happened next is most vividly described in Stuart's own words.

'Rather typical, as everyone else doesn't know what to do, Bobby's straight in there trying to save and trying to look after the kids. Bobby got in the car and got one out and tried to do mouth-to-mouth resuscitation. But that was him. In a way he was showing his leadership qualities, like he used to do on the pitch. If something needed doing, then he would do it. If there was a problem or you needed something doing, he would do it. He has a good heart. I know it was a different situation to playing football, but rather than sit back and let something happen, he tried. He got one of the kids out and tried to give mouth-to-mouth. Although it's a sad story, it's typical of the person, going in and not being afraid of anything. Going in and trying to help or save the situation.'

Perhaps a significant part of the reason why Bobby doesn't mention what he did that night is the fact that his efforts were at least partially in vain. Stuart McCall remembers only too well that one of the children died. The other may also not have survived. An equally likely explanation for his silence is that Campbell doesn't see anything remarkable in what he did that night. 'Not being afraid of anything' is just the way he is.

Back on the football pitch, a week later Campbell's home debut (second time around) got off to a dreadful start. Millwall were 3-0 up and the dismal run of results looked like never ending. He may not have scored, but he certainly played his part in a recovery that saw City come back for a 3-3 draw. Nobody in the ground could have forecast what would happen next. Then....well, then the Campbell memory kicks in, but with a large dose of understatement.

And then we got a bit of a run together.

They most certainly did. Bradford City 1983-84 vintage created a new club record of ten league wins in a row. Remember, Campbell had been part of the team that had created the previous record of nine league wins in a row. In fact, starting with that 3-3 draw against Millwall, Bradford City went 17 league games without losing. The club that nearly went out of business at the start of the season and had been facing certain relegation by November, would finish 7th in the Third Division.

John Hawley, who had signed for City only during the summer months and who had therefore never previously played alongside Campbell, surrendered the number nine shirt to its rightful owner immediately. John had played for Hull City, Sunderland, Leeds United and Arsenal, among others and was nearing the end of his football career, albeit preparing himself for a second career as an auctioneer. He had just returned from a spell playing in Hong Kong for a team called Happy Valley. Eric McManus remembers John as 'the quiet man of the team', who 'couldn't believe the camaraderie both on and off the pitch, especially Campbell's part in it.' But Eric also remembers 'John was a great finisher'.

They'd signed John Hawley. It was Hawley and Don Goodman, who'd come up through the ranks. Goodman the speed machine. One of the best jumpers I've seen was Don Goodman – 5'9" or 5'10". He could jump higher than me. Don had some spring in his legs and he could get up there and head a ball. He's had a marvellous career. I played up front with one or the other of them, mostly John.

He was a good lad, John. There was that time when he put a weight down his pants so he wouldn't have to keep his weight down. We had weight checks once a week. Abbo and Dave Evans were running round with sweat bags on and Mars bars in the bag; they'd had no breakfast. Abbo would be 10 stone 9 and should have been 10 stone 7. They'd knock him for that. 'That's a fiver, Abbo.' Abbo would say 'Look at them fat bastards. They can get to 14 stone and they're alright.' I used to say 'Abbo, we take the knocks so you guys can come running through.' I used to be about 13 stone 10. If I touched 14, I'd go down. You needed big lads up front in those days. You still do to get out of those leagues. You need big strong lads who can take the knocks and guarantee you at least 35 games out of 46. They can miss 10, but they can't be missing more than that. I never missed many, but I was lucky.

Don Goodman was very much at the start of his career, still short of his eighteenth birthday when making his Bradford City debut as a substitute in April 1984. He too was to travel far and wide as a player, as far as Hiroshima and Motherwell, before establishing himself as a commentator on television and radio. Greg Abbott had made his Bradford City debut in the 1982-3 season and was to go on to make over 300 appearances for the club. Dave Evans joined from Halifax Town in the summer of 1984 and was another who played more than 200 games for Bradford City.

Giving up the number nine shirt didn't stop John Hawley scoring the goals. In those first 15 pre-Campbell games, John had scored just two goals. In the remainder of the 1983-4 season he scored another 21. Campbell himself chipped in with 9 in 33 appearances; not his usual high ratio of goals per game, but, as he says

I took a lot of knocks for him and he got the goals. Next year I got my share of the goals.

Anyone who thinks that those words should be interpreted as Campbell being satisfied with his goals tally, even in the whole context of City's successes, needs only to consider another of Stuart McCall's gleeful recollections from that record run - gleeful only because Stuart himself was for once not on the receiving end of this particular Campbell tale.

In the days before football managers complained about too many games in too few days, Bradford City's fixture list for the Christmas and New Year period included games on 26th, 27th and 31st December and 2nd January. In the midst of that winning run City played Wigan Athletic at Valley Parade on 27th December. Wigan had only been admitted to the league for the start of the 1978-9 season and had been promoted from the Fourth Division at the same time as City at the end of 1981-2. City won the Christmas fixture 6-2 and the game was as one-sided as the score line suggests. Once City had scored their sixth goal there had been a certain amount of what would now be called 'showboating'.

McCall, one of the last to get back to the dressing room after the final whistle, expected to be met by scenes of unrestrained joy. Instead, he saw two of his team mates, Garry Haire and Mark Ellis, in a position he himself had once encountered on his very first meeting with Campbell. They were one either side of the striker 'with their feet dangling' and only the Irishman's strong hands, one round each throat, for support. The problem was quite a simple one. The two City wingers had allowed the team to score six goals without offering Campbell a sniff of a chance for himself. Worse still, Garry Haire had been shooting from all angles and Mega had even had the audacity to score one himself. Campbell was not best pleased. 'I'd never seen anyone so upset at winning 6-2 in my life.' Although Stuart has diplomatic amnesia about the actual words being used, it was plain that the displeasure was being spelled out in no uncertain terms. 'Bob had been standing in the box getting more and more frustrated. You'd have thought we'd got beaten 6-2. But that was just him. He loved scoring goals.'

For the record, starting with a 4-1 win against Brentford on 26th November 1983 and ending with a 2-0 victory at Exeter on 3rd February 1984, Bradford City scored 36 goals in those ten consecutive wins. While John Hawley was scoring 14 of those goals, Campbell mustered a measly four. Even Terry Gray, hardly a prolific goal scorer, managed more than Bobby! But Campbell must have made some sort of contribution for the team to win ten in a row and his comparative lack of goals hardly put at risk his place in the side.

Campbell was back at Valley Parade and all was well again. But that 'next year', when he did indeed get his 'share of the goals', is very much another story.

Chapter 13
GLORY AND TRAGEDY

As the 1984-5 season started, Bobby Campbell's career must have looked as though it had already contained just about every possible element in the life of a professional footballer. Fighting back from a career-threatening injury; being rescued from part-time football; going to the World Cup Finals (despite being banned for life from international football); being sold as the only valuable asset to save his club from extinction; being 'repossessed'; and even meeting his French fan club. But none of that would prepare him for what the new season would bring. Campbell and his team mates were about to experience the highs of professional success and the depths of tragedy. Team spirit would create one and get them through the other.

From the start of the 1983-4 season, when the financial crisis first took hold of Bradford City, Trevor Cherry and Terry Yorath had known that there would be no money to spend on transfer fees or wages. Any team rebuilding would have to be done on the cheap. Although Bradford City (1983) Limited were hardly awash with money by the start of the next season, their encouraging performance in the Third Division and the 7th place finish made Valley Parade a more attractive place when it came to signing new players.

Dave Evans was released by Halifax Town and immediately acquired the nickname Dracula. It seems that at that time anyone who went on to play for a team in a higher league after over 200 games at The Shay could well and truly be said to have come back from the dead! Boomer, as he preferred to be called (from his habit of 'booming' the ball great distances upfield), missed just one league game that season and became Peter Jackson's permanent partner at the heart of a defence that would concede under a goal a game. Jacko, by now the club captain at the age of just 23, also played in 45 of the 46 league games. Chris Withe, younger brother of England international Peter, had made the left back spot his own throughout the previous season and also played in all but one league game. Local lad Mark Ellis, 'Mega' to all around him, also figured in every match but one and goalkeeper Eric McManus was an ever present until an injury at Hull in February caused him to miss six games. Greg Abbott, who had come from Coventry City in Roy McFarland's time, also played in forty games, switching as required between right back and midfield.

If those six players were rarely missing, the team spirit and togetherness were typified even more by no fewer than three ever-presents. Bobby Campbell and Stuart McCall were already heroes with the Valley Parade fans. But the third player to feature in every league match was new to Valley Parade at the start of the season and was a virtual unknown, having made just 21 appearances in four years for his only professional club, Coventry City. His name was John Hendrie and he was to re-launch his football career with a vengeance at Valley Parade.

John Hendrie was to create a remarkable list of records, both at Bradford City and later in his career. Just by way of a starter, not only was he involved in every league match of the 1984-5 season, but throughout his four year stay at Valley Parade he was to miss just one league game. The fact that he missed that game through suspension, after one of the most contrived dismissals some Bradford City fans have ever seen, and that the game he missed could have gained Bradford City promotion to the top flight of

English football, only goes to underline his importance to the team.

But, for a player who had struggled to make his mark on the game prior to being snapped up by Trevor Cherry and Terry Yorath, John Hendrie was to go on to even more remarkable feats. He would leave Bradford City in the Second Division for a transfer fee of half a million pounds paid by Newcastle United of the First Division. He would then play for three other League teams – Leeds United, Middlesbrough and Barnsley – each of which, with Hendrie a regular in their side, gained promotion to the First Division (or Premier League as it was to be called by the time Middlesbrough and Barnsley achieved their promotions). Not too bad for a free transfer to Bradford City!

We know that Bobby Campbell has great respect for facts and figures, especially the answers to questions like 'How many games did he play?' and 'How many goals did he score?' But Bobby also admires many of those whom he played alongside. Sometimes Campbell's definition of 'play' might have nothing to do with what happened on a football pitch. But his greatest respect goes to those who showed the skills he aspired to.

John Hendrie was a good signing. I was a bit disappointed with Bradford when they got rid of me, because I'd just got John Hendrie to start crossing the bloody ball! I scored 26 goals that season. I sat John down and I said 'Let's go through my goals. You made me one goal, one bloody goal all season.' One cross and that was against Millwall and I had to bend down to head it in. It was coming in and I thought if I come down on it with my head I can keep it down, but if I try to swing the boot it could go anywhere. I just threw myself down and headed it in. It doesn't matter how you hit them, as long as you get the last touch. But he was a good signing. I think with John he had all the ability, but he used to keep too much of the ball and it used to break down a lot. He was a good player that lad.

Les Chapman, who had left for Rochdale at the same time as Campbell's ill-fated move to Derby County, was, apparently, responsible for giving out the nicknames, like the one given to the young Mark Ellis.

Chappie gave Mega his nickname. Mega was worth his wages just to have in the changing rooms. You'd see Mega there cracking the jokes and having a laugh and he said 'you're not a super star, you're a mega star' I used to call Jacko The Beast, he was that soft. He tried to give me the nickname the Beast. I said 'You're so good looking, you're The Beast.' He had his teeth knocked out as a kid. I had mine knocked out as kid. I always said if I ever met the bastard who knocked my teeth out – bridges, plates, they've cost me a fortune over the years.

Since 'Chappie gave out the nicknames', he must take the blame for what goalkeeper Eric McManus was called.

His nickname was Cash because all he would talk about was how much you got for cash. He was a great line keeper. He was one of the best line keepers I've ever seen.

McManus, another player from Northern Ireland, having been born in Limavady, has very forthright opinions about his one-time centre forward and his role in the team. 'He was a fearsome striker, a different class, a genuine bloke. He never missed training, he lived football. There was a special relationship in that team. We just hit it off. It was a huge factor in our winning the title. We worked hard. We were very serious about our football. But it was an extremely happy time. Campbell was the main man.'

But Eric recalls what many would regard as the other side of Campbell. 'He liked a pint. Unknown to him I was his bodyguard. Others hadn't enjoyed rooming with him, so Trevor and Taff told me I'd be doing it. I had to stay with him. There was mutual respect between us. I was a bit older than him. He never caused any trouble at the club.' So at least one eye witness believes Campbell's other side was a bit less troublesome than some people would make out.

Eric remembers the game at Hull in February 1985 for all the wrong reasons. The Hull centre forward was a man called Billy Whitehurst. 'He was the same size, the same sort of player, just as stupid as Campbell,' recalls McManus. Well, maybe Bobby could point to a thing or two to dispute that last comparison. After all, Billy Whitehurst's career took exactly the opposite route to Bobby Campbell's. Whitehurst spent five years with his first professional club, Hull City, before playing for another eight clubs in England and then going to Hong Kong and South China. And, since Bobby would be quick to examine the figures himself, it should be added that in his 193 league appearances for Hull City, Whitehurst scored just 47 goals. Some others have a much better goals to games ratio.

Going back to that game at Boothferry Park, Eric McManus' participation was brief, to say the least. 'This was a big game. It was top versus second. We'd only been playing 90 seconds or less. It was their first attack. My kids had come on the coach and it had been delayed. They were just coming into the ground as I was getting carried off. I had a fractured shoulder. I needed twelve stitches in my face. It was the sort of thing that happened in those days. The centre forward would want to try out the goal keeper.'

Bobby's own recollection of those events is very similar.
When Cash came out that day, Billy must have hit him in three different places. He did his ribs, he did his collar bone, he did his face. When he came back, he was a mess.

But for the rest of the afternoon it is inevitable that the two of them have different memories, one from the game that continued and one from elsewhere. These were the days when only one substitute could be named and the one substitute was most unlikely to be a goalkeeper. Eric McManus' replacement in goal for 88 minutes was Tony

Clegg, who had started the game at right back.

I've only ever got cut once, and that was my own keeper, Cleggy. I was protecting him from Billy Whitehurst up at Hull. I said 'stay on your line.'

Cleggy didn't take to the advice of the new and very temporary goalkeeping coach and Campbell got more than he bargained for when the equally temporary goalkeeper came off his line to collect a high ball. For the record, Bradford City won 2-0.

While all that was happening at Boothferry Park, Eric McManus was in hospital. 'There was some fighting among the supporters. A few supporters ended up in hospital. I was in a cubicle in A & E. A policeman came into the cubicle and just said 'Name'. I asked him what he was talking about and he repeated 'Name'. I asked him again and he said 'You were at the match, weren't you?' I said I had been and he asked me again for my name. Then I told him I was the goalkeeper who had been carried off. He said he'd just walked into the cubicle, seen the injuries to my face and thought I was one of those involved in the fighting. He apologised, said he must have got into the wrong cubicle and went into the next one.' Whatever other injuries Eric may have suffered, his sense of humour was untouched.

Before leaving the words of 'a great line keeper', there is one more opinion from Eric about the man for whom he acted as minder. Actually, they are the very first words he has to say, even before mentioning Bobby's contribution to the 1984-5 team.

'He has a heart of gold, Campbell.'

There are another two more Campbell tales about those players and their nicknames. The first relates to another former Coventry City player, Martin Singleton, who, like John Hendrie, had played only just over twenty first team games in the previous three seasons. He didn't arrive at Valley Parade until December 1984, making his debut in the 2-1 win at home to Bolton Wanderers and making 19 league appearances that season. Until March 1983 there had been another midfield player at Bradford City by the name of Mick Lester. For reasons lost in the mists of time, he had acquired the nickname Charlie.

And we said we hadn't got a Charlie in the team. 'You'll have to be the new Charlie.' It just stuck like that – Charlie Singleton.

The final word on nicknames relates to Bobby himself. He says simply

They wouldn't tell me which one I was.

And the funny thing is that, even now, not one of the other members of that squad ever seems to refer to Campbell by a nickname. He usually just gets 'Bob' or 'Campbell'. Maybe his fearsome reputation continues right through to this day among his old team mates.

Certainly among the younger players at Bradford City, Bobby's reputation was a curious mixture of fear and admiration. Mark Ellis provides one of the best examples of this. Mega came to Bradford City from amateur football as an eighteen year old. Campbell had joined the previous season and so was the established striker by the time the young winger got into the first team near the end of Bobby's first full season.

'Playing up front I suppose he had to be selfish. Campbell just wanted to score goals. Everyone suffered when he didn't. We got on great, but, for us kids, he could be intimidating, even to his own team mates.'

To illustrate the point, Mark tells a story not unlike the one Stuart McCall remembers, albeit from a different game, but still during that record-breaking ten match winning run. This game was played just eleven days after the Wigan game mentioned by McCall and, despite the team scoring seventeen goals in four games, this was to be the fourth consecutive game without a Campbell goal. 'I remember one game against Wimbledon. We were winning 5-2 with about two minutes left and I had a shot instead of crossing. Campbell chased me all the way back to the half-way line for that.'

This particular game, from January 7th 1984, is also recalled by Bobby, but for a totally different reason. Although Bradford City scored five goals and Campbell himself didn't score, he may be able to claim at least one assist. John Hawley scored four and Garry Haire got the fifth. Campbell does, however, recall with considerable glee the Wimbledon goalkeeper that day.

That day against Wimbledon Dave Beasant came out with his feet up. He did it to Stuart McCall and the referee didn't do anything. He did it me and I said to the referee 'He's out of order'. I got my own back in the second half.

As John Hawley scored one of his easiest goals, a tap-in from inside the six yard box, Beasant was frantically trying to extricate his studs from the back of the net. Just how he had ended up there, with his feet rather higher than most of his body, remains an unsolved mystery, of course. The opposing number nine, however, found something amusing on the day and still smiles at the memory. The goalkeeper chased half the length of the field in pursuit of the referee when the goal was given, only to be met with the inevitable caution for dissent. All a bit unnecessary when the game had only minutes to go and the last goal was the difference between losing by two or three goals.

Mark Ellis also knew that, however fearsome Campbell might seem to his young team mates, his opponents suffered much more. 'He would intimidate opponents by his style of play and his presence. They would be frightened of him.' Perhaps because of the way Bobby dealt with opponents, Mega has at least one memory when Campbell's involvement in the physical side of the game brought a little light relief for the slight winger – although he doesn't say that he told Bobby how amusing he found the incident!

'I remember going down to Millwall for a game in some minor cup competition. They had a defender called

Keith Stevens. His nickname was Rhino. He was a big defender, about 6 foot 2 and a big animal. He usually played right back. All the way down there on the coach, Bob was winding me up, saying The Rhino was going to get me. When we lined up, Stevens was playing at centre half, so it was Bobby who got it from him. He split his lip and had a tooth knocked out. It just shows what a battle that was!'

However much dread Campbell may have instilled into team mates and opponents, those who played alongside him for any length of time always end up concentrating on the positives he brought to the team. Mark's own overall assessment is typical. 'When he went to Derby in 1983, we were quite relieved for a time. We didn't realise how much we missed him. The team suffered until he came back.' The results for the two parts of that season, with and without Campbell, prove how accurate that observation is.

Bobby Campbell is not just a bruising goal scorer in Mega's eyes. Far from it. 'He could control the ball and pass with either foot. Other players were just not in his league,' is Mark's opinion. 'If he had been managed properly, as players are these days with agents and the rest, he would definitely have been in the Premier League. He could do so many things. He would take on anybody in training. He used to have competitions with Terry Yorath for who had the best left foot!'

And in one short sentence, Mega gives an overall view of Bobby Campbell that might surprise quite a lot of people. 'He was an intelligent player and modest off the field.'

While echoing Stuart McCall's story and acknowledging that 'Bob was so keen to score goals he'd start arguing after a 6-0 win if he hadn't scored', Mark goes on to say 'But he'd always rather we won than lost, say 3-2, and he'd scored both goals. It was the team and the result that mattered most. It was more to do with frustration when he didn't score.'

The young players in that Bradford City team have every reason to remember what Campbell was like in training as well as on the pitch. Stuart McCall, for example, looking back on training with Campbell, reveals one telling weakness in a long list of Bobby's strengths. 'I would say Monday was probably his worst day for training. Just looking back now I realise why he never asked for heading practice on a Monday. He trained as hard as he could. He moaned in games because he always wanted to score goals. He cared about it. You get people who are not really bothered, but he always wanted to do finishing afterwards. He was a good role model in the way he trained. He trained hard; he always liked to do some finishing afterwards. He wanted to improve himself. But never on a Monday – and I know why now!'

Both Stuart and Mark recall being 'kept behind' at the behest of their striker. 'After training – nowadays you might finish for 12 and then do some gym work or running or stretching – we used to be out until one o'clock or half past one crossing balls for Bob,' Stuart recalls. 'He'd never get fed up of heading. He regularly used to score with his head from the penalty spot. I used to be down one side after training and maybe Mega down the other, just crossing balls. It's a dying breed now. You don't see Joe Jordan's or Bobby Campbell's any more. It's a dying breed the centre forward. The ball goes into the box, you know what you're getting; he goes up, a great old fashioned centre half versus centre forward battle.'

Mark Ellis also remembers how training might depend on which day of the week it was. 'Bob would sometimes miss training on a Monday. It was usually because he'd had a drink over the weekend. But later in the week, especially on Thursday and Friday, he'd stay behind for extra practice on crosses.'

But Mark is very particular about his description of Bobby's drinking habits. 'I never saw Bob have a drink before a game. He might have had one or two after a match, but Thursday and Friday before a game he didn't drink. It was just stories based on his reputation.' And that reputation has probably never been fully shaken off, becoming almost mythical long after Campbell stopped playing. Myths, it should be borne in mind, are fictional stories, although they are often about someone with superhuman powers.

But that 1984-5 team wasn't a simple case of Campbell and ten others. Far from it. As Mark Ellis recalls 'The team spirit was fantastic. There was a sense of togetherness.' Stuart McCall agrees. 'At the end of the day, football is about the 90 minutes on a Saturday. But to get that 90 minutes, you need camaraderie and team spirit.'That particular Bradford City team was to achieve something so many of its predecessors had failed to do, promotion to the second division. Clearly, good as the players were – and some of them were very good indeed – promotion was won at least to some extent by that team spirit.

Bobby Campbell, keen as he was on scoring, was very much a team player, nowhere better illustrated than in his link with John Hawley. 'John used to feed off him,' recalls Stuart.' He knew where Bob was going to knock it and would always get on the bits. In the second half Bob would always get a battering.'

When he talks about that second promotion season, interestingly Bobby skips over most of the games and even his goal scoring exploits. The 23 league goals he scored made him Bradford City's leading scorer by a considerable margin. John Hendrie's nine goals were the next best, with Jackson and McCall each scoring eight.

He does give a brief mention to the November game against Derby County – for fairly obvious reasons. When Campbell had been at the Baseball Ground during the three months at the start of the 1983-4 season, Derby County had played in the second division. At the end of that season they were relegated to the third division for the first time since 1957. Perhaps Bobby remembers Bradford City's match against Derby County because he had a very particular point to prove to the Derby management. Perhaps he remembers it because he was up against one of the best centre halves, certainly in that division and perhaps even in the division above.

Kenny Burns was a good player.

Burns hadn't been at Derby during Campbell's brief stay. He had moved at the start of the 1984-5 season from Leeds United, but he had made his name in the Nottingham Forest team that won the league title under Brian Clough. He may have been a few years older by the time Derby County were facing up to life in the third division, but he was still a player to be reckoned with. It almost goes without saying that Campbell scored one of the Bradford City goals in a 3-1 win marred only by some trouble among rival supporters which resulted in, among other things, some seats being ripped out in the main stand.

During all his reminiscences about the 1984-85 season Bobby doesn't even mention the goal he scored on Match of the Day. That a third division game was actually noticed by the BBC was quite a rarity in those days, when the Saturday evening programme showed highlights from as few as three games, usually all from the first division. The cameras were attracted to the 1-1 draw with Gillingham on 2nd March 1985 because the visitors were another of the front runners at the time, although they were later to fall away and finish one place short of promotion.

Instead of recalling goals scored and opponents bettered, Bobby and so many of the others from that team go straight to the last few games of the season, the games where promotion was nearly lost, then won and then made to seem irrelevant.

Between 17th March and 23rd April 1985 Bradford City played ten league games. They won seven of them and drew the other three. Promotion was by now almost secured. And then the wheels came off just a fraction. A 4-1 defeat at Bournemouth on 26th April was followed by a home game against Reading on 4th May. This was Bradford City's big chance to make sure that they finished in the top three – there were no play-offs in those days, remember. Campbell's recollection of that Reading game is actually one goal too generous to his team. He also omits to mention that he scored one of the two goals.

We got stuffed at home on the Saturday against Reading, didn't we? 5-3 I think it was. It was one of those days when every time they went forward they scored. It was just a setback.

Then we went to Bolton. That was the Bank Holiday Monday. It was a bad day. Bolton fans were throwing bricks at us. We were getting stoned coming back in.

It may very well have been a bad day off the field, but the ninety minutes on the pitch proved conclusive. Only two days after seeing their big chance missed in the Reading game, Bradford City made both promotion and the third division championship a mathematical certainty. Goals from Campbell and McCall brought a 2-0 win, some of the best photographs any football player would ever want and an inevitable consequence.

We celebrated promotion in Huddersfield because that's where Trevor's car was and mine and a few others. Then on the Saturday there was the big celebration and then everything went to cock.

That Saturday, of course, the day of 'the big celebration', the day when Peter Jackson was presented with the championship trophy and the squad said Thank You to the fans in letters two feet high, was Saturday 11th May 1985. Nobody at Bradford City needs any telling about why 'everything went to cock' and why celebrations were no longer appropriate. Bobby's own reflection on the fire that claimed 56 lives is more than eloquent. In a few words he puts into perspective all those other setbacks in his career.

I had no family in the stand. I said to my wife and the kids 'It's going to be hectic today. There's no way I'm going to take you today.' The eldest was only two; the youngest was only about nine months, so they were at home. As soon as I got out I was on the phone to her.

That was the worst thing that ever happened. Never mind your injuries; never mind your heartache – that's the worst thing that's ever happened in my football career. Everybody was looking forward to such a good day and it was just taken away from you like that. You think to yourself 'Why did that happen here, when it could have happened at any stadium?'

Nobody believed for a moment that the events of that fateful day would end quickly. For Bobby Campbell, the centre forward, there were to be consequences for the rest of his career. For Bobby Campbell, human being, there was only one possible response to such a tragedy.

Chapter 14
BEDSIDES AND PITCHES

As will be obvious by now, Bobby Campbell loves telling football stories, especially those with a joke or a prank in them. He has no such stories to tell about the end of the 1984-5 season and the weeks that followed. Bobby's silence on this subject should not be taken to mean that there are no stories he could tell about those weeks, not least about how he used that natural humour to the best possible effect. But he doesn't say much about the immediate aftermath of one of football's most painful disasters. Then again, he doesn't say anything about the traffic accident on Bonfire Night 1983, the time when he was the one jumping out of the team bus to try to save the children trapped in their parents' car. There are just certain things he doesn't particularly mention.

He will touch briefly on the very short term effects of the fire on the team.

Everybody was looking forward to going away for a week celebrating. It was going to be on the Sunday or the Monday. It never happened. You couldn't be seen to go on holiday, could you?

The team holiday, organised and paid for by the club, was a common reward for winning promotion. Quite apart from any general consideration for those injured in the fire and for those who had lost loved ones, one member of the team, Stuart McCall, had very nearly lost his father. Andy McCall had been very badly burned and there was no possibility that Stuart would have left him for something as trivial as a team's celebration of reaching its highest level in the Football League for almost fifty years.

Instead of going on holiday as a team, the Bradford City players, still very much as a team, were going to funerals and making hospital visits. One of the patients in St Luke's hospital suffering from severe burns was Dave Hustler. In the summer of 1985 Dave was 45 years old. The story of how this slightly built man saved the lives of more than one person who would otherwise have died in the flames of the Valley Parade stand is told in some detail in 'Four Minutes to Hell – The Story of the Bradford City Fire'. It is still a source of amazement that Dave insists 'anybody would have done the same', when he put his own life very much at risk to rescue strangers.

But a man like Dave Hustler appreciates the kindness of others and especially when that kindness is so obviously genuine. 'I'd just had my operation that day when the players came round the ward as a group,' Dave recalls. 'I never actually saw the players come in, because I must have been unconscious that day.' Dave remembers many other visitors, not least Stuart McCall, who would check on the other burns patients whenever he came in to visit his father.

But Dave puts just two particular visitors into a special category, high in his estimation. The two make an unlikely pairing and perhaps neither would be especially keen to be associated with the other. 'To me, being in there,' Dave says, 'there were only two people who came to that hospital who really meant it and really weren't upset about being with you. That was Maggie and Bobby.'

It seems highly unlikely that Bradford City's all time leading goal scorer could ever be bracketed alongside the Prime Minister of the day, not even as being one of just two people 'who really meant it'. The contrast with some of the other visitors remains sharply in Dave's mind to this day. 'The rest of them, it looked as if they were doing their duty. We were getting all these M.P's and what have you. It was their duty, just to show their face. Not Maggie. She stayed three hours over her schedule and talked to everybody at length.'

If the Prime Minister showed her concern by staying so long with the twenty patients in the same ward as Dave, Bobby showed his in a different fashion. Mrs Thatcher had a country to run and couldn't keep on upsetting her entourage day after day by talking to burns victims. In any event, she was never too well known for cracking jokes. Bobby Campbell did things his way.

'One of the players that came in – and not just once,' recalls Dave, 'it makes me laugh every time I think about it now – is a fella called Bobby Campbell. He used to come in regularly.'

And, of course, making a few people that bit happier in their most desperate of times is a rare gift, but something Bobby was predictably good at. Dave remembers one particular visit from Bobby, made while he was recovering from the major surgery performed by David Sharpe and his team to repair his ravaged skin.

'He came in one day and said "How are you, Dave, this morning?" I said "All right, Bobby. Sit yourself down." It was about ten o'clock. All our lockers were full with beer, because a brewery had sent a load of beer in for us. We were allowed to drink. The doctors wanted fluids down us. The only time you couldn't was if you were having medication. So I said "Do you want a drink, Bobby?" "It's a bit early for me," was Bobby's initial response. But, always being the sociable sort, he quickly had second thoughts. "I'll put my watch on an hour." And then he had a drink with me and wandered all round the ward.'

On another occasion Bobby came in bearing gifts. 'He brought a big cake,' Dave recalls, 'a massive big cake in green and white.' 'My relatives in Ireland have sent you this over,' was the Campbell explanation.

But Dave also remembers the day when the 'regular

attender' was not alone in his efforts to cheer up the patients. 'Then he came in one time with a lady in high heels and a short skirt - very, very smart. He walked down the ward "All right today, Dave?" He had a chat with me.' But it was Bobby's introduction of the 'very smart lady' that set Dave off laughing. Bobby tried to persuade Dave that he had 'just seen her on the road down there.' Campbell, who can remember the goal scorers in games played over twenty years ago, then had a remarkable memory lapse about the name of this road where he claimed to have met his companion just a few minutes previously. As Dave recalls things, the nearest that Campbell could manage was that the road was called 'something like Lumb'. Dave wasn't fooled by the comic acting. At least, he hopes he's been right all these years in believing that the 'very, very smart lady' was no less than Mrs Campbell.

So, whether it be to share a bottle of beer, to bring in an Irish cake or just to chat with the patients, the regular presence in St Luke's of a 'smashing guy' over those weeks was something that, as Dave Hustler and others will say, 'you don't forget'. Lest Bobby's regular visits to St Luke's should ever be forgotten, there is no better place to look than at the website that is all about the history of Bradford City. Bantamspast has a section called 'The Front Room of Fame'. (It is considered that the front room is rather more special than the hall.) Within that famous room there are photos of Bobby Campbell. One is on the pitch at Valley Parade after returning from Derby County. Another is of the classic Campbell headed goal. But the other two are from bed sides in that hospital ward from the summer of 1985. They both show Bobby with the sort of smile he used to reserve for scoring or at least knocking the opposition goal keeper into the back of his own net. But there is nothing trivial in the smiles in these pictures, as the patients' own expressions make plain.

As the weeks passed and the hospital visits became less

necessary with patients being discharged, the Bradford City squad had to turn their thoughts back to football, difficult though that might have been. Bobby Campbell's contract was up and, in other circumstances, he might have either left Bradford City or at least held out for a much improved deal, given his obvious value to the side.

They didn't offer me the money for the contract. That's when I should have moved from Bradford, when they didn't give me enough money for my contract. But I stuck it out and more or less signed the same contract again.

With the exception of that short stay at Derby County, Bobby Campbell had by this time been with one club for five and a half years. In the same length of time before his arrival at Valley Parade, he had played for six different clubs, including two separate spells at two of those six clubs. In other words, Campbell had settled at Bradford as he had never settled anywhere else. He was, on and off the field, a club hero. And, although he had just scored most of the goals that won the club promotion and knew he was worth that much more, money wasn't his highest priority.

I took a £100 a week wage drop to come back to Bradford from Derby. I only wish I'd had an agent. Nobody had agents in those days. I think the first was Jacko. He got an accountant. We didn't have an agent that knew the ins and outs. I got the promotion and I expected to be on the money I would have been on two years ago at Derby. But they wouldn't hear of it. We negotiated more or less with the manager. In those days they weren't talking big money. Everybody had more or less a budget. Everybody was on more or less the same. There wasn't anybody who was on more than anybody else.

But while he's on the subject of footballers and their respective values, Bobby has an interesting take on the one player in each team who, in his opinion, should be paid that much more.

The only one that deserved it was the goalkeeper.

Cloughie made Shilton the first thousand pound a week player. You'd laugh at that now, wouldn't you? But he said that guy's worth 15 extra points a season, which proved right, because they won the league and the European Cup. He always said that the main men were your goalkeeper, your centre half, your midfield player and your centre forward. The rest of them you can build round. That's the heart of your team, especially in the lower leagues. You need a big centre half, a big hard midfield player or a nasty little midfield player who can keep everybody going, a big centre forward and a goalkeeper who can handle crosses, because in the lower league it's all about ball in the box. If they could all play passing football, they wouldn't be playing in that league to start with, would they?

While that last assessment might seem harsh on some lower league players, not least the man making the assessment, it's difficult to argue with the general philosophy about the central spine of a team at any level. Not many weeks pass by without a third or fourth division manager telling the media that he's searching for at least one player who would fit one of Campbell's descriptions.

But, coming back to what might loosely be called Bobby's own contract talks in the summer of 1985, once again the Campbell heart ruled the Campbell wallet.

Because of the fire, I didn't want them to be making me out to be the bad boy - 'Campbell's asking for a transfer' – so I just signed it.

So the man famed for his intercontinental wanderings and his occasional confrontation with different managers committed his future to another two seasons at Bradford City - in a higher division, albeit one where he had played previously; with no ground to call 'home'; and with no extra money in the pay cheque. But the team had the sympathy of the football world and their talisman had long since achieved hero status among the fans.

The new season began on Saturday August 17th 1985

with Bradford City's first game since 1937 in what was still properly called the Second Division of English football. The game was away to Carlisle United.

There was a big turn out for that first game. Everybody turned up for that first game. I scored two up at Carlisle on the first day of the season. Lovely pitch up there that was.

Stuart McCall remembers the day vividly. 'Then what a start at Carlisle. I remember a beautiful boiling day. We had lunch in a little hotel in the middle of Carlisle and went out for a walk. There was just claret and amber everywhere. It gave everyone such a lift. How fitting that he scored in the first game back! That just sums him up. I think we had 5000 fans there and he got two goals.'

And yet, despite such a bright beginning and a season when Bradford City consolidated their position in the Second Division with a thirteenth place finish, Bobby Campbell looks back on that season as very much the beginning of the end for his football career. His words are stark and unambiguous.

That was my career finished more or less.

The pitch at Carlisle United may have been just the sort that Bobby wanted to play on, but that experience was not going to be repeated with many other games that season. Bradford City obviously could not return to Valley Parade at the start of the new season. There were serious discussions about whether they would, indeed, ever play there again. Not for the first time, nor for the last, the debate began about the desirability of sharing a ground with Bradford Northern, as the city's rugby league team was then called. Whatever the long term future may have been for Valley Parade, there was absolutely no prospect of first team football being played there during the 1985-6 season. Bradford City would spend their first season in the Second Division permanently 'on the road'.

The first 'home' game, a League Cup tie against Chesterfield, was played on Wednesday August 21st at Huddersfield Town's Leeds Road ground.

It was lovely playing at Huddersfield, where the pitch was always as sound as a pound.

The Huddersfield pitch, at least at the start of the season, must have been very much to Campbell's liking for the single reason that was always uppermost in his mind – scoring goals. He and Stuart McCall both scored against Chesterfield, a feat they were to repeat in the away leg, when Bradford City scraped into the second round after extra time. In the first two rounds of the Milk Cup (one of the League Cup's many guises) games were played over two legs, so there was no way of avoiding a 'home' tie. The Football League did, however, change their fixture list for the start of the season, so that the first three of Bradford City's league fixtures were all played away from home, with City travelling to Brighton and Wimbledon after that first game trip to Carlisle.

The first 'home' league game did not take place until Sunday September 1st. The game against Stoke City was played at Elland Road and two penalties from Greg Abbott and a third goal from Martin Singleton produced a second league win in the first four games. Mid table security had been achieved and, with the usual share of ups and downs, was to be maintained to the end of the season. Of the twenty one 'home' league matches, four were played at Elland Road, six at Leeds Road and the remaining eleven, most relevantly from Campbell's point of view, at the ground that Bradford City might have shared on a permanent basis – Odsal stadium.

After that opening day pair, Bobby scored another eight league goals in eight different games. In that 1985-6 season Bradford City won every league match when Campbell scored. He obviously did like playing at Leeds Road, where he scored three goals in City's six league games. But Bradford City as a team must also have enjoyed the Leeds Road surface, since they won every one of the six league games they played on it. By comparison Campbell scored just three goals in the eleven league games played at Odsal, with Bradford City winning six of those eleven games.

I'm playing up front. Every game was going to be an away game for me. We didn't get the home advantage you really want. There was no advantage playing at Odsal. If anything, we were more disheartened playing at Odsal than the away team. The away team only had to come there once. I did struggle that year. I think I only got 12 goals that year.

There are some strikers for whom 12 goals against tougher opposition (10 in the Second Division and 2 in the League Cup) might not have been such a disheartening return. But when you're Bobby Campbell and you're used to scoring more than twenty goals a season, you look upon a 12 goal season as a great disappointment, no matter which grounds the games were played at or who the opposition were.

Both John Hendrie and Greg Abbott equalled Campbell's league tally that season, even if Greg Abbott's ten goals did include seven from the penalty spot. Despite holding their own in the Second Division, Bradford City had only one 'home' gate, for the league derby at Odsal against Leeds United, which topped the 10,000 mark. While Leeds Road and Elland Road were big stadia for such low crowds, it was the wide open spaces of the Odsal bowl that contrasted so starkly with the tight ground at Valley Parade and the atmosphere that even a four figure crowd could generate back at City's true home. The entire season, despite Bradford City's finishing one place above Leeds and three above Huddersfield, is not one that brings back many fond memories for Bobby Campbell.

There is, however, one incident from the end of the season that is memorable, although it is another example of a topic Bobby himself does not raise. It is, on this occasion, recalled by one of his new team mates, gradually introduced into the first team during the course of the season, having previously played non-league football. The

21 year old Ian Ormondroyd was so different from Campbell that there can be no argument when Mark Ellis describes them as 'chalk and cheese'.

The six foot thirteen Ormondroyd was offered a contract by Trevor Cherry after scoring two goals in a pre-season win at Barnet. He had been spotted by Maurice Lindley while playing several leagues below Bradford City's new status and had initially spent a period on trial at Valley Parade. Having accepted his first full-time professional contract at the age of 21, Stix, as he became universally known, began to train with the first team squad. He remembers only too well his first encounter with Bobby Campbell.

'On my first day of training there was a practice match between the first team and the rest. I was with the rest. As we lined up for the kick off, Campbell said to me "This is my shirt. You're not having it." There were a few other expletives added in.'

If it was Campbell's custom to make sure that any fresh faces knew exactly where they stood, Stix was quick to realise that this gruff individual had much to offer. 'It was all about him scoring, but it was also about the team winning. It was all about him wanting to play.'

Although Bobby never went into a coaching job and may not have been ideally suited to that role, Ian is quick to say 'He was always supportive. He would help with bits of tips. He was good in the dressing room. It was like having another leader after the manager and the assistant manager. He was something of a father figure to the younger players, but he made the wingers cross the ball to him!' Mark Ellis in particular would agree with that comment.

By the end of the 1985-6 season Ian Ormondroyd had become a sufficiently well established part of the first team – eight starts, four appearances from the bench and three goals, but never in the number nine shirt! – to be part of the group that went off on an end-of-season break to Magaluf. There was, however, a price to pay for being the newcomer on this trip. 'I was lumbered with sharing a room with Campbell. He would be going out at night and sleeping during the day.' But it was here that Ian remembers an incident reminiscent of the one described by Stuart McCall from November 1983, another occasion when the Campbell story-telling included a significant gap.

'The club secretary at the time was man called Terry Newman. He was an epileptic, but we didn't know that. We were all in the bar one evening, having a few drinks,' Ian recalls. 'Terry began to slide down the wall to the floor. We all wondered if he was just drunk. But then he was on the floor, shaking, turning a funny colour. He was obviously having a fit. He had swallowed his tongue. Bobby got his hand in Terry's mouth and ripped his jaws apart to pull his tongue out. Terry's jaws were clamping down on Bobby's hand and he was cut really badly, but he probably saved Terry's life.'

It seems that there are some actions, performed perhaps instinctively, that others remember more easily than Campbell himself. For more reasons than one, he is a man who it is better to have on your side.

Not that Ian Ormondroyd wants to make out that Bobby is a saint. 'The juniors used to come with a packed lunch provided by wherever they were lodging. He used to nick the sweets, Mars bars or whatever, and take them home for his kids. The juniors used to try to eat them before he got in.'

Mark Ellis, the sometime victim of the Campbell fire extinguisher and scissors, also recalls the risk of Bobby running off with small items. 'I belonged to a health club and before home games I would call in and pick up a couple of energy drinks for myself and Stuart. Bob used to say that they were "a load of shit", but you still had to keep an eye out that he didn't run off with them.'

Newcomer as he was from the world of part-time

football, Stix would have been advised against taking Campbell as his new professional role model. 'These days the players do a lot of warming up on the pitch before the match. Bobby didn't do that. I can remember him watching the 2.30 at Haydock on the TV. Then he would put his gear on, do a few groin stretches and go out and play.'

There was, however, one vital element in the Campbell pre-match preparation that Stix seems to have missed. Stuart McCall remembers that Bobby would always ask Bryan Edwards 'Have you got the medicine?' Bryan would proffer Bobby a small bottle from which he would take a quick swig. One day Bobby offered the same bottle to the young McCall, who realised for the first time that 'the medicine' was in fact a nip of whiskey. As Stuart says, 'You would never have thought it was alcohol. It was just a nip. Then he'd say to you "All the best" and you'd realise what it was! Then he'd go out and score a hat trick.'

Trevor Cherry and Terry Yorath just knew that with Campbell you had to take the whole package, even if it did include some decidedly unusual habits in among the 20 goals a season.

At the end of the 1985-86 season the main cause for optimism for Bradford City fans, beyond the achievement of Second Division stability, centred on the decision to remain at and rebuild Valley Parade. The rebuilding would not only feature a new 5,000 seat steel and concrete stand on the site of the ruined wooden structure, but would include a renovated Kop, which had new terracing to accommodate 7,000 standing fans and, for the first time in its one hundred year history, a roof.

Despite the speed with which the contractors worked, the delay in coming to a decision to remain at Valley Parade inevitably meant that the 1986-7 season would also start with Bradford City playing their home games elsewhere. This time, however, the 'sound' surface of Huddersfield Town's ground was no longer to be the place where City could rely on winning and where Bobby Campbell could maintain his strike rate of one goal every two games. The first ten 'home' league games and three 'home' cup ties were all to be played at Odsal. Bradford City would win just three of those ten 'home' league games and Bobby Campbell would play no part in most of them.

Chapter 15
AND SO TO WIGAN

By the close season of 1986 Trevor Cherry had been the manager of Bradford City for almost four years. The mid-table finish in the second division, despite having no ground to call home, was enough to persuade Cherry that he need not make significant changes to his playing squad. In particular, his strikers – Campbell, Hendrie, Ormondroyd and Goodman – could carry on from where they had left off.

The new season got off to an inauspicious start, with just two draws and three defeats in the first five games. A 2-1 win at Millwall, almost inevitably featuring a goal from Bobby Campbell, produced the first victory, just in time for the visit to Odsal of Leeds United. The local rivals had played each other only a dozen times in their long histories prior to Bradford City's 1985 promotion. Leeds had been in the First Division since 1964, winning titles and cups along the way, until their relegation in the same 1981-2 season when Bradford City were delighted to be promoted from the Fourth Division. Leeds had won both games in City's first season back in the Second Division and so September 20th 1986 was built up as City's big chance finally to 'get one over' their near neighbours.

For very different reasons the game came to be remembered for rather more than the 2-0 scoreline by which City won that day. Stuart McCall recalls both reasons, neither of them especially fond memories, for the game becoming part of Bradford City folk lore. The

Bradford-Leeds rivalry may have been relatively new, given their lack of previous encounters on the field, but it came into being at a particularly unfortunate time. English football in the mid-eighties was mired in hooliganism. There had been so many incidents of violence that the Conservative government had even passed legislation providing for the creation of a membership scheme to keep potential trouble makers either away from grounds or at least under close surveillance.

However, given their recent history and the enormous sympathy throughout football that emanated from the tragedy of just sixteen months earlier, Bradford City could have been forgiven for thinking that they at least would not suffer unduly at the hands of the hooligan element, even though one or two infamous supporters of the team were well known to the police. The Leeds game was always going to be the most likely scene of any trouble, but no one could have anticipated the precise nature of that trouble and the way it would bring back such vivid memories.

It is often forgotten (and perhaps Bradford City fans might just be forgiven for this) that there were two fatal football matches on May 11th 1985. While 56 people died after the Valley Parade fire, another young life was lost at St Andrew's, Birmingham City's ground. Birmingham were playing Leeds United. Birmingham were already guaranteed promotion to the First Division, but a win could still send them up as champions if Oxford's result went the right way for them. Leeds could yet gain promotion themselves with a win, depending upon the outcome of other games. Some 10,000 Leeds supporters were expected at the game.

There were outbreaks of violence throughout the afternoon. There were two pitch invasions at half-time, one from each set of 'fans'; the referee took the players off the pitch during the second half; there were several occasions when missiles were thrown; and, with the match having run almost half an hour late, a wall collapsed as the police tried to quell the final outbreak of violence at the end of the game. A boy of 15 died. Sir Oliver Popplewell, who conducted the enquiries into both fatalities, concluded in his report

'The reason why there was disorder was that a substantial number of visiting supporters, full of drink, came to Birmingham deliberately to cause trouble, and thereby sparked off the Birmingham supporters whose subsequent behaviour was as bad as, if not worse than, that of the visitors.'

The vast bowl of Odsal Stadium, which had once housed a crowd of over 100,000 for a Rugby League Cup Final, was just ripe for those among the rival 'fans' who might have been determined to fight each other. Inside the stadium, consisting largely of ancient terracing, there was a fast-food van. It became a target for the hooligan element among the Leeds United supporters. It was overturned and began to topple down the terracing. Quite amazingly, for the second time in sixteen months a Bradford City game was halted while a fire was dealt with. For Stuart McCall it was the final straw that broke his hitherto life-long allegiance to his home town club, the team for which his father had played.

But Stuart McCall also remembers that one of the Bradford City scorers in that game was Bobby Campbell. That was his third goal in the first seven games of the season, still not a bad scoring ratio by any standards. But it was, as Stuart recalls, Campbell's last goal for Bradford City. It was, in fact, his last league game for the club. Within a few days he was to become a Wigan Athletic player and that number nine shirt, which Campbell had worn in so many games over the last seven seasons, was to be passed around between no fewer than four different players during the rest of the season.

Trevor Cherry decided that he needed a younger model to replace the striker who had celebrated his thirtieth birthday with the winning goal at Millwall a week earlier. He bought Mark Leonard from Stockport County, a Fourth Division team for whom he had scored 23 goals in 73 games. He was not to hold on to Campbell's number nine shirt with any degree of permanency. Indeed, in the rest of the season after replacing Campbell, Leonard started 16 league games and came on as a substitute in 8 others, scoring a total of just three goals in the process.

Two consequences, neither without their controversial notes, followed the decision to release the club's all-time record goal scorer. On the purchase of the replacement striker Campbell has his own tersely expressed opinion.

Then, just as we were moving back to Valley Parade, they got rid of me and they brought in Mark Leonard. I was a better player with my left foot than he was with two feet!

As a brief aside, mention simply has to be made of the fact that, when Bradford City played an England XI to mark the official opening of the rebuilt Valley Parade in December 1986, the man in the claret and amber number nine shirt at the kick-off was not Mark Leonard. He had to wait for the second half before entering the field of play. There is no need to say who the guest player was who started the game as Bradford City's centre forward.

And then there was another, less emotional, but more ceremonial opening. A new stand was built on the Midland Road side of Valley Parade by the end of 1996. In March 1997 that stand was officially opened by Her Majesty The Queen. Standing in line in the rain, waiting to be presented to Her Majesty, were two men who would always be regarded as Bradford City legends, Bobby Campbell and Stuart McCall. Little over a year later the Rangers midfielder would return to Bradford to cement his legendary status as captain of a team destined for the top flight of English football. Campbell was already long retired, as was the man standing to the other side of McCall, Sir Bobby Charlton.

The second outcome of the decision to allow Campbell to leave was the contentious dismissal in early January of Trevor Cherry, following a run of six draws and two defeats, including a failure to score in either of the first two league games back at Valley Parade. His replacement, Terry Dolan, eventually brought Ron Futcher from Oldham and his four goals and six from John Hendrie in the last ten league matches of the season contributed to seven wins in those games, a run which was to see Bradford City finish tenth in Division Two and set themselves up for a very real challenge in the following season for promotion to the top flight of English football.

Bobby Campbell, meanwhile, had headed off to a very different environment – or perhaps it was somewhere remarkably familiar.

Wigan Athletic had been elected to the Football League, replacing Southport, as recently as 1978, long before the days of any automatic promotion from the (then non-existent) Conference. The Latics had established themselves firmly enough to have shared Bradford City's own 1981-82 points tally and promotion to the Third Division and, in the four seasons since that promotion, had further consolidated their status in that higher league. They were, however, a very long way from challenging for anything above that level and were a solid Third Division team when Bobby Campbell signed for them in September 1986.

The one familiar feature that must have struck the Campbell eye immediately was his new home ground. Springfield Park had been Wigan's home in their various guises (Wigan County, Wigan United, Wigan Town and Wigan Borough all played there between 1897 and 1932), although Wigan Athletic had had to buy the ground from the dog track owners on the understanding that no more greyhound racing would take place there. Campbell must have been haunted by the sight of the wide open terraces at each end of the ground, one of which gave on to a grass bank. The contrast with the newly rebuilt Valley Parade, where he was never to play a competitive game, was stark indeed. Worse still, memories of his hated games at Odsal Stadium could have struck fear into him – well, at least more fear than the average Third Division centre half was ever going to strike.

There was a time, of course, when the man from Belfast wasn't at all sure what to make of a solid Yorkshire accent, especially when used in any phrase including the word 'thee' or 'thou'. But, by the time he was leaving for Wigan, Bobby had lived and worked among the Tykes for so long that he not only understood the accent, but he practically thought of himself, despite his very different manner of speech, as a native.

I think I was their first signing from over this way. That was the thing about Wigan, it was all Scouse rejects.

And he wasn't too far off the mark in identifying a number of Scousers at Springfield Park, even if they would undoubtedly have rejected the notion of being 'rejects'. The manager himself, Ray Mathias, was a true native of Liverpool. His twenty years as a player at Tranmere Rovers, even if the Wirral club would not be recognised by Kopites or Evertonians as being a Liverpool team, would do nothing to diminish his permanent standing as a Scouser anywhere else in the country.

At the time of Campbell's arrival at Springfield Park there was one other particular Scouser who was just making his way at Wigan. Having been a member of Liverpool's youth squad, but never making an appearance for the first team, Campbell's new strike partner had just celebrated his 22nd birthday. Little could either of them know how great an impact on the fortunes of Bradford City this young man would later have. His name was Paul Jewell. As with so many others of his team mates, Campbell has a story to tell about the youthful Jewell.

The Campbell disciplinary record, on and off the field, is discussed on other pages. But he himself firmly believes that if you get sent off in a game which your team ends up losing, then it's your fault and you can't expect sympathy from anyone else. It is in this context that Bobby recalls a game at Mansfield Town which, for some reason now lost in the mists of time, had kicked off at noon on a Sunday – not the best time for Campbell to have to play football.

Jewell was just coming through at Wigan. We were playing away at Mansfield and Jewell was having a do with this lad, who was kicking shit out of him. Jewell scored and he went over to him and had a little spit at him. I went over to Jewell and gave him a crack round the ear. I said 'Listen, if you get sent off, it's Sunday morning, I'm knackered, I don't want to be doing your running.'

He'd left the guy lying on the deck when he knocked the ball in the net. I gave him a crack round the ear and told him to get back to the half-way line. Jewell always remembers that. The referee came up and said 'I'll let it go seeing you've sorted it out.' I don't think he'd seen the spit, but he'd seen the taking the piss.

If there's one issue in football Campbell always has an opinion about, it's training. There was one particular aspect of Ray Mathias' training regime that Bobby didn't appreciate.

Training at Wigan wasn't that good. He was keen, but he was one of these that thought he had to keep you out there for two hours. At Bradford with Trevor and George Mulhall, even at Sheffield United, once you'd done your training, if you'd done it sharp and quick, you were off. He used to linger.

There were several consequences of what Bobby saw as 'lingering' and none was positive. The first of these tells a very different story of Campbell's attitude to training at Wigan to the description of Campbell the trainer given by his old team mates at Valley Parade.

I used to coast in training. I hold my hands up. I never used to push myself in training because, at the end of the day, it's not what you do in training, it's what you do on a

Saturday. There are a lot of guys over the years that I've watched – Barry Gallagher is as big an example at Bradford. He used to look super fit. Come the Saturday he'd be the most knackered one of the rest of us. As they say, he'd left it all on the training pitch. With young lads especially, they've got to be seen to be running about. I'd say it's got to be Saturday's performance that gets me in the next week.

But Bobby could hardly help noticing something else about this different training regime, especially once it affected his own fitness in an adverse way.

There were a lot of injuries at Wigan in those two years. I played most of the first season, but the second season I struggled with my groins. If it had been me, I would have played with injuries. I couldn't train for a couple of days, but I would try to play. Then this one went again, so I had this one stretched; then that one stretched; then that one cut; then that one cut. So they cut it to release it and that put me out for a couple of months. I couldn't do sit-ups. I had to watch myself.

Campbell's fitness record at Bradford City, even allowing for the broken scaphoid, was quite remarkable. He hardly missed a game through injury. After making his debut in January 1980, he played in all the remaining games of that season. In his first three full seasons at Bradford City, Campbell played 46, 52 and 49 games. In 1983-4, after being at Derby, he played in all but one of the team's remaining 34 games. In 1984-5 he played 53 times and in 1985-6, when Bradford City had just 42 league games, he played a total of 47 times, always from the start of the match.

He is not exactly being over-generous to himself, when he says

I didn't miss many games. That season, when we struggled, 1985-6, I must have had five injections in the back of my hamstring to play. We struggled because every game was an away game. Not bad for an injury-prone

centre forward, eh?

Despite his groin injuries, he didn't actually miss all that many games at Wigan, although he was deemed fit enough only to come on as a substitute more times than he would have preferred. Having joined Wigan two months into the 1986-7 season, by the end of the next season he had still managed to take part in 69 matches.

Another small consequence of his injuries was one that only a player with Campbell's outlook on the work-life balance could have thought through.

Your social life goes down the river. You can't be drinking because you're not burning it off.

Whether or not the self-imposed restrictions on his drinking were a contributory factor in the final consequence is impossible to tell. But there is one more outcome of a season which, by his own standards, was injury-hit. And this was the most important consequence of all, as we shall see presently.

I was getting depressed with the game.

But in early October 1986 there was no sign that Bobby Campbell, only weeks past his thirtieth birthday, would ever become depressed with playing football. In typical Campbell style he scored his first goal for his new club on his debut, albeit that Wigan lost 3-1 away to Swindon Town. The Wigan team he joined were in the lower reaches of the Third Division at the start of his new career, but they were not to finish the season in such a perilous position.

Indeed, Wigan's season was to end at the very same place where Campbell played his first game for them, at the County Ground in Swindon, but that would be in the following May. By then they had moved up the table and reached the promotion play-offs for a place in Division Two, a lofty height they had never reached in their short Football League history and, as it turned out, were not to reach for another ten seasons.

It was just a shame we blew it in the play-offs. We were

home to Swindon – that was in my first season. We were winning 2-0 at half-time at home in the first leg and we ended up losing 3-2. I couldn't believe how we didn't shut up shop. We were cruising that first half. We went in at half-time and somebody said another goal would kill the tie off. They got an early goal, then another one and pinched one just before the end. Before you knew it – 3-2. We went down to Swindon and we drew nil apiece. That's the way these things go.

Despite that one major disappointment, Bobby has plenty of fond memories of his time at Springfield Park, including his one visit to play in a competition at Wembley Stadium.

They were a great bunch at Wigan, a good atmosphere. We played at Wembley in a Mickey Mouse tournament. There was a centenary competition in the middle of that season. It was based, starting in October, on the next ten games. Whoever had the best results in the next ten games got invited to this 20-minute each way tournament. This was one of my biggest embarrassments. If you can't laugh at yourself, you can't laugh at anybody, can you?

We played 20 minutes each way. There was a penalty shoot-out. The lad who went up first, Paul Cook, who went on to play for Burnley, came up to me and said 'Bob, you notice the keeper's moved so early?' I set my mind to blast it down the middle. I ran up and he moved back along the line. I thought I only had to side foot it in the corner. I stubbed the bastard and it went nearer the corner flag than the goal. I just stood there. The lads were laughing at me. This was at Wembley!

Although Bobby clearly could have a laugh at himself, he was still a professional footballer and a missed penalty at Wembley hurt, even if it had been in a 'Mickey Mouse tournament.' Just in case the sponsors think their efforts were in vain, this tournament was in fact the Mercantile Credit trophy. It had nothing at all to do with Walt Disney.

By the next morning, when the rest of the squad were set to spend another day away from home, even though the team were no longer in the competition, Campbell had made his mind up that he was on his way back home as soon as possible.

I was disgusted with myself. We got up in the morning; I had my breakfast and said 'I'm off home'. I phoned a taxi and asked him to drop me off at the corner of the A1. I got my thumb out and thumbed it up to Brighouse. I got a couple of lifts. There were some Bradford City fans picked me up. They couldn't believe it. They dropped me off at Brighouse. I was in the pub for dinner time. I drowned my sorrows, went home to the missus and she said 'You're not supposed to be back until tomorrow!' The funny thing was I had to organise a lift on Monday from Huddersfield because my car was in Wigan.

Seasoned Wigan fans do, however, have one very special reason for remembering Bobby Campbell. Early in his second season at Wigan, they were drawn against local rivals Bolton Wanderers in the first round of the League Cup. The previous season, when Wigan had come so close to promotion to Division Two, Bolton had been relegated to the Fourth Division, finishing a full forty points behind The Latics. Suddenly, Wigan were the senior team, although Bolton were to finish the 1987-8 season in third place and thus regain their Division Three status at the first attempt.

The first leg had been played at Springfield Park and Wanderers had won 3-2. The outcome of the two-legged tie must have seemed something of a formality to many, especially once Bolton had increased their lead on their own ground. But the 'many' did not include Bobby Campbell. He scored a hat trick at Burnden Park, including two 'screamers' going in off the underside of the bar, enabling Wigan to win 3-1 on the night and 5-4 on aggregate. The Wigan fans do not forget such feats.

But, as the 1987-8 season went on, Campbell's injuries

began to catch up with him and the disillusionment set in with a vengeance.

Some of the injuries were playing me up. My neck was starting to ping with the cold weather. I was getting a lot of little niggling injuries. I played through injuries and I got off the table. Some players, if they broke a finger nail, they wouldn't play. I played with a bad ankle. I played with everything. I played when I couldn't kick a ball. I played when I could hardly run, but as long as I could get in the box and cause trouble, it was worth it.

Of course, Bobby's definition of 'causing trouble in the box' involved scoring or, at the very least, setting up goals for his team. Disillusioned, injured or whatever, nothing was going to change that definition and nothing changed his responses. In his first season at Wigan, despite his late arrival after the seven games he played for Bradford City, he finished top scorer with 16 league goals from 33 starts and two substitute appearances. Another 28 league starts and six substitute appearances during the next season brought a further 11 goals. But the continuing disruption to his career was about to take its toll.

It more or less made my mind up when I was sitting in the dressing room at the end of the season. I just decided I'd had enough. I would have been 32 in the September at the start of the next season.

And so it was that the professional football career that had seen Bobby Campbell leave his troubled native city as a 16 year old and play on three continents, that had taken him to a World Cup Finals and that had made him a cult hero at Bradford City, just came to an abrupt and, arguably, premature end. He was, as he says, still short of his 32nd birthday; but he was feeling the injuries and getting less and less enjoyment out of the game that he had loved and that, as he himself says, had almost literally saved his life. The decision was made and the wanderer, who had in fact by that time lived in the same part of West Yorkshire for the last thirteen years, settled down.

Chapter 16
A BIG DIFFERENCE

More than twenty years since he last kicked a ball in anger, Bobby Campbell has no regrets about retiring when he did, even though he was only 31 years old. That is not to say that Bobby has no regrets at all, about either his life or his career. He inevitably wishes he had behaved himself just a little bit better when he was younger, although for all the world he wouldn't have missed half of the scrapes he got into. His one big regret in his career comes from the very start.

Of course you look back to the early days and wish you'd done something different. Anybody who doesn't say that is a liar. I'd probably have signed for Man United. I wouldn't have known what might have happened after that. You could have got killed crossing the road in Manchester! But that's where I would have started from. I would probably have chosen Man United. There were more Irish lads there and it would have been easier for me to bed in.

By the time Bobby was making that journey across the Irish Sea, Manchester United had learnt a lot about how to deal with young players leaving their homes and families in Belfast. There were more Irish lads at Old Trafford than at Villa Park, including one or two Bobby already knew. Maybe the regime, a little less relaxed than it had been ten years earlier, when George Best was making that adjustment, would have had the right balance of support and flexibility to allow Bobby's undoubted talents to flourish to their maximum. Maybe he would have come on more quickly. Maybe he would not have been banned from the international team. Or maybe he would have been run over by the proverbial bus while crossing a Manchester street.

But, as you might expect, he's very philosophical about all that. He long ago learnt to take life as it comes. There are, as he points out in a different context, very few choices in that regard.

Even if it had have worked for me at Villa, the money that came into the game didn't come in until I left. Even the top players didn't make a big, big wage. That's the way it goes. We can't pick when we're coming and we can't pick when where going, but we don't want to pick it.

If you look for the biggest changes in Bobby Campbell's life, the most significant in the long term, he will admit to three. The first is still that decision to leave Belfast and to avoid the need to take sides in the increasingly bitter and dangerous civil strife. He will tell you that that single decision almost certainly saved his life. It is impossible to imagine the youthful and headstrong Campbell remaining for much longer in his home city without risking his wellbeing and even his survival. So many of his friends had no such choice. Bobby Campbell's ability to score goals gave him a very special opportunity, something he has never forgotten.

He will also tell you that the decisive moment of his career involved George Mulhall's decision to offer him a trial at Bradford City. Up to that moment, talented as he was, Bobby would accept that he had been drifting. Not only had he dropped to part time football in a country then best known for producing excellent cricket players, but his time at lower league English clubs had been chequered, to say the least. He had been branded a trouble maker, a rogue and worse. A man for whom he retains the greatest respect brought him back from the brink.

And that undistinguished past brings us to the third defining moment of Bobby Campbell's life, the biggest single reason for such reform as he might lay claim to. Her name is Paula and she has been Mrs Campbell since 1982. Indeed, Bobby's bonus for being part of the Bradford City team that won promotion from the Fourth to the Third Division in the 1981-2 season, combined with those additional duty free benefits that a trip to Spain brought in the summer of 1982, paid for their wedding.

But Paula and Bobby may not have got off to the most auspicious of starts.

I met her when I was just recovering from my broken leg. I remember it was a Saturday afternoon, a hot summer's day. I thought who is this young bird? She was 18. All she could talk about was the electricity bill for her flat.

For a young footballer who had just been denied his end of season bonus by a career threatening injury, talk of electricity bills can hardly have been at the top of his list of conversation points. But they soon became enough of an item for it to take an ocean or two to keep them apart.

I was courting the wife when I went to Vancouver. We lived together for five years before we got married.

By the time of their wedding, Bobby's team mates had noticed the difference in him. Stuart McCall, for example, says 'Paula used to try to keep him in check. He could even be a bit frightened of her. He used to speak about her – "Paula this and Paula that" – he obviously had a little bit of respect.' Even then it is worth noting that Stuart says Paula 'used to try' to keep him in order. He doesn't actually say she succeeded! But anyone for whom Campbell has respect must be very special. Respect is not something he gives easily.

With Paula at his side, the man who wandered the globe playing football has never been far from Huddersfield for the last thirty years and more. Apart from those spells in Vancouver and Brisbane, he has lived around the town since leaving Birmingham as an 18 year old. Much of that time has been spent in the village of Lindley. While the village's most famous attraction is a Grade II listed building, The Clock Tower, at least one website guides you to other places of interest, including the 'curiosity' at Lindley Working Men's Club –its steward.

I got settled in Huddersfield. I had a lot of friends and associates. The kids were at school nearby. I went out looking for a few pubs at first. I've been here more than twenty years and took this job more or less straight after retiring from football.

Even in what most people might think would be his natural environment, Bobby acknowledges the vital role that Paula plays.

She's like a queen here. She does that much for everybody. If she'd have gone, she'd have had the biggest send-off round here that anybody had ever seen. Not one person has got a bad word for her. She does everybody favours. She runs about for everybody.

And two short sentences, with a perplexed shake of the Campbell head in between, say it all.

She made a big difference.

I don't know why she married me!

In the distant past, especially when he was in a tight corner or two, Bobby Campbell might have denied the obvious. These days, although he tries hard to keep his family out of the limelight, it is plain that he takes both the joys and the responsibilities of being a husband, father and grandfather in much the same way as he once took his goal scoring. What George Mulhall achieved on the football pitch, Paula bettered in domesticity, even if she hasn't yet completely 'reformed' him. Maybe she simply doesn't want to lose the character she has known for so very long. Or maybe even Paula knows her limits.

Chapter 17
AN INCORRIGIBLE ROGUE

While Bobby Campbell was going through his apprenticeship with Aston Villa, I was embarking on a similar stage of a rather different career. I was what was then called an articled clerk. The modern day terminology, 'a trainee solicitor', explains matters more clearly. I spent much of the 1970's working in Leeds, where I learnt all sorts of odd facts about criminal law. One of those odd facts, a short phrase from a piece of old law, was never again to prove useful after I left Leeds in the early 1980's. But listening to and writing about Bobby has reminded of those few words.

When I first went into court in Leeds, I had to get used to a phrase which was generally reduced to 'deemed R & V' and was written on the court record simply as 'R & V'. Being of an enquiring mind, I asked one of my mentors for an explanation. I was first told that the two letters stood for 'rogue' and 'vagabond'. I was then referred to a bulky tome and directed toward the Vagrancy Act of 1824. The astute reader may have already guessed what brought this expression back to mind so many years after I last wrote it down.

While he would rightly object to being described as a vagabond, Bobby Campbell has even called himself a rogue, although the word changes its meaning a little as the years go by. The older Campbell's roguery was clearly of a more sedate nature than some of his youthful exploits. But that ancient piece of legislation would have found plenty of room for many of his activities, not least because it criminalises 'wandering abroad'. When they introduced this expression into our legal system, I doubt if the 1824 legislators had in mind playing football in Vancouver and Brisbane.

But what our nineteenth century legislators did recognise was that some rogues are not reformed quite as easily as others. Some repeat their offending behaviour despite warnings and penalties. The 1824 Act required a court to deem such a person to be an 'incorrigible rogue', thus leaving him liable to face a more severe penalty for continuing to be a 'disorderly person'. Penalties in those days, of course, were always measured in terms of imprisonment, if the offence was minor enough to avoid deportation or hanging. Supervision and unpaid community work were unthought-of.

But the rogues and even the incorrigible rogues were to benefit from a stroke of good fortune when our more modern legislators passed one of the many Criminal Justice Acts of the twentieth century. A fine could be imposed instead of the previously required prison term and being deemed an incorrigible rogue was suddenly much harder to achieve. And then I was struck by another of those odd facts that came from the back of my memory while writing about Bobby Campbell. That Criminal Justice Act, the very one that made the incorrigible rogue such a rarity, was passed in 1982, the same year as Bobby married Paula. The Act did not quite abolish the incorrigible rogue, so it must have been mere coincidence that it looked upon him more kindly from then on.

There are several essential parts to the character of Bobby Campbell. He will always be one of the best headers of a football of his generation. He will always be a legend to those who saw him play. He will always speak in that unmistakeable voice and style. And, with luck, he will always retain that little bit of roguery that has been so much a part of the man called Bobby Campbell, the character these pages have tried to describe.

BOBBY CAMPBELL'S CAREER

Campbell himself is the first to acknowledge that a footballer's career, especially when that footballer is a striker, is most often summed up by bald statistics. His own career has rather more to it than the numbers, but below are the figures for Campbell's appearances and goal scoring records at the nine different clubs he played for. Although the following covers only club football, his playing record would not be complete without a reminder of the two full international caps he won for Northern Ireland in the 1981-1982 Home Internationals

Seasons	Club	Appearances	Goals
1973-1975	Aston Villa	10	1
1974-1975	Halifax Town (loan)	15	0
1975-1977	Huddersfield Town	31	9
1977-1978	Sheffield United	37	11
1978	Vancouver Whitecaps	13	9
1978-1979	Huddersfield Town	7	3
1978-1979	Halifax Town	22	3
1979	Brisbane City	20	10
1979-1983	Bradford City	148	76
1983-1984	Derby County	11	4
1983-1986	Bradford City	126	45
1986-1988	Wigan Athletic	69	27
	TOTALS	**509**	**198**

BC@BC
(Bobby Campbell at Bradford City)

Bobby Campbell's career took him all over the world, but the longest and most successful part was while he was a Bradford City player. The following few pages provide an account of that career at Valley Parade (and a few other 'home' grounds) in dates, in statistics and by reference to just a few games. They tell rather less than half of the story of BC@BC.

1979-1980
League games: - Played - 21. Scored – 8
Cup games: - None. (Didn't play until after City were knocked out.)
Memorable games: - Debut – 12th January 1980, home to Peterborough. Scored on debut in 1 – 1 draw. Wore number 11 shirt, the only time (apart from one substitute appearance) not to wear the number 9 shirt.
City finished 5th in Division Four, missing promotion on goal difference.

1980-1981
League games: - Played – 41 and 1 as substitute (only game as substitute). Scored – 19
League Cup: - Played – 4. Scored – 3.
F.A. Cup: - Played – 1. Scored – 0.
Season's total: - Played – 46 and 1 as substitute.
Scored – 22.
Memorable games: - League Cup 2nd round 27th August

1980, home to Liverpool. Scored only goal in 1 – 0 win. League 11th April 1981, home to Wigan Athletic. Scored all three in 3 – 3 draw.

City finished 14th in Division Four.

1981-1982

League games: - Played - 45. Scored – 24.
League Cup: - Played – 6. Scored – 3.
F.A. Cup: - Played – 1. Scored – 0.
Season's total: - Played – 52. Scored – 27.
Memorable games: - League 12th September 1981, home to York City. Scored three, including a penalty, in 6 – 2 win. City finished 2nd in Division Four and were promoted.

1982-1983

League games: - Played – 40. Scored – 25.
League Cup: - Played – 5. Scored – 3.
F.A. Cup: - Played – 4. Scored – 2.
Season's total: - Played – 49. Scored – 30.
Memorable games: - League August 28th to October 9th 1982 scored in 7 out of opening 9 league games, including 5 consecutive games. League Cup 3rd Round replay 24th November 1982, away to Manchester United. Scored only goal in 4 – 1 defeat.

City finished 12th in Division Three.

1983-1984

League games: - Played – 32. Scored – 9.
League Cup: - Played – None. (Didn't play until after City were knocked out – see below.)
F.A. Cup: - Played – 1. Scored – 0.
Season's total: - Played – 33. Scored – 9.
Memorable games: - League 5th November 1983, away to Wimbledon. First game back at City after being transferred to Derby County during the summer. Another League game, 27th March 1984, away to Bolton Wanderers. Scored the 94th goal of his Bradford City career,

breaking Frank O'Rourke's record that had stood since 1914.

City finished 7th in Division Three.

1984-1985

League games: - Played – 46. Scored – 23.

League Cup: - Played – 4. Scored – 0.

F.A. Cup: - Played – 3. Scored – 3.

Season's total: - Played – 53. Scored – 26.

Memorable games: - League 6th May 1985, away to Bolton Wanderers. Scored first goal in 2 – 0 win to secure championship. Another League game, 20th October 1984, away to Bristol City. Scored the 89th League goal of his Bradford City career, again breaking Frank O'Rourke's 1914 record

City finished champions of Division Three.

1985-1986

League games: - Played – 41. Scored – 10.

League Cup: - Played – 4. Scored – 2.

F.A. Cup: - Played – 2. Scored – 0.

Season's total: - Played – 47. Scored – 12.

Memorable games: - League 17th August 1985, away to Carlisle United. Scored both goals in 2 – 0 win in City's first game in Second Division since 1937.

1986-1987

League games: - Played – 7. Scored – 3.

League Cup: - Played – 1. Scored – 0.

F.A. Cup: - Played – None. (Transferred before City entered competition – see below.)

Season's total: - Played – 8. Scored – 3.

Memorable games: - League 20th September 1986, home to Leeds United (played at Odsal Stadium). Scored first goal in 2 – 0 win in last league game for City before transfer to Wigan Athletic.

Bradford City career 12th January 1980 to 20th September 1986

League games: - Played – 273 and 1 as substitute. Scored – 121.

League Cup: - Played – 24. Scored – 11.

F.A. Cup: - Played – 12. Scored – 5.

Total – Played 309 and 1 as substitute. Scored – 137. (1 goal every 2.26 games)

bantamspast

The bantamspast museum was conceived following the enormous success of the club's centenary exhibition at Bradford Industrial Museum in 2003. Over ten thousand visitors flocked to the exhibition and there was a widespread desire, from both visitors and those who had loaned some of the four hundred plus objects, that the collection be kept together to form a permanent museum. In 2005 the bantamspast museum was opened as a collaboration between Bradford City AFC, Bradford Industrial Museum and a small group of supporters. The museum is funded by donations, sales of replica badges and relies on the voluntary work of a small number of committed supporters. It is estimated that around thirty thousand visitors have enjoyed the museum during its seven year incarnation adjacent to the club shop. The museum has hosted numerous temporary exhibitions on everything from the pre-Wembley FA Cup Finals to the lost sports grounds of Bradford. Perhaps our finest moment was helping to commemorate the centenary of Bradford City's FA Cup triumph in 2011. A host of events took place including an exhibition, celebration dinner and the release of David Pendleton's book Glorious 1911. We have subsequently celebrated the 125th anniversary of the opening of Bradford City's Valley Parade ground with another book: Paraders, the 125 year history of Valley Parade, once again written by David Pendleton. We now have a trio of books in the bantamspast stable with Paul Firth's biography of Bradford City's record goal scorer Bobby Campbell. Overall, astonishing achievements for what is a grassroots museum reliant on donations and good will.

During the summer of 2012 the space the museum occupies was purchased for conversion into a school by the charity One in a Million. As a result for the 2012/13 season the bantamspast museum will be mainly an online resource as we formulate a plan for the continued future of the physical museum. Our aim is to make www.bantamspast.co.uk the best online museum in the football world and with this in mind we will be retaining the loaned objects as we record and catalogue them. In the late autumn we will begin the process of returning the loaned objects to their owners. The loss of the popular museum and cafe area will undoubtedly be keenly felt by many supporters. But we have been very fortunate to receive the support of Bradford City AFC, Leeds Metropolitan University and One in a Million that allowed the museum to exist rent free for five years. We are grateful for the support of the football club in our efforts to relocate the museum, but commercial contracts and practicalities combined to make a complete relocation impossible. However, we are determined to do our best to make the heritage and history of Bradford City AFC as accessible to as many people as possible during this period of change for bantamspast. Please visit our website www.bantamspast.co.uk for regular updates.

Over the summer of 2012 many of our wall mounted displays were re-erected in Bantams Bar and this location will become a kind of 'museum in exile' as we assess our long term future. Unfortunately, there is not free access to Bantams Bar. The club receives valuable income from users on matchdays and we had to be sensitive to the need to protect that income while considering public access. We will continue to work closely with the club, and the Friends of Bradford City, in considering what offers can be made to the supporters who previously enjoyed the museum and cafe area in large numbers over recent seasons. Quite clearly there is a market for such a facility and we will attempt to draw up a business case to present to the club, but in all likelihood this is a process that will only be fully worked up and available for consideration for the 2013/14 season. For the current season the club will be running six free ground tours (which will be advertised via the matchday programme and the official website) and included in the itinerary will be the boardroom, 1911 Club and Bantams Bar.

Many of our 'crown jewel' objects (the 1911 matchball, exhibits related to the fire, the shield that marked promotion to the Premier League, etc.) are in a display cabinet in the boardroom. It is hoped that in time these will return to a re-established museum, but in the short-term the boardroom seems an appropriate location and perhaps the exhibits will be joined by another piece of silverware in the not too distant future. We are also looking to design a 1911 mural for the southern wall of the 1911 Club. The facility is open to supporters on weekdays, indeed their lunches come highly recommended.

We were delighted to help Paul Firth to publish this long awaited book on the career of City's all time goal scoring legend Bobby Campbell. Plans are also advanced for a book by John Dewhirst telling the history of the club in objects and memorabilia. Finally, David Pendleton's comprehensive history of the development of sporting leisure in Bradford in the Victorian and Edwardian eras, which is currently the focus of his PhD, is likely to be published in late 2014.

PARADERS RETRO CITY BADGES

The PARADERS range of enamel badges was launched in 2009 and has been based on historically authentic designs associated with Bradford City since the club's formation in 1903. The commissioning was in response to the poor choice and quality of contemporary enamel badges and to provide collectors with an alternative to the ubiquitous poor standard Chinese imports, street corner rip-offs and fixture badges commemorating instantly forgettable games.

The range has aimed to fill existing gaps in collections of BCFC memorabilia. It means that every version of the Bradford City club crest since 1903 and every graphic character associated with the club has now been made available as an enamel badge. Promotion and memorable seasons, as well as the rivalry with Bradford (PA) have also been featured in unique designs.

The badges have been manufactured in England by a traditional process and the quality, as well as the investment in design, is immediately obvious. These have been produced in strictly limited, minimum production quantities and although the vast majority have now sold out they will not be repeated. The reproduction of historical badges ensures that long forgotten designs have made available and the policy of limited edition releases and quality manufacture is also intended to ensure that the PARADERS badges become future City collectibles.

In April, 2011 £5,000 from the sale of the badges was donated to Bradford University Burns Unit and further amounts have been donated to BCAFC through programme sponsorship and advertising of BANTAMSPAST activities.

Details of the range can be viewed online: www.paraders.co.uk

Three new designs have recently been released. Again these are limited edition commissions for collectors and any surplus proceeds will be reinvested in BANTAMSPAST. You can register your interest by email: badges@paraders.co.uk The badges are also on sale in BANTAMSPAST before kick-off.

SUBSCRIBERS

The following subscribed to
BOBBY CAMPBELL – THEY DON'T MAKE THEM LIKE HIM ANY MORE
in advance of publication and we are grateful for their support

Martin Ackroyd
Phil Artus
Nigel Bailey
Alan Martin Biggins
Denis Graham Blyth
Ali Bongo
Patrick Brady
John Bussey
Adrian Calam
John A W Clough
Robert Clutchley
Paul G Collinge
Jim Collinson
John 'Growler' Cook
Steve Cooper
Graham Coultous
Michael Crowther
Karl David Cunliffe
Neil Davies
Gary Dixon
Manny Dominguez
Mark Driver
Andrew Ellis
David Fenton
David Firth
Ian Fletcher
George Flyde
Richard Flyde
Robert Flyde
Matt Frith
Malcolm Gardner
Mick Gibson
Bert Glover

Paul A Grace
Rob Grillo
Susan Gross
Paul Guest
Martin Hall
Robert Hamilton
Roger W Hardaker
Chris Hawkridge
Ian Hemmens
Chris Hodson
Darren Holdsworth
John Holman
Bryan Ingham
Norman Jagger
Barry Jump
Mick Kehoe
Dean Kemp
Wayne Kemp
John C Kermode
Pete Knowles
Marko Kristovic
Alex Krstovic
Graham Leng
James Lovedale
Gary Marsden
Revd Nigel F Mason
Lee McCormack
James McLaren
Catherine Mills
John Musgrave
Q K Nash
Phil Neale
Andrew Norton

Chris Overend
Colin Parker
Graham Parkin
Neil Parkin
Chris Pearson
Andrew D Pickles
Stephen Pickles
Chris Pollard
Chris Rattigan
David Rhodes
Andrew Rishworth
Robert M Rishworth
Stewart A Roberts
Mark Ross
P M Sanderson
David Scally
Simon Andrew Scott
Chris Scully
Neil F Shaw
Jonathan Shepherd
Keith Sivyer
Mick Skelton
Johnathan Smith
Paul R Smith
Adam Spolnik
Evie Dolly Spolnik
Jeff Spolnik
Tom Stableford
Andy Stokes
David Storrie
Richard Stretton
Ben Sykes
Richard Sykes

Jack Taylor
Brian Tewkesbury
Mark R Thornton
Eric R Toulmin
Andrew Townsley
David Trudgill
Derek A Vincent
Gareth James Walker
Vicky Wallace
Andrew Waller
Andy Ward
Richard Wardell
Phil Watmough
Chris Welbourne
Dave Welbourne
Sue Wellings
Arnold Whitehead
John Whitehead
Drew Whitford-Bartle
Simon Wilks
Graeme Wolfenden
Stephen Woodhouse
Graham Yaffe

Apologies to anyone whose name has unfortunately been omitted due to publication deadline.

ABOUT THE AUTHOR

Paul Firth first went to Valley Parade as a nine year old, more than fifty years ago. Despite Bradford City's relegation that season, he caught the claret and amber bug. For many years he has displayed the extent of his 'incurable affliction' by travelling over 150 miles for each home game from his Merseyside home.

Paul was brought up in Bingley, from where, as a scholarship boy, he went to school within a few hundred yards of Valley Parade. He married into a Bradford City family and on that tragic day in May 1985 both he and his father-in-law count themselves lucky to have escaped from the burning stand.

After gaining a degree at Oxford, he qualified as a solicitor while working in the Magistrates' Courts, first at Bingley and then in Leeds. Although he worked for five years in Manchester, he and his wife continued to live in Thackley, so that their son could be born in Yorkshire. A move to Rotherham was followed by Paul's appointment as what was then called 'Stipendiary Magistrate' (now 'District Judge') in Liverpool. He later sat in the Lancashire courts.

In 2005 he wrote 'Four Minutes to Hell – The Story of the Bradford City Fire', the only book dedicated entirely to the events of May 11th 1985 and their aftermath. He has taken part in numerous radio and television programmes about the fire.

He also writes occasional pieces on criminal justice matters for newspapers and journals. He is a part-time lecturer in criminology and an Honorary Fellow in criminal justice studies at the University of Salford.

West of
England

The
West of
England

AN ARTIST'S JOURNEY THROUGH ENGLISH LANDSCAPES

SYDNEY R. JONES

SENATE

The West of England

First published in 1950 as *England South* by
The Studio Publications, London & New York

This edition published in 1998 by Senate,
an imprint of Tiger Books International PLC,
26A York Street, Twickenham,
Middlesex TW1 3LJ, United Kingdom

Copyright © 1950 Sydney R. Jones

Cover design © Tiger Books International 1998

1 3 5 7 9 10 8 6 4 2

ISBN 1 85958 527 2

Printed and bound in the UK by
Cox & Wyman, Reading, England

CONTENTS

1. INTRODUCTION

NORTH OF THE THAMES TO THE ROMAN WALL

The kind reception given to my previous records of England, both at home and abroad, has encouraged me to complete this volume. It follows *England— South* and thus makes the second in a set of three books. These are planned to indicate characteristic features throughout the whole country by presenting selections of my drawings and notes collected from many places on occasions both recent and distant. The present pages concern the western half of England, bounded in the south by the course of the Thames and Gloucestershire, and in the north by Cumberland and the Roman Wall. Over this area the harvest of beauty, incident, and story is big and rich. My powers and paper supplies are limited. No more than a general pattern and picture has been attempted from too much known wealth available for use. Notable omissions will be found abundant. For these and other sins I beg a little forgiveness while performing my part as showman of drawings accompanied by words.

My humble offering from the West chiefly concerns old things: portions of the English heritage that are related in one way or another to mankind's acts in hatching chapters, paragraphs, and postscripts of the English tale. The sundry bits and details on view in these pages, as a bagman's samples might be, have been gleaned from the supplies that even to-day seem almost inexhaustible. They come from town and country, from busy highways and quiet places made and developed during the course of past life and history. Although the ancient prophet's idea of "the everlasting hills" is getting somewhat worn and out of date with the advent of bulldozers and similar destructive appliances, some of the originals of my subjects might be considered more or less permanent. The Pennine Chain, for instance, and landscapes of hills and valleys belong to this category; many though not all of the fields are likely to remain intact for some time yet. Other objects shown and described exist on more shaky and perilous tenures. Representatives of presents that have passed away or bloomed anew, they include cathedrals and churches, castles, big houses and small houses, towns, villages and hamlets, and such incidental items as windows once brightened by medieval, Elizabethan, and Georgian suns, chimneys that kept home fires burning for ages, and pubs old in the fame of time-honoured home-brews. Needless to state, a number of the buildings illustrated have been mauled and a few of them no longer are visible.

My subjects, with thousands more to be seen in every part of England, are present witnesses of the nation's passage through its centuries of peace and plenty, trouble and strife, and the ordinary bread-and-butter years sometimes garnished with cake. And as the deeds of individuals and nations generally mean more than their words, these works constructed by men and women and the natural scenes known and fashioned by them constitute infallible indicators of human thought, action, and ideals now and again aimed at. These accumulations of past years, manifestations of humanity's problems, capers, and exploits in living, doing, and dying, could not help being allied to the debatable subject usually termed art. This was inevitable, for it is a truism that art, in common with arms, legs, cooking, and other necessities, is an absolute part of the life of all persons and periods. Whether the general expression is considered good, bad, pretty, or ugly may depend on the spirit of the age that produces it and also what people happen to think of the results a long time afterwards. Art certainly differs in kind. Some of it is thought to have beauty, though what and where that quality is constantly arouses speculations and differences of opinion. Even at this moment sections of the public declare that the present age is one of battle between beauty and the beasts, though the wisest among them disagree on where the beauty lies and whether the fierce animals have lairs in the neighbourhood of Whitehall or elsewhere. This type of warfare did not always develop on the grand scale because the skilled practitioners far outnumbered the mere talkers and writers on art. Existing evidence proves that once upon a time abundant beauty thrived, blossomed, and ripened throughout England as men and women cherished and tended the earth, built homes, towns and villages, created wonders for worship, pomp, and circumstance, and gave to the things for daily use their inborn touch of artistry. An artistic race of the elevated sort evidently then peopled the land. The way of life bred fine artists in tune with the times, prompted truly national and great architecture, and made loveliness shine through the arts and the crafts. Everybody had a hand in the process, kings, nobles, churchmen, big bugs, little bugs, and the rank and file of the Joneses, Browns, Smiths, and Robinsons. Channels of thought and traditions flowed down from the developed culture of the Saxons, absorbed the Norman influence, bounded from strength to strength in the golden Gothic time, and streamed on melodiously through the early and late Renaissance years until the Industrial Revolution and its developments stemmed the current. Widespread beauty, once the common possession and inspiration, sank in shallows and in miseries. The bequest of a thousand years was engulfed in an era of new enlightenment. Truly might a present John Jones (descendant of the Joneses aforesaid) burst into poetic eloquence through his pressed-steel window and shout over the prefabricated party fence to John Smith (descendant of the Smiths aforesaid), "Oh, what a fall was there, my countrymen!"

Still, there is much to be thankful for. Amongst the host of amusing and material conveniences now available it is grateful and comforting to have mass-produced motor cars, charabancs, and bicycles for running everybody all over England to view the relics of beauty formed by the people of long ago. If Henry VIII, Cromwellians, and various ancients and moderns had never been born these relics might be even more plentiful, to furnish "the glittering plains" that William Morris often dreamed of. But the remains yet on view mean more than rosemary for remembrance of old life and times. They still can please and charm. They help to demonstrate that good art, beauty, and life flowed together harmoniously and they signify no reasons why a similar state of affairs may not happen again.

Hazlitt, we know, considered "One of the pleasantest things in the world is going a journey." I certainly agree with him and therefore ask the kind reader of this page to join me in journeys through parts of western England that have continued pleasant since Hazlitt spent his early years on our route at Wem and in 1798 heard Coleridge preach at Shrewsbury. The method of progress is as you wish, by mechanical wheels, in an armchair, or any other way favoured for perambulation or sitting down. My journeys over this area have been going on for some time, either on feet, bicycles, motors, railways, in a pony-trap, and even with a boat, a sketchbook always being handy and something to eat and drink in my bag in case of emergencies. Following the example of showmen who offer programmes to indicate what may be expected or endured, it seems best to begin with a brief outline of our ways and destinations. For present purposes my England of the west is divided from the east with an imaginary line formed by the Pennine Chain from Cumberland to the Peak; thus no more than the western regions of the large county of Yorkshire are included. The line then continues south along the eastern county boundaries of Derbyshire, Staffordshire, Warwickshire, and Oxfordshire.

The southern Chiltern country, the exodus of operations, crosses the narrow leg of Oxfordshire which points to the Thames, with Thame at the knee-joint and Henley and Reading at the foot. Chalk hills sweep in curves to the dips and "bottoms," the quietest and loveliest in the whole line of these heights. Grand beech woods clothe the slopes and juniper-trees stand darkly over the more open places. Villages are scattered and generally small. Farm and cottage walls of flint bonded with brickwork indicate location better than signposts. The Icknield Way, primitive and green in parts, winds an antique course from Cleeve to Chinnor. Escarpments above it, rising to more than 800 feet at Beacon and Bald Hills, offer extensive panoramas ending in distant haze and show where we are to go (23). Little rises and valleys over the near plain mark homelands of quaint and out-of-the-way villages, such as Wheatfield, Newington, and Berrick Salome, clustered round Chalgrove battlefield. The Thame stream divides them from higher ground with spy-points at Stanton St. John and

COTSWOLD STONE. *Tetbury.*

MIDLAND BLACK AND WHITE—*Weobley.*

NORTHERN STONE. *Burnsall in Wharfedale.*

PENNINE TOWN. *Alston, England's highest.*

Elsfield for distant views of Oxford (34–35). The Roman way, with legions of blackberry bushes at Ot Moor, points a straight line to Bicester and Newton of the Purcells. Across the vale the Cherwell flows down; ever winding and never hurrying, it sings a battle-song of 1644 at Cropredy Bridge, smiles at Banbury's fine lady, meanders past pretty borderlands, steeples, towers, and parks, and ends in measured paces at Addison's Walk, Magdalen bridge, and the Thames.

The chalk is no more. Stone reigns in its stead, the oolite stone coloured by nature in lovely tints, yielded at Hornton and a score of quarries, and beautifully worked by man. The land begins to rise in an arc from the Norman tower of Broughton Poggs, Witney butter cross, Woodstock's palace, and Adderbury's choice church and spire. Clear rivers, homes of the trout, sparkle along. The Coln winds through Coln Rogers, Bibury, and Fairford; the Windrush shoots under Bourton's little bridges and Burford's four arches; the Evenlode sweeps round Wychwood Forest. They hasten down from the wolds, for the real Cotswold country lies before us. We reach the uplands, airy and sometimes bleak on the tops and cosy in the valleys, wooded and flowered. Scenes everywhere are gracious with stone. It makes the field boundaries (which Cobbett thought ugly!). Stone walls and roofs, homes of lichen and stonecrop, beautify manor-houses, villagers' quarters, and miles of streets in country towns. Spread out far and wide are the places and spaces of the old wool trade and sheep flocks. Churches show proudly from Chipping Campden in the north to Wootton-under-Edge in the south. Their tall towers, mostly in the Perpendicular fashion, particularly commemorate the woolstaplers and clothmen who worshipped in sanctuaries created and paid for with gains made from wool. The Fosse Way crosses the hills, bearing a burden of history in its immemorial course from the Humber to the Exe. It mounts and dips and leads from Moreton-in-the-Marsh (actually over 400 feet up) to Stow-on-the-Wold, Northleach (43), Cirencester, and just misses rare old Tetbury. (9). Cirencester shoots a straight Roman arm to Birdlip and Gloucester; and at Birdlip Hill we have arrived at the high and final escarpments of the Cotswolds. The wooded and bold lines of the hills jut in and out, stand like cliffs over green oceans of land and the silvery windings of the Severn. Camps crown Cleeve, Haresfield, Uley, and height after height. Broadway Tower, a late addition of 1800, commands the north, and the south has its own tall monument at North Nibley to William Tyndale and the Bible. Every high point shows miles and miles of panoramas over the Severn vale, the Forest of Dean, and away to Abergavenny's Sugar Loaf, prospects fit to bring joy to every heart not made of oolite or any other stone (64).

Down in the fertile vale our routes point onward, past Cheltenham's pump room, terraces, and stucco, and the high fretted tower of Gloucester poised over old streets and an ancient New Inn (88, 89). For the present no more than a thought can be sent to Saxon Deerhurst or Berkeley's castle pile in which a

Plantagenet king was murdered, nor can loiterings yet be made to study the feats of the Severn school of masons from Bristol to Tewkesbury. Across the river the pretty way leads by the orchards of Westbury and the old inn of Newnham to Chepstow and the estuary. Stretches of water and sand, the vale and the Cotswolds combine in wide landscape effects and delicate colourings. The land mounts up from these lowly levels and we find the 5, 6, and 700-feet elevations of the Forest of Dean. Pleasant Stile, near Little Dean, gives the close details of the famous Severn bend, already traced from afar on the Cotswold heights. It turns from Epney's eel grounds, circles in a majestic sweep from Pimlico Sands to Bullo Pill, and winds round The Noose sandbank opposite Awre church. The silvery gleam of water, trees proudly massed, and the accent of roofs at Newnham afford a memorable sight of England. The Forest spreads for miles to the north, the south, and westward almost to Monmouth. Here at all times are dense woodlands clothed in the finery of every season, glorious stretches of oaks, the beech trees, shy ponds, scattered hamlets, and inns under greenwood trees. Ruardean Hill and many a point show where our tracks will be for reaching the winding Usk, Abergavenny, and Llanthony's ruined priory in the Honddu dip between the steep and lonely slopes of the Black Mountains (70). Staunton's 700-feet eminence presents another great and famous river bend, the victorious four-mile V made by the Wye on its way down from Symond's Yat to the bank of Offa's Dyke below Redbrook. The nearness of the significant Dyke denotes that we have gained the border country of earthworks, camps, and castles, to recall the dangerous days, nights, and years of the Marches.

With Geoffrey of Monmouth, Henry V, and Rolls the companion of Royce, Monmouth offers good names to illuminate various historical periods. But as we cannot stop at present to pry into the *Historia*, a royal birth, and Gordon-Bennett races, the fact that the town has two bridges is of premier importance (69). The bridges mean a meeting of waters; and when these happen to be the Wye and the Monnow, with the River Usk not far away, a trio of glorious scenic rivers await exploration. Here are scenes of world renown, the subjects painted by Turner and hosts of artists. Waters trace remarkable windings and beautiful curves. Hills and woods mass in grand vistas to far distances. Crags and heights give viewpoints for wide panoramas (81). Vales expand between Monmouth, Abergavenny, and Usk. It is a land of castles. Raglan (75), Chepstow, and others of fame, castles less well known at Grosmont, Skenfrith, White, Caldicot, and elsewhere, add the spice of romance to nature's store of loveliness. Enchantment ever triumphs at the popular Tintern ruins. St. Pierre with a gatehouse is but one of the gabled homes that suggest how peace and quiet indoors needed defence from without in the good old days. Stone walls at Caerwent, or the traditional landing-place for the conquest of Siluria near the Severn Tunnel at Sudbrook, bring a tinge of Roman hours to present days.

An approximate 40 miles upstream from Turner's "Junction of the Severn and the Wye" brings us to Tewkesbury, another meeting of waters. The Avon, "the soft-flowing Avon," joins its greater brother, the Severn, where the bells of the Norman abbey chime benedictions of peace over the meadows, grave-yards of the last hopes and petals of the Red Roses in the battle of 1471. Across the vale the Malvern Hills screen Herefordshire from the Worcestershire plain and Warwickshire, and the Avon, turning a slow movement from Watling Street near Rugby, glides sweetly through these two Midland counties spelt with the capital W. It waters quiet scenes of nature's beauty beautified by man; it shows England's true rural heart while leading across the centre of England.

Thatched roofs, timbered walls, and big chimney-stacks indicate our arrival

WARWICK
—Sydney R Jones

in Warwickshire. The Central Plain, extending beyond Birmingham, Coventry's spires, and Atherstone, holds the characteristic old homes of the district, often moated and framed in oak, as at Grimshaw (95) and Baddesley Clinton. North and south in the county rise stately mansions, such as Stoneleigh Abbey (96) and Compton Wynyates (115), to recall bygone times when a peer of the realm was a king in his own little kingdom. Warwick stands for a real castle that is lived in, but at Kenilworth no more than ruins and ghosts will wel-come our footsteps in treading the halls of John of Gaunt and Queen Elizabeth's Leicester (112). Beyond the Vale of the Red Horse and the Fosse Way we dis-cern one more battle point, Edge Hill, in command of rich landscapes and long distances patterned with the Midland fields and hedgerows. The Avon ever calls, flowing between leafy borders through the vale. It skirts Dunsmore Heath, where the Gunpowder Plotters hoped to proclaim a new queen but didn't, washes the otter's lairs at pretty Bubbenhall, divides Leamington from Warwick, winds through the Lucys' park at Charlecote, leaps the weir at Stratford church (107) bound for Bidford bridge and Worcestershire. Near and far stand the oaks and reminders of the Forest of Arden—Hampton-in-Arden, Henley-in-Arden, gnarled trunks in Packington Park, the Shakespeare oak in Stoneleigh Deer Park. These place-names of course tell that we are right in the heart of Shakespeare's England, a smiling countryside in which "the lark at heaven's gate sings" when the weather is warm and decent. At and round Stratford, in towns, villages, and fields that Shakespeare knew and loved, we can join with people of all nations and pay homage to the immortal name.

Elms, hundreds of them lined on the hedgerows and gathered in massy clusters, meet and greet us in Worcestershire. No county is richer in these noble trees. Like gallant soldiers on the march they stride across the plain which spreads out luxuriantly from Bredon Hill and the Clent Hills to Wyre Forest, Woodbury Hill, and the Malverns (132). On a downward course out of Warwickshire the Avon bends and curves a 25-mile sweep in sight of Bredon Hill and meanwhile graces an English fairyland of present comeliness and past memories. Here are villages to show pictorial combinations of oak timbering against white, thatched roofs, mingled colourings of old bricks and grey stone everywhere embowered in greenery. Cleeve (116), Cropthorne, Elmley Castle, Throckmorton, Birlingham, and a dozen more homely places will tempt any wanderer from hastening on. Evesham names its own vale, one that will offer wonderful sights when nature weaves films of snowy whiteness over the orchards in plum-blossom time. The good earth, praised for fruitfulness in the twelfth century by William of Malmesbury, continues to yield as if by magic. Evesham's ruins and standing buildings, including the Bell Tower (114), mark the sad ending of a mighty abbey, and fresh grass on Green Hill hides red stains where de Montfort fell in 1265. One more abbey relic a few miles away at Pershore and the Norman splendour of Tewkesbury further downstream complete this trio of abbeys, fragments of once great institutions that suggest how alluring the Avon must have been for monks dedicated to the quiet life with fish on Fridays.

The long course of the Severn continues. Passing between the woods of Wyre Forest and Areley, Layamon's dwelling-place "upon the Severn's bank," the river waters the fertile plain bounded by the hills of Abberley and then enters Worcester (108–109). Cathedral and stream unite in the memorable scene that has been responsible for pictures by the hundred before and since B. W. Leader put it on canvas. The great tower, the early Perpendicular masterpiece, stands nobly over the place of Cromwell's crowning victory and Charles's flight of

1651. Another hurrying can be traced from Alcester to Huddington, Hanbury, Burcot, Hagley, and Stourbridge, part of the route galloped hell for leather by the Gunpowder Plotters in November 1605. Huddington Court (124), home of Winter the Plotter, in but one of many timbered and moated houses standing in our tracks through the county. In fact, timbering is on view all the way from Birtsmorton in the south to Chaddesley Corbett in the north, shown by farms, cottages, and manor-houses, Dormston and other dovecotes framed in timber, and a timbered church tower here and there to partner the one at Pirton. In country and town the Midland brickwork appears, of Georgian and earlier dates. Though big castles and very great houses may not be found, such parks and places as Hagley, Westwood, and Croome visibly represent the aristocratic grandeur of a bygone classic age.

On the summit of Malvern Hills a mere step will take us out of Worcestershire into Herefordshire. The bird's-eye view is over one of England's fairest counties. We look towards the birthplaces of William Langland, John Abel the carpenter, Nell Gwyn, David Garrick, John Masefield. The slopes meet the wide vale broken by hills. Brockhampton, Dinmore, Wormsley, Haugh, and more miles of high woods, sportsmen's paradises all, are rarest among the rare in rich colourings and patterned shadows. Offa's Dyke and the Roman way from Leintwardine (*Bravonium*) to Kenchester (*Magna*) mark old boundaries. Beyond Abbey Dore, the Golden Valley, and ruined castles in the Marches, the hills mount up to join the heights of Wales. With many a graceful curve the Wye leads on from de Clifford's Castle of Clifford, bound for Hereford bridge (130–131) and Ross (137). The pretty Lugg river joins it after a long wandering from the woods of Aymestrey and Edward IV's battlefield at Mortimer's Cross. Cattle grazing in the meadows tell that we are among the Herefordshires. Orchard trees, growing hops, and pointed kilns promise cider, perry, and ale to lubricate happy wanderers in snug towns like Leominster, Bromyard, and Ledbury. The cathedral tower of Hereford stands for a centre-piece of the ball-flower ornament displayed in the churches. Nobody can fail to see the black-and-white, the oak and plaster, brave, dazzling effects in town and country scenes.

Leaving reminders of once live strongholds bunched together at Richard's Castle, Wigmore, and Brampton Bryan (149), we cross into Shropshire to find more and more castles standing in various stages of dilapidation from Clun (150) to Oswestry and Whittington (175). These, with camps and ditches on high points, may prompt sentimental romancing on Llewelyn ap Gruffydd, Owen Glyndwr, Roger de Montgomery, and earlier legendary giants who once enlivened the Marches with rows and raids until retirement in the numerous tumuli ended their expressions of brotherly love. The country, here rugged and mountainous, certainly has a warlike aspect. The great Dyke of Offa, worn and weary sentinel, presents its best section from Llanvair Hill into Montgomeryshire. Solitude reigns about the earthen rampart. The air is bracing, landscapes are fine, and slopes and woodlands of exceptional grandeur, almost untrodden by man, lead on through Clun Forest to the Black Mountain. The Stiperstones, the Long Mynd, and Caradoc (158) call us away from the borders of Wales into the wild Shropshire of *The Golden Arrow* and Mary Webb. The River Clun hastens from the mountains. Rippling, it sings a Housman song through "Clunton and Clunbury, Clungunford, and Clun," then swells the waters of

LVDLOW

the Teme. The stream meets Ludlow, perfect in situation and contents, and still haunted by Milton's *Comus*. Corve Dale opens out between Brown Clee Hill and Wenlock Edge. It promises a little world of natural and man-made beauty from Stokesay Castle (149) to Much Wenlock abbey. We meet the Severn once more, see it flowing by woods and ruins in the memorable view of Buildwas Abbey. Downstream, Bridgnorth castle and rebuilt church top the hillside town (163). Higher up, the river touches Wroxeter and its load of Roman deadness, but light and life greet us where the stream circles round the two hills, the spires, the winding streets and fascinating buildings assembled round Roger de

Montgomery's Norman castle and abbey foundation of Shrewsbury (156–157). Near at hand are the ruined abbeys at Haughmond and Lilleshall, and Battlefield church as well, still fine as it was when built for Henry IV to commemorate the victorious day in which Hotspur Percy fell and Falstaff saved his paunch. The broad plain extends from the Severn vale across north Shropshire. On Grinshill Hill at Clive (164), William Wycherley's birthplace, we can see at a glance this tranquil countryside. It is a land of wide pastures, many trees, secluded villages, sandstone Gothic churches and Georgian towers, quiet country towns like Wem and Whitchurch (170), and a little lake district owned by Ellesmere.

The bold, straight line of Watling Street takes us into Staffordshire. A Black Country to the south and the Potteries to the north of the Roman highway introduce our first sniffs of industrial England. But as these signs of the country's greatness do not suggest what Hitler called "strength through joy," we can ignore the scenic effects of smoke and arid earth, follow the Romans to their station at Wall (*Letocetum*), and then ruminate on uneconomic products of old England, here visible in the unique triple spires of Lichfield presiding with grace over Dr. Johnson's own city (182–183). Cannock Chase is in sight. This elevated tract, even now largely unspoiled by coal-loving man, shows diversified surfaces, woods and parks ringed round pretty Penkridge, Beaudesert, Rugeley, and Milford. Views from the uplands extend away over the western scene, a quiet, rural country notable for the churches at Gnosall and Eccleshall, and a battle-point of the Red and White Roses on the higher ground at Blore Heath. Up on the moors of the Staffordshire Highlands the River Trent begins a long course. It passes through Trentham Park, greets at Tixall the River Sow, fresh from Izaak Walton's birthplace and the shoemakers of Stafford. The stream glides between wooded banks past Cannock Chase, adds pleasantness to the village acres of the Ridwares and King's Bromley (189), meets the Roman road pointing to Derby, and sends the gypsum water along to the brewers at Burton-on-Trent. Landscapes across the vale denote the aged limbs and remnants of Needwood Forest, and limbs and features of gentry who owned the oaks we shall find wonderfully represented inside Hanbury church. At that high point, with Derbyshire in full view, the River Dove shows itself after coming down in lovely measures from the Fishing House of Cotton and Walton in Beresford Dale. Winding, ever winding, the stream leads us to Tutbury's Norman church and the castle, a smashed memorial of John of Gaunt.

Derbyshire promises the mountains, dales, and rivers for which it is famous. But first, if we cross from Staffordshire to south Derbyshire in the neighbourhood of Newton Solney, the landscapes there and beyond show in lowly key through the sandstone vale of the Trent. A pastoral stretch of England is this, true to the Midland type. Miniature hills break the level lines at such points as Findern, Ticknall, and at Chellaston Hill. Swarkeston's long and ancient bridge marked the limit of the Young Pretender's advance. The Church of All Saints, Derby, keeps the pride of Perpendicular towers for many a mile (195). At this point, where Prince Charles Edward came to a stop in 1745, the railway sheds and industrialism may not detain us, so we can advance in the tracks of the Pretender's hasty retreat, leave the sandstone, meet the mountain limestone and millstone grit, and enjoy a complete change of scenery. The hills grow higher and bigger. Upward from Belper and Ashbourne groupings become varied and bold. Darley, Monsal, and the dales and vales that everybody knows open out, fast streams and the Rivers Dove, Wye, and Derwent hasten from the moors, impressive panoramas fill the distances. Above the magnificence of crags, rocks, glens, and leaping waters the Peak rears its wild heights to more than 2,000 feet, the southern culmination of England's great backbone along which our northward quest will be through the Pennines to Cumberland. Buildings and field boundaries of stone rule again. Bulky walls, heavy roofs and low-pitched gables begin to show that we are meeting the northern expression in masonry. Stone greyly colours Stanton-in-the-Peak (207), Eyam, Bakewell, Tideswell; it tones scores of places settled round valley streams, on hilltops, and across the county to the vicinity of Chesterfield's crooked spire. Properly situated in nature's bounteous settings stand the great houses, relics of systems now worn out. Historic and renowned, they include Chatsworth, very splendid (201), and Haddon Hall, romantic and picturesque (202), two of England's great sights. The Norman ruin at Castleton, representing one of the old brigade, occupies a position dramatic enough either for William Peverel or *Peveril of the Peak*.

In Macclesfield Forest, at the *Cat and Fiddle* inn, or perhaps with a look back from Alderley Edge, we bid a temporary adieu to the mountains and dales, then descend to the plain of Cheshire. Wide flat landscapes broken by a few sandstone hills make the landscapes on our route to the River Dee and the Wirral peninsula. Level, rich farmlands stretch for miles. Gothic church towers, built pink and red from the native stone, give touches of colour to the villages and towns and locate the cathedral at Chester (221). Trees in Delamere Forest and elsewhere remind that dense woodlands once covered the county, and "magpie" buildings, plentifully in view, show how the earlier inhabitants used the timber. Their efforts promise exciting moments at Moreton and the group of noted halls, at Marton and Warburton churches, and inside and outside the unique rows of Chester (208–209). Malpas (215), and towns and villages in all directions, contain their particular specimens of oak used without stint, sixteenth- and seventeenth-century interiors, and massive low beams devised for bumping people's heads; perhaps the old timbers of Knutsford prompted unrecorded comments from Mrs. Gaskell and the taller ladies of *Cranford !*

On Merseyside and north of the High Peak we gird our loins to meet and leave the drab concentrations of industry in Lancashire and Yorkshire. Hemmed in stand reminders of times gone—cathedrals at Manchester and Bradford, Perpendicular churches, old halls well cared for by new owners and municipal authorities. Forests of chimneys, smoke, vapours, and twinkling lights by night yield characteristic effects, peculiar yet fascinating for those who appreciate them; and at least these areas of cottons and woollens demonstrate how far we have travelled since Adam and Eve first set the fashion with pristine leaves. Moors, valleys, and farms on hillsides (241) surround and neighbour the masses of stone, bricks, and mortar. The sandstone, extended from Cheshire, ends on the coastal belt at Morecambe Bay. Speke, near Liverpool, and Hall i' th' Wood at Bolton are among the last of the timbered houses before the reign of the northern stone buildings.

Clear of the signs and portents of manufacturing towns we meet pure air, prepare for mountains, rocks, passes, moors, torrents, and the tumbled stone that makes nature's own grand architecture throughout the Pennines and the Lake country (258). Great Whernside, Ingleborough, Helvellyn, Skiddaw, the fells and the highest peaks in England will point directions and serve for milestones. Villages, towns, lonely farms, and cottages crouched on the slopes and all built of gray stone present man's handiwork dwarfed by the bigness of natural shapes. Boldly constructed with massive walls and low roofs, the buildings seem to stand defiant to wind and storm. The dales run down into Yorkshire (247), to Grinton, to Wensley, and to the memorable scene at Bolton Abbey on the Wharfe (242). Rivers of fame and beauty, including the Ribble, Turner's Lune, the Eden, and Wordsworth's Duddon, leave wild birthplaces for luxurient vales. In this land of poets, song, and story the castles, peel towers (262), and fortified homes may stir thoughts on moss-troopers, raids, and strife. At scores of points between John of Gaunt's Lancaster (234–235), Appleby, and Carlisle (260–261) we can meditate in safety on times that were dangerous. More pleasantly perhaps if the Lakeland wet does not descend, the roofless halls of Brougham Castle will suggest a few lines from Wordsworth on the Shepherd Lord Clifford (263).

Legends of a Roman Wall now gone can lead our imaginations past the red city of Carlisle (260–261) and through the pleasant green vale to Gilsland, the village in which Walter Scott met and won his bride in 1797. The River Irthing leaps the rocks, shoots the bridge, then curves fast below the bluff of Birdoswald. On the height are stones and broken masonry, all that remains of *Ambloganna*, once the largest Roman station on the Wall (264). We stand on the ruins, look towards Bewcastle Fells and Scotland, see where the Ninth Legion advanced for conquest in the second century—and never came back. Strife not recorded in history or ballad brings this sketch of our itinerancy to a full stop.

2. WESTWARD FROM THE CHILTERN HILLS

OXFORDSHIRE, GLOUCESTERSHIRE, MONMOUTHSHIRE

Good honest ground, real English, makes this area for exploration indicated on the map below. It spreads beyond the River Severn and is washed by the tides of the Bristol Channel; the Thames and Oxfordshire form boundaries in the south and east. Chiltern chalk, Cotswold oolite and lias, sandstone beds from the Severn vale to the River Usk and the mountains tumble geological time down the ages. Landscape shapes and patterns are richly varied by these formations. Combinations of nature's handiwork and the labours of man account for a wealth of attractive scenes. Many of the great sights, such as Tintern and the Cotswold towns, have worldwide repute. Early dwellers and Romans found the high points and big panoramas; they travelled along the Fosse Way and other routes now in use. Fine architecture developed through the local products of stone, chalk, flint, and plentiful woodlands. It is shown by splendid churches, towns, villages, and country houses built of stone, flint walls and timbered dwellings. Spoliation by modern industry is not generally well represented, but a number of objects, including the crop of aerodromes in operation, temporarily defunct, or captured by squatters, signify a district abreast of the times.

SOUTHERN CHILTERNS AND THE OXFORDSHIRE VALE

OXFORDSHIRE VALE from
the Chilterns at Beacon Hill

Nowhere do the Chiltern Hills show better than on the 20-mile stretch in Oxfordshire. Landscapes are both widespread and intimate. The line of escarpments from Swyncombe to Chinnor Hill can give one the idea of being on the top of the world to view kingdoms; the seclusion in such parts as Bix Bottom (25) and Maidensgrove Scrubs may rouse a suggestion of being the only inhabitant on earth. All the best characteristics of chalk country are here— heights and distances, rises and falls blended in subtle curves, close valleys enclosed in steep banks, heaths, commons and airy spaces, hollow ways, hanging woods, and some of the quietest places under the sun. Mother Earth pervades the colour-schemes. Spangled tints on turned ploughlands, the opalescent shine of field greens, and bright accents of exposed chalk offer the thought of a divine artist at work and using white freely with the pigments on the palette. Brilliant effects are amplified by the stately depths of woodlands, the undergrowth of thorns and bushes; yews and hollies make their own deep notes, and juniper-trees, darkly clad, are regimented like soldiers on slopes of whitened green.

The south Chiltern woods are glorious. Where could be found more gracious massed patterns of trunk, limb, and foliage than in the sequence which extends from Crowell Hill and Aston Woods to Stonor Park, Nettlebed Woods, College Wood near Hardwick House, and the hill of St. Birinus at Berins? Oak and ash, sycamore, cherry, and a mixture of trees thrive. The beeches of course hold pride of place. Their branches and new greenery shoot up over the haze of oceans of bluebells in spring; summer warms the luscious tints; autumn decks the beech foliage with gold beyond price. November tunes its symphonies to golden showers, and all through the winter pearly smooth bark gleams like silver above carpets of rich brown leaves that rustle and prance in the wind.

Alas! many of these noble trees prematurely die. The woodman spares not the axe. Men wearing official hats walk round and pronounce doom far and wide. Dreadful slaughter happened during the war years; now the high price of nationalized coal has brought further degradation by reducing the beauty of branches to mere blocks of wood for fuel, scurvily sold at one penny each.

Old-fashioned craftsmen also do their bit, a very little bit nowadays, for their race is becoming extinct. Though they turn the growth of nature's patient years into legs for chairs to accommodate human beings in the passage from the cradle to the grave, these acts may be excused by realizing that they represent last skirmishes in a lost cause pitted against the conquering monarch called machinery.

Samuel Rockall, the old friend of H. J. Massingham, has been fighting this losing battle all his life. For this reason I set out to find him just beyond Stonor Park and discovered his flint cottage and wooden workshop on the edge of a heath fringed with beech trees, the ammunition for chair-leg bodgers. A knock at the door and an enquiry brought the reply, "You'll find him down the garden"; which to me seemed just as it should be when seeking a true child of environment who drew the essence of life from the earth, its gifts, and skill of human hands. Among spring cabbages and sprouting onions I met a hale, shortish man whose merry eyes, characterful features, and air of sturdy independence evidently were not born of a safety-first and penny-in-the-slot decade. He talked of plants and weather, trees and wood. We went to the workshop. Outside on the heath grew beeches. Trunks, felled by the bodger, lay piled on the near grass. The door of the workshop led to a cave fit for Arcady, Pan's very own, conglomerated with blocks for chopping, horses for sawing and shaving, the lathe for turning, tools suspended from beams and hung on walls. When the lathe spun round for my particular benefit the prime moments had come. The pliant wood yielded. Curly shavings scattered. Deft hand movements made the shapes. A chair-leg, properly finished off, finally was mine. I received more than that, held in my fingers a last link in the chain of traditional workmanship that brought pride and pleasure to both makers and users, and thus garnished life through past centuries in England. Here was exemplified the ageless economy of divine provision: growing trees outside, felled trunks, the wooden workshop, right tools, finished products, joy in work, seasonable beauty visible always, sweet air around, little money for labour, and—happiness. Natural supply, place, and pride in doing accounted for the man standing before me. He represented the end of a line that made the national folk art and from which sprang a Hugh Herland, a John Abel. His accomplishment, simple though skilled, offered one of those little episodes in ordinary workaday life such as Chaucer knew and an artist vignetted on the parchments of the *Luttrell Psalter*.

Whether Samuel Rockall still works in beech I do not know. The memory of my visit lives, a reminiscence formed in the mind like a faded cameo set in a Chiltern scene of springtime. Many winters have come since then. Sad to relate, chair-leg bodgers do not fit into new times. Machinery has conquered them one by one. If any survive, they might be thought just archaic and out-of-date jetsam by the human flotsam buoyed pleasantly or otherwise on progressive currents agitated by electric drills, prefabrication, and other diabolical inventions. Tears

BIX BOTTOM, *a secluded section of the southern Chilterns with a ruined church below Maidensgrove Scrubs. The woods of Stoner Park show in the distance.*

WATLINGTON. *The lines of the Chiltern escarpment seen from above the site of the old castle.*

HORLEY, *a stone village in north Oxfordshire near to the famous quarries for Hornton stone*

for the passing of an old brigade are therefore superfluous, nor is it heartening to sentimentalize on ancient and hand-made Windsor and rush-seat chairs, once eagerly sought by young folks and grandfa's with whiskers. Yet if any of my readers fancy an antidote to things as they are, or would like whiffs of old life and freedom before they are as extinct as the dodo, I recommend a journey to Summer Heath, beyond Stonor Park and just in Buckinghamshire, to see if the chair-leg bodger is still on view. If he is not, the Chiltern views will repay all the petrol expended.

Little of historical consequence belongs to this section of the hills. Grim's Dyke, fringed with beeches, holds its antique line from Nuffield to Mongewell, keeps secrets and tells nothing. The Icknield Way, senior in service, cuts the Dyke, skirts Ipsden and Ewelme; rising in elevation and beauty, it strides the greensand belt where the chalk promontories push out at Swyncombe Downs and Watlington, Beacon and Chinnor Hills. Lovely and silent in green and white stretches, the route invites no olden confidences among the solitudes. Gone are the signs and footprints of the unknown figures that went up and down from Salisbury Plain, the Berkshire Downs, and Norfolk in the forgotten centuries of B.C. Conscious of age and purpose, the primeval track still asserts authority, fixes parish boundaries, demands respect for original uses, laughs as it were at modern times. More than once it has done this to me while bringing discomfort for not using the Way as first planned. In wet weather the putty-like surface has clogged my bicycle wheels to a standstill, literally given the command to propel myself on Shanks's and carry the machine. In an age of human frailty it is sometimes salutary to be thus reminded of elemental origins and natural forces. White sticky mud in the Chiltern area is good for this purpose, having been puddled for about 100 million years if geologists speak the truth.

Neither villages nor population crowd the high lands. Settlements usually keep to the early arrangement of scattered hamlets grouped round greens and commons. The little collections of habitations, each decently small in the bigness of natural environment, make pretty pictures of houses, cottages, and barns properly featured in the native fashions, simple schemes of bright flint and brick walls, tiled roofs browned and mossy, bits of plasterwork, and timbering here and there to emphasize respectable lineage. The place-names, sampled by Hollandridge, Pishill, Maidensgrove, and Huntercombe End for a representative of the numerous "Ends," exactly fit Chiltern locations and qualities. Cosy pubs serve the district. At one of them recently, when the tough Argentine bulls were in short supply, I met a brave salmon in cut. I do not give the location of the fish because that announcement might cause an invasion; his presence is mentioned only to prove that a wayfarer may thrive quite well while exploring these sequestered haunts in which the finery of nature's work predominates. Architecture takes second place. It had little scope to develop strongly. In past times the

27

district was remote, a camping-ground for robbers and odd sort of people, and the Chiltern Hundreds in the next county even now keep old memories green by accommodating extinct politicians. A sprinkling of lowly churches offer what might be expected in form and style—Norman arches at Checkendon; Early English windows at Ipsden; Swyncombe in a divine situation and interesting throughout from early walls to the fine modern rood-screen; and no more than a tangled ruin in Bix Bottom to recall Thomas de Belesham, the first rector in 1236. The idea of hearth and home, expressed in a bigger way than was usual in village and hamlet, brought the very good house at Turville Heath, a Georgian specimen open to the sky and the trees and in view for all to see.

And there is Stonor House in its park, a grand sight of lordly home and natural beauty blended to a high note of harmony. The footpath from the clap-gate in the village to Balham's Wood yields visions all the way, stately measures offered by the Restoration house and the chapel, gardens meeting grasslands, wide green slopes curving down, patches of shade from isolated trees, deer ambling in line, and the great semicircle swept majestically and toned with deep woods that mount to the rim marked out against the sky. Of all the combinations of homes and parks in England, few, if any, can excel this one for the artistry of leaving much alone and adding little. Tranquil and secluded, the scene remains an emblem of past spacious years. Yet in spite of the perfection and visual delight presented it seems ghostly to me now, a faded relic like a human beauty mellow in age but with course run and purpose served. Dead as a doornail are the inspirations and uses that caused and maintained the like of Stonor House and Park. My first visit of long ago suggested an ideal frontis-piece for *Burke's Peerage*. A school was in possession on my last visit. What next? I wonder! All who wish to see this rare sight intact should hasten there before the spoilers get to work.

Away to the west the Chiltern ramparts point their bosses and combes to the cornlands and the vale. Magnificent panoramas from every vantage point sweep over the great plain punctuated here and there by what Horace Walpole called "the dumpling hills." Eye and fancy travel over the valleys of the Thame stream and the River Cherwell, to the moated castle of Shirburn, Chalgrove battlefield, Oxford, Marlborough's and Vanbrugh's Blenheim, to Roman roads and coaching roads, towns, houses, and villages of long standing. Fine, too, are the looks back at the bold line of wooded heights when we say good-bye to the Chilterns and descend to the Lower Icknield Way running through Ewelme, Watlington, and Chinnor (25).

The mention of Ewelme reminds me that the showpiece of the neighbour-hood is handy, one justly famous and much visited by the knowing ones from English counties and foreign countries. Pretty cottages and houses, clear streams, little bridges, watercress beds, the site of a palace, a peerless group of fifteenth-century school, almshouses, and church (31), trees everywhere, downs around—what more could desire hope for on this earth, unless it be that the Benson aerodrome might retire instead of thrusting into the very borders of this demi-paradise. The story of Ewelme since its Domesday years already has been printed in dozens of books. It is therefore needless to slip back to the year 1428, when William de la Pole, Duke of Suffolk, married Alice Chaucer, the grand-daughter of the poet. Nor can anything new be said on their palace above the stream, the school and courtyard almshouses they caused to be made in lovely brickwork, the church they rebuilt in the Perpendicular style, and the treasures of craftsmanship it contains in monuments, hundreds of carved figures that include real masterpieces, sixteen brasses, old glass, the fifteenth-century font cover, the timber roof panelled and enriched. This village group gleams like a jewel, wonderfully wrought, finely set, toned by age; of all the places I know, marooned in the backwaters of an era distinguished for ugliness, few can awaken keener joy in past beauty. The palace of the Duke and Duchess, and later of Queen Elizabeth, gave up the ghost early in the seventeenth century. The only relics of it survive in the manor-house. It was from this palace that the Virgin Queen rode away on a pillion with her gallant Earl of Leicester to inspect the remarkable monuments of the de la Beches in Aldworth church, ten miles distant in Berkshire.

A ride in Kemp's bus from Ewelme will deposit those of us unfortunate enough to be without cars into Watlington. The end of the journey thus made can also provide some people with an anticlimax to the haunts of the late lamented Duke and Duchess of Suffolk. One-eyed, deadly, off the map—all sorts of laudatory expressions I have heard bestowed on this little town lying snug below the Upper Icknield Way and Chiltern slopes. Such tilts of language imply peace, charm, desirability. Watlington has these and other good qualities, even if it does not rank tawny and full-bodied in the choice vintage of small country towns. It centres round the market hall, arched below and built of 1664 brickwork, with the Georgian front of the *Hare and Hounds* conveniently placed opposite. Timbering, thatching, walls of flint, and plaster, and a sprinkling of good Georgian houses can be tracked in curious back ways and along the winding streets through which John Hampden made his last ride to Chalgrove battlefield in 1643. All in all, this one-eyed and deadly little town of much desirableness, near to the sources of bacon and eggs and far removed from tax inspectors, seems to me just the place that any harassed slave of the present dispensation might choose for ripening in age, comfort, and oblivion without even noticing explosions from Parliament Square, Russia, and other directions. The church, being largely rebuilt, need not make unusual demands for devotional exercises. Nicholas de la Beche and his castle, built in 1338, threaten no more, because both have completely gone (25); the site of their alarums is merely guarded by an artist of great distinction (Harold Speed), but he is quite inefficient in the arts of murder and only keeps watch when perched up a tree writing his books. In case of temporary ennui the little buses could show how the big world wags in the market on Fridays at Wallingford, or at Woolworth's near the Bodleian in Oxford. Now and then the funny railway train, after much labour, might promise connections for Fleet Street and a banquet at Guildhall. Not very often though, for I'm sure that any nice and wise person, once properly settled amongst old cronies in Watlington, would rarely dream of leaving them.

Shirburn Castle, really a fortified house of 1377, towered, moated, and built to replace a Norman stronghold of the mighty Robert D'Oilli, lies in aristocratic seclusion two miles along the Lower Icknield Way from Watlington. Next in order on King Cymbeline's road is Lewknor church, a beautiful reminder of the monks of Abingdon and very interesting, followed by the Lambert Arms. The inn, long famed as a port of call, marks a meeting of roads at the foot of Aston Hill, so we will follow the one that first leads past notable Tudor survivals of a Cistercian abbey in Thame Park, then enters the town settled near its namesake, the Thame river.

Thame is the jolliest place imaginable, whether in spring, summer, autumn, or winter, and the pubs will supply anything from tea to French wines of right vintages, at least one of them could when Landlord Fothergill reigned at the *Spread Eagle* and My Lord Asquith might be spotted making for the dining-room to tuck in. This bright collection of streets and houses meets the country and the country comes into the town, hinting a kind of marriage between corn-fields and shops, live beasts and roast beef, hay smells and petrol stinks. Hearty, browned, and healthy people walk up and down; scythes, bill-hooks, hoes, wheelbarrows, hedging-gloves, straps, buckles, and all sorts of marvels offered for sale spiritually belong to the world of soil and singing larks; signs up aloft embellished with painted symbols, such as black horse, nag's head, swan, eagle, and birdcage, keep up the nodding acquaintance with the beasts and birds of the field. Thomas Hardy's immortal Casterbridge always crops up in my mind when in the wide main street of Thame, a worthy rival of the one at Marl-borough (32). Having settled down before the Conquest, the town of course is full of old things to show just what it should do for a marketing centre of mellow years. Inns, shops, and houses revive aspects of home life from the tim-bered and gabled period to the era of very good brickwork and eighteenth-century doorways. The reign of Queen Elizabeth brought the two school-houses; John Hampden attended one of them and, after the Chalgrove battle, returned to die in a timbered house near. A pretty picture riverwards through the trees includes the Prebendal House and Early English chapel, the work of Bishop Grossetête in the thirteenth century. Best of all and bordering the open

EWELME, *a gem of a village, has stood prettily at the foot of the Chiltern Hills since Domesday times. The church is a treasure-house of craftsmanship in stone, wood, carved tombs, and brasses. Adjoining are the quadrangle of almshouses and a school. All these buildings were schemed in the fifteenth century by the Duke of Suffolk and Alice Chaucer his wife, a grand-daughter of Geoffrey Chaucer the poet.*

STANTON HARCOURT. *Part of the church, Pope's tower, and remains of the Harcourt's early home. The church contains notable Harcourt monuments. In the tower Alexander Pope completed his translation of the fifth volume of Homer in 1718.*

THAME. *Tuesday market in the wide main street. The town is noted for its agricultural show, a noble church, prebendal chapel, abbey remains, Elizabethan grammar school, gabled and Georgian houses, and numerous inns including The Spreadeagle (right) and The Bird Cage (left).*

CHAPEL HOUSE NEAR CHIPPING NORTON. *Relics of the old coaching establishment at which, in 1776, Dr. Johnson delivered to Boswell his celebrated panegyric on the hospitality of inns and taverns.*

BANBURY. *Inn yard of the Reindeer showing the Globe Room before it was spoiled. The room had panelling of 1637 below an exceptional plaster ceiling, and served for a council of war at the time of the Battle of Edgehill. The entrance doors to the yard are dated 1570.*

OXFORD FROM ELSFIELD. *A distant impression of the city of towers and spires backed by the Cumnor Hills. One of the memorable views visible from the higher surroundings in the north-east.*

LOWER HEYFORD, *on the Cherwell stream. The parklands across the valley lead to Rousham House, a Jacobean home of the Dormer family with gardens laid out by William Kent.*

NORTH LEIGH, *near the Evenlode valley, Wychwood Forest, and the remains of a Roman villa. Stone houses and cottages neighbour the Saxon tower of the church, a building with medieval wall paintings, alabaster monuments, and beautiful fan-vaulting in the Wilcote chapel.*

ASTHALL (*above*) *and* BRIZE NORTON (*below*). *Two of the manor-houses that add distinction to many of the Oxfordshire villages. Next to Asthall the Windrush valley contains Minster Lovell and the ruined home of the Lovells.*

BURFORD. *Cotswold towns offer some of the most wonderful streets*
England. In and round this High Street are Elizabethan and later dwelling
the Tolsey with a clock (above), a remarkable church, the Priory house a
chapel, the bridge over the River Windrush. Walls and roofs of local sto
harmonize with the wold setting.

green is the big church, a noble structure begun by the Bishop of Lincoln just mentioned. From the wealth it contains I can only indicate particular preferences—the central tower and lantern, Early English arcades, a rare south porch and parvise in the Decorated style, the Perpendicular rendering of the nave clerestory and roof, richness in the tracery of the south transept window, and the panelled tomb in the chancel with effigies of a lady and gentleman carved in alabaster. This monument, like a good many more, commemorates the art of getting on in the world, though more than alabaster perhaps may be needed for success in the hereafter. The gentleman in life secured the manor at the Dissolution, served Queen Mary only too well, assisted in burning martyrs at Oxford, became Lord Williams of Thame for services rendered, and finally retired into the gorgeous tomb at the opening of Queen Elizabeth's reign in 1559. His money built the almshouses, since defunct, and also the boys' school, now devoted to the book-learning of commercial Dr. and Cr. My Lord and My Lady continue intact. They are wonderfully presented, properly dressed, attended by greyhound and unicorn, railed in for privacy, and no suggestion of conducting bishops to martyrdom appears on the graven images. In a charming thatched house across the green lives Herbert Norris, the famous authority on English costume. Anybody lucky enough to meet him may learn all that can be known about the fur cloaks, armour, dress, and the trappings on the tomb of these great ones, once living figures in the lovely church.

Thame's present, however, is quite as thrilling as its past. In addition to Thame Show, an exciting and annual spectacle, every Tuesday market-day stages first-class shows all the year round, agog with cars, horses, traps, and waggons, country people shopping and bargaining, stalls in the street laden with gew-gaws for every taste, pavements strewn with agricultural and household fancies. A general liveliness prevails, made all the merrier by the music of cattle, sheep, sows, and little porkers penned in wattles. And what is this? Myself wedged in a crowd of farmers round an auctioneer and a cow. The bidding starts: "18, 10 —18, 15—19—19, 5" and so on to "25—26—26, 10. Any more bids on 26 pounds 10 shillings?"—and in the excitement of the moment I nearly bid higher and might have secured a brown and white heifer, though what on earth to do with it would have sorely troubled my brain! A great place is Thame, both for past and present. Go there as soon as you can, dear reader, look well around, lunch with jolly farmers at the *Spread Eagle* or the *Black Horse*, and perhaps return with a pig or a cow to help out the rations!

South-west of the town true rural country stretches in peaceful and quiet acres to the Thames valley. Remote villages and hamlets continue from the Miltons, Wheatfield, Cuxham, Britwell Salome, Newington, and on to Warborough, prettily clustered round a stone and flint church tower and a big green, the local focus for cricket and August feasts of tremendous gusto. Buildings begin to show that we have reached the oolite stone. Many thatched roofs indicate an old craft still alive. Men can be met and talked to while they fix yelms and sprays and carry their burdens. The thatchers' "burden," it may be explained, is the wooden frame used for conveying heavy loads of straw up the steep angles of roofs. This implement resembles a large edition of a boy's catapult; it is rightly named when loaded, as I have discovered while lending a hand to one of these thatchers who is a friend of mine. Interesting sights and scenes are plentiful in this district, but my space only permits the bare mention of a few of them—Jacobean woodwork in Rycote chapel; the church of Henry VIII's brave topographer, John Leland, at Great Haseley; the wedding-house of John Hampden at Pyrton, good for Tudor chimneys and brickwork; an old barrel-organ for Sunday voluntaries in Brightwell Baldwin church; the big eighteenth-century house in full view at Newington; gatepiers, a pigeon-house, and a granary at Ascott, only survivors of the home of the Dormers, built in 1662 and immediately burned down. Those who prefer lunch before devotions can aid digestion by attending the only Sunday service inside Berrick Salome church at three o'clock; this permits meditations on the woodwork of the seventeenth-century gallery and roof. The name of Salome hereabout, be it noted, owns no connection with the wicked lady of the Bible. It survives from the Sallom family and the local pronunciation of "Saloom" is near the mark.

On the old London road over the Chilterns and near to the Thames stands Benson, though it might have stood no more when the Benson aerodrome expanded by pinching part of the historic highway and Beggarsbush Hill. Happily the village survived, just as Offa did in the year 777 after trouncing the West Saxons at the Battle of Bensington and thus pinching for the Mercian kingdom the district now called Oxfordshire. The battle is a forgotten thing; Benson's place on the great coach road is not. The bow of the *Castle* inn, the white front of the *White Hart*, timbering at the *Crown*, odd openings, long yards, and the nice architectural assortment in houses and inns clearly belong to a horsey past. While the new cars and red coaches swish past, stop, and go on, an air of departed days breathes balmily about this very good village street. Standing evidences trace back to the ages of roadside life agog with packhorses, heavy waggons, latten bells, chaises and sixes, flying-machines, and parsons jogging along with Mrs. parsons behind on pillions. And the following words told to me recently, and handed down from Landlord Costar who kept the *White Hart* in Georgian days, preserve what transpired when a large personage drove down from London.

"Good morning, landlord. Have you got any boiled bacon to-day?"

"Yes, at your service, your majesty," replied Costar, with a low bow.

"Let me have some, please. Don't forget the pickled cabbage. Never mind about the Majesty. I'm tired of that. Call me Farmer George down here."

OVERY MILL *on the Thame stream.*

After that dialogue King George III was known by his farming title whenever he called for the famous boiled bacon and cabbage of the *White Hart* at Benson.

Three miles distant towards Oxford, and near the end of the Thame stream's course, another faded relic survives in a backwater quiet as one could hope for in a noisy and hustling age. This is Overy Mill. It had a mention in Domesday Book, and William the Conqueror's scribe did not forget to put in a good word for the eels; natives who do not worry about Doomsday still say, "It's a good place for eels." Many a long year has passed since the monks of Dorchester Abbey went "over the rie (water)" to grind their corn at Overy. It is a long time, too, since Master William Turner, last of the line of millers of that name, passed in and out of the doorways, ground the corn, and, whitened from cap to boots, looked over the mill-dam and perhaps pondered on stewed eels. Nothing is doing now. A silent wheel in a gloomy chasm and bits and pieces tumbled down give suitable elements for the sentimental kind of picture favoured by Victorians and titled "Life's work ended" or something like that. Yet of all peaceful spots this is one of the rarest. You may sit for a whole day where I sat to sketch with never a human being in view, watch patterns of light and shade change on the weathered mill and the trees, hear water for ever singing into the pool. Hour by hour minnows turn and sparkle, tadpoles burrow, moorhens dart gracefully. Descendants of the Domesday eels of course do not show themselves, nor, fortunately, do the hasteners along the polished tarmac of the busy London–Oxford road only a quarter of a mile away.

Dorchester's splendid abbey and choice houses, and Oxford too, are beyond our present tracks; both these points properly belong to my previous book, *Thames Triumphant*. Divergent roads, or the Roman way from Dorchester, will lead us from the Thame valley to higher ground and on to Ot Moor, a fine solitary expanse in my youth, then marvellous for blackberries and quietude, and now marked on the map, "Bombing Range"! This way also goes perilously near the unlovely sprawl that demonstrates how an incomparable city is treasured by the English race. Nevertheless a number of distant prospects of Oxford seem to have escaped the notice of the spoilers. Round about Stanton St. John, Elsfield, and Beckley you see visions of towers and spires dreaming in the vale (34–35). Distance, lending enchantment to the views, softens the excrescences and surrender of beauty outward to Marston, the village with the manor-house in which Oxford surrendered the sword of war to Cromwell. Away to the west, and beyond the range of these views over Oxford, the upper Thames valley expands to meet the uplands. Here is announced the long course of stone building awaiting ahead. Stanton Harcourt (32), Bampton church, Brize Norton (37), Witney, North Leigh (36), and houses, cottages, and churches on every hand begin to show the delicate tints of oolite and the work of

NORTHLEACH. *A sermon in stone from the great days of Cotswold wool. The fifteenth-century reconstruction of the church seen from the south. The window traceries and porch are finely designed and executed and the interior contains famous memorial brasses to the woolstaplers.*

STANTON, *a village with charming homes and two manor-houses placed on a spur of the Cotswolds above the Vale of Evesham.*

old-time masons who shaped doorways, mullions, chimneys and carvings, graded slates from ridges to eaves, and cunningly laid boundary walls without mortar.

These pictures in stone continue up the pleasant valley of the River Cherwell. They sparkle in meadows, on wooded ridges, and feature brightly in villages and hamlets from the Heyfords (36) and the Astons to the gables of Fritwell manor-house. Rousham House, erected early in the seventeenth century and furbished in the eighteenth by William Kent, supplies a touch in the grand manner; complete with gardens designed by Kent, it moved Horace Walpole to prate of "Daphne in little" when he wandered among groves, fountains, and statues in 1760. Cool uplands over the stone lead to Bicester church, an interesting structure near to the meeting of Roman roads and within hail of meets of foxhounds. More than once the sporting Bicester pack has urged me to Cropredy Bridge, the exact point held by Waller after the fighting on June 29, 1644. The venerable church in the village keeps many good things, including a cannon-ball to recall the battle. This inspected, and without more thoughts of war, we advance to realms of peaceful stone, trouty streams, uplands of departed sheep flocks, with the Cotswold Hills calling in the distance.

COTSWOLD COUNTRY

The oolite stone land to the north of the Thames mounts up towards the west. It begins to rise in a rough curve marked by Cirencester and Fairford in the south, and continued through Witney, Woodstock, and Deddington to Banbury in the northern tip of Oxfordshire. After meditations on the cannon-ball, the genuine old eagle of the brass lectern, and other attractions at Cropredy, a few miles onward will lead us into Banbury. But first, bound as we are for delectable harmonies in Cotswold scenes and stone, glances through the villages spread round Banbury Cross will give foretastes of joys to follow. Great Bourton, Horley (26), Hornton, still famous for quarries, and place after place grouped on slopes and in valleys glow with the delicate colouring of the local product. They exactly fit their natural environments. The brilliance of the golden tints on the walls of Deddington is so arresting, one almost forgets to find the parsonage house in which King Charles slept after his short-lived victory at Cropredy. Much of the masoncraft in the district is remarkably good; it rewards a constant lookout for walling laid in trim coarses, arched doorways, gable adornments, and the artistry of stone slates laid in diminishing sizes from eaves to ridges of roofs. Little date panels give inklings of human lives, make one wonder who answered to the initials of W. M., G. B. H., or R. A. I. and caused their monograms to bloom on the homes they reared and evidently loved.

Among the village churches Bloxham and Adderbury are splendid. The local saying tells of three spires in a line,

> Bloxham for length,
> Adderbury for strength,
> King's Sutton for beauty.

The last one, perfect in grace, is in Northamptonshire and therefore outside my present borders, yet the other two churches lack nothing in beauty. John Harvey, scholarly champion of Gothic art, traces the fineness of Adderbury's chancel to Richard Winchcombe, a master craftsman working early in the fifteenth century. Homes schemed on the bigger scale for squires and notables add particular sights to these pleasant north Oxfordshire scenes. One of them, at Hanwell, is no more than a relic of the courtly Copes' Castle; seen from the churchyard, it makes a pretty picture of Tudor stone and brick. Another churchyard view includes Wroxton Abbey, fortunate in continuing much as it was when built in 1618 on the site of a priory. Jacobean gables rise and big windows glisten just as they did for earlier owners, Lord Keeper North and George III's Prime Minister, Lord North, director of the Boston tea-party. Broughton Castle is the prize of the neighbourhood, an early fourteenth-century foundation reconstructed by the Fiennes family in the sixteenth century and fully meriting all the expressions of admiration already aimed at it. Complete with moat, gatehouse, hall, oriel windows, and a hiding-hole up aloft, here are all the elements for "a haunt of ancient peace in the good old days!" Even so, peace did not always reign. One member of the family lost his head during Jack Cade's rebellion, another fell in the Battle of Barnet, and mysterious visitors used to mount a secret staircase to plot Civil War conspiracies. The household also provided a "Fiennes lady on a white horse," the one that made any precocious infant "Ride a cock-horse to Banbury Cross." Doubtless due to the rise of democracy and the consequent eclipse of nobility, the "Fiennes" lady slipped in the social scale to become merely "fine," just like any June Smith with a flaxen perm riding in Hollywood. This loss of caste is a pity because it has flattened an elevated point in the nursery rhyme.

Banbury, ancient in fame for cakes, ale, and cheese, thrives to-day at the centre of old coach roads and new motor highways. In certain particulars it is a town of has-beens, a cemetery of late lamenteds without gravestones or epitaphs. The castle, erected in 1125 by a bishop of Lincoln and heroically defended without hope for the King in 1646, merely survives as somebody's doorstep. A mid-Victorian erection, often called bad names, serves as best it can for "the goodly cross with many degrees (steps) about it," seen by Leland and later knocked down by local vandals. The big church rears its masonry over the ashes of a splendid medieval predecessor, one hardly excelled in all Oxfordshire and therefore blown up by the Banburyites in 1790. All the town gates have disappeared and the stone town hall obviously dates from the modern sham Gothic period. The Globe Room no longer adorns the *Reindeer* inn with panelling of 1637 and a plaster ceiling that was good enough to be copied for the South Kensington Museum; this room sailed away to America within my recollection. Nor do the above complete the town's losses. In past years of fruits and fats my visits to Parsons Street were schemed for gormandizing the same kind of Banbury cakes that Ben Jonson and George III relished. My appearance at the same spot for the same purpose in 1947 ended in disappointment. The welcoming fragrance had departed from the threshold of Lamb late Beesley. Brutal printed words barred the way. They read, "No Banbury Cakes for Sale." I turned from this emblem of those who arrange our bodies and souls, and consigned modern times to the devil for these particular reasons. Cakes eaten in Banbury were scrumptious and unique; made from a secret and traditional recipe, they proved how well people filled their insides in the happy ages of Unsocial Insecurity; while consuming and gloating you could ponder on the old wool trade by recalling that the peculiar shape of the Banbury cake derives from the weaver's shuttle.

Enough of Banbury's losses. The town retains plenty to mark its continuance and gains. Even the ponderous church, spacious and theatrical inside as planned by the Cockerell architects, attracts admirers to-day, probably because we have gone from bad to worse. Fashion is fickle, has changed since 1810 when a writer to the *Gentleman's Magazine* thought the church "more like a gaol than a Christian temple." Below the heavy tower the vicarage stands meekly, a charming survivor from the blow-up of 1790 and preserving gables and windows characteristic of the mid seventeenth century. Church and parson's home face a capital stretch of historic highway joining North Bar to the Cross; generous in width, good for the red buses and motor cars, it yet looks just the thing for shades of phantom horses and coaches between the wide verges, and ruby coachmen, too, who of course used to wink at pretty maidens fresh from matins in the departed Gothic shrine. Streets, Church Lane, Butcher Row, and curious ways keep tight to the medieval town plan and consequently offer antiquity nicely blended with modernism. For instance, pointed gables, curved windows, and external plasterwork look very well above the bright colours of agricultural implements arranged by Messrs. Neale and Perkins. Those who require them can swallow Mr. Goodman's pills behind the same square window-panes that attracted gouty and dyspeptic Georgians. Best of all is the Market Place. It upholds ancient custom, continues true in deed as well as name. Grouped around are reminders of past marketing days, the gabled and Georgian frontages, Jacobean timbers, pierced wooden pendants, the panelled and carved doors of the *Unicorn* inn perpetually guarded by heraldic animals under the date of 1648. When the stalls are set up in the open, the hubbub of chattering, jokes, laughter and shouting echoes round the mature background, just as it must have done for centuries. A great sight is this market, jolly, crowded, and assorted with bloaters, ice-cream, the Women's Institute, flowers, fruit, gospellers, suspenders, and every known commodity for mankind's pleasure, profit, and discomfort. A power for starting movements in cash is irresistible. As sure as eggs are eggs and sometimes bad, few human beings could conquer parting with money for things needed or never likely to be wanted. One day while there my publishing friend acquired two fly-catchers for useful service in sultry London; at the same time I gained two religious tracts (for nothing).

In spite of the above acquisitions a suggestion of the town's losses persisted on that occasion until my departure from Banbury. For accuracy of facts in this book, I went to the *Reindeer* to ascertain if the historic fame for ale had disappeared like the actual Banbury cakes. Though shorn of its treasure, the Globe Room, the inn yard had not been completely spoiled (33). The doors to the yard remained intact, fine solid doors generously made of oak. There was the date, ANNO · DIN · 1570, and the carved names as well, IHON KNIGHT · IHONE KNIGHT · DAVID HORN, each separated by a little carved heart. A pretty fancy, I thought; but while wondering who the owners of these names might have been an aged man fresh from the bar said to me, "Make a fine lot of firewood!" Perhaps he felt impelled to uphold the town's reputation for destruction? Certainly he mentioned the coal shortage and quite confirmed my intuition that Banbury ale had not vanished.

The uplands spread southward from Banbury. Landscapes shape in gentle slopes. Streams water green valleys. The Evenlode river makes lovely windings. Big and little woods mount to particular richness at Great and Little Tew, Blenheim Park, and Wychwood Forest. The local stone colours the villages, mutely tells the annals of rural centuries. It amplifies stories of country squires, as at Chastleton and Shipton-under-Wychwood, locates the home of Lucius Cary, Lord Falkland, at Great Tew, and stone walls round Blenheim Park, extending for furlongs beyond Woodstock and laid in the best dry stone walling I have ever seen, enclose Vanburgh's immense palace reared for the great Duke and Sarah.

All the villages in this region repay exploration, either for beauty in stone, history, and sometimes for surprises. Idbury, for example, one of the high places facing the Wychwoods and the Evenlode, has the customary curiosities—a clerestoried church partly Norman, stone cottages, and a manor-house. Yet this manor-house, though correct in traditional masonry, once helped to give me quite a surprise. Enquiring at this home of *The Countryman* for the founder and then editor of the quarterly, the reply was, "He is in the orchard pruning fruit-trees." Very strange that seemed! The words shattered my belief that editors of works on every known subject drew inspiration from Fleet Street and similar

CHIPPING CAMPDEN, *the old wool town prime with the fineness and pattern of stonework. Its distinctive features include the church rebuilt by the wool merchants, a fourteenth-century woolstaplers' hall, William Grevel's medieval home, the market hall (above), lovely seventeenth-century almshouses, and remnants of Viscount Campden's mansion, burnt down in the Civil War.*

WINCHCOMBE *lies in a hollow on the fringe of the Cotswolds. Once it was an important Mercian town and the place of a Benedictine monastery with a shrine to St. Kenelm. The great abbey has gone but a wonderful fifteenth-century church remains unspoiled. Picturesque houses line the streets. The inns show a stone frontage of The Old Corner Cupboard and the courtyard gallery of The George, a reminder of the pilgrims.*

conglomerations of bricks and mortar. How and why *The Countryman* evidently "comes from the country" needed no further explanation.

Another cause for surprise, not to my knowledge previously illustrated, exists at Chapel House, a draughty hamlet on the old coach road directing past the Rollright Stones to Birmingham. This object, being an archway the worse for wear (33), keeps so many memories inside its worn stones that I specially followed in the tracks of the coaches on the good motor road through Woodstock and Enstone to Chapel House. When centuries oozed with big joints of roast beef and pork, port wine in cobwebby bottles, etc., etc., for the delight of man's internal apparatus, and until after a princess, later Queen Victoria, honoured the spot, this archway and adjacent buildings, once components of a very celebrated inn, welcomed alike travellers of great, famous, notorious, and inconsequent stature who arrived variously sun-burnt or blue-nosed, according to the behaviour of Sol or Boreas on the bleak Oxfordshire uplands. And lo! on one memorable day, March 21, 1776, to be exact, the bulky Doctor dined excellently, so Boswell related, soared to the heights of inspiration on wings developed by a satisfied tummy, and uttered his immortal panegyric:

"There is no private house (said he) in which people can enjoy themselves so well, as at a capital tavern. . . . You are sure you are welcome: and the more noise you make, the more trouble you give, the more good things you call for, the welcomer you are. No servants will attend you with the alacrity which waiters do, who are incited by the prospect of an immediate reward in proportion as they please. No, Sir; there is nothing which has yet been contrived by man, by which so much happiness is produced as by a good tavern or inn." He then repeated, with great emotion, Shenstone's lines:

"Whoe'er has travelled life's dull round,
Where'er his stages may have been,
May sigh to think he still has found
The warmest welcome at an inn."

Every true explorer of England knows these words by heart; yet they are so wedded to my soul through benefits enjoyed and in expectation, pardon is asked for quoting them again. Johnson, Boswell, coaches, horses, chaises, callers, landlords—all semblances of their ghostly selves and dinners have faded from Chapel House. Now the chapel of the priory of Cold Norton merely marks a ground-plan under a lawn. The archway with a leaky roof looks likely to tumble down. A solitary pull-up at the cross-roads alone struggles to keep alive the spirit of hospitality. Therefore, on the December day of my sketching, when the wind blew chill from the north-east, I went down the hill to Chipping Norton and fed in the modern fashion behind a good old frontage of the *White Hart*.

The airy and spacious centre of Chipping Norton, a combined High Street and Market Place lined with stone buildings sprinkled with seventeenth- and eighteenth-century features, is so contrived on a slope that masculine dwellers downstairs on the high side could study their feminine neighbours in bedrooms opposite; this may be possible, but of course does not happen in a town so respectable. The new Post Office, built of stone in the Georgian Style, is nearly good enough to be an old one. Things more hoary include dull earthen relics of a castle erected during the reign of Stephen, a guildhall with mullioned windows, Middle Row obviously in the middle, a pretty lot of dormers and chimneys on the seventeenth-century almshouses, a fine big church entered through a notable two-storied porch and wonderfully lit in the nave from a fifteenth-century clerestory daringly constructed of more glass than stone. In addition to sculptured monuments the church contains a collection of memorial brasses. One of them, to John Yonge, with woolpacks at his feet, has particular interest for us at this stage of our progression. The gentleman's footstools imply that we are reaching the true stone land of Cotswold sheep and wool, a land in which you now can wander from morn until eve without seeing a flock of sheep or a shepherd, more's the pity.

Everybody knows that onward from the fourteenth century this wool trade rose to be a prop and mainstay of the country's prosperity, and the immigration of foreign weavers, first encouraged by the Edwardian kings, developed the great cloth industry. The peculiar constitution of Continental towns, each jealous of independence and continually at war with each other, made keeping sheep flocks in western Europe a hazardous enterprise. Thus England gained the advantage of being the chief supplier of wool to the weaving countries beyond the Straits of Dover. The woolpack on the brass in Chipping Norton church, similar tokens elsewhere, and emblems throughout the wold country related to this story of wool can summon speculations on a multitude of things. One can think of the Cotswolds, once a vast sheep walk; the port of Bristol, an early staple for wool; the staple established at Calais in 1363 for the European market; merchants and nobles trafficking in wool and kings doing likewise (before the battle of Crécy Philip of France sneered at Edward III, "the royal wool merchant"); the rise and expansion of the home cloth industry; the decree for everybody to wear woollen caps and be "buried in woollen" to keep trade thriving; Queen Elizabeth, ever sagacious, planting her Lord Chancellor on the Woolsack in the House of Lords, ever to remind him of the white source of golden prosperity in case his mind went woolgathering elsewhere. Standing evidences in these Oxfordshire and Gloucestershire lands, now awaiting our exploration, emphasize the tremendous importance of this olden industry. Reminders abound to vitalize anew the centuries when "Cottys" fleeces were in high favour, great demand, and called buyers from the Continent and home centres, sent strings of pack-horses laden with precious burdens over the wolds to the ships at the ports, and fed weavers in Cotswold valleys and more distant

Cottages at BIBURY

53

parts of England. So much is on view for delight, suggestion, and contemplation, it is rather nice to be reminded of sheep, shepherds, and tinkling bells on the open wolds under the broad sky, billowy wool on pack-horses, merchants mixing bargaining with attending mass, and other aspects of man's work and enterprise in the process of making money and buying immortality. This way of life, indicated by the weathered properties of its stages, even gains in romance when spied from this era of clattering machinery, assembly lines, murky industrial towns, dull suburbs, and times of advantages now enjoyed while all bodies and souls are manœuvred as economic robots for equation on the national balance sheet. Even the words current in those past days of trading vibrate cosily. Woolly brains like mine can sometimes weave fantasies from the very sounds of "fells" (skins with wool on them), "in pile" (wool heaped up), "tod" (28 pounds weight, usually made of three or four fleeces, valued in 1481 at 13s. 4d.), "woolpack" (about 250 pounds of fleeces), "poke" (a small sack, nowadays usually associated with buying a pig), "sarpler" (a large sack containing 80 tods); and the word "woolstapler" itself always rings a tuneful note.

Sheep farming, trading in wool, and the consequent flow of prosperity influenced the development of architecture as a matter of course, for religious worship and artistry belonged to the accepted scheme of daily life and work. Nature not only provided the sheep walks; it also gave good stone which was turned to advantage through the wealth, devotion, labours, and talents of men. The buildings that constitute the unique charm of the Cotswold scene therefore did not happen from tricks of luck, accident, or sentiment. They were the logical result of divine provision, fortunate circumstance, enterprise, skilled work spiced with genius. Masonry served for a true expression of a people who made the towns, villages, and manor-houses while they chiefly depended and thrived on wool, or were connected with the commodity in one way or another. Their story is told by villages high among walled fields and lying in wooded valleys watered by clear streams—at Snowshill and Stanton (44), Bibury on the Coln, Chalford in the Stroud valley (55), and everywhere throughout this area bright with walls and steep roofs of stone. Streets of the incomparable towns, ringed by Chipping Campden (49), Burford (38), Cirencester, Tetbury (9), Wootton-under-Edge, Painswick, and Winchcombe (50), send their messages from halls of woolstaplers and marketing, from gable, archway, and pediment. Churches, responsive one to another with arch and tracery, embattled parapet and crocketed pinnacle born of riches accumulated by the woolmen, join in harmonies of grey and golden beauty over hill and dale. Frequent manor-houses and the larger dwellings in the towns bespeak a spacious and cultivated life. They localize families and names, show home quarters such as those of William Greville of Chipping Campden, "the flower of the wool

CHALFORD, *stone built and steep, in Gloucestershire's Golden Valley.*
The cloth industry, introduced by the Flemings and Huguenots,
brought centuries of prosperity to this bright vale of the River Frome.

OWLPEN MANOR-HOUSE *near Dursley. Secluded on a slope below high woods, it was built in the sixteenth century and occupied by the Daunt family for generations. The clipped yew-trees in the gardens are ancient and noted.*

merchants of all England," Daunts of Owlpen (56), Fettiplaces of Asthall (37), who owned "all the parks and all the places," and the gables and towers at Chastleton remain as built and occupied by Walter Jones, the Witney woollen merchant, before he retired to a heavenly woolsack in 1633.

The building style that developed, marked strongly with local characteristics, was a true child of the English tradition. It matured late in the fourteenth century, rose in the full flower of grace and majesty during the fifteenth, and the native manner of work continued through Elizabeth's reign until the Restoration. Old in years when Queen Anne and the Georges ruled, the style then gained new delicacies with pilasters and angle quoins, classic doorways and eaves cornices, now often to be viewed standing beyond formal paths and pillared gateways. Obsequies these might be called, wreaths for the final page of the great English epic that came to a full stop in the wars waged by economics, competition, and the coal, smoke, and mechanical industrialism of England's northern towns.

To paint the lily is wasteful and ridiculous, wrote Shakespeare. It would be equally foolish for me to attempt additions to the words already available on the jewelled stonework set in the Cotswold scenes. Since Guy Dawber produced the volume on Cotswold architecture nearly fifty years ago and Arthur Gibbs penned *A Cotswold Village* in the manor-house at Ablington bearing this inscription carved over the entrance, PLEAD · THOV · MY · CAVSE · O · LORD · 1590, writers have issued acres of pages on the delights, and also the defects, presented by these wolds and valleys. Some of them, clear of vision, have told all that can be known on the lie of the land, craftsmanship in stonework, and fertility of design in masonry. Others, looking through mental eye-pieces coloured rose-pink, perceived much ammunition for sentimentality in mossy walls and roofs overgrown with roses. A writer here and there merely found the wolds bleak and draughty, and certain silly individuals, armed with smoky spectacles and minds insensible to colour and beauty beautifully rendered, discovered no more than an absence of damp-courses and articles dependent on drainpipes. The poets, perhaps, have most nearly revealed the Cotswolds' heart and spirit of place—John Drinkwater in *Cottage Song*,

> When down the silver tides
> The moon on Cotswold rides.

Odell Shepard on Bibury in *The Harvest of a Quiet Eye*,

> I shall remember cottages
> Carved out of silver and gold,
> And how the great beech-darkened hills
> Tenderly enfold
> That little human island
> Washed round by meadow and wold.

And surely John Masefield must have had his own Cotswolds in mind when he conceived,

> For they'd the skill to draw their plan,
> And skill's a joy to any man;
> And they'd the strength, not skill alone,
> To build it beautiful in stone;
> And strength and skill together thus . .
> O, they were happier men than us.

Better than any word or drawn pictures, best of all it is to explore the Cotswolds, the real thing. You can put up at the *Lygon Arms* in Broadway (if it is not full up), at the *Lamb* in Burford, dating from the fifteenth century, the *Bull* in Fairford (oh! my trout for breakfast there!), at any of the inns and anchorages of ancient peace for ancients not in a hurry. What is seen then can be enjoyed and admired. Mind and memory are enriched with impressions gained from churches, manor-houses, towns, and villages left by earlier dwellers, the standing memorials of themselves, their lives and thoughts, evidences clearly and strongly made in stone and incapable of telling fibs or proving that white was black or black was white, a trick so easily done nowadays by manipulators of modernism. Amongst all the loveliness it may be difficult to ward off sermons in stone and that sort of preaching. Such temptations nearly captured me at the moment of gathering these words while sitting on a wall of stone. Swinbrook, Asthall, and the ruins of Minster Lovell manor-house glinted in the sunlight down below in the Windrush valley. The hill behind me hid Coln Rogers, Winson, and Bibury. Uplands spread in curve after curve to meet the Rissingtons and Bourton-on-the-Water. Very quickly all chance of attack from sentimental moodiness retired before the onslaught of a string of lorries snorting past my stone wall and bearing sections of the prefabricated houses! Yet these emblems of house and home did preach a jolly good sermon on ugliness allied to convenience in this epoch of England's progress. They reminded me that the Cotswold tradition of building is as dead as anything can be. Attempts to revive it were made by Sir E. Guy Dawber at Coldicote and elsewhere, C. R. Ashbee at Campden, Ernest Gimson and Ernest Barnsley of Sapperton, Charles Bateman (who owned a delightful house at Bourton-on-the-Hill), and other architectural friends of mine. They did splendid work, brought new life to a building style evolved in past generations and exactly suited to the local scene. But their efforts represented no more than individual specks in the ocean of a lost cause. Modern thought and conditions have no affinity with the way of life that adorned the Cotswolds with golden glory.

The main routes for Cotswold exploration are good, and very obliging for our purpose of finding and seeing the landscapes, the villages and towns built of stone. The Fosse Way bisects the area from north to south. It mounts from the

Vale of the Red Horse to Moreton-in-the-Marsh, then points up and down in an immemorial line to the end of Gloucestershire near Tetbury. The Way sends out arms right and left to Bourton-on-the-Hill, Upper and Lower Slaughter, Bourton-on-the-Water (prettily grouped round the stream crossed by little bridges and once likened to Venice by somebody who had not seen the Grand Canal), Chedworth noted for the Roman villa, Coln St. Denis and Coln Rogers, North Cerney, Ampney Crucis, and many more villages of attraction and memories. Stow-on-the-Wold, perched high, stands like the hub of a wheel with spokes radiating in every direction. These promise yet more notable villages, among which are Wick and Little Rissington; Naunton and Seven-hampton; Temple Guiting, screened in woods once owned by Knights Templars; Stanway; Broadway, still a charmer in spite of popularity; and Stanton (44), Weston-sub-Edge, and the villages grouped round Chipping Campden in a locality which I think exhibits the stone architecture in its very best mood. Witney lies at the fringe of the hills. A stone town throughout, it possesses a good church under the high spire, the seventeenth-century butter cross neighboured by a quaint town hall carried on pillared archways, and most unusual, a new and convenient housing scheme built to tone and harmonize with the work of the ancients. Here old fame is kept alive by manufacturing the "Earlyworms," in which we awake somewhat later than the birds; and my mind went wandering down centuries when in Bridge Street I read a notice, "Weavers wanted." The highway at the butter cross, finger-posted for Cheltenham, is a capital leader to Cotswold moods and graces. It mounts above the Windrush valley, shows village after village from Minster Lovell to Barrington and Windrush, rises higher and higher, skirts the vale of the Coln bound for Fosse Bridge, Bibury, and Quennington. Turnings on each side will take you over the wolds and into a quiet world of soft green pastures, warm-coloured earth, lucious shades of spinneys and woods, and dry stone walls follow the curves of the land to collections of cottages grouped round churches. More to the south the route from Cirencester to Birdlip Hill and Gloucester cuts a straight and bold Roman line through finely wooded hill and dale scenery; attractions to the left and right include Daglingworth, the Duntisbournes, Norman sculpture at the highest wold church of Elkstone, and the halt in King Charles's wandering at Coberley rectory. The Golden Valley holds treasures at Chalford (55) and up the Frome stream to Sapperton; and for the romantic scenery of the southern Cotswolds a fine round I can recommend shows the beech woods down to Owlpen and Uley, North Nibley, the tower of Ozleworth, Boxwell, a hiding-place of King Charles after the battle of Worcester, and a view of the historic keep and gatehouse at Beverston before reaching Tetbury.

Here, there, and everywhere are the famous manor-houses, one and sometimes two in most of the villages, and exhibiting all the variations of local style in gables, kneelers and finials, windows divided by mullions, entrances made by old squires for their ladies (and themselves), the matchless stone roofs, and squared chimneys finished with moulded caps. Those who know the owners of these houses can see stone fireplaces, panelling, and all sorts of wonderful things inside; less fortunate wanderers, not on visiting terms, usually may squint at these lovely homes from roadsides or neighbouring churchyards. The number is so large and my stock of paper so small, I can only mention this short selection from my choices to send my readers in search of more: Snowshill, high at 850 feet; Stanton Court, built in the sixteenth century to serve prisoners of war and their hutments in the twentieth century, and Warren House, of 1577, round the corner; Stanway, with a gatehouse, a notable group erected by a land-owning Tracey early in the seventeenth century; Upper Swell, Upper and Lower Slaughter, three prizes close together; Whittington Court, mainly early sixteenth century with a later wing added, poetically connected with the names of Denham and Dobell; two specimens previously mentioned and illustrated, at Asthall and Owlpen; Bibury Court of 1623, and Ablington, dated 1590, a mile distant; Moor Hall, in a very bad way at my first introduction, but now happily thriving after being re-christened More Hall; Little Sodbury, a fifteenth- and sixteenth-century house in which Tyndale began translations of the Bible. The later style of building to balanced and classic designs brought charming results. One of the best is at Lower Lypiatt, near Stroud, erected in 1717 behind a sweep of stone piers and a gateway made by Warren, the celebrated smith. Medford House, Mickleton, re-fronted in 1699, also shows a very pretty face within a walled forecourt; it so attracted me at first sight in years long ago that I explored beyond, slept under the stone roof, sketched the doorway and the urns, and of an evening walked in the manor park up and down the fine avenue of elms planted by Shenstone, the poet, to get a kind of feeling of being Morgan Graves, the eighteenth-century squire. That did not come off. Times had changed. Evidently the defunct squires of these manor-houses never would do for modern days, based on the sacredness of one vote for every one man and woman and the omnipotence of political fry. Members of an extinct race, their years and deeds are remembered by the homes they made and memorials in the near churches where they worshipped, and sometimes slept, in big family pews while the sands of the hour-glass trickled down. Their courses run, they retired to the places of worship to sleep for good. Now we can gaze on graven images and records of the Trinders of Westwell, Fettiplaces of Swinbrook, and their like, who passed quiet country lives on ancestral acres, built in faith with durable stone for themselves and their progeny, reared sons and daughters to follow on, set examples both good and indifferent for neighbours, tenants, and the nation, farmed and planted, tickled

CLIFTON. *The Georgian and Regency terraces high on the bank of the River Avon near the Gorge and Suspension Bridge.*

BRISTOL. *The cathedral from the south-east and ruins of the bishop's palace wrecked by Reform rioters in 1831. The cathedral has the remarkable late Norman chapter house and medieval choir aisles of unique design. It remained without a nave from the dissolution until 1868.*

BRISTOL. *St. Mary Redcliffe, the famous parish church of rich Perpendicular architecture which commemorates the piety and munificence of the merchants. Notable memorials include the Amerycke brass. Here Coleridge and Southey were married.*

The Gloucestershire vale, the Severn bend, and the Forest of Dean viewed from the Haresfield escarpment of the Cotswolds near Stroud. Abergavenny Sugar Loaf and the Black Mountains show in the far distance.

the trout, shot the birds, and then departed to spheres of silence, commemorated with little more than monograms and dates figured on gables and porches, and inscribed slabs and carved effigies in churches, to inform posterity that they had breathed, lived, and died.

From villages and manor-houses we reach the towns, grey towns, golden towns, shining out from sunlit landscapes in exquisite harmonies of tone and colour. Evening light amplifies their mellowness; on moonlight nights I have seen pearly shades and slanting shadows blended mysteriously; and even in dull or wet weather there is a good deal to be said for a fine stock of masonry as an outlook. Children of time, these aged towns speak volumes. Their weathered stones in churches, dwellings, inns, and halls of trading offer solid stuff to illuminate the annals of communities that prospered during centuries of summers and winters while Tames of Fairford, Sylvesters of Burford, the Grevilles, Torteys, Midwinters, Smalwoodes, Biddles, and hosts of notable and workaday natives spread their family trees and built for comfort and beauty. It is no cause for wonder that Cotswold towns have charmed writers, artists, and lookers from all corners of the earth, choice specimens as they are in the collection of smallish and little towns so remarkably matured in England's past years. No towns in the country quite equal this Cotswold group and their contiguous neighbours in Wiltshire and Somerset. Built with stone throughout, the most expressive material used in building, they rose to the highest point of excellence in what may be termed democratic architecture ; that is to say, a regular method of building devised and encouraged for the uses of the common life. These towns still accurately reflect the guiding motives that made them. Particularly do they show the influences of local product, climate, environment, and the degree of material prosperity and spiritual enlightenment attained by a people naturally bright in temperament and invention.

Lack of space again forbids me even to mention all the Cotswold towns that have given me hours and days of pleasure; but they have wide fame and no doubt a map and the joy of finding will direct my readers to them. One is tempted to say that the main street of Chipping Campden cannot be bettered in England (49); pardonably the town may claim to be the most perfect small one on earth, with its combination of seventeenth-century market hall, Greville's fourteenth-century house, Woolstaplers' Hall (where I gossiped with C. R. Ashbee in distant days), inns, house fronts gabled and square (behind one of which F. L. Griggs used to hide), gardens and vistas at the backs of the said houses, and for a climax the almshouses and church, acme of magnificence, facing all that is left of Sir Baptist Hicks's mansion, burnt down by Royalists in the Civil War to cheat Roundheads of a prize. Then you light on Burford High Street (38), and Sheep Street too, waver, do not know where to award the palm, and retire inside the *Lamb*, the brick-fronted *Bull*, the *Cotswold Gate*, the *George* (King Charles's pub), or the *Bear* to think it over. Here, again, is the delicious cohesion of stonework grouped down the slope to the Windrush stream crossed by the old bridge; and lots of sights, too, with one of the largest and most interesting of the Cotswold churches, the Warwick almshouses founded in 1457, Symeon Wysdom's Elizabethan grammar-school, the Tolsey, houses for beauty and stories, and the Priory and seventeenth-century chapel combined, tumbling to pieces when I first found it, but now intact to recall the Elizabethan mansion of Lord Falkland and the safe retreat for Speaker Lenthall after the Restoration. Tetbury is another charmer, not widely known to the outer world and therefore deficient in "luncheons and teas provided." It crowns the hillock surrounded by valleys; thus elevated and topped by the church spire, the groupings from the Bath and Malmesbury roads and other directions compose remarkably well. Spire and tower developed from a rebuilding to the old pattern in the 1890's. The body of the church is an amusing curiosity. Designed and built by Francis Hiorn, of Warwick, it has spaciousness and a certain dignity, in spite of the spindly piers made of wood and iron and the spiritless window traceries in the wiry "Gothick" style fashionable during the ascendency of Horace Walpole and the "Committee of Taste" who cultivated romantic sentiments as an anchorage from classicalism. The present building followed a medieval predecessor, so large and handsome that it was knocked down in 1777 to enable Tetbury to change a real monument into a sham one. Genuine articles are offered in the picturesque, hilly streets and byways round about. Gables, Georgian façades, shell door-hoods, and a mixture of features seem to tell of an easy-going past while the town clock bell pips out the hours in high, squeaky notes or you look out on placid scenes from under the arches of the seventeenth-century market hall (9); placid scenes, that is to say, if the outlooker is not perpetually spied on, as I was, by a bright youth with a bicycle, a local scion of the ubiquitous tribe specially created to terrorize artists with such expressions as, "Mister, what are yer drawin'," "My! Rosey, isn't it lovely!" or more politely, "Pardon me, may I look?"

Other sights, scenes, and interests are unending in the complete group of Cotswold towns. Certainly the collection is remarkable when one remembers Stow-on-the-Wold, "where the wind blows cold" in winter, dreaming away summer days on the height mellowed by the houses round the Market Square and the church, used in 1646 as a cage for Royalist prisoners after the last battle fought in the Civil War; Moreton-in-the-Marsh, by no means marshy, but situated over 400 feet high on the march or Cotswold boundary; Winchcombe (50), the old Mercian town, pilgrim point for St. Kenelm's shrine, a name-place for Jack of Newbury, the town with the perfect fifteenth-century church, stone houses, inns, and the *George*, the pilgrims' rest, where you can sleep above timber inscribed with the initials of Richard Kyderminster, past landlord and

SHIPTON
OLIFFE
13c. bell turret

WINCHCOMBE
Arms panel
Chandos
Almshouses

NORTHLEACH
15c. porch
Upper figure Blessed Trinity
Lower Virgin & Child.
Bell turret above
Left pinnacle pierced for chimney to parvise

PAINSWICK
18c. House near church

COTSWOLD NOTES

STOW on the WOLD
Renaissance house
Market Sq

67

wealthy Tudor abbot of the departed monastery; Painswick, very arty, and particularly good for eighteenth-century houses; Stroud, more remarkable for its situation between the hills than for the contents centred round the Elizabethan town hall; Minchinhampton with a good seventeenth-century cloth hall standing on columns and arches; Nailsworth, surrounded by fine heights, and perhaps most curious for a street which natives say is like a penny because they can have a pint at the *King's Head* at one end and another pint at the *Britannia* at the other end; Dursley, thriving afresh with engineering in place of wool, yet still sedate with its town hall and market house presided over by Queen Anne; Fairford, known throughout the world for the glass windows in John Tame's "wool" church, a late-fifteenth-century shrine most handily placed for reaching the ancient *George* and the *Bull*, cherished in my memory for pre-war comfort, chicken and trout; and Cirencester, the villagers' Ciren, the Cicester of the nobs, entrancing always, and briefly noted in my earlier book, *Thames Triumphant*.

Northleach, situated right in the middle of the wolds, demands more than two words. This large village-cum-small town has kept a warm place in my heart since I first found it in the 1890's, then a Rip Van Winkle kind of spot lost and forgotten in a pushing age. Grass actually did grow in the streets. Apparently strangers were rarely seen, for the welcome given to me by the natives mounted almost to a point of embarrassment. The landlord at the *Wheatsheaf*—I can picture his cheerful, hale, and bearded features now—treated his only guest with the devotion of a loving parent; the huge sirloin of roast beef presented for my solo performance is yet tender in memory, and companions in the smoke-room assured me of ample provision for whatever might happen because the town was noted for a workhouse at one end and a prison at the other. Northleach has a different look now. If the workhouse exists no doubt it is otherwise and beautifully named, perhaps a St. Christopher's home schemed to serve democratic travellers. Judging by the meal consumed before writing these words, roast-beefy savour is not even on smell. Below the stone walls the main road is principally tarmac. Coaches, lorries, and cars buzz along for Cheltenham, Oxford, and London. The coaching days of petrol have livened up the town that was left high and dry when the coaching days of the horses faded. Go-ahead fogies must be pleased with the town's progress, even though Northleach may be less fascinating than in my earlier years, when it advanced backwards.

A number of years ago, say four or five hundred, this town probably flowed with milk, honey, beef, mutton, sack, and malmsey. Without doubt it was then right on the top of the times; in fact, it appreciably assisted in making those times what they were. The church most distinctly proclaims this fact. It is a glorious work of art, a pride of Cotswold; it illuminates more clearly than

MONMOUTH. *The defensive tower on the medieval bridge over the River Monnow in the birthplace of King Henry V.*

The valley of the River Usk and the Sugar Loaf (1955 feet) near Abergavenny.

LLANTHONY PRIORY, *romantically situated in the Honddu valley of the Black Mountains. Built about 1115, it was largely*

words can tell a tale of men's worldly striving and prosperity, religious devotion, and trust in things beyond this earth (43).

In common with other Cotswold town churches, this one represents great dignity of thought expressed in local stone by exuberant craftsmanship. Brief particulars of the edifice are these. Little remains of the twelfth-century building. At a later date a great reconstruction happened. The present tower, nave, and clerestories, the south choir aisle dated 1489, and the south porch, mounted up in new splendour between the approximate dates of 1400 and 1500. That means about one hundred years to create a joy for ever, if mankind ever should think it worth while to keep such things of beauty for so long. The nave interior is lofty and spacious, wonderfully lit by the clerestory windows. Arcades of singular pillars and arches plainly denote the late Perpendicular style; they closely resemble those at that other grand Cotswold church of Chipping Campden. The timbered aisle roofs adorned with carved bosses may cause the eyes of shrewd worshippers to wander upward from prayer-books. One boss, quite noticeable, flaunts the bear and ragged staff; this symbol of the house of Warwick, with others at Cricklade, Chipping Campden, and elsewhere, recall the past mightiness of the Beauchamps and the Grevels in this land of wool and denote how useful sheep were for brightening earl's coronets. Window traceries, particularly in the nave aisles and east chancel, are good enough to be called remarkable. Two choice works appear in the chancel sedilia crowned with canopies and the original fifteenth-century pulpit. The font, very gracefully supported and probably of early-fifteenth-century date, is peculiar for the series of heads carved all round it. These curious faces may represent benefactors to the church. It is very thrilling to trace the masons' marks scratched on many stones and so unite the building with the makers of it, almost say "How d'you do" to William Nutto, Simon White, and the skilled company whose brains and hands created this emblem of faith and work. Amidst all the finery they left for posterity it is difficult to stop even making a catalogue of things to be seen. The most marvellous one of all, however, must be mentioned. This is the south porch, the late-Gothic masterpiece. To find its equal in inspired masoncraft would mean searching through all England. So much for a story in stone of past times. At present a notice in the porch reads: "This is a large church and costly to maintain. This is a small and poor parish." Any charitable soul who now scans this page of mine and straightway tips up to the Vicar a fiver, or more or less, for the preservation of this noble structure will thereby do high service for God, England, home, and beauty.

A sermon in stone is not the only one here. A complementary story is told in brass. The numerous and famed memorials of Northleach preach from the floor all about the building. As a good structure must always depend on its foundations, so these brasses represent the foundations on which this rare church was built. They commemorate the power of wool, the prosperity, benevolence, and piety of those who traded in it. Looking down, or crawling about the floor, you can actually meet the woolstaplers, see depicted the men who thrived, grew rich, and with profits made paid for a worthy monument to the source of all goodness, or in the idiom of their own age of faith and religious fervour, "To the glory of God." There they lie, set out here, there, and everywhere, engraved at full length in brass as if awaiting their final earthly call and meanwhile offering themselves for inspection. Notable among them is John Fortey at the east end of the same nave that he directed to be made "lightsome and splendid" with the contents of his purse before he departed this life in 1458. Himself, Thomas Bushe, with a bush, William Midwinter, and others in this crowd of forty portraits repose with feet on sheep and woolpacks, their emblems of comfort on earth and perhaps of joy in heaven. Very fascinating are the particulars displayed, the details of costume and the merchants' marks.

The good folk of Northleach fully realized the importance of wool, the source of their own and the country's wealth, and the brasses in the church show that they took care to depart this life with representations of their feet still firmly planted on the sheep and the woolpacks which had served so well in the passage on earth. The situation of the town gave it particular importance. Burford, Chipping Campden, Winchcombe, Cirencester, in fact most of the old wool towns stand at the fringes of the hills. Northleach alone is right in the middle of the Cotswolds. It therefore developed into a famous collecting point. Wool poured in from every direction. Merchants flocked there to secure the prizes stored by the local woolstaplers in great stone warehouses. Bustling must have been the scenes when the inns were crowded and woolstaplers offered hospitality in their stone houses as buying, selling, and packing progressed and pack-horses set out on their journeys. The published letters of the Cely family, London merchants of the staple with business in Calais and Bruges, afford interesting sidelights on a busy Northleach in the 1480's. They introduce the actual person of William Midwinter, with whom the Celys principally dealt, and for a pretty garnish they illuminate a flirting interlude between young Richard Cely and Miss Lemryke during matins and mass inside the church of my illustration. These figures and the wool trade vanished years ago. The great warehouses went to pieces; only the relics of one did I discover and record. Northleach dwindled into a phantom of its former self. No longer the merchants passed into the church under the Blessed Trinity and Our Lady carved on the lovely porch. Those of my readers who travel that way I trust may follow in their footsteps, stop, admire, and put a big or little something into the box to help preserve this beautiful monument erected through the piety and generosity of the woolstaplers in spacious times when grace and devotion had a real place in day-to-day life.

Away to the west the Cotswold escarpments sweep in bold succession across Gloucestershire, growing richer with trees and verdure in the southward march. Camps crown point after point, tumuli are in good supply, archæologists crawl into the long borrow near Uley to inspect funeral arrangements made in the year goodness knows when, and the stone implements and iron currency bars which I handled evidently had been made and left on Meon Hill by Neolithic and Iron Age ancestors. The Romans provided more recent proof of occupation. They found and adapted what they wanted in the way of ancient earthworks and sites, reconstructed, planned afresh, and so left their unmistakable signs all along this impressive line of defence which directs through Meon Hill, Shunbarrow Hill above Stanton, Hailes, Haresfield Beacon, Uley Bury, and Little Sodbury. Within reach, and handy for military leave and week-ends, lay the cities of Gloucester and Cirencester, and the villas known to-day by remains at Chedworth, Elkstone, Charlton Abbots, Woodchester, Witcombe, and elsewhere. Very big snails now living at Coberley, thought to be descendants of those first introduced from Italy in early years of A.D., indicate how Roman epicures tickled their palates. Apart from antiquated associations, these camps repay finding because the ancients had such good eyes for country. Uley Bury, for instance, occupies one of the grandest of fortified sites. To climb up into it means enjoying the present in finest mood, breathing pure air high above the vale, and meanwhile treading fresh green turf that rooted in man's centuries years before Romans used the great camp of about half a mile long from earthwork to earthwork. In addition the Bury served for a kind of Aldershot to the chain of forts extending between Meon Hill and Clifton Down.

While bits and relics left over from early days may be very entertaining to those who like them, more important for ordinary mortals are the panoramas in view from the Cotswold escarpments. Heights and the places of forgotten wars emphasize in breath-taking fashion that there are visible, and always have been, the miles and miles of vales, hills, and woods fading away to blue distances and grey horizons, the work of powers greater than those possessed by insignificant humanity. Romans and their predecessors looked far to the west over these expanses. We do the same to-day, see what they saw, and newer patterns added with centuries of patient labour to glorious wide stretches of peaceful and smiling landscapes. I illustrate one only (64), a scene from the Haresfield Beacon enclosure embracing the River Severn and its famous bend at Newnham, the Forest of Dean, the River Wye country in Herefordshire and Monmouthshire, with the Abergavenny Sugar Loaf and the Black Mountains in the distance, both plainly obvious on clear days. Similar view-points over these coloured miles can be found by the score in following the escarpments of the Cotswolds that guard the river vales of the Avon and the Severn from Meon and Broadway Hills to the high lands leading to Clifton and Bristol.

LOWER RIVER SEVERN, ITS
TRIBUTARIES AND BORDERLANDS

A watery line for the Severn, hills and woods beyond, distant mountain shapes on the Welsh border, and the pattern and colour seen in the panoramas visible from the Cotswold escarpments call us to rare scenery further west. Passing the near stretch of country for the present, extending from Bristol to Gloucester and Tewkesbury, we will in reality or fancy find ourselves on the far side of the River Severn where it bisects Gloucestershire and bounds Monmouthshire.

We see a proper vale, real English in character and of the kind that Tom Hughes loved—wide, flat, fertile, and bounded by hills. You can sample its true quality all the way along the high road bordered by orchards and pastures from Gloucester to Westbury, Newnham, Blakeney, and Chepstow. The road also offers ways down to the tidal river. Here the stream and sandbanks are a good mile in width at The Noose, Oldbury Sands, and other points; level lands on our right bank lead to the heights of the Forest of Dean and the ridges between the Wye and Usk rivers; eastward the green miles of the Berkeley Vale meet the wooded slopes of the Cotswolds. These elements yield land-scape effects of peculiar quality, rarely spectacular, but charming always. Horizontal scenic lines combine with passages of water and sand. Big skies form overhead. Sunlight and shadows from clouds variegate the widespread subtilty of colouring. The pictorial motives suggest subjects by a Dutch painter of the seventeenth century or from our own school of great water-colourists; in fact, Turner, Peter de Wint, and Patrick Nasmyth painted in this neighbourhood. These expansive and pastoral lower Severn scenes, the Cotswold escarpments we have just travelled, and nature's demonstrations of the grand manner await-ing to be seen in the near Wye valley, each emphasize England's trick of ringing the changes and presenting much variety in little space.

The annual exploits of the Severn bore foaming past the golden sands of the Noose, salmon fishing at Beachley and Awre, eels at Epney, and other distinc-tions and peculiarities of the lower River Severn are too well known for me to dwell on. Of less widespread renown, yet of unique interest to students and painters of birds, is the long stretch of low land called the New Grounds, facing the river below the very pretty village and big green of Frampton-on-Severn. The Grounds are "new" because they were reclaimed from the water in the fifteenth and seventeenth centuries. For hundreds of years they have been a sanctuary for birds, protected and cared for by the Berkeley family. Here in winter gather the greatest collections of wild geese in England, wildfowl, and migratory birds from near and distant countries. Most wonderful sights can be observed. Whether you know all, as Peter Scott does, or nothing whatever about pink-feet and white-fronts, the birds feeding, flapping their wings, flying,

RAGLAN. *Ruins of the stately pile erected in the last years of great castle building. It developed in the fifteenth century, an elaborate construction of lofty walls, machicolations, courts, the moated keep and fine gatehouse.*

TINTERN. *The ferry arch near the ruined abbey.*

MATHERN. *Moynes Court, a stone home with a gatehouse built in 1603 by a bishop.*

and circling round thrill beholders with their expressions of grace, strength, and beauty. Gratefully remembered is my own experience on a December day when a pale, wintry sun glinted through wisps of mist and on to the white wings of the moving life gathered on this quiet and secluded lowland. The Severn bend begins here, a very notable scenic composition and one of England's best. Its course has been noted in the Introduction (pp. 13–14) and already we have traced the distant curve from the Cotswold camp above Randwick (64). A closer and best point of view is from Pleasant Stile on the upward road from Newnham. The majestic sweep of the stream winds round the peninsula; rich passages of woodland and trees, vivid green of pastures, and the accent of roofs clustered at Newnham combine in a memorable prospect, one that would fire any enthusiast who performs on big canvases and large areas of drawing paper. Such performers might feel happy settled at Newnham inside the old inn adorned with a stone pediment, vases, and an eagle over a porch roomy enough to shelter a mayor and corporation. These functionaries, alas, and the ceremonial sword they liked to think was presented by King John, disappeared when the town lost its ancient status. The spacious main street remains none the less pleasant in spite of the loss of a mayor and the kingly days, too, of Henry II, who sailed away in 1171 to annex Ireland after Dermot MacMorrogh ran off with O'Rourke's wife and O'Connor went to the rescue.

Pointers of our arrival in the Forest of Dean are given by the names of Little Dean near Pleasant Stile, once a Roman station, the quiet old town of Mitcheldean lying between the groves and the tump, and Ruardean heights, in command of wide landscapes patchworked with fields and woods to the foothills of the Black Mountains. Stretching for about 20 miles in length and 10 in width, the Forest is big, a worthy rival to the New Forest. Large enough for the flight of arrows from the bows of strong kings, at an early date it acquired royal standing as a hunting ground. No arrow here deposed a Rufus by disposing of him, but a like fate befell the Earl of Hereford while hunting on Christmas Eve in 1143; the remains of the Cistercian abbey at Flaxley, founded by his son, commemorate this mishap. For centuries verderers and miners assembled to guard their traditional rights and privileges. Where the verderers eventually met in the reign of Charles II, and still do so, can be inspected under the timber roof of their Court Room at the Speech House, an interesting survival of old English custom. Harking back towards the beginning of A.D., the most exciting archæological curiosity to my way of thinking is at Blackpool Bridge, about 3 miles from Blakeney. Here you can walk up and down a section of road trodden by the Romans, paved as they left it, and well preserved for a hale old article aged more than 1,500 years. Farther on, between Bream and Lydney, a spooky hollow shrouds dark holes dug by Romans who searched for iron ore with oak spades. The coal-mining district of Cinderford, useful though it is just now, may not be ideal for holidays or honeymoons, and parts of the Forest are popular with human beings and much frequented by them. But many ways, far from madding crowds, remain unspoiled. They lead to the Forest's heart, where silences are broken only by rustling leaves and songs of birds, and the majesty of nature's own work rises supreme in tree forms, leafage and flowers. Above the glades and the ponds the ridges are prolific for near and distant views. Eastward is the Severn and its vale bounded by the Cotswolds. In the west the River Wye sweeps from Welsh Bicknor and Symonds Yat to the great vista visible from Staunton, and cliffs and woods massed in peculiar grandeur indicate the river's southern course past Offa's Dyke and the height crowned with the castle and Norman church of St. Briavels.

The narrow streets at Monmouth, reckoned to be on a Roman site, are just outside the Forest at the junction of the Monnow with the Wye. Needless to state, the present natives do not wear the Monmouth caps trimmed with leeks that Fluellen told Henry V were so becoming, but the town retains other past adornments for observation. Castle ruins, mouldy for a birthplace of the gallant Henry V, show best from the opposite side of the river, and a representation of the hero of Agincourt decorates the early eighteenth-century town hall supported on an open colonnade. Geoffrey's window, an enriched Perpendicular oriel of five lights, presents historical complications; it would be nice to think that Geoffrey of Monmouth worked hard on King Arthur behind the mullions and produced one of the earliest best-sellers, but this attractive piece of masonry obviously dates from years and years after the daring fabulist's own twelfth century. The River Wye accounted for the seventeenth-century bridge, since widened. River Monnow did better, caused the town to get its best present showpiece. This bridge, guarded by a medieval gateway, is picturesque when seen from the waterside. Thus it has been presented by thousands of artists of varied abilities and sexes in many periods. For the sake of variety I tackled the subject from the King's highway while in a motor car (69). Turner's fine drawing of the arches and gateway grouped from the usual angle afterwards convinced me that in affairs of art, as with things in general, it is better to be conventional and good than unconventional and shaky.

Whatever of fable may have hitched on to the Monmouth oriel, the name attached to it, Geoffrey of Monmouth, hints with truth that we are at the gateway to a home of old romance. Geoffrey, with Walter Map, born in the neighbourhood, and Layamon, who lived on Severn bank, make a valiant trio among writers of twelfth-century truth and fiction. Celtic vivacity, continually exploded in the racial wars of the Marches, gave moving incidents and names to history. The face of the land hereabout tells its romantic stories without aid of words from romancers. Offa's Dyke bordering the Wye is visible upward from Chepstow. Dozens of earthworks and camps show on vantage points. Castles on the Wye, the Monnow, and the Usk bristle up over rippling waters, and castles on hillocks and with moats in peaceful rural landscapes look quieter now than they used to do. All of them exactly fit the type of scene, here mounted romantically in natural effects of hills, woods, and winding rivers (69, 81). Ruined, picturesque in decay with towers and walls fallen, the castled pictures are just the subjects for ruminations on Normans and Lords Marchers who continually harassed the natives, and in return were harassed by visitors from the Black and other mountains looming dark in the west. It is quite understandable that George Borrow, when he groped round Chepstow Castle, fell to repeating for nearly one hour *The Norman Horse-shoe*, remembered from Scott:

> From Chepstow's towers, ere dawn of morn,
> Was heard afar the bugle-horn ;
> And forth, in banded pomp and pride,
> Stout Clare and fiery Neville ride.

Stories and views of FitzOsborn's and de Clare's castle at Chepstow are famed, and the superb combination of ruins and setting at Raglan (75), fitting last scenes for the last act of medieval military architecture, quite rightly attract the gaze of multitudes doomed to inhabit a mundane age deficient in knightly and heraldic trappings. Upward from the castle of Prince Hal's birth in 1388 at Monmouth the windings of the Monnow, and of Time, offer further warlike embellishments. They present a round Norman keep at Skenfrith, the keep with adjacent thirteenth-century ruins at Grosmont, and a moated White Castle remarkably preserved 6 miles inland from the river. Each lovely and away from beaten tracks, these units in a triangular system of Border defence give little hint of past hurryings and scurryings. Only in fancy can be pictured Henry III personally in charge at Grosmont, the surprise attack launched on him by Llewelyn ap Iorwerth at night, warriors minus clothes stampeding into the darkness, and a probable quick exit of Queen Eleanor covered only with the medieval equivalent of a Burberry, for of course early-English ladies, even if French, did not favour nightdresses or pyjamas.

Castles again are framed in the River Usk's settings. Running fresh from the mountains, the stream sweeps and curls grandly through its vale, brightens Llanover, Llanbaddock bridge, and other joyous spots, passes the Went Wood ridges and reaches Roman *Isca* at Caerleon. Abergavenny's ruined walls and towers and the pretty town of Usk with its keep and gateway figuring in the ruins, each offer old stonework suitable for pictures or for souls with a romantic tilt. William de Braose, a most horrible knight, furnished at least one appropriate episode at Abergavenny when he invited seventy Welsh warriors to dinner and had all of them murdered after the coffee and liquors. No such misfortune is likely to occur in Usk to-day. Historic and charming, the town amply compensates for any stains on hospitality in the past by affording comfort without murder and much more than safety in food at the *Three Salmons* hotel. More castles and signs of perils and surprises appear towards the Severn estuary in the neighbourhood of Roman conquest at Caerleon and Caerwent. Penhow Castle occupies a hilltop; the early walls, round tower, and fourteenth-century gatehouse at Caldicot make a memorable group; and houses near and far, as at the Bishop's Palace, Mathern, and Moynes Court (76), show that the old inhabitants felt most comfortable when behind gatehouses and fortifications. Even Llanthony Priory, wonderfully situated in the Honddu valley of the Black Mountains, is more piquant with the romance of strife than of holiness (70). Built by Augustinians in the first half of the twelfth century with the powerful de Lacy's money, and at a site thrice blessed with traditions of St. David of Wales, a hermit's cell, and a church of 1113, "savages, thieves, vaga-bonds," weather and wolves soon made things either too hot or too cold for prayer, meditation, or praise. Rather than be doomed to purgatory before it was due, the monks flitted from the Honddu (black water) to Gloucester, left their temple to go to ruin. Early in the nineteenth century it became an un-fortunate plaything for Walter Savage Landor, who in due season flitted also. Now you can settle inside upstanding leavings of the monks and perhaps feel quite as romantic as Geoffrey of Monmouth in surroundings that surely are unequalled by any other hotel in the land. You live in the prior's own quarters, go out to fish, scale Hay Bluff and the mountains, wander away to find de Lacy's castle at Longtown just in Herefordshire and the fifteenth-century rood loft at Partrishow church. At night, without being modernized by thoughts of bathrooms, you wind up the circular stone stairway, stepping in correct transitional Norman–Early English style. And so to bed, to wing afar from these dull times into dreamlands, chivalry's own, romantic with Queens of Love and Beauty, fields or, plumes waving argent and gules, and proper charges of fierce warriors, villains, dragons, wolves, and heavily armoured knights tumbling off hefty horses. Whatever Augustinians and W. S. Landor may have thought of Llanthony Priory, I call it a charmer.

My space, like Time, flies. Reluctantly I must leave the mountains, the rivers, the rural scenes and the grand scenes of these Monmouthshire lands, telling of much more than pillage by Lords Marchers and onslaughts by Welshmen. The Wye, guiding to Gloucestershire again, cannot be praised afresh; it is Richard Wilson's "River Wye," Turner's "River Wye," Wordsworth's "Sylvan Wye," the river of countless pictures and innumerable books, the famous valley for the charabancs and motor cars, yet still continuing sublime and perfect. Hastening on I pass Tintern (76), the Wyndcliff (here the wind cost me one hat while drawing for p. 81), Chepstow, and reach the camp at Sud-brook where the conquering Roman general, Julius Frontinus, is supposed to

RIVER WYE FROM WYNDCLIFF *and overlooking Chepstow,*
the Wye and Severn confluence, and distant Cotswold Hills.

New Inn
Teatime
Three Choirs Festival
Sept 1947

Sydney R.
Jones

Timbering in
SOUTHGATE St.
House of Robert Raikes

15th century
Angle Post
New Inn

GLOUCESTER

have sat after crossing the New Passage nearly 2,000 years before I sat there myself, to construct a picture of a new Severn Bridge which threatens to desecrate the watery landscape. A dive through the Severn Tunnel and my arrival under the trees on College Green permits me to introduce—Bristol.

Contrasts Bristol certainly offers after the country pictures, broken-down castles and deserted monks' quarters of Monmouthshire. Here is the romance, if any, of modern times in exchange for our recent encounters with ruins. Situated close to the River Severn, the estuary, the Cotswolds, and glorious Somerset, it is well placed for living in or getting out of. Being very big, this is the first centre of commerce and industry that we have met as yet in our wanderings through western England. It savours of both the land and the sea; you can stand on pavements or look out of factory windows and see ships. Streets are busy, packed, full of hair-breadth escapes from motors; and commotion, noise, a fine high tower of a new university, a cathedral half modern, factories in view, and a hundred sights give lively impressions of a city right on the mark and up to date, the embodiment of that peculiar, illusive, and often very unsatisfactory quality called progress. Bristol kept in the vanguard of progress for centuries. Merchants, explorers, sieges, riots, wars, politics, and a constant lookout from presents into futures helped movement forward. Thus Bristol rose to be the second city in England during the seventeenth and eighteenth centuries. When steamships were born Bristol founded a new era with the first regular service to America. Railways developed, so Bristol produced the biggest goods shed in the world. Much earlier, before William the Conqueror arrived or Britons had learned to sing *Rule, Britannia*, Bristol held foremost fame for being the principal slave market in England. Much later, even in the 1940's, Bristol East sent a Chancellor of the Exchequer to Westminster to improve on the pre-Conquest idea by manufacturing Britons into slaves out of the azure main while singing *Rule, Britannia*. Such happenings and notable records during a very long time certainly entitle Bristol to its pride for progress.

Bristol does not suggest, as many old towns do, an ancient dependence on royal, feudal, or ecclesiastical privilege. Two rivers, the sea, and trading made the city. Its character was developed by people of commerce and enterprise who knew how to act, get things done, to adventure and prosper, and who found time and means for piety, charity, and culture. Before the German raids this city and port, with buildings old and new ringed by a group of fine churches, reminded me most of the City of London, itself a growth of trade and settled by the river leading to the oceans of promise.

Though merchants and trade ruled in Bristol, footholds of aristocratic overlords and the monks accounted for a castle and a monastery. The castle ended with Cromwell's order for demolition after the memorable Civil War siege. Relics exposed by German bombs and the name of Castle Street are the inglorious reminders of the Conquest stronghold that was rebuilt in the twelfth century by Queen Matilda's half-brother, Robert, Earl of Gloucester, and used by the queen for keeping King Stephen quiet while chained round the feet in a dungeon. Books on the brave old days explain how Robert also got himself into a similar uncomfortable position and thus enabled the king to regain the use of his legs and walk on to his throne again.

Works built by the monks fared somewhat better than those made by the feudal lords. Although another destroyer, Henry VIII, finished off the monastery when he turned the abbey church into a cathedral in June 1542, ancient beauty has survived from the great Augustinian foundation of Robert Fitzhardinge, first Lord of Berkeley, which began to shape in 1140 on the border of College Green at the traditional place of St. Augustine's preaching in *circa* 602 (62). Before the Tudor plunderers appeared the Norman great gateway had been rebuilt in 1515 and a demolished nave awaited reconstruction. Thereafter time and circumstance dealt hard knocks to the cathedral and precincts. From the Dissolution until the nineteenth century the church remained without a nave. Reform rioters, Bristol's harbingers of progress, wrecked the bishop's palace in 1831, but failed to reduce the cathedral. Gothic revivalists duly arrived. G. E. Street designed the nave and western front for completion in 1868 and J. L. Pearson reconstructed the bulky central tower in 1892. These and other alarums completed, memorials of monkish years and the prime time of English art survived in the choir, chapels, transepts and chapter house. Beauties now displayed particularly include the Elder Lady Chapel of about 1200, the four-teenth-century Berkeley and Newton Chapels, fifteenth-century transept roofs rich in carved bosses, canopied tombs, with the one to Abbot Newland, very splendid. The chapter house, with vaulting, arcades, and surface patterning, is one of the most impressive late-Norman interiors in the land. Very ingenious, and not to be seen elsewhere in England, are the arrangements of stone arches, beams, and spandrels in the choir aisles. Here is evident the bold originality of the progressive school of Bristol masons. Though these features may be more notable for novelty than beauty, they do show the birth of an idea, one that is found fully developed in the choir of Gloucester Cathedral.

Through the ups and downs of early castled and monastic years the townsfolk reigned top dogs. Neither wars and rebellions, very severe devastations from the Black Death, nor whiffles of other sorts quelled the people's progressive spirit and independence. When necessary, as in 1312, they ran a siege on their own account. Their ships sailed the seas, carried the English wool, fought in the wars of Plantagenet kings, and for services rendered to Edward III Bristol was created a self-contained county in 1373. A hundred years later legends and rumours stirred these dwellers by the Avon Gorge. They dreamed of a golden West. John Jay's two ships set out in 1480. John Cabot followed in 1497. They led the way for adventurers and explorers to scour uncharted oceans. The Armada threatened, so Bristol ships fought for Queen Elizabeth as they had done for Plantagenets and were destined to do for the hero of Trafalgar. While merchants and seamen, their foresight, commerce, and hard work continuously brightened national glory and local fame from century to century, Bristol developed into a place of close-packed streets on the peninsula formed by the River Avon and a new channel cut for the River Frome in the early days. A bridge led over the water to Redcliffe. Tall masts at the quays meant prosperity and enterprise, and ships safely in port savoured the native air with a fragrance of distant lands. Many churches enriched by merchants graced the scenes below the downs. Merchant venturers, coopers, cutlers, and the good companions of various guilds met in their halls; no doubt they mixed business with jolly times and Bristol milk, then a convivial kind of punch inspired by the West Indies trade. The fruits of individual effort and adventure in active life prompted kind thoughts and deeds. Hospitals, almshouses, and other quarters were created and endowed for the sweet advancement of charity, education, the arts, and citizenship. Thus the people advanced the place and purpose of their home town, made it of importance second only to London. Events, like years, pointed forward. Bristol marched with times on the move. The *Great Western* forged new links with America in 1838 by starting the first steamship service across the Atlantic. Docks expanded, the railways came, the Suspension Bridge begun by Brunel was completed. The *Greyhound* and numerous coaching inns changed tactics, and the *Royal Western* hotel on College Green boldly informed all and sundry, "Omnibus to and from every train. R. P. Ham, Proprietor, Turtle and Wine Merchant." Modern Bristol developed and spread in size if not in beauty. Industries grew and multiplied. The name of the ancient and ever-new city went round the world on chocolate boxes, cigarette cards, motor vehicles, aircraft, and a hundred and one big and little products carried to the ends of the earth from the docks on the Avon. The year 1940 brought a new kind of interlude. During thirty raids Hitler's bombs churned up signs of past and present. Much remained steadfast. Representatives of the early lights, the lords spiritual and lords temporal, retained position, and the real makers of the city, trade and worldly enterprise, carried on. The monastery-cum-cathedral therefore stands. Castle relics are on view again. A progressive municipality forges ahead with all latest developments in welfare; and a civic restaurant, in which I observed fish and chips in great favour for tea, daily operates a parable of loaves and fishes, But the busy scenes, the general alertness, and gaunt gaps made by the German raids hardly imply the glamour of those far-off years that made Bristol.

Sitting under the trees on College Green, an oasis in the middle of noise and hurrying, it may be pleasant now and then to get back a bit; to fancy, for instance, the year 1756 transported from the first chapter of *The Virginians* and alive again with Mr. Trail, merchant, large and grave, Harry Warrington in mourning, their talk on negro slaves, and all the vividness of Thackeray's picture of Bristol on that summer morning when the *Young Rachael*, Virginian ship, came up the Avon on her return from the Potomac with Edward Franks captain, in charge, who invented the wonderful advertisement for W. D. and H. O. Wills when he said, "There's no sweeter tobacco comes from Virginia, and no better brand than the Three Castles." Mr. Pepys may help a more distant mental flight and with facts rather than fancies garnered onward from 2 p.m. on June 13, 1668, after being "parboiled," dried, and sweated in Bath at four o'clock in the morning. Thus fortified, he decided that Bristol was "in every respect another London." He saw where the merchants met in Corn Street "and a fine cross yet standing, like Cheapside" (since counterfeited on College Green). He walked through Marsh Street (now drab with garages and a waterworks department), visited the "most large and noble quay," inspected "the new ship building by Bally" (a naval architect of the time). "No carts, only dog-carts" in the streets recalls the fact that horse-drawn vehicles were prohibited for about three centuries because their iron tires damaged the street paving. Deb's uncle, "very good company," pleased him mightily, and the merchant's "good entertainment of strawberries, a whole venison-pasty cold, and plenty of brave wine, and above all Bristol milk" evidentally cheered the cockles of the Pepysian heart.

Charming times! Still they dimly echo in streets, byways, and quiet corners on the flats and up the slopes. You can dodge about in the traffic, at the same time see quays, water and ships, and easily twist a thought back to wooden bulwarks, spreading mainyards, "argosies of magic sails." Broad Quay expands wide in centuries of fame, peopled with visions of John and Sebastian Cabot looking to the promised west, Martin Pring bent on discovering a landing-place for Pilgrim Fathers, Admiral Penn's son finally destined for Pennsylvania. Stones, bricks, mortar, and dirt are telltales for stages in long development. Courts (Dusty Foot and Pie Poudre are good names for two of them) and narrow streets that have survived efforts for destruction by municipal authorities and Hitler preserve the lines of the packed and close planning mentioned in medieval records. Christmas Steps—a quaint bit—show the "steppering" done in 1669. Development beyond the city walls produced King Street at the restoration of King Charles, the spacious quadrangle of Queen Square fixes a building line for the reign of Queen Anne, terraces above the Avon at Clifton mark the outward stride for Bristolians and fashionable spa visitors in Georgian and Regency years.

Progress and the recent raids have not helped to preserve original works

THE CHELTENHAM VALE *and distant line
of the Malvern Hills from Upper Dowdeswell.*

GLOUCESTER. *The fifteenth-century tower, finished with pierced masonry of*
splendour in choir and Lady Chapel, Norman piers in the nave, the shrine of Edwa
the city preserve the Roman plan and old buildings show a

"Gloucester coronet," predominates in the vale below Cotswold Hills. Perpendicular
and the finest cloisters in England are among the riches of the cathedral. Street lines in
of medieval stonework, timbering, gables and Georgian fronts.

TEWKESBURY

A group at King John's Bridge. Many old houses line picturesque streets leading to the abbey church, celebrated for the Norman tower and west front, tombs and chantry chapels. The battle here in 1471 ended the Wars of the Roses.

created after the fashion usual in old English towns. Survivors include the eighteenth-century façade of Coopers' Hall; an open timbered roof of the Cutler's Hall in Rosemary Street; the Exchange well designed by John Wood of Bath and amplified on the pavement outside by curious posts dated 1594, 1625, 1631, known as "nails" and used by merchants for settling bargains "on the nail." Oldest institutions of their kind in England are the Library, patronized by Wordsworth, Coleridge, and Southey and built in the local classic style pre-eminent in Bath, and the Theatre Royal of 1766. The home and domestic front has its reminders of fashion and period. There are the notable Regency and Georgian terraces and crescents at Clifton (61), sedate white walls with cornices in Berkeley Square, Queen Anne houses in Queen Square. No. 6 King Street leads the fine series of doorways with shell hoods. Excellent Georgian rooms and fittings are open for all to see at No. 7 Great George Street, the house in which Wordsworth first met Coleridge. The homebred earlier manner of beam, oriel and gable has a showpiece in the timbering of 1664, which includes *Llandoger Trow*, the inn with the strange name derived from Llandoger, in Monmouthshire, and trow, a type of boat sailed long ago by a nautical landlord. Older still are the remarkable pavings of tiles removed from the Canynges house and now in the British Museum, proofs that the homes of great merchants did not lack beauty and luxuriance in the fifteenth century.

Churches: they have held their places well enough to suggest the towered scenes that were the city's pride when nineteen of them stood within the walls and ringed the space with high masonry and joyful chimes. Loveliest of all rises the great collegiate Church of St. Mary Redcliffe, spired over the city and the docks, an emblem of faith for both (63). Choir, transepts, nave, and porches extend in a noble design; arcades, clerestories, and vaults soar to lofty heights, and traceries, pierced parapets, flying-buttresses, and pinnacles unite in the resplendent harmony born of the late Gothic time. It is a true expression of the merchants, a memorial to the Canynges family and their fellow citizens, who determined to have and to pay for the best that money could buy. The spire collapsed in a storm soon after completion and awaited the nineteenth century for renewal, but the splendour seen and praised by Queen Elizabeth remained and has continued in this "fayrest and most famous parish church." Memorials inside, puppets and properties of old tales, commemorate priests, knights, sailors, soldiers; the Medes, the Jays, and the prolific offspring they could afford to have in the fifteenth century join with the company of merchants that added lustre to their own years and church. Thoughtful, blest by angels, lies William Canynges, the merchant prince of his day, patron of this architecture at St. Mary's and with enough spare cash to entertain a luxurious Edward IV, himself a fellow merchant in wool. The brass face of Joan Brook looks outward, raises but never solves the enigma on the origin of America's name; for of

Joan
dau. of Richard Amerycke
Sheriff of Bristol

from
the Amerycke brass
St. Mary Redcliffe

course a few old Englanders and all New Englanders know that the living Joan was daughter of Richard Amerycke, Sheriff of Bristol and John Cabot's friend. Memorials such as these, screened from outside noise and visible in the dim religious light of church after church, perhaps best of all afford the liveliest commentary on the years and the spirit of Bristol's great past. They represent the actual people who traded, adventured, brightened the fame of their city, added passages to England's far-flung story; men who did very well for themselves (and others) and went inside churches pretty often to offer prayer, praise, and thanksgiving for benefits received (and expected). Among this crowd of silent figures are Martin Pring, most admirable and impudent of navigators, and George Snygoe at full length in a furred robe, both at St. Stephen's; Edward Colston, grand old benefactor fresh from the hand of Rysbrack at All Saints; Henry Gibbes in the skull-and-hourglass fashion at St. James's; John Whitson at St. Nicholas's, famed for naming Whitson Bay, Massachusetts, in 1603; John Aldworth, clad in scarlet at the Lord Mayor's chapel of St. Mark's. Knights, mayors, aldermen, merchants, seamen, even the Canynges's cook, all are there cut in stone and brass. You can go close up to them, look into their characterful faces, see how they dressed, study the arms they bore, and feel all the fresher for a breath of valiant times that neither knew nor desired safety first from the cradle to the grave.

Away from sepulchral gloom and facing the four winds of heaven the Cabot Tower stands high in elevation and fame on Brandon Hill. It commands a range of towers, spires, chimney-pots, factories, miles of green England, silvery streaks of water. The structure is not particularly beautiful nor older than the year 1898. Even so, a very noble tower is this. Placed high for all to see, it symbolizes dreams, memories, the spirit of a city whose pioneers began to make the English tongue a language of the world. A penny-in-the-slot fitting and a lift will raise sightseers up to the top. There, if the earth were not round and human eyes could see better than they do, the United States and Canada might be discerned far away in the west.

Neither tower, tablet, nor flourish commemorate Bristol's first brave attempt in 1480 to conquer the West. John Jay's two little ships, the *George* and the *Trinity*, piloted by Thomas Lloyd, then "the most scientific mariner of all England," sailed the uncharted Atlantic and failed to reach their goal, a legendary "Isle of Brasile." They gathered little glory and no medals. But they went not in vain. The spirit of hazardous exploration, already astir, was quickened. What happened seventeen years later every schoolboy knows; and some oldsters remember that John Cabot, the Venetian, settled in Bristol, made a friend of Richard Amerycke, the Sheriff, obtained letters patent from the King for himself and "his sonneys" to sail for the discovery of islands and countries then unknown "to all christians," left Broad Quay in the *Matthew*, manned by an English crew, discovered new-found lands in North America, and on St. John's Day, June 24, 1497, a year before Christopher Columbus discovered the South American mainland, John Cabot unfurled the Royal banner on Cape Breton Island and "took possession in the name of King Henry VII." This feat of tremendous promise brought Cabot a reward of £10 from the King and a pension of £20. The second voyage, more discoveries, a safe return in the autumn of 1498, then death removed the brave adventurer from the stage of worldly history. Better than the cash reward and pension is John Cabot's credit in perpetuity, brightly kept on Brandon Hill and at Cabot Straits leading to the Gulf of St. Lawrence.

On a September day after the close of this last world war I walked to the base of the Cabot Tower and there met two strangers, a pretty girl dressed in blue, evidently English, and an officer from overseas. We talked together, admired the views. Then I said, "You can see even more from the top of the tower and the lift will take you up."

"Fine," answered the man. "We'll go."

He looked through his cash without finding coppers for the penny-in-the-slot, asked me to change a shilling; I couldn't, so gave my only pennies, for which he offered the shilling.

"No thank you," I said. "This is my privilege. If we happen to meet in New York we'll make up the change there!"

"Do you think I come from Noo York?" he asked laughingly.

The enormity of my military crime at once was obvious on noticing that he wore the uniform of a Canadian officer. "Well," I added apologetically, "in Toronto, Montreal, or wherever it may be."

He laughed again, the girl smiled roguishly, click went the pennies into the slot. With a mutual, "Until the next time," they disappeared upwards. I went downward to find the relics of the fort, defences of Bristol during the sieges of 1643 and 1645. "Halloo! halloo!" and words shouted down made me look up. The words were lost on the wind, but two figures on the tower, clear against the sky, waved again and again. I hallooed and waved in return, then finally descended the hill. With a last look back I saw the pair up aloft, lit by the western sun and faced towards the Atlantic. "A very pretty picture and an emblem," I thought. "Charming young England and brave young Canada, just suited for an Atlantis up-to-date and not according to Plato or Bacon. Perhaps they are engaged, maybe just married, and bound for a united adventure. Wouldn't old John Cabot have loved to see them, 450 years after his own adventure!"

Northward from Bristol level and wide landscapes border the Severn leading to Gloucester below the southern and best wooded scarps of the Cotswolds. Villages look snug with thatching, timbering, warm-coloured brickwork, and tiled roofs. Grouped round church towers and manor-houses, they give the local type of rustic pictures that continue through Gloucestershire to Shakespeare's land and Worcestershire. Black and white and the thatching at Frampton-upon-Severn are wonderfully set off by the long and wide green— Rosamond's Green by name, one of England's biggest. Slimbridge, a traditional birthplace for William Tyndale, has the old cider mills, tools of time-honoured industry which remind of being in the apple and orchard country. Thornbury and Berkeley, each picturesque with a splendid church and a castle, and both creepy through murderous associations, keep the flame of history lurid. Tudor battlements, bays, oriels, and moulded brick chimneys at Thornbury, begun in 1511 by Edward Stafford, third Duke of Buckingham, localize a noble work never finished because the duke provided the farewell speech for Act II in *King Henry VIII* and expired on the block at the Tower in 1521. The embattled and buttressed pile pierced with squint-holes seen from the meadows at Berkeley is proper material to shake up notions on chivalry or bloodthirsty crimes of a long time ago; quite enough to send shudders down anybody's back is the knowledge that these fourteenth-century walls screen Fitzhardinge's Norman tower and the place of Edward II's murder in 1327, where shrieks broke the stillness of a September night and Bristol citizens came on the morrow to view the distorted face of a King of England who had refused to be bullied, starved, or tortured to death.

Travelling in the footsteps of Abbot Thokey we next reach Gloucester and see one result of this murder at Berkeley. John Thokey ruled in Gloucester's Benedictine abbey church of St. Peter, a rebuilding begun in 1089 and now partly visible in the strong Norman design of the nave. The abbot was loyal and apparently cute. More than once he entertained Edward II at the abbey. One day, when the king mentioned the absence of his own painted portrait in

MAXSTOKE CASTLE, *a moated fortified home begun by William de Clinton in 1345 and still inhabited. Two Kings of England slept here; Richard III on his way to Bosworth Field and Henry VII on the night after the battle.*

GRIMSHAW HALL, *probably the finest timbered hall of the sixteenth century in the Forest of Arden country.*

Ford's Hospital founded 1529

Bablake Hospital founded 1506

Priory Row

S R S

Palace Yard

COVENTRY. *Notes made before the war raids.*

STONELEIGH ABBEY. *The classic frontage of 1704–20 adjoins remains of the Cistercian abbe*
King Charles stayed in the older rooms with the loyal Leighs at the opening of the Civil War in 16

the hall where they dined, the abbot replied that his royal master's features should adorn a more distinguished position—as in fact they did, though for reasons then never dreamed of by the speakers. The murder at Berkeley accomplished, followed by refusal from the monks of Bristol and Malmesbury to bury the remains of an unpopular and deposed king in their abbeys, loyal Thokey himself fetched the body "from Berkeley Castle in his own chariot" and with procession and solemnity buried it "in the north aisle, hard by the high altar." During 1329–34 the abbot's earlier wish came true. Edward II, in the alabaster effigy of death, occupied a place of honour by the high altar; sublime in repose the figure still sheds royal dignity with features finely tooled and enclosed in a canopy of pinnacles richly carved in Caen stone. Time and popular feeling quickly elevated the murdered king to martyr and saint. The relics were thought to work miracles. Pilgrims flocked to the shrine. Wealth thus accumulated enabled the great reconstruction to proceed on the eastern Norman fabric. The Severn masons advanced their experiments made at Bristol. They developed the transepts, achieved the choir lit by the immense and superb east window, memorial to Edward III's victory at Crécy. Thought and execution brought the spaciousness, the brilliant lighting; high vertical lines to piers and mullions, windows of many lights cut by transoms, surface panelling lightly worked in stone, urged fine architecture forward into the revolution of the Perpendicular style. Fan-vaulting and pierced screens in the cloisters, unsurpassed in the world, led the way for similar triumphs elsewhere. Onward from 1450 the central tower rose predominant over the composition, elevated 225 feet high and crowned with the pierced parapets and pinnacles of the famous "Gloucester coronet." Late to arrive, the detached lady chapel and the gallery-bridge set the seal of delicate grace on this grand scheme in 1500. Glory accumulated in chapels, screens, tombs, stalls, misericords, and the marvels of stone, wood, metal, and glass, carving and imagery that have been described again and again since Henry VIII turned the Benedictine abbey into a cathedral of the new foundation on January 4, 1540.

Stone gateways and curious exits lead from the spiritual calm of the close to the twentieth-century air and crowded pavements of the secular capital of Gloucestershire. Here are pleasant and lively mixtures of the old and the new. Northgate, Southgate, Eastgate, and Westgate Streets follow the exact lines planned by the Romans for *Glevum*. At their crossing the curfew bell in the old tower of St. Nicholas still tolls the knell of parting day. A lot of church towers, medieval masonry, timber framing and Georgian brickwork keep their places shoulder to shoulder with modern erections, areas of plate glass, and an outer fringe of those skimpy little houses in which happy people now enjoy life. The charming local burr is heard spoken in the streets, though not by the nobs who patronize the collection of good shops and county doings; and of the city's good days, which are many, those of the Three Choirs Festivals cannot be bettered for music, grand effects, and human sights. Things of the old order include remnants left by the Black Friars, the Grey Friars, and the monks who removed from Llanthony. The Robert Raikes house (82) faces the Crypt Grammar School of 1539. Timbers and good wooden windows overhang at the house in which Bishop Hooper lodged on the night before his martyrdom in 1555. More interesting buildings of various shapes and periods reward the seeker in this ancient place that accommodated William the Conqueror when he issued orders for compiling Domesday Book. The *Fleece*, with a courtyard and vaulted cellars, the *Bull*, *King's Head*, *Leather Bottle*, and *Greyhound* are samples from the nice collection of names for hospitable institutions. As for the *New Inn*, this is one of the oldest and finest survivors of the ancient type and one of the jolliest providers for modern days in all England. It has a gorgeous fifteenth-century angle post outside, an inside courtyard introduced by the archway (82); there are snug rooms to eat in, the courtyard gallery for going to bed and perhaps finding a wrong bedroom in Pickwickian style, and the general mellow atmosphere can make one feel either Johnsonian or Elizabethan, or just as cobwebby and medieval as John Twynning, the monk, to whom the foundation is traditionally ascribed. The city is difficult to see whole because it lies in the flat vale. The top of a tower or something high, such as I found, can be handy for spying down to discover wonderful and unexpected groupings (88–89). More distant compositions seen from the Severn meadows show the cathedral's tower, clerestory and broken roofline soaring above clusters of domestic roofs, calling to mind Peter de Wint's picture painted in 1840.

The end of this chapter brings me to the river and valley country from Gloucester up to Tewkesbury, the beginning of the noble vale that sweeps away between the Malvern and Bredon Hills into the heart of the south Midlands. A fertile and well-tilled countryside, and the buildings on it, give the quality of more to follow in our course northward. Pretty villages have pretty names—Stoke Orchard and Woolstone are two samples. Cottages and houses show the black-and-white and the red brick constructed and grouped in the homely Midland manner. Upleadon introduces one of the church towers built of half-timber, and at Hartpury begins the series of tithe barns conspicuous for great length. Pauntley old court, dovecote, and church are London-ish with fourteenth-century associations of Sir William Whittington and his son, the real but not fabulous Dick. A spirit of longer ago still haunts the Saxon church and chapel in quiet meadows by the stream at Deerhurst; it is no ordinary experience to see the walls undoubtedly used by St. Alphaege for worship, to be in this place of pre-Conquest times, to recall an abbey's thousand years of romantic vicissitudes which came to an end when George Throgmorton obtained the buildings and the tithes at the Dissolution. Two towns hereabout represent a small and a large one. Newent, little, historic, and surrounded with bloom in spring, marshals itself round the spired old church and timbered market hall. Cheltenham, big, clothes its own piece of the vale below the Cotswolds and in sight of the Malverns (87). Those who like the stucco and verandah grace overflowed from the age of elegance will find the correct doses in this early example of a garden town; the delicate combination of Promenade, Regency terraces, Papworth's villas architected for Lord Sherborne, tree-lined avenues and gardens, now gracious in maturity, may stir a thought for old tunes and gaieties, Byron and celebrities, "Indian" settlers conscious of livers, and the fashion that flocked to the spa after George III drank the waters in 1788, benefited his inside, and caused the town to rival Bath.

Lastly Tewkesbury, rare old Tewkesbury, where Severn and Avon meet and dozens of artists could fill dozens of sketch-books. Everything is here—beauty, history, memories, river and waterside, King John's Bridge (90), picturesque inns, streets of timbered houses and tall brick fronts. For thoughts and emotions beyond the scope of words there is the abbey church, its Norman tower, western arch, vaults miraculously poised, the flowering of architectural styles as at Gloucester, the marvellous chantries, perfect carving in miniature, old glass in the Despencer windows. But I must tear myself away from my beloved, as we are overdue for Warwickshire. Merely can be mentioned the *Black Bear* under the sign of the house of Warwick, the *Berkeley Arms*, *Wheatsheaf*, Clarence House and Cross House in the specimens of timber and plaster of the sixteenth century and pre-Cromwellian period; the half-timbered *Bell* for "Abel Fletcher's home" in *John Halifax, Gentleman*, the *Hop Pole* for Mr. Pickwick's dinner, "Thick as Tewkesbury mustard" from Shakespeare; and my inadequate words on a treasured English town end with a homily for my readers, painted in medieval lettering on plaster behind a High Street frontage,

> Three thinges pleseth booeth God and Man. Concorde Be twene bretheren Amytie betwene nayghbowers : And A man and his wyfe that agreeth well to gether.

3. THE MIDDLE OF ENGLAND

WARWICKSHIRE, WORCESTERSHIRE, HEREFORDSHIRE, SHROPSHIRE

Mapped below, this is an ideal land for oaks and glades, leafy lanes, elms and orchard trees. Footpath ways to jog on, and the intimate scenes characteristic of the Midlands, we like to think bred and helped to make Shakespeare. The Midland Plain meets the noble vales expanded round the Avon and Severn rivers. Clee Hills and Wenlock Edge, leading to the rugged heights of the Marches, divide the vales of Hereford and north Shropshire. From Warwick to Worcester, Hereford and Shrewsbury buildings show this area to be chiefly on sandstone. It is also a great district for seeing past timber construction; names of Arden, Wyre Forest, and the general woodiness explain why. Henley-in-Arden, Evesham, Ledbury, and Ludlow are samples of the lovely old towns, and scores of villages are so pretty that explorers may wish to stay in them for ever. One reminder of early days is the straight line of the Fosse Way across Warwickshire. Watling Street and Wroxeter stand notably for Roman years. Offchurch, and Offa's Dyke suggest being in ancient Mercia. The crop of castles, war sites from Edge Hill to Battlefield, monastic relics, two cathedrals, moated houses, mansions in parks, and expressive architecture typify the human motions and ideas that constantly stirred at this heart of England.

WARWICK. *Beauchamp Chapel, the glory of St. Mary's Church completed in* 1464. *The superb tomb and effigy of Richard Beauchamp, Earl of Warwick, occupies the centre, and an ornate Elizabethan memorial commemorates Robert Dudley, Earl of Leicester.*

ASHOW. A scene in the Stoneleigh Abbey domain near to Leamington.

LEEK WOOTTON (page opposite). "The Skylark," a study in the upper Avon country.

WARWICK CASTLE. *Cæsar's tower built by the first Thomas Beauchamp about 1360. The castle, developed round a Norman mound above the River Avon, was successively held by the Beauchamps, the Nevilles, and the Grevilles. It is one of the great monuments of chivalrous splendour that remains habitable to this day.*

WARWICK. *The Leycester Hospital, an ancient foundation re-established by Queen Elizabeth's favourite, Robert Dudley, Earl of Leicester. It then became what it is now, a home for pensioners under the badge of the Bear and Ragged Staff.*

STRATFORD-ON-AVON. *The Birthplace in Henley Street associated with the birth of William Shakespeare on 23rd April, 1564. With its museum and garden, one of the most famous goals for pilgrims in the world.*

STRATFORD-ON-AVON. *Holy Trinity Church on the riverside, Shakespeare's last home in 1616. This celebrated building is distinguished for thirteenth-, fourteenth-, and fifteenth-century architecture, chapels, tombs, and the modern screen. The graceful spire, erected in the eighteenth century, replaced a timber steeple.*

WORCESTER. *The cathedral, much restored throughout,*
window between turrets distinguishes the west front design, a
dicular features. "The Faithful City," true to the Royal

Sydney R Jones
Worcester.

*fully on the bank of the River Severn. A vast Geometrical
us tower of circa 1365–74 is the earliest of these great Perpen-
Cromwell in his "crowning mercy" on September 3rd, 1651.*

STRATFORD-ON-AVON. *Harvard House of Shakespeare's time adjoins the*
Garrick Inn. The elaborate timberwork was built in 1596 for Rogers, the
Stratford alderman. His daughter Katherine married Robert Harvard, and
Harvard University in America is a perpetual memorial to their son John.

SHOTTERY. *Anne Hathaway's Cottage, the most visited cottage in England and once the home of the bride who married Shakespeare by licence when he was eighteen. This characteristic specimen of Warwickshire rural building, its contents and garden are perfectly maintained by the Shakespeare Trustees.*

III

KENILWORTH CASTLE. The keep (centre), the beautiful fourteenth-century hall (left), Leicester's Elizabethan buildings (right), and site of the great lake in foreground. Cromwellians ruined the castle. No ruins in England are richer in associations with the great names of English history. These extensive remains stir memories of kings, queens, de Clintons, de Montfort, John of Gaunt, Robert Dudley, and the Wizard of the North, Sir Walter Scott

THE VALE OF EVESHAM, *a land of rich cultivation, old fame and beauty. A view over Offenham, Evesham, and extended to Bredon Hill.*

EVESHAM. *The most conspicuous reminder of one of the mightiest medieval abbeys, founded on Avon bank about 702 and once the shrine of Simon de Montfort. The Bell Tower belongs to the brilliant years of tower design in the Perpendicular period and was still incomplete at the Dissolution in 1539.*

COMPTON WYNYATES. *The moated home of the Comptons and the Spencers, one of the finest Tudor examples in England, has remained practically unaltered since the reign of Henry VIII. The name is derived from the vineyard that once existed there.*

ABBOT'S SALFORD, *an Elizabethan Roman Catholic home that came to the Eyston family, descendants of Sir Thomas More. It is full of surprises in panelled rooms, a long gallery, odd staircases, a hiding-hole, and additions of different periods.*

CLEEVE PRIOR. *One of the many picturesque villages in the River Avon borders below Stratford. Cleeve has a good church, farms and cottages of timbering and stone, the old King's Arms, and a manor-house framed in clipped yews.*

LONG MARSTON

HILLBOROUGH. *Pigeon-house*

PEBWORTH CHURCH *with dormer windows*

BIDFORD Bridge

S.R.J.

IN THE SHAKESPEARE VILLAGES

Piping Pebworth, Dancing Marston,
Haunted Hillborough, Hungry Grafton,
Dodging Exhall, Papist Wixford,
Beggarly Broom, and Drunken Bidford.

117

WICKHAMFORD, *one in the series of pretty villages near Bredon Hill.
Penelope Washington lived in this manor-house and her memorial in the
neighbouring church shows the stars and stripes of the Washington Coat of arms.*

OFFENHAM, *traditionally associated with King Offa,
and now in the centre of market-gardening and orchards.*

SHAKESPEARE'S COUNTY

Warwickshire has been so prettily made by God and man and so often written of, it is difficult for me to decide on a point for opening this page or to think of anything that has not been stated before on the county which is sometimes presented as the private property of William Shakespeare with an entail on his name for ever. Yet my beginning must be made somewhere; so I will imagine myself where I have often sat, under the Shakespeare Oak, gnarled and bent over the River Avon in Stoneleigh Deer Park. Nobody can say with certainty that Shakespeare ever saw it. Only foolish people own this truth. For wiser folk the truth about the oak is just as you like it. It even may be the very tree used by Orlando when billposter of rhyme to Rosalind,

> Hang there, my verse, in witness of my love.

Shakespearean or not, the tree serves very well for a starting-point into one of the most wooded of English shires. It stands at the heart of England. A few miles away are the Lillington Oak and the archery turf of the Woodmen of Arden at Meriden, each claiming to be the centre of our island, whose irregular shape could not possibly have a fixed middle. Approximately central, and appropriately so, the Forest of Arden extended. Not very definite in boundaries, it seems to have spread over most of Warwickshire north of the River Avon, but not quite so far distant as Michael Drayton poetically fancied,

> Her one hand touching Trent, the other, Severn's side.

In other ways the Forest had no limits. It set no bounds of space or time for romance, love-making, deeds aboveboard and below, and the frolics and mysteries of life adapted to shades under the greenwood trees. We know that a banished duke, "his co-mates and brothers in exile," Touchstone the clown and Phebe the shepherdess did very well here and found the uses of adversity sweet. When required the Forest could produce ragged staffs for bears to maul; a particular one was embellished for the Black Dog of Arden when he proved to be one too many for Piers Gaveston at Blacklow Hill in 1312. Another aspect of the Forest's usefulness, dated just over a century ago, is given by a letter now before me.   The writer was my ancestral relative, then on a visit from Shropshire to Malvern Hall, Solihull, to attend the Musical Festival at Birmingham. Travelling through the Forest near Solihull, a village even at that time almost lost in the woodlands, highwaymen attacked the coach. The lady arrived intact at Malvern Hall, but alas, she sadly wrote,

> I have lost all my smart clothes, five best gowns & my two fine Bonnets & the handsome silk lace veil. I cannot go to any of the concerts not having an evening gown left! All my nice new Canezous are stolen and all my blonde trimmings!

To-day there is still no doubt of being in Arden when in Warwickshire. The old tract, which in fact was well wooded but not an impenetrable area of dense forest growth, is suggested on moving from place to place, from Morton Bagot, Beausale, Forshaw Heath, Temple Balsall, Berkswell or Wishaw, for example. Scenes are close, intimate, friendly, near at hand, rarely expanded in great widths and distances; they would have suited Birket Foster, or David Cox when in his home county. Trees in abundance, and especially oaks, border the lanes and group in the fields. Landscapes show leafiness everywhere, sturdy grace of boughs and trunks, all the harmonies of greens and browns, patches of grassy heath. Villages, hamlets, cottages, farmsteads, and moated houses with walls timbered in oak look just right in their woody settings. Oaks in the glades of Stoneleigh, grand aged monarchs at Packington, a deer park at Combe Abbey, Lady Luxborough's retreat and immense double oak at Barrels, ancient acres of the Archer family at Umberslade, wooded slopes of the Dugdales at Merevale, the old grounds of "Syr Thomas Malory, Knight" at Newbold Revel, and more of the parks for which the county is remarkable preserve the true Warwickshire glory of fine trees. Many of the place-names have a woodland ring in this district stretching east and north from Aston Cantlow, Henley-in-Arden, Tanworth-in-Arden, Packwood, Hampton-in-Arden, and Acock's Green, Birmingham, marked on old maps for a boundary of the Forest.

Apart from the Arden Forest, typified at my starting-point under the Shakespeare Oak standing over bracken on the Stoneleigh bank, this Warwickshire ground is well stored with more vernacular features of locality. One of these is the celebrated river, the Avon. Others are the villages and towns of distinct native flavour, and picturesquely made. They show harmoniously in wooded field and hedgerow surroundings, the characteristic scenery of the Midland Plain; they continue at about 200 feet lower level across the Leamington and Red Horse vales to their boundaries at Edge Hill, Burton Hills, and the hills of Shuckburgh. Standing on these hills, or at such points as Liveridge Hill above Henley-in-Arden, the eye travels far over the rich and patterned lands of Shakespeare's country. Throughout this district of vale, plain, and forest are the sites, mansions, houses, and buildings of sundry patterns, altogether a notable lot, which accommodated the human resources of the neighbourhood and also served the splendid people, likewise a notable lot, who helped to make these Midland shires a cockpit for the action, enlightenment, and success that illuminated medieval, Tudor, and Civil War times and the later years of intellectual polish, invention, and commercial prosperity. But observers topographically minded sometimes have said, and perhaps a few of my readers may think, that the splendour of persons never can equal the splendour of oaks, elms, hedgerow flowers, rivers, or sermons in stone, timbering, and brickwork. Whether this idea be true or not we will at this page-point of progress look around for objects other than people, spy along rivers, rushy banks and meadows, meet villages and towns of old standing, and here and there notice houses with low beams, classic heights, hiding-holes, and various inconveniences once enjoyed by the defunct splendid persons.

The Warwickshire Avon, weighty with fame, in spate from beautiful expressions of Garrick and other poetical admirers, and the recipient of very bad words from dwellers in the houses it regularly floods in rainy seasons, has managed to keep fair and lovely along most of its winding course. Though it has been useful in attracting dollars from American tourists, the river is not considered an ideal economic proposition by the modern type of iconoclast because it is not especially fitted to make man work harder and harder or influence international rates of exchange. Hence factories, gasworks, and such monuments of progress are not well presented. It is true that the lords of Nationalized Electricity lately conceived a notion for erecting monstrosities to blear miles of placid beauty round Hill Wootton, Leek Wootton (103), and Guy's Cliff (rightly called by Leland "a place meet for the Muses"); an historic region thus might have gained things most horrible and sufficiently terrifying to send jerks through the ghosts of Piers Gaveston and Guy the Hermit while prowling about the riverside at midnight. Through the valiant acts of the Mayors of Leamington and Warwick these arrangements have not yet come to pass. The river at present generally keeps out of date, flows and curves placidly, delights with quiet scenes, charms from the source to the end. Graceful in motions and decked with rushes and arrowheads in the stream, it passes wide stretches of pasture, ploughland, and orchard, snug villages, old church towers. Willows, hundreds of them, stand in lines and avenues, joined one to another to show green arches like Gothic arcades. The stream meets the bridges of ancient towns and reflects on its surface the tapering spire of the national poet's shrine (107).

Coming into Warwickshire the Avon makes one Roman point at the bridge on Watling Street near to Rugby, Charles Dickens's "Mugby," in the "dull-ness of the scenery" disliked by Arnold; the river passes a second Roman point on its last stage out of the county from Bidford's fifteenth-century bridge (117) and the ford, which mark the line of the straight road leading through Alcester and Beoley to the stretch of original track preserved in Sutton Park close to Staffordshire. The stream's infant prances, begun in Leicestershire, continue round Dunsmore Heath, a bleakish region and bleak indeed on the 5th of November, 1605, for Sir Everard Digby and the one hundred conspirators who assembled there, only to learn that the gunpowder arrangements entrusted to Guy Fawkes had not blown up the King and the Parliament. Past these spaces of gloomy remembrance the Avon shows off its own true qualities. At Bubbenhall it has grown in width. The real vale begins to open out. The stream ambles down to Ashow (102), bound for Warwick and Stratford, Wasperton, Luddington, Binton bridges, Cleeve Mill, and more shy haunts fit to love and retire in for ever. Scenes have that delicate beauty that is so very English, exactly right for this heart of England. The waters move placidly between low banks, chatter over little weirs and mill-races. Bushes and branches screen the holes of fishes, and eels and tench hide in the mud. Willows and alders wave silvery leafage in the breeze. Hedgerows, oaks, and bosky shapes of elm and ash mark out broad meadows painted with the colours and wild flowers of the seasons. Quiet places abound in which to forget and remember. Lazing in one of them under a willow near Charlecote (Shakespearean name!) I saw a sleeping fox in the next tree wake up, stretch himself, jump down, give me a sidelong glance, then trot leisurely across the grass, turning his head now and again with as much as to say, "Catch me if you can!" Such a meeting with Reynard may not happen twice in a lifetime.

Otters live at Bubbenhall. I've seen them under the river bank just below the place where Alfred Parsons sat to picture the church tower and cottages amongst trees beyond the greensward. This mention, not of otters but of a Royal Academician and a village, reminds me of scores and scores of pictures offered by these villages on or near the Avon, and of hundreds of artists who have had a go at them. Early sketching-grounds of mine, these villages and their border-lands embrace Stoneleigh and Ashow, the winding stream from Barford to Wasperton, Weston and Welford below Stratford, Salford Priors and Abbot's Salford, and

> Piping Pebworth, Dancing Marston,
> Haunted Hillborough, Hungry Grafton,
> Dodging Exhall, Papist Wixford,
> Beggarly Broom, and Drunken Bidford,

the Shakespeare villages popularly but doubtfully associated with the poet's pub-crawling and his meditations on the morning after the night before under a crab-tree by the roadside between Bidford and Stratford (117). Full of pictorial motives, and also furnished with ancestral antiques and antiquated human descendants of ancestors before antique dealers and weekenders dissipated both, this attractive area has been well spied on by artistic professionals and amateurs. It rose to much favour in the days when Edwin Abbey and Alfred Parsons penetrated over from Broadway, and Yeend King might be noticed under an umbrella; artists then strewed the earth round the mill, the medieval lych-gate and the timbered cottages at Welford, while now and again white ponies pranced gaily along with Marie Corelli, out for a talk to the old sea-captain by the maypole or bound for Dorsington in search of copy for God's Good Man. Natives, properly featured and dressed without need of make-up, were ready at hand for painters of the subject pictures liked and bought by the public before the advent of world wars and atomic bombs; pictures of the popular kind titled in the style of "Gleaners returning," "At

GORCOT HALL. *Built of brick and timber, and full of oak inside, this old home of the Chambers family stands on Gorcot Hill near Redditch. One window of 365 panes shows the arms of Queen Elizabeth. A spider dial painted on another window tells the time when the sun shines into the room.*

HUDDINGTON COURT *prior to restoration. The moated and timbered house with an elaborate Tudor chimney, once the home of Catesby's cousin, Robert Wyntour, a conspirator in the Gunpowder Plot. After the capture of Guy Fawkes, thirty fugitive plotters sheltered here on November 6, 1605, attended Mass, and prepared for death.*

milking time," "By candlelight," "When all the world was gay." In these figured the glove-makers, whose work done at cottage doorways went to Worcester; William, heavily whiskered, and voluble with "O blame, O day!" "Odds rat me!" and explosions in speech apparently derived from Elizabethans; the rosy-cheeked dame who expanded marvellously after sundown on the laying of ghosts with parsons and bottles; and a range of local types, young or ancient and suitable for all sorts of artistic occasions and pigments. Now it is nice to remember them, the last of a generation and a race extinguished by progress; soothing it is to recall their features, whiskers, stories of their day-to-day life, "the short and simple annals of the poor," which in narration sometimes were very long indeed and full of truths stranger than fiction.

Since these good folk went to quiet acres where rude forefathers sleep many of their haunts and habitations have continued whole. Though perilously near progressive districts full of people that specialize on spoliation of landscapes and weekends, symptoms of auld lang syne still persist in villages of the Avon vale and throughout the Warwickshire countryside. Local conditions and old-fashioned influences are clearly defined. They are well suggested north and south in the county and particularly mark such regions as Curdworth, Berkswell and Tanworth, Newbold-on-Avon, Lighthorne and Preston-on-Stour. In all directions stand the typical timber-framed cottages, houses, and farms with panels of plaster or brickwork, the thatched roofs, the coloured tiling. Big chimneys tapered upward to the stacks denote open fireplaces inside, the vast apertures that provided natives with warmth, smoked bacon, downdraught, smoky atmosphere, and gave Shakespeare a reason to write,

> Though little fire grows great with little wind,
> Yet extreme gusts will blow out fire and all.

Sightseers who quiz Anne Hathaway's Cottage (111) and Mary Arden's Wilmcote cottage, at least cannot fail to notice two good specimens from the local hundreds of these framed and thatched providers of home, sweet home. This mode of construction in oak and panel, elaborated to gables, bargeboards, brackets, porches, and windows divided by wood mullions, served for the larger village homes and small manor-houses. Often moated for security in Arden, now frequently used as farmhouses or freshened in age by new and enthusiastic owners, they are to be seen at Bott's Green, Grimshaw Hall (95), Berry Hall, Gorcot Hall (123), Clifford Chambers, in parish after parish and always worth finding for the pictures they yield, the stories and names they recall. Southward, where the lias of the hills meets the vale, stone chiefly rules for building. It colours adorable villages, named to include Shuckburgh, Burton Dassett, the Tysoes, and Tredington. Yet the prevalent Warwickshire timbering is not absent; the fifteenth-century and haunted manor-house of the Ingrams at Little Wolford is but one instance of the effective combination made with stone and oak. When timber for fuel absorbed by the near centres of manufacture made oak scarcer and bricks and tiles became generally used, the later Midland style for house and home spread through the towns and the villages. It developed the characteristic red-brick walling, string courses, tiled roofs with dormers, little bay-windows for cottages. Bigger bays and taller windows lighted the larger houses. Moulded hoods protected Georgian and Regency doorways. A few entrances had shell hoods, like the one you can see by the roadside at Wootton Wawen, prettily adorned with modelled fruit and flowers for pretty brocades and wigs to pass under when dishes of tea went round and gossip expanded Mr. Knight's South Sea Bubble money spent at Barrels or glorified young Mr. Jago's Beaudesert poems.

It comes easily in Warwickshire to make a transition from small to large, to pass to bigger things from the circumscribed signs of even and long-settled life in hamlet and village. The country invites this. Central, old in use, rarely has it been out of touch with national expansion and temper. Much fought over, the land long knew the alarms of war and political intrigue. In years of peace and plenty alarms no less exciting sprang from industry, invention, discovery, and intellectual ardour urged forward by a shrewd people disposed for action, enlightenment, and material advantages. The local spirit of time and circumstance reacted far beyond the local fat pastures and borders. Joseph Priestley and James Watt perched statuesque at Birmingham, a birthplace of trade unionism at Joseph Arch's Barford cottage, the Jennens family home of great iron-masters at Nether Whitacre, Sanderson Miller's centre of polite intellectualism and Gothic Revival sproutings at Radway Grange—such outward forms with big meanings are expected constituents of the scenes, belong to them no less naturally than a birthplace for Shakespeare fits Stratford, Warwick Castle stands for Richard Neville the King-maker, Kenilworth recalls Simon de Montfort, pillar of English freedom.

The bold stretch of the Fosse Way from south to north gives to the county a sure mark of immemorial importance. Speculators handy with cars, or, better still, good on their feet, can spend happy and full hours tracing this straight life-line. It runs off the Cotswold stone at Stretton-on-Fosse, enters the Vale of the Red Horse, continues past Compton Verney house and park, Chesterton Roman camp, the site of a forgotten battle at Offchurch, the fortified mound of Brinklow, and at High Cross meets a hoary comrade, Watling Street.

Far and wide passages of national history can be read without books. Pages of it open at Warwick Castle (104). A modest 2s. 6d. per head delivered at a turnstile of romance will assault and carry the barbican and fourteenth-century gatehouse to the stronghold of the Beauchamps, the Nevilles and the Grevilles. Early walls and towers joined to later additions and rebuilding stand firm and erect high over the River Avon and the original medieval bridge, now broken down. As plainly as can be, the battlements, machicolations, and masonry carry the flow of centuries through the years of the Black Dog of Arden (slew Piers Gaveston, 1312), the King-maker (slain at the battle of Barnet, 1471), Queen Elizabeth entertained with fireworks, peaceful penetrations by later royal guests; re-created are seasons of "grim-visaged war" and many a "piping time of peace" to elucidate the words of a Shakespearean Richard III, himself Richard Neville's son-in-law and a visitor to this castle. At Kenilworth walls of the castle are ruined and baileys overgrown. Cromwellians drained the great lake and destroyed the park (112). Unlike Warwick, the placing of Kenilworth Castle in a hole is not spectacular, nor have the relics the advantages of charges at 2s. 6d. per head to stem assaults in close formation by crowds that may or may not know of a book by Scott called *Kenilworth* and what Simon de Mont-fort did for all of us. When I lived within two miles of these ruins, and therefore was liable to brood over them at all hours of days and seasons, it was remark-able to discover the peculiar feelings aroused inside the human apparatus by these pink and grey stones and grassy mounds, particularly when the sun was low or the moon was high. These effects may have proceeded partly from the state of vision, liver, and mind, but no doubt very much more from the unseen yet potent spirit of the still air, the stuff of remembrance born of past years and deeds that helped to fill chapters of England's story. Few acres in the land are richer in meaning, great names, and memories than these at Kenilworth. Outer towers, the tilt yard, inner and outer courts, wreckage of de Clinton's Norman keep, John of Gaunt's beautiful hall (c. 1390), and Leicester's Elizabethan build-ings abide like a fabric of dreams. Robert Dudley's gatehouse continues intact and fitted with finely sculptured alabaster and oak chimney-pieces, prime from the grand days of Queen Elizabeth's visits in 1566, 1568, 1572, and in 1575, when 320 hogsheads of beer celebrated that great occasion, and very likely young Shakespeare, aged eleven, yelled with delight while the wonderful fire-works exploded into "birds flying and cats and dogs fighting, serpents of fire, a dragon as big as an ox." No fireworks illuminated the historic occasions of Maxstoke, a dozen miles distant, when dynasties fell and rose and the first Tudor succeeded the last Plantagenet. One night in 1485 Richard III slept in the castle on his way to Bosworth Field. Immediately afterwards Henry VII did likewise —on his way from Bosworth Field. Begun by William de Clinton in the middle of the fourteenth century, wonderfully preserved, and still a home, Maxstoke Castle is a perfect survivor of a moated Edwardian quadrangle with embattled walls, angle towers, a gatehouse and living quarters made more for days of peace than of fighting, a fortified house but weak for war's hurly-burly. It is the most lovely and quiet retreat imaginable. You can encircle the walls on the path by the wide moat, look out for dragonfly blue, peer down at the fishes, the only signs of armies that I or Henry VIII's commissioners discovered (95).

Differences of opinion between Royalist and Roundhead impressed later stamps of history on these lands. Few parts of Warwickshire escaped the hammerings and turmoil of the Civil War. Not everywhere is one conscious of the ghosts of kings; yet when I used to work in the panelled room at Stoneleigh Abbey near to the Norman stonework of the Cistercians, it was sometimes enervating to fancy time set back to the fateful year of 1642 and to wonder if Charles I's silk nightshirt rustled inside the four-poster just behind me. To this mansion grown from an abbey (96) Sir Thomas Leigh welcomed the King when on his way to set up his standard at Nottingham after the citizens of Coventry had shut their gates against the King. At Radway Tower, built by Sanderson Miller on Edge Hill in 1750 (a wonderful viewpoint for Warwickshire's patterned miles), you can stand where King Charles stood on the day of the first Civil War battle. The near beacon on Burton Hills signalled news of the conflict; soldiers sleep in Warmington churchyard. About the Fosse Way beyond the county boundary near Stow-on-the-Wold the last local fight of the conflict ended in 1646, when Astley, the silver-haired veteran and captive of Morgan the Cromwellian, sat on a drum and said, "Gentlemen, yee may now sit down and play, for you have done all your worke, if you fall not out among yourselves." Open war on Warwickshire soil thus temporarily closed until recent displays from the air spread ruin in Coventry and Birmingham, and the windy batteries of politics and economics opened up on the mansions and the landscapes.

Messages of the Warwickshire churches seem to be mostly of peace, though fighting knights lie inside them, grooves on outer stonework show where archers of Arden sharpened their arrows, and Civil War bullets and bullet-marks are in Tredington church door. Gothic forms, solid and workmanlike, group well among the timbered and brick homesteads of the villages and country towns. Far and wide stand the embattled towers, locally very characteristic, fine at Kineton and splendid at Brailes. Here and there a spire is seen far off or near, and well shown at Southam and Tanworth. Out of the ordinary are some of these churches. One at Wootton Wawen developed remarkably from Saxon and Norman times. Knights Templars achieved dignified expanse and the series of wheel windows in the thirteenth century at Temple Balsall. Lapworth gained the beauty of a detached tower and spire, the high Perpendicular clerestory, the chantry chapel over a western porch. Snitterfield (the church of Shakespeare's uncle Henry) acquired carved wood figures, panels, and heraldic shields when Renaissance design mingled with the Gothic. Masterpieces arose in the great Perpendicular style. One was the Beauchamp Chapel, Warwick (101); another, the tower and spire of St. Michael (1394–1433), subtle and superb, and still erect at Coventry. Later on the alert people in this district of progress and expanding industry naturally followed the fashions of

BROUGHTON HACKETT, *one of the secluded villages between Alcester and Worcester. Hundreds of nesting-places are inside the pigeon-house illustrated. The district preserves several of these survivals of manorial privilege.*

KYRE WYARD *near Tenbury. The pigeon-house and great barn of the older buildings. The main front of the house dates from the eighteenth century. Capability Brown laid out the grounds, and the park is notable for grand trees, including fourteenth-century oaks.*

HEREFORD. *The fifteenth-century bridge over the River Wye leads in* *the fourteenth-century cathedral tower is remarkable for ball-flower decoratio*

pleasant capital city of the orchard and hop country. Broad and sturdy,
rises over the largest collection of chained books in the world.

GREAT MALVERN, from the Worcestershire Beacon. The view includes the priory and Perpendicular tower of the mid-fifteenth century, the Worcestershire plain, and the Severn Vale.

Stuart and Georgian times. Good crops of eighteenth-century churches matured. They ripened in fair or strange growths, harvested a kind of Christianized paganism. The English soil bore Corinthian pilasters at Honily in 1723, a classical temple of 1731 at Castle Bromwich; Bonomi, the Italian, devised Doric columns at Great Packington in 1790 for the Earl of Aylesford; and a masterpiece was completed after 1725 when Thomas Archer's tower rose over the west end of St. Philip's, Birmingham (195). From early to late centuries simple folk, gentry, and splendid persons made last visits to these churches in the way common to humanity. Little stones on churchyard grass, memorials on sacred walls and floors, tombs in suitable and superior positions alike record inevitable fate. Carved effigies, lifelike or from stock patterns, heraldic ordinaries and charges, brasses, and inscriptions present opportunities without formal introductions for making silent acquaintance with once live beings who kept their little worlds moving and bright while they answered to such names and places as Boughton (Newbold-on-Avon), Fulke Greville (Alcester), Lucy (Charlecote), Compton (Compton Wynyates), Verney (Compton Verney), Throckmorton (Coughton), Ferrars (Baddesley Clinton), Shuckburgh (Shuckburgh), Holte (Aston), Adderley (Lea Marston), the incomparable Dugdale (Shustoke), and of course Shakespeare himself at Stratford. Worth a day's march or a ride is a call on the Peyto family in the perfect seclusion of Chesterton, a remarkable crowd with two members made by Nicholas Stone. A visit to Richard Beauchamp's brass portrait in St. Mary's, Warwick, superbly rendered by John Massingham in 1450, and a study of every figure and detail on this marvellous tomb, means a revelation of how things were done in England's golden age of craftsmanship.

A good showing is made by houses of families commended in the churches, homes nice in size, but never so gigantic that inmates felt little in stature and puny of mind, as for instance anyone might do under the four acres of roof at Blenheim. Compton Wynyates (115), Stoneleigh Abbey (96), and other mansions in the vicinity certainly are quite big enough. But nobles owning such large titles as Compton, Leigh, Hertford, Willoughby de Broke and Craven, their relatives and friends no doubt were not overpowered by mere extent and shape in abbey remains, courtyards, long galleries and rows of gables; quite easily would they breathe and live while living up to Cipriani's ornate Labours of Hercules in the white saloon of Stoneleigh, Palladian impressiveness and Homeric decorations of Ragley, mixed Vanbrugh and Adam effects at Compton Verney, brilliance of gilt, rococo, and Captain Wynne's front at Combe Abbey, Grinling Gibbon's carvings at Arbury.

If Compton Wynyates is the prime showpiece of this district, well worth finding and rightly found by the many who appreciate a jewel of Tudor loveliness beautifully set, ordinary mortals perhaps may derive most satisfaction in seeking the less pretentious establishments, the expressions of home that so admirably fit the leafy scenes and symbolize past day-to-day life and sentiments of substantial families comfortably placed or settled in squirely fashion on ancestral lands. Masters and mistresses then did not do all their own housework and washing-up. Servants were plentiful in that lost age of willingness when everybody either had to be willing to work or was quite willing to be worked for. Even passing glances at the large areas that evidently were dusted and polished, or the very size of the kitchens can act as sedatives to minds fashioned by the present era of domestic terror governed by the non-appearance of "chars and dailies." The manorial and secluded homesteads have a fragrance of old years about them, suggest calm and manageable days and quiet, sleepful nights. Few parishes have not one of these homes representing the local architectural currency and the changes of schemes in living. Biggish or medium in size, some are timbered, some are moated; many have the brickwork and stone of the sixteenth, seventeenth, and eighteenth centuries. Grimshaw Hall (95), Gorcot Hall (123), and a few more specimens have been indicated on earlier pages. Another one is the Catholic family home of the Eystons at Abbots Salford, captivating both outside and within, and offering the chance of getting lost in a hiding-hole (115). Among the large number that have kept status, lost it, or continue in useful ways for farmers, you may light on the fashions of domestic years in all directions and range through generations and periods. The farmer's home at Wormleighton, for instance, has Tudor brickwork and stone erected by the Spencers, and through the arched gateway, dated 1613, Prince Rupert rode when he arrived to spend the night before the Edge Hill battle. Arlescote, on the roadside below Edge Hill, evidently fits the late seventeenth century with nicely balanced hipped roofs, dormers, projecting wings and walls of stone, and a similar effect in brickwork and tiles, though somewhat larger, appears beyond iron gates at Clifford Chambers. With quoins at the angles, eaves cornices, chimneys prim and uniform, Honington by Shipston-on-Stour is fully developed; busts of Roman emperors on outer walls and lavish decorations inside evidence the Italian tint of mind once so fashionable with the English. Foxcote, in the same neighbourhood, points the eighteenth century onward with the pilasters, pediments, and stone urns of the Cannings, a family descended from the famous merchants we traced at St. Mary Redcliffe, Bristol. Pinley Priory in Rowington parish tumbles time back to the close timbering period, while Coughton Court of the Throckmortons offers an impressive choice of style in Tudor, Jacobean, and the "Gothick" locally popularized by Sanderson Miller. The Lucy's Charlecote (noted for the Shakespearean deer-stealing fable charmingly resurrected by Washington Irving) clearly indicates the first year of Queen Elizabeth's reign and offers one hallmark of that period in the gatehouse elaborated with ornamental parapets and octagonal corner towers. It is joyous to thread the Arden lanes and suddenly discover the groupings of gables, Restoration brickwork, gates and piers, and the topiary garden of seventeenth-century yew at Packwood House, reminders of the Featherstone squires who were followed by the Ash family. Old centuries belong to the battlements and brick walls of Pooley Hall, Polesworth, a place of the Cockaynes in the reign of Henry IV and rebuilt by them in 1509; here Michael Drayton served as page to Sir Thomas Cockayne, and theorists also like to fit in young William Shakespeare and thus account for the poet's evident personal knowledge of north-east Warwickshire.

Of the ancient houses Baddesley Clinton, rarest of the rare, diffuses a spice of late medievalism. It lies secluded. Walls rise steeply from a broad moat. A Queen Anne bridge, in place of the old drawbridge, leads to the massive fifteenth-century oak door of the gate tower. Beyond is the courtyard built round three sides of a square in a mixture of sandstone, timber, and brick. The hall with a carved and dated fireplace and room interiors have all the elements for anything you like to think of or fancy from past Catholic days when bearers of the name of Ferrers had good uses for the secret staircase and the priests' hiding-holes. One still evening while I was there and a low sun mellowed colouring, a lady dressed in black velvet looked down into the courtyard, smiled from an upper casement, and made one of those pictures that stick in memory. To me the scene appeared just such a one that Edwin Abbey might have penned for an illustration to Shakespeare, with perhaps a title inscribed "O mistress mine" or something like that. An opposite point in the swing of architectural time is marked by Malvern Hall, Solihull, classic with wings right and left, the eighteenth-century home of the Greswoldes, proud in one of those broad and wooded parks typical of Warwickshire when I knew it a long time ago. Afterwards a secondary school took possession, a housing estate developed. Fortunately, before the years of myself, school, or housing, John Constable finely painted a characteristic and rich canvas of the hall, park, lake, and superior sky, thereby preserving the aristocratic bearing that a system of living once could impart to English landscape. The National Gallery is the place to see how Malvern Hall looked before it actually and figuratively lost an upper storey and came down in the world.

Church bells merry at midnight to welcome Christmas morning in Southam; Shipston-on-Stour good for Georgian stone houses; brickwork and black-and-white round about a seventeenth-century town hall in Alcester; Henley-in-Arden's long and picturesque highway below de Montfort's castle mound of Beaudesert; a medieval bridge over the river, the Georgian houses, a lovely church spire, fifteenth-century windows and Digby tombs on the hill at Coleshill; and much more I remember and might write, if my short space did not forbid, would be in praise of Warwickshire's little towns, examples of those special products of England that are nice to find, pleasant to look at, comforting to stay in, perhaps for ever and ever.

The larger towns of Rugby, Leamington, Warwick, and Stratford line across the county on or near the River Avon. Leamington continues in popularity, thrives, keeps a spa look even in these degenerate days. The gardens and groves are fresh and bright. The Old Well House and the Royal Pump Rooms stand firm and imply that the beneficent waters have not yet evaporated under the stress of national economy. When in the town I never fail to sip the unpalatable liquid, though not for the good it has showered on so many human insides or might do on my own, nor because it enabled John Ruskin to write, "I have gone back to brown potatoes and cherry pie!" Rather does the magic water, just one taste of it, set my mind thinking of the sprouting spring discovered by the shoemaker, Benjamin Satchwell, and those other springs that sprouted in unison to shower not only water but honour, fame, and success. Royal honour flowed in with the Prince Regent in 1819, followed by more from princes and princesses, and fame and popularity streamed along, while the nobility, notables, and all sorts and conditions of gay, sober, and liverish water-drinkers and abstainers came and stayed in the procession of nineteenth-century years, filled the Assembly Rooms built in Bath Street in 1821, promenaded up and down the Parade, found the Metropolis repeated at their own doorsteps in such quarters as Oxford Street, Regent Street, Euston Place, and even a miniature Covent Garden Market. At the appointed times the throngs departed, left their ghosts behind to haunt the Regency and Victorian villas that stand elegant, shapely, and creamy-faced with stucco make-up in Clarendon Terrace, Waterloo Place, Newbold Terrace, Willes Road, and other well-planned groupings embowered in greenery. In their own particular years Charles Lamb, truly great essayist, made a first acquaintance with Elliston, truly great comedian, "over a counter in the Leamington Spa Library"; Nathaniel Hawthorne settled at No. 10, Lansdowne Circus, in "one of the cosiest nooks in England or in the world"; Charles Dickens fitted Mr. Dombey and Major Bagstock inside the "Royal Hotel," found for Edith Granger and Carker "a deep shade of leafy trees" (locally fancied to be in Holly Walk). Yes, it is quite amazing what a mere glass of water can do when taken in this trim and attractive town. While benefiting the digestive apparatus, it also may act as a tonic for travelling a long way from to-day through the avenues and terraces of white and green, or to the Regency days of the little square window-panes and covered walks in Covent Garden Market behind Warwick Street; anybody who likes to do so can slip out of the present and enjoy re-creating yesterdays at the first hotel, the *Bath*, erected by William Abbotts after the discovery of the waters in Bath Street, at the very good frontage of the *Clarendon*, at the *Regent*, so named by command of George IV—and where, in good old days

ROSS-ON-WYE. *Market day at the pillared market hall, a building dating from the reign of Charles II.*

CRADLEY *near Bosbury, two picturesque villages below the Malvern Hills in Herefordshire.*

Weather vane
Grange Court
LEOMINSTER

Church Lane, LEDBURY

ORLETON Court

Porch dated 1674
The Ley near
WEOBLEY

Brackets & post
Market hall
LEDBURY

SRJ

15" sq.

HEREFORDSHIRE DETAILS

before the advent of world wars, I used to consume grilled salmon steaks without need of the chalybeate spring for a sedative. They (the steaks) have since retreated to my ventricle of memory. If one of my readers now happens to find more of them at the *Regent*, and can generously spare and forward a slice of the browned pink delicacy for my consumption in this epoch of collapsed currency and short rations, I shall feel deeply grateful and acknowledge an act of remembrance for happy days spent, long ago, with the pretty white features and green leafage of Leamington Spa.

At Warwick, adjoining Leamington, we hitch on to the touring circuit of the Shakespeare Country proper, an event signalized by the ceaseless clatter of every known kind of thing on wheels up and down High Street. This proof of much coming and going—it has robbed me of sleep on more nights than one— relieves me considerably at this page on the county town, suggests getting away with it lightly because dozens of written guides and critical surveys already exist for the benefit of sightseers and seekers after knowledge who are delivered on wheels or otherwise. Humbly, therefore, I merely present my pictures (15, 101, 104, 105). Robbed of ammunition by previous explorers, I am left with nothing new to disclose on the castle, St. Mary's real Gothic and its peculiar Gothic finished in 1704, the Earl of Leicester's Leycester Hospital, two town gates existing and two missing, Sanderson Miller's fine Shire Hall completed in 1753, the dignified eighteenth-century birthplace of Walter Savage Landor in which he now could have said, "Put me amongst the girls," the antiquated appearance of Mill Street, the view from the Georgian bridge on the Banbury Road. These and more sights and associations make Warwick adorable when touring crowds have gone; then Leicester's pensioners in blue gowns saunter on shady sides of pretty streets, and the van Dycks and the Canalettos radiate glory undisturbed inside the castle. The bits of less common information, summarized below, are all that I can safely offer without endangering my life through knocks on my head from ragged staffs directed by captious bears and highly informed experts. 1. The great fire of 1694, which destroyed about 250 houses and caused St. Mary's to lose a medieval nave and tower, cleared spaces for the later frontages, doorways and fanlights that look so well in Church Street, High Street, Jury Street, and a perfect Northgate Street. Behind are dainty, well-proportioned rooms, and even an early Quaker meeting-house of 1695, so secluded, private and silent amongst clipt yews and hollyhocks that I will not disclose its whereabouts. 2. Can any town in England show a better interior than Sanderson Miller's masterpiece at the Shire Hall? It's a tremendous sight at night with dancers, music, and soft lighting. 3. Quaintness at the eighteenth-century law courts is so arresting, any lawabiding citizen might be pardoned for doing a murder or other crime for the chance of appearing inside the criminal or civil department. 4. Whatever may be said for or against Sir William Wilson's architecture of the spacious and high nave of St. Mary's, it makes a wonderful setting for ceremonial occasions of the Mayor and Corporation, soldiers, sailors, crowded congregations, the organ pealing, and parade hymns. 5. The *Warwick Arms* has been done up very nicely since the lords of war departed.

And so to Stratford-on-Avon, as Mr. Pepys might have said, though apparently the busy traveller was one of the few illustrious persons who left no mention of Shakespeare's town. Dr. Johnson, who did, because it lay on his posting route to Lichfield, I think told somebody that to marry once is brave, twice, heroic, or words to that effect. Yet of greater courage would be the man or woman bold enough to think of presenting any facts or fictions not already offered once, twice, or a thousand times on what has been called the play town of the world. Much more than that is this ancient place. Known by evidence from Saxon and Domesday years, rich in a long and prosperous medieval history, standing in the heart of a true countryside, and settled on the tree-lined banks of the Avon between Sir Hugh Clopton's bridge and Lucy's mill, if bombs or other destructive inventions by man remove all else but Stratford, still will remain an epitome of England. No doubt the powers of destiny acted on that assumption when locating a birthplace for Shakespeare.

It is often said that popularity has spoiled Stratford. I do not think so. I have known the town at all times and seasons, in the quieter past years, in the later phases of invasions by crowds, ice cream, chars-à-bancs, restorers, antique shops, and a commercial vitality that has driven me to Keith Prowse in London for the only hope of securing a theatre seat at Stratford. Yet to me the town ever seems impervious to spoliation. In the face of popularity and other adversities it has kept a heart and spirit pure, fresh and permanent as its poet's works. To seekers and lovers it speaks like Rosalind, "Can one desire too much of a good thing?" Would-be spoilers it can reproach and lightly drop a hint from *Henry IV*, "I know a trick worth two of that."

Forestalled by distinguished producers of facts and fictions that have made Stratford the matter for square miles of printed and drawing paper, my task at Shakespeare's town already has been done for me. Apologetically, therefore, I offer my handiwork of scenes known the world over, coupled with a spice of Shakespearean advice for my reader to follow,

> I'll view the manners of the town,
> Peruse the traders, gaze upon the buildings,
> And then return and sleep within mine inn.

Tales twice told again and again then will be remembered and located in their famous places—Holy Trinity Church, one of the most beautiful in Warwickshire (107); a group to fascinate at the fifteenth-century Guild Chapel, Guildhall and Shakespeare's school; nothing to see of New Place, the house built by

Sir Hugh Clopton, purchased by Shakespeare in 1597, knocked down by Parson Gastrell in 1759; Shakespeare's birthplace in Henley Street (106); the Hathaway Cottage outside the town at Shottery (111); Hall's Croft in Old Town, finest of the Tudor houses, probably lived in by Shakespeare's daughter Susanna; Harvard House built by Alderman Rogers in 1596 (110); pictures unending in streets of timberwork, brick, and stone; the gabled *Shakespeare*, a timbered *Falcon* (supposed to have been Shakespeare's pub), the *Red Horse* (with Washington Irving's "little parlour"), and more inns galore of all ages and patterns with provision inside them for all sorts of tastes. There is also a Memorial Theatre, a recent product of "this iron age." This intruder in the gracious scene of river, bridge, trees and meadows incorporates bits left over from the burning of an earlier erection, its predecessor. The bits are liable to remind old fogeys of the glamorous days and nights of the Bensons, George Weir, Oscar Asche, Frank Rodney, H. O. Nicholson and attendant hosts, when all and sundry, including myself, made annual and joyous family parties of players and audiences in the odd and spiky old theatre, one equally inglorious with its successor for a worthy tribute to the creative genius and immortal memory of the great Elizabethan Englishman.

Without presuming to offer one word on the ancestry and life of Shakespeare, why he married Anne Hathaway, deer-stealing, pike called luce, who wrote the plays, and other subjects reserved for minds of the very learned, I now say with Gloster, "Enough, enough," repeat Hamlet's last words, "The rest is silence," bid a temporary farewell to my lifelong friend, Stratford-on-Avon. In so doing I gratefully remember that many people are quite satisfied to have the plays whether written by one Shakespeare or not, that Stratford exists and is lovely, and that a railway porter named Shakespeare used to direct pilgrims from Warwick station platform to the shrine of a man for all time who was bred on Warwickshire Bacon.

A suspicion of smokiness must dim the end of these notes on Shakespeare's county. Geographers know of the existence of Nuneaton, Bedworth, Coventry, Birmingham, and their environs; geologists tell of a Warwickshire coalfield; and political economists have expended much wind, ink, and paper on a number of things since Adam Smith, a Scot, and the Industrial Revolution began to tackle the green lands of England. Places and views in north Warwickshire illustrate various aspects of the matters above-mentioned. Invasions of industrialism on nature's landscapes nevertheless are not quite my subjects for these pages, though the Nuneaton district might have offered an excuse for expanding my memories of South Farm, the birthplace of Mary Ann Evans, "Cheverel Manor" at Arbury, the "Hall Farm" at Corley, and Chilvers Coton for "Shepperton" in the George Eliot books. Coventry, the ancient city of religious, civic, and domestic treasures related to spires, friars, royal visits, guilds, pageants, mystery plays, charities, wool, cloth, watches, and ribbons, by good fortune could have remained one of the most wonderful town sights in all the land. It didn't. Destroyers obliterated city walls, ten of the twelve gates, the cathedral of St. Mary, built with three spires like Lichfield, Butcher Row and other things; factories that revolutionized the uses of human legs surrounded the city's heart, and German raiders did their dreadful work. The spires, St. Mary's Hall, and Bablake are among the standing reminders of old glory, and casualties such as Ford's Hospital and Priory Row I am told yet may be kept from falling (96). But my own constant reminder of intimate Coventry years is an old patchwork quilt that covers me up at night with silken bits of the true "Coyntrie Blewe" praised by Michael Drayton and Ben Jonson, a very cheering sight to see when waking up in the morning in these days of the blues.

Lastly, it would be foolish to deny the existence of smoke for a halo to Birmingham, great and beneficent city though it is, one certainly never seen by Shakespeare but now possessing the best library of Shakespearean books in the world. To penetrate within this halo is not quite the thing for these pages of mine, most unsuitable sheets for papering large industrial cities. Nor are the following words interposed for the reason that first impressions of the Midland metropolis when gained from railway trains romping in from Euston, Paddington, or Wolverhampton sometimes offer satisfactory suggestions for a Dante's *Inferno*, just as first sights also can do at Manchester, Leeds, Sheffield, and other monuments of England's greatness and commercial prosperity. Rather does Birmingham now figure here because it will be my one sample, my representative of more of the kind to be seen in our progress northward, and at places where it is not my purpose to tarry long. And further. This city ranked second in the kingdom, with a University, and a famous School of Art guided years ago by Edward Taylor, first directed me along the thorny ways of drawing, architecture, and the crafts. Gratefully I salute thee within thy smoky nimbus; and also recall that my illustrious namesake with a hyphen, Edward Burne-Jones, here had his natal habitation, discovered the *Morte d'Arthur* of Malory at Cornish's in New Street, began to devour it free gratis in that bookshop until William Morris appeared and bought the copy. Thereafter the magnificent Burne-Jones windows appeared in the church of St. Philip, and the artist endures perpetually bright in the unique collection of Pre-Raphaelite works kept at the city's Art Gallery—or rather, in parts of the fine gallery left intact after the German raids.

The strength of Britain depended on coal, said George Stephenson, when he suggested that the Lord Chancellor ought to sit on a bag of coals instead of on the Woolsack. And if England's early source of wealth and good fortune,

KILPECK. *The Norman sculptor's genius for decoration and surface pattern.*

ROCHFORD *church on the bank of the River Teme. Norman pattern in the tympanum, one of the twenty-seven English representations of "The Tree of Spiritual Life and Knowledge," a mystic device deep rooted in antiquity.*

MANSELL LACY. *A village with timbered buildings in the notable Herefordshire group which includes King's Pyon, Weobley, Pembridge, and Eardisland.*

144

wool, prompted glorious memorials in the Cotswolds and elsewhere, the country's later epoch of greater worldly prosperity that developed under the rule of King Coal, steam, and the steam engine created its own monuments, of which Birmingham obviously is one. When coal ousted wood for smelting iron, and consequently shifted the centre of the iron industry from Sussex and Kent to the Midlands, Birmingham rose on the swelling tide of fortune. Its long record of ceaseless industry, busy workshops, alertness, and spirit of advancement marked the point for a meeting-place of ideas, invention, scientific discovery, and a certain brilliance of intellectualism. Statues of James Watt and Joseph Priestley in the squares, reminders of such men as Matthew Boulton, William Murdock, John Baskerville, and Francis Eginton recall shining lights that fired minor revolutions and affected kingdoms.

"The toy-shop of Europe," so named by Edmund Burke (and called "Brum" by the vulgar), has projected the fangs of industry far and wide, both within and outside Warwickshire. Manufacturing "toys" of steel and iron not intended for children's playthings, ramifications of a long-established armoury, and a thousand trades ever expanding have wiped out fields, farms, woodlands, villages, changed them into things quite different. If the builder of a Jacobean Aston Hall, Sir Thomas Holte, Lloyd the banker, Squire Taylor of Moseley Hall, David Cox of Harborne, or even Joseph Chamberlain returned again to look round their former haunts they might blink and rub their eyes more than twice at the sight of the widespread agglomeration.

As years count in a superhuman world, it is not long since the glitter of iron, steel, and brass outshone the jewels of nature's providing in and around Birmingham. Cherries grew in Walker's orchard in the eighteenth century on the site of Cherry Street, and less than 200 years ago the present fine thoroughfare of New Street was bordered with farmlands and barns. Nevertheless Birmingham is old enough though it may not look so to-day. First a Saxon settlement, the Bermingeha of Domesday Book early developed the long main street from Deritend to Dale End. For reasons on which history is silent the town undoubtedly rose in wealth and importance through the medieval years, had markets by royal charter from 1166, fairs from 1250, a considerable Gothic church with a spire and chantry chapels, religious guilds, and a priory founded in the thirteenth century. One significant record of growing status was a permission to pave the streets granted by Edward III, evidentally a beginning of the ways cobbled with the "petrified kidneys" that generated ill fame, odium, and bad language for centuries afterwards. Subsequent to the Conquest the family of de Byrmyngham held the manor. The manorial home stood at Smithfield Market, where cattle and cabbages now change hands for cash within the limits of Moat Lane and Moat Row, names of course derived from the de Byrmyngham's moat. Next door to the cabbages knightly effigies repose inside the rebuilt church of St. Martin, the supposed memorials of the Edwardian lords of the manor. More names recorded, of esquires and persons of local consequence, emphasize that the town got on well in the world, first trading principally in leather and later in metals. Nobody thought of trading in pen and paper to tell us what their early habitations and hovels looked like. Certainly they must have been of the traditional kind determined by the use of Warwickshire timber, wattle and daub, and sandstone. Leland, who arrived in the reign of Henry VIII and so wrote the earliest description, saw these buildings or their successors when he noted "a mansion house of tymber" at the end of "Dirtey (Deritend), a praty street as ever I entered." The "smithes and cutlers" observed on the same occasion were sure signs of the flourishing metal industry. "Anvils" and "great numbers of smiths" impressed Camden when he followed in the 1580's, and at that time he must have noticed the timbered houses which I sketched years ago in this same street. The growth and success of the town in the early years wholly depended on a self-reliant population. Here existed no castle or powerful monastic constitution with people inside to meddle and dominate outside. Neither were there trade guilds or a corporation, local government being done in the usual manorial way by a high bailiff, low bailiff, two constables, meat conners, bread weighers, ale tasters, and odd-jobbers. Sadly deficient in controls and limitations imposed by wicked feudal capitalists, ecclesiastical overlords, or guild ranters on labour, the town was one of freedom in which, to use the words of my old friend Howard Pearson, "any man might work at any trade at any time," produce high quality like that of Benedict the Cutler, and live laborious days and nights without hindrance from jealous rivals or the scum of the earth. Therein lay chances for prosperity. The local circumstances, then different from those at the greater centres of trade like Coventry, naturally spurred effort among the natives and attracted free and skilled artisans from elsewhere. Thus it is quite easy to understand how and why the inhabitants acquired their traditions, their sterling human qualities, and the independence of thought and action that early and late landed them into all sorts of scrapes, riots, and tremendous successes.

Following the visits of Leland and Camden, time swinging along brought one of the rows and planted its mark at a spot still called Camp Hill. There Prince Rupert squatted on Easter Monday, 1643. With him were 2,000 horse and foot, 4 drakes, 2 sakers (small cannons). The townsfolk with muskets numbered only about 140, but decided "to stand it out, stay and trie the issues rather than be so perpetually reproacht." Twice they beat off the invaders, called them "Cursed doggs, develish Cavaliers, Papist Traytors." Then numbers told. The Royalists broke through, murdered, burnt about 80 houses to ashes, thieved, raped, got drunk, did all the correct things that victorious warriors usually did, and generally delivered unpleasant medicine to the enthusiastic

Parliamentarians and Puritans who had forged 15,000 swords for the Earl of Essex but refused to make one for their King.

The wonderful increase of trade after the Restoration expanded the town over the top of the hill. There, early in the eighteenth century, dignified lay-outs developed, charming and spacious effects that now, alas, can be gleaned only from copper-plate prints and "prospects." Sedate house fronts, the Bluecoat School (1724), and avenues of trees lined the square about St. Philip's Church, consecrated in 1715. Shorn of all but one or two of its original frontages, the square at least remains, and the church continues to show the tower, dome, and cupola, a most original and masterly composition designed by Thomas Archer, uncle of Lord Archer of Umberslade (195). The Old Square, an open space still, developed in similar style with Queen Anne and Georgian houses all round and lawns in the middle, pleasant features long since engulfed by commerce. Here the earliest houses, due to William Wesley, a forgotten architect, were occupied by 1713. The last of them to stand, the demolition of which I witnessed from the site of the priory, made a home for Hector, Samuel Johnson's lifelong friend and brother of Ann, the wordy master's first love; there in 1733 the Doctor produced his first book, the translation of Lobo's *Voyage to Abyssinia*.

Carried onward by the Industrial Revolution, the splendid and tragic event that brought so much and spoiled so much, the town grew bigger and bigger. Fame spread out, wealth poured in. The eighteenth-century increase of inhabitants from 15,000 to 73,000, made Birmingham one of the foremost places in the kingdom. Trade advancement and multitudes of people meant more streets and more and more buildings—premises and workshops for little and big manufacturers, artisans and merchants; homes for masters, homes for men, homes for inventors and thinkers; a place for Joseph Priestley's laboratory and one for the library of William Hutton, the historian (both burnt down by rioters in 1791); an establishment at Easy Hill for John Baskerville after he had risen from teaching writing in the Bull Ring to be a very prince of typographers, friend of Shenstone, Dodsley, Benjamin Franklin, and Horace Walpole. Substantial houses with classic doorways approached from iron gates and forecourts made comfortable and elegant residences for the men and women who helped to forward the great centre that sold "what all the world desires to have— Power," as Boulton told Boswell in 1776. Some of these roomy abodes continued a chequered existence into this present century in shabby surroundings, then gave up the ghost as their former prosperous owners had done. The de Byrmyngham's moat was filled up in 1816; it's a long time since Mrs. Gillott called orders to the workshop upstairs "Another pen, Jo"; and many a year has passed since the town developed into the colossus that offered a sure mark for German raiders. But the city with a Royal Charter, and ever marching forward, keeps a sentimental thought for its early days by stimulating crotchety old ages for the timbered Golden Lion Inn and for Sir Thomas Holte's Aston Hall, built in the full Jacobean style of mullions, curved gables, long gallery, elaborate staircase, and fine interiors, nowadays sadly rattled by the yelling and cheering from the Aston Villa football ground.

New triumphs in the nineteenth century brought new faces of people and buildings. Among them were George Borrow to see "the greatest workshop of England," Cardinal Newman at the Oratory, J. Henry Shorthouse to weave the romance of Rome into *John Inglesant* at Edgbaston. Peculiar things of a peculiar architectural period developed. Now they are particularly remembered by Francis Goodwyn's 1823 Gothic at Holy Trinity Church, the Roman Catholic cathedral known as one of Pugin's "spiky 'uns," Barry's rebuilt Grammar School of King Edward VI (recently destroyed), which enabled Archbishop Benson, Burne-Jones, and other celebrated and ordinary mortals to swot up their first Latin pronouns and verbs. The Town Hall made an effective display with the imitative classicalism of the 1830's; it was all ready for Mendelssohn to go inside in 1846 and first produce *Elijah* at one of the Musical Festivals, the celebrated events to which sensitive early Victorian ladies arrived from miles around and took their pleasures in the manner indicated by these words written to my grandmother

I never heard anything so splendid as the music, it was overpowering. One of the Miss Cliffords fainted and was taken out, and her sister soon followed in strong Hysteria from which she fell into an Epilepsy and continued insensible for three hours.

The writer, Lady Boyne, added, "I could not bear the excitement every day but to-morrow I will go to the *Messiah*"; evidently she was one of the brave women of the period. This classic hall on an island site, designed by Hansom, producer of the Hansom cab, brings to an end my slight notes on the Midland metropolis, my one sample of a great industrial city offered in this book.

EAST AND WEST OF THE MALVERN HILLS

When days are bright and clear you may stand on the Worcestershire Beacon above Great Malvern Priory, one foot in Worcestershire, the other in Herefordshire, look eastward over the great Severn–Avon plain, spy over a grand cathedral tower and across Worcestershire bounded by the Clent Hills, Lickey Hills, and the Cotswolds (132), then turn eyes west to see the rich green vale of Herefordshire with another cathedral tower, broken configurations, courses of the Rivers Wye and Lugg, and distances of hills and mountains that lead into Wales. Doubtless Will Langland had looked both these ways when he slumbered and "dreamed—marvellously," saw in a vision *Piers Plowman*, the "fair felde ful of folke," kings, nobles, bishops, monks, squires, merchants,

BRAMPTON BRYAN. *De Harley's ancient stronghold, stubbornly defended in the Civil War, aligns with Richard's Castle and Wigmore in the castled country of the Marches.*

STOKESAY CASTLE. *This rare survival of a fortified home was erected by the de Ludlow family in the thirteenth century. Later builders added the overhanging timbering and an Elizabethan gatehouse.*

CLUN. *Lofty ruins of Fitz-Alan's Norman keep in the gaunt little town near Offa's Dyke and entrenchments ascribed to Caractacus. The castle probably figures in "The Betrothed"; Scott stayed at the local inn, The Buffalo, when writing the novel.*

freemen, and serfs, the society of his own time in the reigns of Edward III and Richard II. At this beacon top of 1395 feet, showing more than a dozen counties, anyone still can see visions, dream dreams, in the reign of King George VI. Spread out below are many of God's own fair scenes not yet spoiled by man, cathedrals and churches of old faith, Evesham, Worcester and Mortimer's Cross where battles were fought, time-honoured houses, country towns, secluded villages, and particular homelands to be pried at, if desired, for reminders of Richard Baxter (Kidderminster), David Garrick (Hereford), Walter Savage Landor (Ipsley), Elizabeth Barrett Browning (Hope End), Edward Elgar (Broadheath), A. E. Housman (Bromsgrove), John Masefield (Ledbury), and other gifted folk about whom much or little is known.

First of Worcestershire. Wanderings through the county have given me excitements now best recalled by things of this sort—glorious trees and orchards everywhere; masses of yellow plums here and there; loveliest reaches of the Avon through the vale in sight of Bredon Hill (113); a sequence of two centuries beautifully shown by the towers at Pershore, Worcester (108-109), Malvern (132) and Evesham (114); Tenbury, Bewdley, Upton-on-Severn, Pershore and Evesham for representatives of country towns with old pasts; half-timbered houses and historic homes (118, 124); tithe barns at Littleton and Bredon; dozens of pigeon houses from Avon to Teme (129); the general prettiness of the villages (116, 118); Croome D'Abitot, Naunton Beauchamp, Grafton Flyford, Chaddesley Corbett, and Hanley William for samples of the good-sounding, double-barrelled place-names; Green Hill, where Simon de Montfort tragically ended his fight for English freedom; Worcester's standing reminders of Charles's getaway from Cromwell, which enabled England to continue with a King later on; the Gunpowder Plotters' route of flight after a mad bid for religious liberty; the kindness of a lady met at Hampton Lovett, who suggested the possibility of meeting Sir Roger de Coverley's ghost at Sir John Pakington's tomb if I waited in the church until midnight—a prank I didn't fancy; facial and phychological studies offered by natives under the royal sign of the *Queen Elizabeth* inn at the most precious of villages, Elmley Castle, on a night after a Boxing Day meet of foxhounds on Bredon Hill; an anchorage from a night of deluge inside the *Union* inn, Flyford Flavell, when more human impressions were accumulated from local patrons, who spoke the speech of their fathers and did not wear Worcester gloves while mixing Worcestershire sauce with their stories.

Signs of the quiet life and nature's luxuriance pure and undiluted might not be considered the particular attractions for visiting the Worcestershire regions of Dudley, Oldbury, and the outliers of Birmingham. But once clear of industrial bulwarks and urban sprawls a good deal is visible that cannot have greatly changed since the Papist historian of Hindlip, Thomas Habington (1560-1647), made his observations while captive in his own county after being involved in the Babington plot. Through Worcestershire, and onwards into Herefordshire and Shropshire, the farther west you go the better are the chances of finding the things that some people think made and make England. Stanley Baldwin, Earl Baldwin of Bewdley, evidently found them and thought so. Hereabout it is appropriate to recall the statesman's words spoken in 1924. "To me, England is the country, and the country is England," he said; no doubt memories of a native Worcestershire were in his thoughts then voiced on an England known through the various senses—sounds of the corncrake, the scythe against the whetstone, the hammer on the anvil, sights of wild anemones in April, the plough team, the last load of hay,

"and above all, most subtle, most penetrating and most moving, the smell of wood smoke coming up in an autumn evening, or the smell of the scutch fires: that wood smoke that our ancestors, tens of thousands of years ago, must have caught on the air when they were coming home. . . . These things strike down into the very depths of our nature, and touch chords that go back to the beginning of time and the human race. . . . These are the things that make England."

Or, I humbly beg to add, the things that did make England before the tractors and combine harvesters arrived, before the last few generations converted fields into towns to engulf the bulk of the population without day by day chances of seeing wild anemones, hearing corncrakes, or sniffing wood smoke.

Except at the northern tip, verging on the Black Country, Worcestershire is blest with the kind of ground and scenes that did and do make the best of England, real English in essence and on hand-shaking terms with Herefordshire, a county known to knowing ones as the most beautiful of all. Without extravagant scheming for startling effects nature showered her gifts with a loving hand over the Worcestershire plain, and man has been working hard at it ever since William of Malmesbury found the Vale of Evesham fruitful and lovely in the twelfth century. Landscape forms, far extended, mark the variegated mixtures of pastures and ploughlands, miles of orchards, trim patterns of market gardens. Strings and poles train green avenues of hops westward from Worcester into Herefordshire. Trees in abundance add full and rich colours, bright, deep green, and golden in changing seasons, gracious with trunks and branches in their winter garb. Elms ranked like standing sentinals or trusty warriors on parade, the elms which I adore, give to the county a special character. The River Severn traces a strong and bold line from north to south, from Wyre Forest to Tewkesbury's meadows, an immemorial line of strife and fighting when wars swayed to and fro over the Marches, and a water-line of thriving trade in the later days of the prows and busy wharves, now grass-grown, at Bewdley. The Avon, river of peace, curves and winds below Bredon Hill, where, long ago, the soft valley air rang with melodies of abbey chimes

from Evesham and Pershore, and monks passed over the four bridges at Offenham (now gone), Evesham (replaced 1856). Pershore (c. 1413), and Ecking-
ton (rebuilt 1729). The Teme hurries down from the high lands of romance;
rippling along from Tenbury to Powick old bridge, it is nice to fancy the eddies
circling to a haunted strain of *Comus* caught from Ludlow,

> Sweet Echo, sweetest nymph, that liv'st unseen
> Within thy airy shell.

Rivers, little streams, rich leafiness, haunts of quiet, lands of diligent labour,
church spires and embattled towers, towns and villages of black and white and
brickwork, old manorial homes—all the wealth of the plain is set out like a
green bowl of golden promise sheltered below the ring of hills. It can be looked
into all round, from the Malverns, Bredon Hill and Broadway Beacon, from
the Ridge Way used by ancients laden with Droitwich salt, from the Lickey
Hills above Bromsgrove's Gothic steeple, from Woodbury Hill, where Owen
Glundwr mustered his forces against Henry IV and a future Henry V.

Though not an exceptional group, most of the Worcestershire old parish
churches are interesting and many occupy very rural situations. Developed in
the usual medieval styles onward from Norman, a sprinkling of Georgian
effects rounded off the periods. Lowish and embattled towers of the fifteenth
century are characteristic and plentiful (as at Alvechurch, Astley, Bretforton
and Berrow) and Bredon, Halesowen, and Bromsgrove have the less frequent
spires. This wooded county gained uncommon features with the five towers
constructed of sixteenth-century timbers, two of which sparkle in black and
white at Pirton and Dormston. Eighteenth-century modes are well illustrated
in several places and notably at Worcester. The church on the hill at Tardebigge,
produced by Francis Hiorn of Warwick and sat in by the Earls of Plymouth,
followed the classic fashion of 1777 and mounted one of the most graceful
spires of the period. Some years earlier, in 1763, the Earl of Coventry fancied
and paid for an essay of "the Gothick" at Croome d'Abitot. Prettily placed on
the edge of "Capability" Brown's park, the goodish tower, the outside of the
church and its amusing interior may have been designed by Robert Adam.
Sanderson Miller, both, or neither. That's a secret. These two churches keep a
stock of Coventry and Plymouth monuments. In other directions there is no
lack of display in reminders of pride departed. Samples are offered by the
tombs of the sixteenth-century Blounts at Astley, Talbots at Bromsgrove,
sixteenth- and seventeenth-century Biggs at Norton, Savages at Elmley Castle.
Impressive Sheldon monuments at Beoley recall originators of the celebrated
tapestry weaving begun at Barcheston in the middle of the sixteenth century.
The Russells assembled a large family party at Strensham. First arrivals turned
up in armour and brass onward from 1375 and so provided Worcestershire with
its oldest memorial brass; Sir Thomas (1618) and Sir Francis (1704) appeared

later with sculpture most cunning, but eventually the line wore thin, went feminine, and the gathering tamely ended at a wall tablet of 1774. During four centuries, however, this party made up a remarkable display of costume, heraldry, and craft expression. Earlier members observed the traditional solemnity of their occasions, reposed flat, with hands at prayer in hope and expectation. Not so Sir Francis. He lived through the Restoration, had known the disillusions of experience. He kept to his curled periwig, cravat and breeches, lolled comfortably on a cushion, figured in a kind of conversation piece with his wife under the eyes of plump heavenly cherubs instead of a neighbour ancestor's skulls, with as much as to say that even a tomb, while symbolic of vanity, virtue, and joyous immortality, can be quite a human and sociable affair if properly schemed in the round to the many dimensions of earthly life. Sir Joshua Reynolds did not think this sort of thing seemly. Others may agree with him. Yet this figure represented in a wig, reclining, and talking perhaps can be just as allusive for immortality as one portrayed lying flat and silent, particularly if it is reckoned that some people at least will go on talking for ever.

On the right days for scent very good scenes were made by the Croome Hunt; fox, hounds, master, huntsman, and riders extended in a swift line from the fox's nose tip, with Besford church for a static and secondary accent in the background, gave me one of the best hunting pictures I ever saw, a proper Herring or Crawhall effect only, being the real thing, much better. The memory of it also reminds me that the secular rather than the ecclesiastical department of life had the best architectural run in Worcestershire. Pursuit in that direction brings plentiful rewards. Manor and country homes, villages, hamlets and towns, offer in total a well-defined expression of vernacular building conspicuous for timber construction and brickwork and bearing a family likeness to similar work in Warwickshire, features of which I have tried to indicate in the previous section.

Neither my space nor the need exist for enlarging on words already written by experts and others on the great houses of Worcestershire, mansions which include the Lyttleton's home of Hagley Hall, lively inside with Vessali's plaster decorations and Chippendale's fittings; Witley Court, produced out of the iron industry by the Foleys; Croome Court, standing in the park created out of a swamp by Lancelot Brown; Hanbury Hall, correct to the year 1701 with angle quoins, eaves cornices and dormers; and best of all, Westwood House, made vivacious by Pakington owners, Elizabethan four-square in plan with Restoration additions set diagonally at each corner, and containing elaborate oak interiors and the best of late seventeenth-century plasterwork. These big effects are not for everybody to see. Soon they may be widely available. At Croome, for instance, delinquent juveniles were to follow the earls; they did not arrive, so now sub-normal boys will inherit the works made in a noble past by Robert

The Feathers Hotel

The Angel Hotel
before renovation

Lane's Asylum

The Reader's House

NOTES IN LUDLOW

SHREWSBURY. *Wyle Cop, the ancient and picturesque street leading down t*
when travelling to Bosworth Field in 1485. Apartments occupied by Charles Di
stayed at this famous coaching establishment, De Quincey slept in the elegant eighte

nglish Bridge and the Abbey church. The central timbered house lodged Henry Tudor
t out beyond the main frontage of the Lion Hotel. Disraeli and a host of celebrities
ntury ballroom, and Paganini played in the musicians' gallery.

CAER CARADOC FROM SHARPSTONES. *The reputed fort of Caractacus, entrenched on the height of 1506 feet, commands Church Stretton and Mary Webb's country.*

Adam and "Capability" Brown for the sixth Earl of Coventry and Maria Gunning, the famous beauty painted by Reynolds.

Ordinary mortals, in possession of their senses and out of the peerage, are better suited with the lesser sights to be seen at close quarters or spied at from respectful distances. Village streets at Cleeve Prior (116), Ombersley, Rous Lench, and Ripple; villages like Abbot's Morton, Himbleton, Naunton Beauchamp, or Broughton Hackett (129) away from beaten tracks; adorable villages spread below Bredon Hill from Offenham (118), Cropthorne, Hinton-on-the-Green and Great Comberton; very many old family houses that offer such pictures as an early hall and screen at Eastington, a moated Birtsmorton known to chaplain "Thomas Wulsey" before he was a cardinal, Talbot's sixteenth-century oak and bargeboards at Salwarpe, Mere and Middle Beanhall both conspicuous for black and white gables, the Washington's home at Wickhamford (118), Kyre Wyard joining the work of earlier and eighteenth centuries (129); these, with more and more similar sights, give the truest architectural pattern of Worcestershire. Aspects of past day to day life are accurately set out by the plentiful sixteenth- and seventeenth-century timber construction, brickwork made to the fancies of late Tudor and Stuart builders, the more formal arrangements that served in Georgian and Regency times. Rarely out of sight is the prevalent black and white. It happily blends in landscapes and brightly groups in villages and country towns.

In this prosaic age, with little better than B.B.C. voices on the air or red traffic lights winking in the dead of night to give a body shudders and creeps, the old sort of phantoms, ghosts, hobgoblins and night fears shrouded in dim halos of the past may seem to be interesting and even sprightly. Worcestershire acres and houses had a good share in accommodating such spectral visions. No doubt ghosts as well as history were supplied by King Charles bolting from the battle of Worcester and Simon de Montfort trapped at Evesham; in quite early days the Conqueror's cousin, Urso the Bear, over from St. Jean d'Abbetot in Normandy, planted something more than the village names of Croome d'Abitot and Redmarley d'Abitot with his harryings, cruelty, and rapacity that earned the curse of the Saxon Archbishop of York,

> Highest thou, Urse,
> Have thou God's curse.

The district was long a centre for dissent, religious and political upheavals. Sins of Catholics, Protestants, and Puritans in the space of a hundred years from the time of Queen Mary to the Cromwellian interlude made life very uncomfortable for a great many people. Foxy houses developed, spooky places with mysterious insides hidden behind innocent oak and plaster, picturesque brickwork and big chimney-stacks. In one of them my body slid under movable stairs down a black bogey-hole, but hit neither fire, brimstone, nor clanging chains. That happened at Harvington Hall near Chaddesley Corbett, moated, timbered, reconstructed with brickwork in the seventeenth century, and successively lived in by the Pakingtons and the Throckmortons. At Huddington Court, 5 miles from Droitwich, I disappeared behind a wainscot into a secret gloomy recess, only to come out unharmed and make a drawing of the old walls from the edge of the moat. Tricks like these once could be performed all about Worcestershire, and nowhere better than at John Talbot's Grafton Manor and Thomas Habington's Hindlip House, monuments to the Jesuit archpriest of bogey-hole construction, Nicholas Owen, alias "Little John." Nobody used to get into these places for fun. They were risky necessities in the daily lives of most of the important local families who, after the close of Queen Mary's reign in 1558, clung to the old faith—sincere and devout men and women who worshipped in secret, suffered the religious persecutions under Queen Elizabeth and James I, were styled "Popish recusant convicts" and fined £20 a month for their belief, or endured, as Sir Thomas Tresham did, years of imprisonment and a fine of £2,080 annually for not attending the particular kind of church service dictated by the ruling power in control of the rationed religion. From these conditions, intimately connected with Worcestershire, grew the historical event now celebrated by juveniles with much hilarity, guys, and blacked faces. Of all the flights, escapes, captures and hidings that made nights shimmer with spectres for years afterwards none had more dramatic incident or even now offers better matter for hair-raising, none ever made more rubbish and fireworks to burn and explode than the one historic occasion remembered by the wild stampede of desperate fugitives galloping across the counties after the London news had spread on the fifth of November, 1605, "There is treason discovered! The King and the Lords should have been blown up."

Quickly the drama developed. Guy Fawkes, captured almost at midnight, went to the Tower. Soldiers guarded the 3,000 billets of wood, 500 faggots, 36 barrels of gunpowder. Catesby and John Wright, followed by Christopher Wright, Percy, Keyes, and Rookwood rode with haste and more haste from London on the relays of horses earlier placed by Rookwood at certain hostelries along the Holyhead Road. Travelling furiously in the wind and the rain of that November day, they reached the *Lion* inn, yet standing at Dunchurch, early in the evening, met the large company of Catholic gentry assembled there, told of the failure of the plot to proclaim the Princess Elizabeth queen. Ill news and forebodings dispersed the company. Forty members that remained by ten o'clock determined on flight westward, took horse, disappeared into the night.

Modern conspirators who disappear from Dunchurch in daylight to follow the tracks of the Gunpowder Plotters can cover their ground and find properties to fit this exciting old story; also, not being chased, more than once I have known there are opportunities for enjoying rural scenes and the sights of a very attractive locality. Even the charms of Warwick may suggest the fugitives helping themselves at midnight to remounts from the stables of Benock, the horse-dealer. Four miles on, at Northbrook below Sherbourne Hill, the early Victorian farmhouse locates the home of John Grant, brother-in-law of Robert Winter, at which arms and ammunition were collected; the moated grange of this wealthy squire long since shared the doom of its owner. The Plotters' route onward, started before dawn and laboriously followed during a wild wet day, lay through Snitterfield, the swollen ford of the river near Great Alne, Alcester's picturesque streets, and along the pretty Worcestershire lanes around Dormston to Huddington Court (124), a timbered house with a fine Tudor chimney, the home of Robert Winter, ardent Catholic and large landowner, Catesby's cousin, and married to the daughter of John Talbot of Grafton. Moated and forlorn, this manor-house as I first found it on a damp autumn day years ago seemed the most melancholy yet intact reminder or the beliefs, hopes, and crime that made the Gunpowder Plot. Though in need of repair the house kept the general look it had in 1605. Rain teemed into the moat. A kind country woman asked me inside out of the wet and also to see interiors fitted with contrivances for concealing Papists. A decayed window in the east gable, called, she said, Lady Winter's Window and originally made for lighting the hall, no doubt had been looked through by Robert Winter's wife when she saw her husband and the weary, travel-stained fugitives arrive in the afternoon of that Wednesday, November 6, later to be joined by the fearless Thomas Winter, the last in flight from London. A stone fireplace showed the arms of Edward III, the Huddingtons and the Cromleys carved on the mantel. Round it had gathered and dined together for the last time the thirty brave Englishmen who had risked all and lost all in the cause they believed to be right, conscious of the impending fate earlier voiced by Catesby to Winter at Warwick, "What, hast thou any hope, Robin? I assure thee there is none that knowest of this action but shall perish." At three o'clock the next morning Mass was celebrated in the house. The conspirators confessed, re-armed, rode away in the darkness before dawn. Meanwhile an armed force prepared for pursuit, commanded by the Sheriff of Worcestershire, Sir Richard Walsh, over from his timbered Court House at Shelsley Walsh, where motorists now meet for car trials.

"It's a pity the old place is in such a bad state," a friend said to me at Huddington.

"Yes," I replied. "Whether you like the Plot or not it did cause the annual search and spring-cleaning of the Parliament cellars, besides suggesting a possible good way for posterity to deal with redundant politicians. This house has a niche in our history. Also, it is very pretty to look at. Something ought to be done about it."

An appeal in a responsible quarter to save the house brought the reply, "Let the damned thing perish," evidently sent by an unbeliever in Gunpowder Plots or Plotters! I did not see Huddington again. It suits me best to picture the scene through the eye of memory, particularly after reading this news in John Russell's *Shakespeare's Country*, "a house whose restoration is more than usually to be deplored . . . uniform Trust House black-and-white, walls being broken and extra gables inserted in existing bays."

The desperate ride of the Plotters continued. Dumpy hills, green vistas and the elms, thatched roofs, brick cottages, the black and white of houses mark their route past Hanbury, Tardebigge, Hewell Grange (here arms and gunpowder were stolen from Lord Windsor), Burcot to Clent in sight of the Lickey and Clent Hills, onward through Hagley and Stourbridge (where the ford in flood damped the stolen gunpowder) and lastly to Holbeach, five miles within Staffordshire, Stephen Littleton's home, in which the gunpowder exploded while being dried and burnt Catesby and Rookwood. Soon the Sheriff appeared, set fire to the house, captured prisoners; before Catesby was shot dead he said to Thomas Winter, "Stand by me, Tom, and wee will dye together." Only relics of the original house and two hiding-holes survive from that final scene on November 8, 1605. Apart from the London executions of the conspirators, including Thomas and Robert Winter, and also of the celebrated Father Garnet, the Jesuit, who was captured at Hindlip after hiding in a hole for eleven days, the end of this sad, eventful history in Worcestershire leads us to the county town where John Winter and Humphrey Littleton met their end at the scaffold on Red Hill.

Less than fifty years after these executions, when Cromwellians had murdered a king and accomplished a deed that plotters failed to do, Parliamentarians at the Battle of Worcester crowded the cathedral with 6,000 prisoners, wrecked "Popish" imagery, plundered and damaged the interior of the fabric. Hardly less destructive were the onslaughts of restorers. From the middle of the eighteenth century until 1874 they attacked and transformed the exterior, but did earn thanks for keeping the building upright. In spite of these varied attentions, gifts from the golden age are visible in the grandeur of immense expanse, length and height, the noble proportions created in the rebuilding begun in 1224 and culminated in 1374 with the completion of the glorious tower, the earliest of their great Perpendicular masterpieces. Beauty and craftsmanship tell of the bygone time in the long nave, double transepts, the Norman crypt, clustered shafting in the thirteenth-century choir, Prince Arthur's magnificent chantry, the cloister complete, and a fourteenth-century refectory now part of the school. Great church and tower dominate the famous views seen from the Severn bank (108–109). Possibly they did not attract the plotters of ugliness, who usefully could have applied gunpowder on completing their power

BRIDGNORTH. *The up-and-down town on the River Severn has queer stepped byways and the leaning tower of a Norman keep. Good examples of timbered houses include the birthplace of Bishop Percy, famed for his poetical "Reliques."*

COALBROOKDALE. *The early iron industry settled here, marred beauty on one of the finest stretches of the River Severn. A mile away the ruins of Buildwas Abbey in a glorious setting offer one of the sights of England.*

163

THE WREKIN *from Grinshill. This volcanic mountain, isolated 1335 feet over the Severn plain, stands for the Shropshire toast, "To all friends round the Wrekin."*

NORTH SHROPSHIRE PLAIN *from Clive, near Wem, and backed by the Welsh mountains beyond Ellesmere. Clive was the birthplace of William Wycherley, the Restoration dramatist.*

station with four circular vomit pipes alongside the bridge. These utilitarian objects belched forth like hell upon earth during my sketching operations, sent filthy vapour towards the grand symbol of faith stronger than kilowatts, emitted smoke over the cricket ground where the Fosters merrily knocked up centuries in the summer suns of yesterdays.

Though smoke and manufacture exist elsewhere in this active county capital, no lack of pleasant things remain left over from candlelight years. Eighteenth-century houses in the close, a good collection, have the proper calm and cultured outside demeanour for their situation, whatever may happen inside them to-day. The Edgar gateway of a destroyed castle opening into the court of the King's School, buildings extending to the cloister and spread below the grand cathedral tower, give scenes gracious enough to make anyone wish to live school days there for ever. Conspicuous among the early churches is the fifteenth-century spire of St. Andrew's, notably visible above the bridge and the houses in one of the river views. For those who like the idea of Christian worship without soaring Gothic vaults and mysticism there are the Georgian churches of St. Nicholas (1730), St. Swithun (1736), All Saints (1742), and St. Martin (1772). These add particular character to the city's skylines. Most impressive is the steeple of St. Nicholas, obviously adapted from a design by James Gibbs for St. Mary-le-Strand, London. St. Swithun's interior, delightfully intact as completed in 1736, mounts a *tour de force* in the imposing three-decker with pulpit perched high under a sounding-board, the dove above, an eagle below, and enough carved devices and etceteras all round to illustrate any parson's texts and thirdlys. Inns abound; before visiting all of them an explorer might first sample the timbering of the *Farrier's Arms* in Fish Street, effects reminiscent of a Cecil Aldin at the *Crown* yard in Broad Street, the big and solid front of the *Star* that used to intrigue me inside for sirloin in the merry decades when Englishmen could enjoy real roast beef. New Street, Friar Street, and Silver Street show off the old fancies for black timbers, white panels and overhanging beams. The Commandery, a rare English treasure, stands at the site of the Saxon Bishop Wulfstan's charitable foundation; history's tales are told with Tudor hall and oriel, hammer-beams and wall paintings, an Elizabethan staircase and the room in which a Royalist duke went to die after the fighting at Fort Royal. In this "Faithful City" you appropriately read carved on an old beam in Cornmarket, LOVE GOD—WB 1577 RD—HONOUR YE KING, and perhaps at the same time think that Charles bolted from a back door behind the said beam en route for the Boscobel Oak. Round about ancient streets are mazes of narrow passages and courts unaltered in plan from early centuries, the death-traps in the hand-to-hand fighting and the carnage of that awful September day in 1651, proudly called by Cromwell his "crowning mercy." But merrily rang the bells of Worcester on May 29, 1660. The Stuart had come back to roost to be merry. "FLOREAT SEMPER FIDELIS CIVITAS" blazed resplendent from the Guildhall in 1724, when Thomas White, designer and stone-carver, completed the brightest and most loyal of civic buildings. Arms, trophies, cupids blowing trumpets, urns, and a lantern high up aloft join in the felicitous, even giddy, display behind the railings and gates made by the famous smith, Robert Bakewell. Royal with figures of Charles I, Charles II, and Queen Anne carved by White, the classic centrepiece also offers warnings to evil doers with the scales and sword of justice and Cromwell's head nailed up by the ears. And a warning, too, for me. We are long overdue for Herefordshire.

Particular people who know what's what, therefore not very numerous, have no doubt that Herefordshire is the most beautiful of all English counties. Some of them have told me so, and why; but with Shropshire on one side and Monmouthshire on the other, to award the laurels seems as difficult as the predicament of Paris faced with the girls and the apple. Other people, not very particular, titled M.P.s for short, and given to talking overmuch when the face of Big Ben is lit up, wish to wipe this very beautiful county clean off the map of England. To them, and all others who threaten Herefordshire's right and just place in the country's cartography and record of history, home and beauty, I say go to the — that is, go and look for themselves if they have eyes to see and vision to understand.

For Herefordshire is a comely county, friendly and kind to be in, just the place for enjoying orchards and gardens, trees magnificently grouped and shaped, great big woodlands stretching for miles, tumbled hills and high places commanding wide panoramas. Ridges, steep valleys and mountains of the Marches can lead weary souls clean out of this troubled century into the back ends of nowheres. From the fastnesses of Wales the River Wye flows down past Hay and the Edwardian castle relics of the mighty de Cliffords, Lords Marchers; tracing curve after curve and many a horseshoe bend the river crosses the county through Hereford and Ross (137), turns a romantic course below the wooded promontory capped with the Norman keep and broken towers of Goodrich, triumphantly meets the borders in the grand and famous sweeps at Welsh Bicknor and Symonds Yat. The River Lugg, fresh from the Radnor mountains, courses through Byton and Aymestrey between hill slopes verdant with the finest woodlands imaginable, then bounds the battlefield of Mortimer's Cross, handsome young Edward's victorious point for the White Rose and the Throne in 1461; the waters divide the flattish and fertile vale to and past Leominster, circle round the hill and the church of the Knights Hospitallers at Dinmore, and finally swell the Wye at Mordiford. Where the Black Mountains show in the west the little River Dore leaves the heights, the tumps, and the cromlech near Dorstone for the Golden Valley; the stream babbles through Peterchurch, gathered round the slender Decorated spire pointing over an unspoiled Norman church interior, meets Abbey Dore, rare with the Early English loveliness left by the Cistercians—and it's golden in the vale when cornfields ripen for harvest, apples colour, and beauty mellows on the hillsides showering gold, gold more precious than old-time sovereigns. Beyond the valley's eastern end is the rarest of rarities, Kilpeck church (c. 1150–75), standing by the Norman fragments of Hugh FitzNorman's castle; humans, beasts, birds, fishes, beak-heads, a monkey, a bull, a pig, warrior knights thought to be Welshmen, all manner of features, shapes, and grotesque, here and there looking rather paganish, show what the Romanesque carvers could do in the way of rich decoration when they really meant to show off (143). There is no suspicion of paganism over the neighbouring hill by Garren Brook at Orcop when the Christian message perpetually freshens around midnight on Old Christmas Eve and the miraculous symbol of the Holy Thorn blooms year by year, so the oldest inhabitants say.

The wide vales centred round Leominster, Hereford, and Ledbury give pastoral landscapes of the real Midland sort, softly coloured with field and hedgerow, pastures where the Herefordshires feed, climbing leaves and catkins criss-crossed in the gardens near the pointed cones and cowls of the hop-kilns. Cloud effects form and change above these green levels—I've spent hours sketching them over by Pembridge, Eardisland, and Ashperton—and the Arrow, Frome, Leadon, and smaller streams wind in and out past feathery trees, banks speckled with wild flowers, and rushes in sight of sporty trout that send rings circling through watery reflections. Wars, "grim-visaged," rather than the piping times of peace, are definitely hinted when you find Offa's Dyke above the Wye at Mansell Hill, the point at which the defensive ramparts turned north from the river in advance of the Roman line through Kenchester and Leintwardine. Not much of the Dyke is on view until Shropshire is reached. But banks, ditches, and broken-down castle relics crown height after height from de Lacy's Longtown in the south to the northern reminders of the Mortimers and the de Harleys at Wigmore and Brampton Bryan (149). These bristle up in quantities prolific enough to satisfy all romantic enthusiasts who like to ponder on warriors that faced, fought, and chased each other, raided east through Hereford to the Severn, raided west into the mountains, and regularly killed each other when English, Welsh, and Norman blood flowed through the Marches. Ravens feasted and widows wept in the "days of old," now tinted with romance only because they occurred such a long time ago.

Often it is prettier and much more romantic to find still in commission amongst peaceful green backgrounds and orchards the black and white buildings, the remarkable and conspicuous features in the Herefordshire make-up, which show how the native carpenters developed timber construction to its zenith from the trees of the woodlands. At Cradley (137), Bosbury, Church

LOWER BROCKHAMPTON HALL

Lane, Ledbury, Mansell Lacy (144), Pembridge, Luston, Dilwyn—here, there, and everywhere shine the magpie patterns on houses, market halls, cottages, farms, barns and dovecotes, lively with the particular turns the craftsmen gave to posts, braces and brackets, windows, bays, doorways, and gables (138), all held together with mortice and tenon, an invention in use from the beginnings of history. You can admire the brightness of timbers, light panels and carved fancies in manor-house after manor-house; for instance, at Wythall near Ross, Orleton Court, The Ley near Weobley, Staik House, Eardisland. Perhaps you may find Lower Brockhampton in a woody hollow near Bromyard, the fourteenth-century hall of the Brockhampton family, and the gatehouse reflected in the moat, a sight liable to make anyone gasp, as I did on first discovering this prize more than forty years ago. It is as many years since I found Weobley (10), one of the most remarkable townships in any shire. Then it was quite fantastic in black, white, and aged unrestored wobbles. Rarely visited by antique hunters of black or white intellects, meals had to be found and eaten under hoary timbers in the smelliest of bar parlours, remarkably queer for the pungent and beery atmosphere of centuries. All that remained of John Abel's town hall made a weathercock on the roof of a shop; but to wander in the old town below the perfect Decorated church spire brought a feeling of being a real Elizabethan or Jacobean prowling about in settings correct to period. Now tidied up, it's no longer

> Poor place, proud people ;
> Low church, high steeple.

The *Red Lion* is delicious for more than outside appearance, and the sparkling streets and byways still constitute an English wonder. The weathercock abovementioned reminds that Herefordshire was the homeland of John Abel, "one of His Majesty's carpenters," creator of a splendid town hall framed in timber at Hereford (demolished), another one at Leominster (now Grange Court of

Castle Gate, 1601

High St. Ireland's Mansion, Elizabethan

Butcher Row. Abbot's House. 15th cent.

Frankwell. 1576

School Gardens. Jacobean

SHREWSBURY DETAILS IN TIMBER

WHITCHURCH. *A Queen Anne group of old school (1708) and St. Alkmund's Church (1713). John Talbot, the great Earl of Shrewsbury who figured in Shakespeare's "Henry VI," was buried under the porch of the earlier church after he had fallen in battle near Bordeaux in 1453.*

1633), the screen at Abbey Dore church. the old school-house at Weobley, many more local halls and houses. This master constructor whose work and fame have lasted also, alas, concocted his own epitaph to commemorate a long span of ninety-seven years from 1577 to 1674. To demonstrate how the mighty may fall I quote the first two lines from the inscription at Sarnesfield church,

> This craggy stone a covering is for an Architector's bed,
> That lofty buildings raised high, yet now low lies his head.

Much more than is slightly noted on my pages does the face of Herefordshire present and suggest. While the early houses developed the ball-flower ornament flourished for the cathedral and churches in the fourteenth century. Poetry— the land has bred and inspired poets for England since Langland's summer days on Herefordshire Beacon until "Ledbury bells broke forth" for Wordsworth and chimed "sweetly, slowly" over John Masefield's birthplace. The county gave Kembles and David Garrick for the stage. It has fermented cider for centuries, grows hops, shows "Hop Pole" inn signs, breeds the white-faced cattle. This countryside of promise and delight, one that keeps beauty unalloyed and does not advertise itself, offers wealth more than enough to convince any- one, even M.Ps., that Herefordshire should be treasured, kept intact on the map of England, preserved from robbers just as the unique world map, the Mappa Mundi, has been guarded at the cathedral since about 1290.

While Adam and Eve and the Ark on Richard of Haldingham's map in the cathedral concern a time somewhat earlier than the beginning of Hereford's long past, a great deal of history belongs to this ancient town of King Offa, its see claimed to be one of the oldest, its shrine famed in the Middle Ages, its sieges, Border strife, and burnings, its buildings that once made streets of black and white, and the generations of men and women who did deeds remembered onward from the days when Ethelbert, King of East Anglia, made love to Offa's daughter, Altrida, lost his heart followed by the loss of his head, consequently expired in 794, caused a shrine to be erected and the cathedral to be dedicated to St. Ethelbert as well as to St. Mary. It is not for me to enlarge on such matters of general knowledge, nor to resurrect the Norman keep and great stone towers demolished by Cromwellians at Castle Green, medieval town walls reminded by Wall Street, the lost six gates, John Abel's large, timbered and departed town hall, all now invisible, merely notable for remembrance, possible lamentation, and rosemary. Rather do I put down quickly a few im- pressions likely to be gained in this city now busy, flourishing and attractive on the banks of the Wye plumb in the middle of the county.

The cathedral precincts, the fifteenth-century bridge, and the river walks afford the prime viewpoints (130–131). Byways and the quieter thoroughfares best show the timbered and Georgian brick frontages; survivors in High Town, and conspicuously the capital black and white of the former Butchers'

Guild House constructed in 1621, indicate the earlier pattern in this central and generous space. Widemarsh Street has the Coningsby Hospital with the Black-friars ruins adjacent. Interesting woodwork and misericords belong to St. Peter's Church, and to All Saints; the latter also possesses 313 chained books. The *Green Dragon*, the *Mitre* with a gay sign, the *Tabard*, the *Hop Pole*, and a crop of significant inn names aptly commemorate various happenings and blessings bestowed on this centre of holiness and knightly deeds where cider has been on draught since the fourteenth century.

Human departments of life in various ages and stages are available for observation and speculation. Contemporary natives and country folk in the streets, at the race meetings, adorned for Three Choirs Festivals, in juxtaposition with animals at the celebrated livestock markets; famous singers visible every third year over breakfast bacon and/or one egg each at the *Green Dragon*; men, women, innumerable brats, their bundles, meat pies, and speech, arrived at the railway station for the hop-picking; these and other effects regularly or periodi-cally in view naturally suggest earlier celebrities who, though not on view, probably at midnight haunt certain places that are obvious in daylight. One of the latter is or was, David Garrick, born in Widemarsh Street; here, while Captain Peter Garrick looked for army recruits, Mrs. Garrick produced her own recruit for the stage in 1717. Four years later Mrs. Kemble continued the good work by presenting Roger; and he, conscious of duty, fathered twelve more lights for the footlights, including John, Philip, Stephen (baptized at Kington), Charles, and the divine Sarah (Mrs. Siddons). Corinthian capitals, frieze, and pediment at the Kemble Theatre in Broad Street classically stand for the classic name—but I wept to find the movies featuring in the place of Sarah's Desdemona. Not so classic, yet not void, is the long blank wall beyond the west end of the cathedral. There, years ago, an old, old man of whom I sought knowledge about this wall merely said he was very deaf, felt very middling; and a grubby young angler carrying a jam-jar by a string brightly answered my questioning by asking, "Say, mister, have you got any cigarette cards?"—two encounters which proved that prophets, even shady ones, are not without some sort of honour save in their own country. Unaided I found the expected object, the lettered tablet prophetic of oranges in Old Drury, red coats in Chelsea, bar-sinister babies, all dependent on "The site of the birthplace of Nell Gwynne, founder of Chelsea Hospital and Mother of the first Duke of St. Albans. Born 1650. Died 1691." Nice it was to think that "pretty witty Nell" did infantile capers and practised on this wall in preparation for King Charles over the garden wall in Pall Mall; nice to stand at the very spot, while also careful to forget that perhaps she never did, didn't found Chelsea Hospital, didn't even die in 1691, because the funeral happened in 1687!

A matter of boiled bones of a much earlier date rounds off my meditations on the human species in Hereford. Thomas de Cantilupe, the good bishop with the long nose and red hair, went to see the Pope in 1282, died on the way back, was promptly boiled down by his chaplain, Richard of Swinfield, afterwards bishop, and the bones reached Hereford Cathedral for burial. Very soon things began to happen. Miracles of healing occurred. Pilgrims consequently arrived from far and wide. In the medieval period the abode of the bones achieved a popularity and knack of gathering gold, silver, jewels, and cash only excelled by the shrine of St. Thomas at Canterbury. The shrine's base, now in the north transept, richly carved and unrestored, is one of the very few examples existing in England. More valued to-day than old bones are the jewels and treasures in stone left after severe maulings and restorations at this small cathedral. It remains intact with strong Norman masonry, and is proudly marked on Wye bank with the broad and sturdy tower, rebuilt about 1310, a premier specimen of ball-flower enrichment. Perhaps the most precious possession of all is the largest and most wonderful library of chained books in the world. Now, having just come out of it filled with admiration and despair at the sight of superb lettering, illumination, and printing, and without hope of bursting the chains to pinch even one book, I must away from Hereford, its beautiful county of vales, hills, timbering and castles, to continue my own inferior work.

IN SHROPSHIRE

Here again, beautiful to see and explore, is another claimant for England's most beautiful county; those like myself, with Shropshire ancestry and blood in their veins, of course rank it first, A1, nonpareil. Hills and mountains for grandeur, solitude, and wide-swept panoramas, miles of wooded banks, exquisite dales and rich vegetation fill the south from the Severn to Offa's Dyke where successively mount the heights of Clun Forest, Stiperstones, Caer Caradoc (158), Wenlock Edge, the Brown and Titterstone Clee Hills, grand viewpoints all for spying far and wide from camps and trackways made by early ancestors. The Marches in the west, scarred from old wars but dreamlands now in the quietest places under the sun, bristle with earthworks and ruined castles from Hopton Castle keep and Fitz Alan's Norman tower at Clun to Oswestry and Peverel's Whittington (175); over these scrapping grounds of vanished Lords Marchers and the fiery Welshmen who rarely disgraced their condition of birth by dying in their beds,

> The vanquished eve, as night prevails,
> Bleeds upon the road to Wales.

Northward from the Severn the big plain stretches in level miles and little rises to the lakes round Ellesmere and the Cheshire border; true pastoral country is this, patchworked with pasture, ploughland, and farms, the parks and the places, timbered and brick homesteads in the villages, pleasant towns old with streets for marketing and country folk to meet in at Newport, Hodnet, Wem, Whitchurch, and round the butter cross at Market Drayton. You can stand on Grinshill Hill above Clive (William Wycherley's birthplace) to see the vistas, the bird's-eye views over this plain, east and west from the aged volcanic Wrekin to the mountains of Wales, expanses from the Stretton hills in the south to the northern levels fading away in blue distances (164).

This county of mountain and hill, dale and plain, with heights for wide panoramas and shades for high romancing, has all sorts of wonderful things there for the finding. You can speed along Watling Street, Telford's Holyhead Road below the oldest English rock, Shropshire's very own Wrekin, enter and look round Roman *Uriconium* at Wroxeter, then with map handy, spirits up, and promise ahead follow on the tracks of the Fourteenth Legion along their route controlling the frontier, stopping on the way to look over many a fine view, remarkable half-timbering at Pitchford Hall, ruins of Edward I's council hall for the Statute of Acton Burnell, Caradoc oval camp and double ditches, black and white at Little Stretton, a Jacobean Sibdon castle, the rare fortified home of the thirteenth century at Stokesay (149), and Clungunford in the Clun valley. Ruined castles and signs of wars, though very plentiful, are matched by the works of men of faith and sometimes of peace who made the abbeys, now beautiful in decay and showing their Norman beginnings at Lilleshall, Haughmond, Much Wenlock, and loveliest of all, Buildwas, where the Severn swings round between the woods in a scene rarely equalled in England. Churches of all periods tempt church-hunters. Diddlebury has one of more than a dozen churches with Saxon masonry and herringbone work. Lydbury North, Edstaston, and frequent hill and valley places keep their Norman features of characteristic sturdy towers, Romanesque arches and carving. Of Gothic churches visited and remembered I can only mention the beauty, dignity, and sculpture at Tong and Shifnal, a fourteenth-century rebuilding at Chelmarsh, Battlefield Church commemorating the victory of 1403 (and Shakepeare's *Henry IV*), the spire at Worfield, Tudor roofs at Selattyn, a fifteenth-century screen and roof at Bettys y Crwyn high and remote by the Black Mountain; and of churches built in the classical period. St. Alkmund's in the eighteenth-century group at Whitchurch is one of the best (170).

Churches are not for everybody now we no longer expect to be Saxons, Normans, medievals, Georgians or Christians, but for travellers all on wheels or hiking, good to discover, nice to be in, and often difficult to leave are the villages, old houses, and country towns about which Salopians have lived since Saxon and Norman times and in which they continue to thrive. There are the villages of the plain, cosy groups of black and white, red walls, tiled and thatched roofs, not particularly distinctive or spectacular, but quiet, rural, and

OSWESTRY. *Timber window, Lloyd Mansion.*

WHITTINGTON CASTLE *between Oswestry and Ellesmere. The Plantagenet gatehouse to the ruined Norman stronghold, rebuilt after the Conquest by Peverell, kinsman of Peverel of the Peak.*

HAMSTALL RIDWARE. *The Hall Farm, once part of the manor-house with a watch tower. The farm contains linen panelling and carved roundels of the Tudor period.*

KING'S BROMLEY. *The green and the fifteenth-century church tower. The village, a royal possession in Norman years, stands on the River Trent within reach of the parks and oak-trees of Needwood Forest.*

fitting the wide landscapes broken by sundry bumps, the Hawkstone ridge, and the abrupt sandstone at Grinshill. More exciting, especially for those who carry fly-rods in addition to sketch-books or cameras, are the villages partly stone-built in the Clun valley, Corve Dale, Ape Dale, and more dales and vales, never far away from quick streams chattering along for sporty trout—and for you and me. In out-of-the-way villages high up and sometimes bleak—Clee St. Margaret, Easthope, and Ratlinghope are three—the summer air is as stimulating as the great ranges of scene offered; draughty seasons there and keen wintry days may bring an idea of Mary Webb's Deborah gazing out from John Arden's stone cottage "when grey rainstorms raced across from far Cader Idris," or can suggest Old Thomas Parr lustily thriving on good Shropshire air to the age of 152 years at Glyn. Practically every parish has its larger houses or a manor-house. Either built of native sandstone, patterned with black timbers and white panels in the west Midland style, or schemed to the local ideas of the early and late Renaissance, they stand all about Shropshire, often beautiful, always interesting, mostly dating from the easy sixteenth- to eighteenth-century times when prosperous people then knew that to have was to hold without being unduly skinned by harebrained politicians and ubiquitous tax-gatherers. Scores of these emblems of hearth and home can be tracked far and wide; some of my favourites are the sixteenth-century Wilderhope grim and high on Wenlock Edge, Elizabethan stone and broad bays at Shipton Hall in Corve Dale, Elsich very picturesque and moated a mile from Culmington, the Tudor hall at Willey south of Broseley, Whitton Court's fourteenth-century, Elizabethan, and Stuart features, Richard Baxter's timbered house at Eaton Constantine, many gables and high chimneys at Minsterley, a stately eighteenth-century brick and stone front at Halston Hall, Whittington. Numerous homes famed for associations, architecture, or the charms of noble situations can urge a leisurely wanderer to the Walcots' Walcot Park, the Plowdens' Elizabethan and Jacobean Plowden Hall, brave Viscount Hill's Hawkstone Park where the Red Castle (1232), the rocks, and the caves awed Dr. Johnson, Styche Hall of the Clives, the Corbetts' Longnor Hall perfectly preserved from 1670, Apley with the terrace and hanging woods, an eighteenth-century Attingham Hall, splendid Elizabethan stonework at Condover Hall (1586–1598), and one of the timbered gems of England, E-shaped, at Pitchford Hall. Within such houses, great and small, of course toasts have been drunk from generation to generation "To all friends round the Wrekin," ceremonies at which in my own time I have joined. The sight of these old homes, their smooth lawns, flower borders, roses, and topiary trees can send one's thoughts rambling back a bit. Easy it is to imagine successions of country squires settled on ancestral acres; their progeny, like Robert Clive and Rowland Hill, going out into the world to brighten the country's fame; bookish gents in panelled libraries; ladies furbishing by candlelight in powdering closets; original sitters for family portraits I have discovered here and there painted. by Thomas Hudson, Gainsborough, and lesser lights—to say nothing of cellars of canary, old port, and cobwebs that I never discovered, and their departed patrons, rakish, horsy, and hard-drinking sportsmen who may have bullied their wives, frightened their children, and possibly ended with poisoned pottage, as the *Gentleman's Magazine*, dated March 31, 1773, reported of my ancestor, Edward Fleming, lord of the manors of Westhope, Sibdon, and Shadwell.

Memories of Shropshire towns make me wish for the dozens of pages I cannot have to praise them. Shrewsbury, friendly rare Shrewsbury, shines like the jewel it is amongst English county capitals. Ludlow leads the country towns (page 18, 155). Almost matchless, it has the great castle ruined yet rich in pictorial motives to reanimate past glory, historic deeds, young Philip Sidney and Milton's *Comus*; grouped around are treasures of beauty at St. Lawrence's Church, the *Feathers* and the *Angel* for looking at and going inside, timbered buildings, Georgian houses, Broad Street and Broad Gate, every joyful sight imaginable mounted on, and in view from the rock above Ludford and opposite Whitcliff where the Teme circles round, running fresh and clear from the rugged steeps of Bringewood Chase and Downton. Towns on the Welsh border, peaceful now, keep a grim suggestiveness of stormy pasts in this tilting-ground of old feuds. Oswestry, where Penda of Mercia killed Oswald of Northumbria and nailed the body to a tree years before I can remember, even now looks crouched and ready for anything that might threaten from the mountains and Offa's Dyke; but the castle used for battles by Henry II, John, and Richard II has fallen to pieces, the presence of a lady mayoress on my last visit (1948) ensured no fighting in the streets between the friendly English and Welsh, and from the comfortable *Wynnstay* hotel you can safely emerge to see the few sights at the Lloyd mansion (175), Holbache's old school gables facing the churchyard, the Griddle Gate (1631), the great tower dating from about 1200, survivor of the church mostly demolished in the Civil War battle of 1644. Southward and beautifully set near the lonely Welsh border ridges lies Bishop's Castle with town hall Georgian, church tower ancient, and for the inevitable signs of fighting the scant relics of the Norman fortress of the mighty bishops and their outwork keep at Lea. South again, beyond wooded slopes and the high entrenchments of Bury Ditches, Clun fits its own wild valley: sleepy old Clun, hoary to summon the romantic mood and make you not wonder a bit that Walter Scott stayed in the *Buffalo* inn to write chapters of *The Betrothed*. Interesting for the church, a fine timbered lych-gate, the stone bridge, and charitably graced with the court-yard Trinity Hospital of 1614, its inmates and the kind master parson who used to give me nice teas, the grey little town has quite forgotten the turbu-

CLUN

lent years of fighting round the Norman keep (150) and the fortress-like church tower begun by the Saxons. You can sally forth westward without need of helm or armour for battling fiery warriors, climb heights studded with camps and tumuli, see from Hergan's 1342 feet the great Dyke of Offa still on guard facing the Caer Din Ring, idle away hours in the solitude and silence brooding over Clun Forest; if the tinkling bells of the Clun sheep tumble you to sleep on a grassy bank you may dream of the Fitz Alans, De Says, Prince Rhys, ghosts of hosts of raiders and fighters who used to prance about dangerously—even revivify old Caractacus himself in his camp of Caer Ditches, or perhaps at Coxall Knoll, making the last stand against the Romans, when the blood of the three days' battle dyed the stream that flows down from Llanvair Hill and to this day is called Redlake. Away from these borderlands of bloodthirsty fame captivating points abound in more historic towns. The wrought-iron bird of the *Raven* inn sign at Much Wenlock welcomes you to streets of old houses, the timbered guildhall, the Cluniac abbey ruins, the lovely prior's house. Queer stepped byways at Bridgnorth mount up from the Severn bridge to pretty and queer sights on the hilltop, handy to the black and white frontage of the *Swan* (163). Shifnal retains the "old houses crossed and recrossed in a great many directions with black beams" that Charles Dickens found useful for *The Old Curiosity Shop*, and not far away are more black beams at Boscobel, where King Charles hid in the oak tree (189). The pleasant and wide main street of Newport leads to the big fourteenth-century church tower and the school founded in 1657 by William Adams, the haberdasher (189). Another High Street, in Whitchurch, has one of those rare and curious shops called "penthouse-like" by Shakespeare, and at St. Alkmund's Church, rebuilt by Smith of Warwick in 1713 for £4,287 4s. 2d., all who enter by the porch must pass over the relics of John Talbot, thus obeying the dying wish of this Earl of

Shrewsbury, the foe of Joan of Arc that strides, fights, and dies across the pages of Shakespeare's *Henry VI*.

You may come to Shrewsbury from Shropshire's northern plain or the western hills, along Watling Street, or very attractively by following the Severn's course from Wyre Forest through Bridgnorth, Coalbrookdale (163) and Wroxeter, the lost Romano-British *Uriconium*, once a walled city of 170 acres for a highly developed civilization that vanished after thriving through four centuries, yet one of the most thrilling places in England when I saw Bushe Fox excavating this station of the Fourteenth Legion called Gemina. Six miles from these ashes of the dead the river curves to greet *Uriconium's* rival in age. Past the abbey church and stone relics of Roger de Montgomery's monastic foundation you reach the English Bridge, and lo! alive, thriving, lovely in features, steeped in old dreams stands the goal promised in A. E. Housman's lines,

> High the vanes of Shrewsbury gleam
> Islanded by Severn stream;
> The bridges from the steepled crest
> Cross the water east and west.

Worthily crowning its own delectable shire, here present delight joins with beauty, history and legend to yield everything that any respectable heart could desire for looking at, probing into, finding out. About the two immemorial hills almost encircled by the river, at every turn the past springs to life.

Shrewsbury pictures and stories could fill volumes of a long and full record. Early times developed in the Pengwern of the British, Scrobbesbyrig of the Mercian Saxons, Edward the Confessor's town recorded with 252 dwellings of wood and thatch. Middle and later ages are marked by the Norman castled stronghold of the Conqueror's kinsman, Roger de Montgomery; existing town walls of *circa* 1220; visible reminders of Austin, Black and Grey Friars; colours in windows and sermons in stones at churches founded by Saxons at St. Mary's, St. Julian's, St. Alkmund's, St. Chad's (classically rebuilt in 1790); Wyle Cop, High Street, Mardol, Frankwell, and more streets rarely equalled, and nowhere bettered for the timbered mansions, halls and houses of Tudor, Elizabethan, and Stuart years (156–157, 169); dignified homes erected with brickwork in Belmont, College Hill, The Crescent and elsewhere when Charles, William and Mary, Anne, and the four Georges sat on royal perches; the lodging in Wyle Cop for Harry Richmond before the Battle of Bosworth, the old school of Philip Sidney and Fulke Greville, the departed place for Pailin's Shrewsbury Cakes in Castle Street, Charles Darwin's birthplace at The Mount, the great market in which Mary Webb sold carrots; and, most wonderful, a dive out of Pride Hill under the sign of "The Fifty Shilling Tailors" into the medieval and Elizabethan atmosphere of Butcher Row, Fish Street, and Grope Lane, where it would seem most natural to meet an abbot of Lilleshall

PILLATON HALL, *near Penkridge, below the wooded uplands of Cannock Chase. The chapel (c. 1480) and the Tudor gatehouse are relics of the moated mansion lived in by the Lyttleton family for 300 years. Numerous Lyttleton monuments are in Penkridge church.*

THE FOUR CROSSES, *dating from 1630, an inn on Watling Street patronized in the coaching days by the London–Chester coaches. Tradition credits Dean Swift with a rude couplet scratched on a window-pane after spending a night here.*

LICHFIELD, *the city of Dr. Johnson's birth and Joseph Addison's child*
English and Decorated architecture. It was commenced in the twelfth cer

he cathedral with the only group of triple spires in England is notable for Early
mpleted in the fourteenth, wrecked by Cromwellians, and restored by Victorians.

LICHFIELD. *The Georgian front of the saddler's shop adjoining the archway to " The George" hotel (left).*
LICHFIELD. *Entrance to Michael Johnson's house and the place of Dr. Johnson's birth in 1709 (right).*

lolling against his own angle-post or spy Falstaff in for a drink at the *Bear* after his alarums and excursions at Battlefield. But words, mere words, never will do for this treasured town. It is one to be seen, explored, and inevitably loved.

To end my deficient babblings on one of the most fascinating large centres left in England, and for you, kind readers, and travellers all who merrily refresh and gratefully rest on their journeyings, I conclude by mentioning that Shrewsbury's remarkable, interesting, and historic inns include miniature forests of timber at the early *Golden Cross*, *Trumpet*, and *King's Head*, the *Old Post Office* grouped round a courtyard, the *Cross Keys* highly ornamented, a late Elizabethan *Nag's Head*, and the restored *Unicorn* of 1603. The *Lion* (157), a prince of its race, rebuilt over ancient cellars late in the eighteenth century by a prince of landlords, Robert Lawrence, has one of the rarest ballrooms on earth choicely decorated in the Adam style, a room in which Paganini played, De Quincey slept, Prince William Frederick (later William IV) danced, followed by generations of the fair and the brave twirling round and round on the oak floor until this present year of grace. "The strangest little rooms" upstairs, numbered 27 and 27a, were occupied by Charles Dickens; and the drive-in through which you now steer your car served the mighty coachman, Sam Hayward, in his supreme moments when townsfolk kept out of bed o' nights to see this artist of the ribbons spring 'em up Wyle Cop, majestically circle his team at the top, shoot the opening with bare inches to spare, and deliver the speedy "Wonder" coach into the inn yard at 10.30 p.m., Shrewsbury time, to complete the 158 miles from London in 16 hours. Lastly the *Raven*, where I write these words. Not an architectural masterpiece is this hotel. Though the black bird has perched there since the fifteenth century, his plumes were plucked and curled afresh in Victorian style, accompanied by a sad laying of those ghosts that make chains rattle and teeth chatter at midnight. No longer is visible the room of Dr. Sacheverell's explosions on local parsons in 1709. But above the chatter and pleasant tinkle of coffee cups in the lounge I seem to fancy hearing an old strain—surely it must be Captain Plume singing,

> I still will complain
> Of your frowns and disdain,
> Though I revel through all your charms:
> The world shall declare,
> That I die with despair,
> When I only die in your arms.

The notion sets me thinking of Justice Balance, Justice Scruple, Mr. Worthy, beloved Melinda, loving Silvia, all the jolly puppets that George Farquhar romped round the Market Place, in the streets and by the Severn when he wrote *The Recruiting Officer* in 1706 "at the sign of the Raven in this good town of Shrewsbury" and properly dedicated the Restoration concoction of wit and naughtiness "To all friends round the Wrekin."

4. CENTRAL AND NORTH MIDLANDS

STAFFORDSHIRE, DERBYSHIRE, CHESHIRE

The sandstone of the Central and Cheshire Plains meets the limestone and millstone grit of the hilly districts in north Staffordshire, east Cheshire, and about the end of the Pennine Range in Derbyshire. Clear rivers, including the Dove and Derwent, flow fast from the heights to swell the winding Trent; other streams go west from the moors to the Mersey. The Dee curves in from Wales, bound for Chester and the sandy estuary. Scenery is varied. It offers wide vales and plains richly cultivated, the celebrated dales and highlands leading up to The Peak. There are quiet rural expanses, grand trees of the old woodlands and forests, river landscapes placid and charming or beautifully wild, long views from high points, and gloomy sprawls of brickwork, factories, coalpits, ironworks, and sundry allied effects contributed in mining and industrial areas. Local stone made the interesting series of sandstone churches, and the grey towns, villages and boundary walls in the dales and the hills. Oak trees, once very plentiful from Needwood Forest in Staffordshire to Delamere Forest in Cheshire, framed the black-and-white buildings and famous timbered halls.

186

THROUGH STAFFORDSHIRE AND
TRENT VALE

If all my readers carefully followed the instructions and routes to Shrewsbury given at the end of the last chapter—and of course they have done so—certain peculiarities of scene may have been noticed. These include smokiness round Oakengates on Watling Street, a cast-iron grave slab facing the west end of the dull Georgian church at Wellington, ironworks in Coalbrookdale, the pioneer bridge built of cast-iron by Abraham Darby in 1777 at Ironbridge. Adjacent in South Staffordshire lies the Black Country, an area well supplied with arid ground, mean streets, blue bricks, chimney stacks, slag heaps, and other contributions made by the Industrial Revolution and its developments. These topographical features denote that in the Midlands and over many murky miles in the North things exist to scare even the bravest modern Doctor Syntax in search of the picturesque. Splendid though the scenic effects may be for those who like beauty decked drab, ugly, plain or 2d. coloured, my modest pages never would do them justice. Therefore, now casting my mental eye over particular regions in Staffordshire, among many omissions of products made by the peculiar human arrangements known as civilization and economic progress I do not illustrate (1) the view from Hanley church tower ("Indian-red architecture, tall chimneys, rounded ovens, scarves of smoke," *vide* Arnold Bennett); (2) monuments dedicated to Bass, Allsop, and the Burton-on-Trent brotherhood; (3) gloomy Brownhills in which I first saw Joseph Chamberlain and heard about Karl Marx; (4) scenes in Swan Village.

The Black Country lies mostly to the south of the line made by Watling Street from Fazeley to Weston-under-Lizard. You can observe its scenes from afar and hurry on, look into them at close quarters, admire or condemn; for myself I incline to a remark Shakespeare might have quoted from his own play if he had hopped over from Warwickshire into Staffordshire later than actually happened, "We are not the first who, with best meaning, have incurred the worst." Nevertheless sundry articles merit inspection in many places. St. Peter's Church, Wolverhampton, for example, has the fine interior with double clerestory windows, chapels, tombs, and a remarkable fifteenth-century pulpit on the first column of the nave. The high mound of Dudley castle retains the ruined keep of 1264 and extensive relics of buildings begun by Normans. Other objects of interest include overhanging gables below a black-and-white lantern of the Oak House, West Bromwich; crow-stepped gables and brickwork at the Old Hall, Old Hill; the *White Hart* inn, Walsall, in which Charles I's queen stayed before the battle of Edge Hill in 1642; an Elizabethan Moseley Old Hall that obliged Charles junior with a couple of nights hiding after the battle of Worcester; and it pains me to mention the first steam engine sold by James Watt on view at Tipton, to recall one of the causes for urging to full blast the catastrophe of the Industrial Revolution.

Beyond the smoky pall nice country opens out, particularly towards the Shropshire borders. Kinver Edge commands miles of views over Wyre Forest, Enville Chase, and the Stour valley. Hilton mound, near Shareshill, is another good viewpoint for countless acres farther north. Here are eighteenth-century Patshull, Sir John Soane's design at Chillington reached by grand avenues, lordly Weston Park, the Vernons' home at Hilton, Stourton castle, birthplace in 1500 of Reginald Pole, the Archbishop of Canterbury during the martyrdoms in Mary Tudor's reign. These stately homes in private parks give promise of many more to follow, built by the ancient families on their broad lands in Staffordshire. Countrified villages begin to appear. They show features common throughout the lower regions of the county—timbering and brickwork of the larger houses, tiled roofs, thatching here and there, cottage walls of brick or oak timbers divided by panels of light plaster, churches made of the local sandstone and often dating from the fourteenth and fifteenth centuries. A number of hoary inns with black beams continue to distribute liquids. They are fitly represented by the *Whittington*, Kinver, and the *Four Crosses*, dated 1636, at Hatherton, near Cannock (181), an historic centre of roadside hospitality claiming a couplet attributed to Dean Swift. In happy past years I used to imagine the rev. gent posting along the straight miles of Watling Street bound for the deanery of St. Patrick, spending an uncomfortable night, fuming over breakfast, and scratching on a window pane with a diamond this expression of regard for his hostess,

> Thou fool ! to hang Four Crosses at thy door ;
> Hang up thy wife, there needs not any more.

From the Dean's years to those of Nero means a jaunt of only a few miles along the Roman highway to Wall, once the busy township and posting station of *Letocetum*. Traces of the walls or barricades of oak trees, remained until the eighteenth century. More recently the busy spade has turned up many things for inquisitive people to see and remember—pots and tiles and hypocausts— why the baths were hot or cold—where the bones and ashes went—in the glory that was Rome.

Near to these lifeless curiosities of a lost empire living reminders of the medieval golden age shine in beauty. Clear of the Black Country's gloom, and to the north of Watling Street, the remark made to Boswell hereabout in 1776 might yet be appropriate, "Now we are getting out of a state of death." The air is salubrious. Ridges of Cannock Chase show beyond flattish fields and woods. A trio of spires stand out. Sandstone coloured and graceful, they beckon to the shrines of St. Chad and of Dr. Johnson, to the homes of

> the most sober, decent people in England, the genteelist in proportion to their wealth. " Sir," said Johnson, " we are a city of philosophers ; we work with our heads, and make the boobies of Birmingham work for us with their hands."

NEWPORT. *The pleasing front of the grammar school situated near to the interesting church in this Shropshire market town. The school was founded in the seventeenth century; famous scholars included Sir Oliver Lodge and "Tom" Brown, the Restoration wit and satirist.*

BOSCOBEL. *Home of William Penderel, one of the family that sheltered Charles II in September 1651. The house contains the hiding-hole used by the King, and near is the descendant of the original oak-tree in which the King hid.*

MOW COP *in the Staffordshire high-*
lands overlooking the Cheshire plain.

CANNOCK CHASE *at Milford Hill.*

Lichfield has the tranquil and comfortable aspect common to most of our major cathedral cities. Streets and pavements are narrow enough to give fellowship with yesterdays; their frontages of Midland brick and timbering, here and there notable, can flit the instant and proximo down Georgian, Restoration, and earlier years. A number of shop windows, bowed and bulging, emphasize the unloveliness of adjacent plate glass; so attractive in this wise is the establishment of Mr. Mercer, the saddler, that any enthusiast, albeit horse-less, could hardly resist going inside to buy a bridle (184). Behind the streets are gardens and green stretches for those who fancy action, peace, or meditation in sunlight and under shady trees. Stow Pool bounds a graceful town scene, and the Minster Pool perpetually reflects the spires locally called the Ladies of the Vale. With many attractions and charms Lichfield must be pleasant to live in; no doubt environment partly accounted for Dr. Johnson's praise and high opinion of the inhabitants. Certainly it is a nice spot for a temporary anchorage, for pottering about to look at this and at that. Modernization has not achieved spoliation so well here as elsewhere. The gasworks hardly show, and though bars for fish, chips, milk, and similar contrivances exist for those who esteem them, the modest appearances of these present necessaries do not especially offend the senses of sight, smell, and gentility. Modern times have not dimmed all the freshness and purity of the city's heart. This is remarkable when one reflects that Lichfield for many years past has stood near to the gates of money-getting beyond the dreams of avarice and grime beyond the imagination of chimney-sweeps; it has managed to continue placid and aloof outside the very portals of the mechanical industrialism which made England great, glorious—and in vast areas, ghastly.

If a middle point can be found in the irregular shape of England, the three spires must very nearly mark it. This particular situation, adjacent to Wall at the junction of two important Roman roads pointing east, west, north and south, and the city's position on the old coach route from London to Holyhead via Chester, made Lichfield a centre of travel onward from dim ages. Saintly Chad, settled in a cell by a well that sparkles to-day as it did in A.D. 669, planted the banner of faith; he sanctified the ground for the line of Mercian bishops and Offa's archbishop. Norman and successive prelates devised the beauty of arch, vault, and soaring masonry. They surrounded the city with a moat to keep nasty people out, and a gate near St. John's Hospital served for entry and exit until it disappeared in the eighteenth century. While the cathedral grew in dignity and magnificence, buildings and homesteads rose round about it. A piece of walling now preserved marks the place of a friary founded in 1229. Tudor brickwork and eight gallant chimneys all in a row stand over the thirteenth-century site of St. John's Hospital. Gables and timbers, and pleasant seventeenth- and eighteenth-century houses, still attractive and worth finding, took shape and place on old foundations as the years passed on. Within their walls lived churchmen and laymen, tradesmen who flourished well on the old-established market days, and prosperous men renowned for brewing very good beer. "I remember," said Johnson, "when all the decent people in Lichfield got drunk every night, and were none the worse thought of"; and Boniface in *The Beaux' Strategem* recommended the local tipple with eloquent jollity. Some of the buildings acquired the nameplates of fame. The grammar school, founded soon after those at Eton and Winchester, nurtured bishops, judges, Addison and Garrick. At Priests Hall, now quartered with an auctioneer rampant, Elias Ashmole took preliminary breathers before being Windsor Herald to Charles II and founding the Ashmolean at Oxford. Almost next door Mrs. Michael Johnson (*née* Sarah Ford) produced the infant Hercules of Toryism (184). The presence of extraordinary powers of mind at that corner of Breadmarket Street soon placed the possessor at the head of a juvenile kingdom. Down those steps the youthful genius went, to receive the homage of his schoolfellows and be borne shoulder high in triumph to school. The original bookshop and birthplace, lit by ample windows, white-faced up to the late seventeenth-century cornice, and rich inside with personal relics handy to the immortal teapot, is the premier milestone in the Johnsonian pilgrimage. Statues of Johnson and Boswell outside in the market place rise silent and curiously over animated scenes and buses loading up. Further afield ways lead by Stow Pool to the descendant of the Doctor's beloved willow tree, to Michael Johnson's ill-fated parchment factory, Dame Oliver's school, and various reminders of Lichfield's and England's illustrious son, Samuel Johnson.

This city of age and fame, centrally placed and served by ancient routes as I have stated, must have known a medley of arrivers and departers that popped in and out or halted for high business, ordinary business, or with no business to be there at all. Monks and clergy, the mighty and the lowly, pilgrims to St. Chad's Well, country folk amarketing, packmen and waggoners, martyrs doomed to be burned outside St. Mary's, Lord Brooke at the head of fanatical Cromwellians mad for the destruction of the cathedral, and all sorts and conditions of men and women came and went. Some of them brightened and others darkened the scenes in the watered vale. The late 1600's opened the reign of the coaching years. Teams of horses and the merry toot of horns enlivened the Holyhead and other tracks that led to Lichfield. Coachmen, delivered their passengers. One day Captain George Farquhar alighted in search of recruits and chanced to find *dramatis personæ* for the Haymarket stage. A few years later Captain and Mrs. Garrick drove in from Hereford and deposited the infant David for a twenty years' stay. An actress arrived, and played under the name of Mrs. Siddons for the first time. Some travellers, like young Samuel Johnson and younger David Garrick, set out for London and conquest by coach (3rd class). And some, including the celebrated Doctor Johnson and the Honourable James Boswell, sped down from the metropolis by post-chaise at 2s. a mile (1st class).

These evolutions of trafficking on the roads naturally caused an adequate supply of inns, just as motoring does to-day. Here then, in Lichfield, are numerous old established and coaching inns built in a variety of fashions. Only to look under archways and down long yards can rouse up all sorts of fancies. Remembrances develop. In the dim shades riders trot out, coaches swing in, leaders start off, horses reach journey's end; and the merry, merry years and the dreadful past years yield up once again their stocks of coachmen, guards and passengers scrambling down; pretty chambermaids by candlelight and feather beds up aloft; highwaymen off duty looking bland; snug quarters bursting with old English plenty; and possessors of frost-bitten or sunburnt noses stoking up copiously with the local home-brewed to warm or cool the cockles of their hearts. There stands the *Swan* with an archway and a spacious cobbled yard leading to the boots only knows where, the establishment that provided a breakfast for Johnson when he flared into satire at the sight of Mrs. Thrale's riding-habit and delivered a lecture on "propriety of dress." Next door a drive-in leads to the *King's Head;* and another opening at the *Three Crowns* in Breadmarket Street accommodated the bulky Doctor and Boswell on their visits to greet and stay with mine host Wilkins.

And there is the *George*, a saintly and royal George, Georgian fronted on an ancient hospitable site, with an archway and yard of its own, passages to get lost in, and lo! a ballroom too, with mirrors to reflect beauty, and a frieze giddy with demure cupids that must have winked over sentimental sights and nights by the score during their perpetual young years. If you stay in this comfortable haven, treat with propriety its joyful provision, retire to room No. 47 or thereabouts, repose sweetly, rival the lark in her waking, you can leap out of bed to behold a vision fit for the upper place promised to some of us later on. Soon after the sun begins his day's work the cathedral can be seen glittering in brightness and shade high over trees and roofs (182–183). Should the night mood develop a bit more shifty than above-mentioned you may or may not in the small hours dream of queer happenings, Landlord Boniface shuffling about with his three wicked conspirators Highwaymen Gibbet, Hounslow and Bagshot, or even Archer warbling to Cherry,

> But you look so bright,
> And are dress'd so tight,
> That a man would swear you're right,
> As arm was e'er laid over.
> Such an air
> You freely wear
> To ensnare,
> As makes each guest a lover!

For George Farquhar, rambling about this very inn and through Lichfield, discovered more than a landlord, his daughter, and the fleshy beings of common life. His creative mind conceived phantoms and pageants to flit airily through *The Beaux' Stratagem*, the sprightly Restoration comedy that delighted audiences throughout the eighteenth century and in later years made Charles Lamb the gayer for reading it. Cruel fate intervened after the author's best and most successful work was first produced at the Haymarket theatre on March 8th, 1707. "Poor, nature-loving, cheerful, melancholy Farquhar!" wrote Leigh Hunt. "He took to his sick chair; retained enough of the blissful abstraction of genius to write the 'Beaux Stratagem' in six weeks; and died during the height of its success, before he had attained his thirtieth year." How many more visitors of fame have halted at the *George* since Farquhar's years and the appearance of Boswell and Colonel Stuart in 1779? When a Prime Minister arrived during my sketching operations in 1947 I recalled Dr. Johnson over the way at the *Swan* in 1774 and then almost shuddered to think of the explosion that might have burst if the Hercules of Toryism had come to life again, crossed the street, and bumped into the Achilles of Labour!

My last Lichfield sight, the cathedral, of course ranks first in the order of spectacular appeal. But the central monument of the diocese, a magnificent heirloom of England, already has worthy champions wiser than myself to relate all of the history, beauty and falsities of this warm-coloured creation in sandstone, survivor of one of the loveliest of our smaller cathedrals and unique in the grouping of triple spires. It represents man's virtues and vices, is symbolic of inspired creation, worship, destruction, restoration, and hope perpetual.

The cathedral's ages, briefly stated, fall into a number of periods. The Saxon church or churches appeared after the death of St. Chad at Stowe on 672. A cathedral of the first Norman bishop followed. The present form of the structure began to develop late in the twelfth century and was finished about 150 years later. Building thus progressed through the times of Early English and Decorated architecture, both of which styles are well represented. A hint of the Perpendicular style came in 1337, when William of Ramsey, King's Master Mason to Edward III, started the four bays of the presbytery to complete the edifice; these four bays connected the superb Lady Chapel of *circa* 1330 to the original three western bays of the choir. A costly shrine to St. Chad and an embattled wall to fortify the close were provided by Bishop Langton (1296–1321) of splendid memory.

One of the thirteen cathedrals served by secular clergy, Lichfield escaped the grabbing propensities of Henry VIII. Similar good fortune did not happen in 1643. Cromwell and his minions then met to plan foul deeds in the Tudor house at Mavesyn Ridware, six miles from the city. Lord Brooke, zealous to abolish "all decent order in the service of God," determined to destroy the cathedral

TWO MIDLAND CATHEDRAL TOWERS. *St. Philip, Birmingham* (left), *a masterly design of 1710 by Thomas Archer, courtier, architect, and uncle of Lord Archer of Umberslade. All Saints, Derby* (right), *the finest Perpendicular tower in the district, designed early in the reign of Henry VIII.*

STAFFORD. *The College, founded in the middle of the seventeenth century by Sir Martin Noel, built of local stone and well preserved.*

STAFFORD. *Chetwynd House, a dignified example of Renaissance building in brickwork and stone, and formerly the town house of the Chetwynd family. Richard Brinsley Sheridan used to stay here when M.P. for Stafford.*

held for the King by the Royalists. With his forces outside the close he set about the work in grim earnest. A sniper, however, perched on the parapet of the central tower, spotted my lord and shot him dead; the site of this fall from grace can be inspected in the street suitably named Dam. Nothing daunted, the Roundheads continued to bombard the building and close. After three days the besiegers conquered. They advanced in fanatical triumph to do devilish work in their customary way, wrought havoc unthinkable, chased cats with hounds through the vaulted aisles. Battered, roofless almost everywhere, treasures smashed, archives and historical documents burnt, the close walls down, the central spire gone, the once glorious pile was reduced to the worst of all the cathedral wrecks made by Puritanical madmen.

With King Charles safely restored to home sweet home, the cathedral obviously needed a restoration too. Those gayer years brought along Bishop Hacket—all hail to thee, excellent Hacket! For the glory of God and the honour of man he determined to revive the cathedral of his see, then standing gaunt and ruined in 1662. With right good will he collected vast sums for the enterprise; and if the pretty story of the prelate's own coach and horses bearing away rubbish and hauling in stone may be no more than a fable of good intent, a likeness of the original Gothic splendour and ancient dignity had been recaptured after seven years of great labour. Again the central spire completed the trio, reconstructed it is thought by Sir Christopher Wren. A lapse followed. Long periods of neglect caused masonry to decay. More restorers arrived in the 1850's to undertake tasks long overdue. Doubtless their intentions were good. But these Victorian architects and craftsmen represented the spirit of their own time, a hard, mechanical time dead to the true meaning of medieval thought and inspiration. Not only was the building rescued and strengthened; it suffered such a dose of inharmonious reconstruction, furbishing and touching up that the results, only too obvious at present, and the names of the gentlemen responsible for them need not be dwelt on by me.

Yet Lichfield cathedral continues glorious. It has triumphed over destruction, restoration, and other deadly sins, is of the noble things on this earth, permanent in appeal. The grand medieval masses and compositions captivate beholders to-day as they did in the old time. The grouped spires, lovely from every angle, point heavenwards above lengths of roofs and clerestories, geometrical traceries in the nave, tall choir lights and the long windows of the Lady Chapel. The majestic west front, finished early in the fourteenth century, keeps its original scheme of surface decoration, gable, beautiful doorways, the spire-capped towers concealing the ends of the aisles. A hundred memorable sights are presented within. Arches and ribbed vaults spread from west to east; they emphasize the full design of the nave (*circa* 1250–1280) and grandeur at the crossing where the transepts open out. The choir, remodelled onward from 1337, terminates in the east with the cathedral's great treasure, the Lady Chapel (*circa* 1320–1330), aglow with exquisite colours of sixteenth-century Flemish glass. Where so much that is fine remains, inharmonious restorations and falsifications need not be noticed.

Time and again during visits to Lichfield I have experienced the thrill of turning from the main street between pretty brick and timbered houses to see the cathedral's western front, rich, warm-coloured, and with symbolic beauty leading the eye and mind upward. Round the great church extends the close, bordered with Restoration and Georgian houses and, tucked away in a retired quadrangle, the little Vicars' close patterned with timbers, flowers and greenery. Wandering here and there you can easily imagine Dr. Johnson shambling along his favourite Dean's Walk or picture pale young Joseph Addison, son of the Dean, making his way to the grammar school. This close charms at all times and never more than at the end of a spring or summer day. Then it is very quiet. The sightseers have gone. The spires catch the late evening glow as the sun goes down. Lights begin to twinkle from casements and window panes. Night deepens. One by one some of the lights pop out. Lively cherubs, angelic choristers of the *Magnificat*, have finished their larks and gone to roost. The big bell booms. The last loiterers in the walks depart. The shade of Johnson has gone home and Addison's ghost is tucked up in the Deanery. The cathedral spires and the great western front loom in silhouette from a darkened sky. You seek your host or inn and, grateful for impressions stored in memory, sleep in peace. Dawn and sunshine light another day. Ways lead to pastures new. The spires lessen in the distance. As they fade from sight I say "Amen" to Lichfield—until the next time of asking!

Enthusiasts for Mercians or for coal are both suited with routes from the seat of Offa's defunct archbishop at Lichfield. The Mercian-minded can travel east to Tamworth, the place of Mercian kings more than a thousand years ago; then, as now, handy for Watling Street, and now, but not then, valued by archaeologists, with whom I have climbed the high castle mound to inspect Saxon, Norman and later masonry. More than once Shakespeare found the old stones useful for Act scenes and war's "noises off." In the town below may be noticed good fourteenth- and fifteenth-century work at the church, the glass windows by William Morris, Ford Madox Brown and Burne-Jones, a William-and-Mary town hall, St. James's Hospital in an incongruous hiding-place. From the castle mound you look over the champaign country. Little streams wind down to the green meadows of the Tame valley. The fertile earth, garnished with woodlands, sets off villages, hamlets, churches, Clifton Campville's slender spire, and Elford, worth a day's pilgrimage to see the carved alabaster effigies of the Ardernes, Stanleys, and more knights and ladies of the 1400's and 1500's.

Westerly routes from Lichfield are satisfactory for those interested in coal and the defilements on land achieved since economists set out to plan the labours of man. Travellers not so minded and content with God's free air and nature's bounties can still find plenty of both on the undulating plateau of Cannock Chase. This ground accommodated myself and legs on the longest day's walk of my life, more than forty miles of it and egged along by an athletic young man down from Oxford who nearly hobbled me to premature doom. I mention this exploit merely to indicate a few points we then saw and which yet may remain unspoiled and worth finding: Hammerwich overlooking miles of Chase scenery; Farewell, once a priory of Lichfield, quiet in the meadows by the stream and Georgian hall; Castle Hill earthworks and acres of bracken round the early Renaissance hall of Beaudesert (now *ichabod*); the pleasant placing of Rugeley and the town's unpleasant reminders of William Palmer, the poisoner; lovely woods and parks, in parts dating from Domesday, stretching in fine succession at Hagley, Wolseley, Oakedge, Brockton, Milford and Shugborough; views of the Chase presented from Milford Hill (190); timbered cottages at Acton Trussell; wooded slopes of Teddesley Park; black-and-white houses and Littleton monuments at Penkridge; St. Modwena's chapel and Pillaton Hall gatehouse (181), survivors of the "antique mansion residence of the respectable family of Littleton Baronets . . . standing marks of convivial mirth and good old cheer" (*Gentlemen's Magazine* 1789).

West of the Chase the country to the Shropshire boundary is pretty and pleasant, true to the Midland character. Quiet lanes and footpaths wind among meadows, rushy streams, woods, lowly heights. Railroads are few. Villages and hamlets, often marked with the local brickwork in cottages and houses, keep prime and secluded. Adbaston is one good specimen; "Dear native Adbaston, remote from care," wrote Bowker Ash, the poet whose verses pleased Coleridge. Lands of the flattish south lead northward to the broken tracts of hills and extensive woods about Whitmore, Ashley, and Blore Heath, where Richard Neville's White Roses defeated the Lancastrian Red Roses in 1459. The sandstone churches continue. Gnosall tower stands out conspicuously; it marks a notable building of the centuries dated from the Norman to the fifteenth. Norbury and other church interiors have more monuments of the old gentry on view. Great parks are not so frequent here as in the county's centre and east; those at Keele and Swynnerton make good in quality, and a once ducal Trentham now has risen to the heights of democratic sociability.

Stafford, the county capital in the middle of the shire, lives on the Sow, a tributary of the Trent, whose name does not properly advertise the town's raw material of leather. Here we meet sniffs of industry again. But the smells of tanned hides of the horse or the cow are grateful, even comforting, when compared with the odours compounded in the Black Country or the Potteries. That peculiarity I noticed with a degree of pleasure on the spot during endeavours to cobble my own offerings of art with the local products. The reason for the hides, shoemaking, also seems to be an historic craft. According to *Exodus* Moses wore shoes and according to Webster Anglo-Saxons had *sceóhs;* without dwelling particularly on feet so ancient as theirs or who fitted them, it is evident that shoemaking has benefited all sexes throughout all ages. Long after the Industrial Revolutionists rode their iron horses shoes continued to be made by hand; they enabled Stafford's M.P., Richard Brinsley Sheridan, to invent the neat toast, "May the trade of Stafford be trod underfoot by all the world." To-day, though mechanized, shoemaking is a clean job not unduly burdened with smoke, fumes and smuts. That is why it is not in the least unpleasant to walk about Stafford and to track more scents than those of leather by following in the shoeprints of Saxons, Normans, Tudors, and staunch Royalists.

The castle mound leads back to the Norman years of Lord Robert, who settled himself on the Conqueror's reward for accomplishments. The existing masonry is a nineteenth-century reconstruction made on the foundations of the Edwardian keep, a square structure of 1348 with octagonal corner towers, duly blown up by Cromwell. Two notable churches have weathered centuries. St. Chad's interior is magnificently Norman; St. Mary's remains impressive throughout from its Saxon beginnings to the nave arches, Tudor clerestories, and the noble octagonal lantern erected over a spacious cruciform plan. Numerous gabled and timbered houses tell of times from 1475 to Elizabeth's reign and the seventeenth century. One of the casements first lighted the infancy of the valiant Cavalier and saintly brother of the angle, Izaak Walton; thus undying fame came to the town in 1593. A show-piece for black-and-white, the High House in Greengate Street, made a lodging for King Charles and his friends in 1642; Prince Rupert, always looking for sport, then fired a couple of bullets over the garden wall into the weathercock's tail on St. Mary's. Later days brought Chetwynd House, town quarters of the Chetwynd family, a Renaissance effect of much dignity and charm schemed in brick walling, stone features and pilasters (196). This home and other Georgian houses fronting the streets remind of little seasons in the county town, elegant gossip, scandal over port by candlelight, and occasions made brilliant through the presence of Sheridan, the local M.P. from 1780 to 1812. More lowly inhabitants whose bottles were few settled in the Old College in Mill Street (196); the almshouses have been well preserved since Sir Martin Noel in the mid-seventeenth century provided the doles, the stone gablets, and armorial embellishments.

The town, busy enough now and busy for centuries past, accumulated a good supply of inns and coaching establishments. They continue visible and serving. A

CHATSWORTH. *Ducal, classic and renowned, the stately palace is beautifully set above the River Derwent. Designed for the first Duke of Devonshire by William Talman, the Restoration architect, it dates from 1687–1700
on the site of Bess of Hardwick's Tudor house.*

HADDON HALL. *The seat of the Vernon and Manners families is justl*
famed for picturesqueness, beautiful situation and romantic suggestion
Always planned for domestic use rather than for war, this home of lovel
buildings stands round two courtyards. It was begun in 1070 and finishe
during 555 years.

few, like the *Vine*, are very ancient. Dickens knew the *Swan*, called it dowdy as "the Dodo," thereby implying extinction. George Borrow thought otherwise, brightened it for ever in *The Romany Rye*.

> Truly a very great place for life and bustle. was this inn. And often in after life, when lonely and melancholy, I have called up the time I spent there, and never failed to become cheerful from the recollection.

My exact sentiments, dear George! During my past artistic and leathery adventures in Stafford the shoemakers often entertained me at this inn. Full of life, bustle, plenty, and good fellowship it was then. At the long table in the dining-room talk bandied round—of shoes—and ships—and sealing-wax—over cabbages and English sirloin. Then I gleaned two weighty secrets. They are now exposed to the world as I bow adieu to the town : (1) Tanning with the bark of oak, a method possibly dating back to the year when Queen Nefertiti donned her first pair of "Lotus" shoes, is still the most satisfactory way of converting hides into leather. (2) A tip to reimburse my readers for the money spent on buying this book. New soles of shoes wear best if the wearer first walks through grit or fine gravel. The grit works into the leather. Soles thus last longer. There's nothing like leather! so they say in Stafford.

The near "Trent, by Tixall graced"—that's how Michael Drayton put it—is also graced with more fine parklands at Ingestre and Sandon. Admirers of Wren's City churches should not fail to visit the church at Ingestre. While examining the interior screen and pulpit made of Flanders oak, the general richness of work in stone, wood, metal, and plaster, I certainly felt transported from Staffordshire to my *London Triumphant* days. Often attributed to Sir Christopher, the building is the most finished and elaborate country example of his period. It was due to Walter Chetwynd, the lord of the manor whose Stafford house we have seen in Greengate Street; after the consecration of the church this squire gave a "splendid dinner for the Nobilitie, Clergy, and Gentry, both men and women." Everything, except the dinner, remains much as it was on that August day in 1677. Thrice historical Chartley and its old woodlands lie a mile or two from the river. Upstream is Stone, abode of more shoemakers, and bright with the halos of a painter and a poet, Peter de Wint, born there in 1784, and Richard Barnefield, the Elizabethan, who sang,

> As it fell upon a day
> In the merry month of May.

Beyond more parks and Trentham neither merry months of May, June, or July will conceal Industrial Revolutionary features and charms, nor dispel the gloom and vapours diffused over the concentrated and packed five towns of the Potteries. Of them Arnold Bennett wrote, "Beauty was achieved and none saw it," and noted "the chequered sky," a "scarlet market-place." And if artistic history was made by William Littler of Longton Hall, Josiah Wedgwood at Etruria, Spode, Minton, Copeland, and other giants in transforming clay, the landscapes have been considerably upset in providing for the uses, washing and peculiar needs of man. Therefore I hastily retreat and pass onward.

The Staffordshire highlands spread from the Potteries to the county borders. Ah! it is clear and fresh up there. Nature offers beauty and wise people from the towns take care to see it. You meet broad open spaces, moors, rocky shapes, woody gorges, miles of distances; you can trace the lapwings' rapid flight overhead and the flash of trout in clear pools of valley streams. Hills fill the area. High elevations are broadly marked by the Weaver Hills, Ipston Edge, Morridge, Merryton Low (1603 feet), and the fantastic outlines of The Roaches, all spectacular points to be on and to look from. Moorlands extend to Flash, quaint little Longnor, and to Mow Cop (190), where the eyes at least seem to be in possession of all Cheshire. New patterns of England open out. Grey stone churches and villages climb the slopes or nestle in glades and dingles. Native stone colours field boundaries and the walls and roofs of cottages and farms. Leek, the capital of the district and famed for the silk manufacture first introduced by the Huguenots, stands out on its slopes facing the heights. Here the Young Pretender came in the advance and the retreat of 1745, but probably had no time to admire the pinnacled Gothic church tower or the interesting seventeenth- and eighteenth-century houses and domestic architecture.

Infant waters flow down. The Trent begins a long course from Biddulph Moor, near to the Elizabethan hall ruins wrecked when a Royalist Brereton faced a Parliamentary Brereton. The Manifold, Hamps and Churnet, lovely rivers all, leave the heights. They descend to green borderlands and woods, swish below crags in deep valleys. Circling and rippling melodiously, the clear streams perform remarkably well in amplifying the stuff of picturesqueness, romance, history, and memories. At Beeston Tor nature's towers crown a memorable scene at the meeting of the Hamps and the Manifold. The Churnet's divine loveliness at Alton is piled with the Talbot turrets, battlements and dogs rampant, Pugin's chapels, de Verdun's ruined Norman keep, immense and singular effects that might do for a fabled vision, castles on the Rhine, or a nightmare in fairyland. Apart from prehistoric finds in Thor's Cave, high on the bold rocks above the Manifold, and remains left by Saxons and Danes in the cave at the base of Beeston Tor, previous distinguished arrivals and their places are remembered. Copper miners, for example, delved enough cash value out of Ecton Hill to enable Carr of York to design and build the fine eighteenth-century Crescent at Buxton for a Duke of Devonshire. The Manifold's disappearing trick below ground at Ilam completely mystified Dr. Johnson in 1774; many years earlier underground rivers probably had no effect on William Congreve sitting in the grotto writing *The Old Bachelor*, the play that delighted London, shocked the Jeremiah's, and made the author's name when produced at the Theatre Royal in 1693. Mary Howitt liked to climb and write on "the top of Caldon-Low" above the River Hamp, and Ellastone, between the Rivers Churnet and Dove, gave George Eliot "Hayslope" for *Adam Bede*.

The River Dove, a joint possession of Staffordshire and Derbyshire, hurries down from Dove Head to Beresford Dale, a beautiful combination of stream, green slopes, woods and rocks. Here, on Staffordshire soil, is just the place to dip into *The Compleat Angler* and pay homage at the little stone Fishing House dedicated to "I W—C C—Piscatoribus Sacrum—1674," to visit the hiding-hole used by Charles Cotton for dodging creditors, and amble over his deserted bowling-green on the height above. Experts perhaps may succeed in catching trout; seekers for less elusive prey will be quite content to follow Cotton's example,

> Oh, my belovèd nymph, fair Dove,
> Princess of rivers, how I love
> Upon thy flowery banks to lie,
> And view thy silvery stream
> When gilded by a summer's beam.

Past the "Pike Pool" and lower downstream is the wild scenery of Wolfscote Dale. Mill Dale comes next. Then begins Dove Dale, the sylvan and precious jewel of nation-wide fame needing no poor words of mine to sing its praises. The waters flow on in sight of the Weaver Hills. They circle past a Roman camp and Norman abbey foundations at Rocester, just miss Uttoxeter, once Roman, but better known for ancient markets and the present contents of the *White Hart*; at the carved panel on the conduit in the market place tears may be deposited for the sad story told by a penitent old man, Dr. Johnson:

> "Once I was disobedient; I refused to attend my father to Uttoxeter market. . . .
> A few years ago I desired to atone for this fault; I went to Uttoxeter in very
> bad weather, and stood for a considerable time bareheaded in the rain, on the
> spot where my father's stall used to stand."

Gliding along, curving endlessly through its lower wide vale, the river offers rapture here, joyous scenes there, and meets romance and history at Tutbury. Norman arches and rich carvings of the church remain from the priory founded by Earl Ferrers soon after the Conquest. John of Gaunt's castle, grim and ruined, crowns the height dominating the stream, the follower of two earlier strongholds destroyed in the years of the Normans and Simon de Montfort. Here was Mary Stuart's prison; ill, her beauty faded, the Queen of the Scots left through the gateway for the last time in 1585. King Charles came in 1645, hid after the disaster at Naseby. A year later General Brereton arrived and Cromwellians achieved the wreck now to be seen—proud Lancaster's two stately halls, window traceries, carved fireplaces, vaulted undercrofts, the stone gateway, buildings round the tilt-yard, all shattered and mouldy relics. Latterly the yard

Reynard's Cave DOVEDALE

Sydney R. Jones

has staged only tilts, arguments, and a fight or two between antiquaries who mediate on mounds, stones, usually disagree on everything, and retire to the *Dog and Partridge*, an inn with black timbers intact after centuries of wear.

South of the River Dove lowish hills stretch around Marchington Woodlands and Hanbury. You spy over the Trent vale and far across Derbyshire. Near trees beautify the uplands. Names locate Bagot's Wood and Park, Woodend, Holly Bush, Abbot's Bromley, and Bagot's Bromley, where Bagots lived before Domesday Book was made. Trees and names remind of a pre-Conquest Needwood Forest, with 24 miles of it left in Queen Elizabeth's reign and recorded for 47,150 oaks in the time of Charles II. Oaks as big round as any number of men's bodies, and antique holly bushes here and there may be discovered and admired; but many of God's high standards have gone the way of other beautiful things that are slaughtered in man's quest for low standards of high living. Ancient families, settled hereabout almost as long as the oaks, are remembered by their effigies in the churches. At Blithfield in the Blythe valley, for instance, memorials to the Bagots portray members of the line that figured all down the pages of English history; on Hanbury hilltop repose carved monuments of the Hanburys, Adderleys, Agardes, and the Egertons. In the early days, when sport was state controlled, kings hunted deer through the Forest. To enable them to do so men were deprived of their homes and means of livelihood, even lost eyes, hands, life itself under the cruel Forest Law rigidly enforced before *Magna Charta* was sealed and Henry III reigned in King

DRONFIELD WOODHOUSE. *A farmhouse example of the stone tradition in east Derbyshire, a local style of building that is not widely known.*

STANTON-IN-THE-PEAK, *a stone-built village with cottages and three halls high above the Lathkill Dale. Many prehistoric remains in the neighbourhood include those on Stanton Moor and the great stone circle of Arbor Low.*

WATERGATE STREET, CHESTER, *has the best preserved sections of the R*
originated in the thirteenth or fourteenth century, were erected on the top of R

se unusual arrangements in streets are unique in England. They probably
dations, and have been continually transformed in succeeding centuries.

CARTLEDGE HALL *on the heights between Chesterfield and Sheffield probably dates from the early 1500's. Inside are panelled interiors and enriched plaster ceilings. It was a manor-house of the Wolstenholme family and thus is linked with Canada by the name of Cape Wolstenholme at the head of Hudson Bay. The author Robert Murray Gilchrist lived here in the present century.*

EYAM HALL *in the Derbyshire dale country. The manor dates back to Saxon years. This hall was erected 10 years after the Plague had spread from London in 1665 and devastated the village.*

John's stead. That is why inquisitive people, including myself, have gone to see a type of larking which originated in those misty years of Merrie England. Pranks are presented in the venerable little town of the abbots of Burton, Abbot's Bromley, on the Monday of the September Wakes. Then the deer-skulls with antlers, bows and arrows, and the hobby-horse come out of store from the church tower and the Horn Dance is performed. Now the dance is an amusing and lively caper through the streets in front of the black-and-white gables and spectators gladly pay tribute into a funny old bowl. But in the reign of Edward I the buffoonery had a real meaning. The natives danced with joy to celebrate their grant of the *Charta de Foresta*, which mitigated the severities of the Forest Law and restored their freedom.

Below the uplands of Needwood the Trent vale opens out wide. The river bends remarkably through level miles and winds out of Staffordshire and across south Derbyshire, reinforced first by the Dove and then by the Derwent. Landscapes are homely rather than spectacular. Flattish, with rises here and there, and far extended to distant low hills, this unmistakable Midland tract of pastoral country offers just the effects that might be expected. Scenes and features make pretty pictures of old villages, shady greens, halls amongst trees, church towers like the one at King's Bromley, a spire or two as at Repton, fields divided by hedgerows, quiet buttercup meadows, the wide deep Trent flowing between low banks, and the cows I saw lazily paddling in the stream on a hot summer day near the hermit's Anchor Church at Ingleby—pictures all very nice and very English. They can be sampled in pottering about the three Ridwares—Mavesyn, Hamstall, and Pipe—Yoxall, King's Bromley, and Alrewas, Staffordshire villages in the pastures watered by brooks and little streams running into the Trent. Mavesyn Ridware has a Tudor gatehouse, a dovecote, and carved armoured knights in the church, well worth finding and meaning that a Malvoisin left France in 1066, fought at the Battle of Hastings, and then settled his family in the parish. A quarrelsome lot were these Mal-voisins; some of them continued to live up to their French name for "evil neighbours," one derived from the movable engines used by old-time warriors for battering down walls, anything, and anybody standing in their way. To me this ominous tinge in the sweet air also seemed suitable for the place selected by Oliver Cromwell for hatching his plans to destroy a cathedral, mentioned previously in my note on Lichfield. If asked very politely the kind farmer at Hamstall Ridware manor-house (176) may show a visitor the good panelling and carvings of Henry VIII period, and the lofty watchtower too, relics of the departed mansion of the Leighs, whose Warwickshire home we round at Stoneleigh. Perhaps nicest of all in this part of the river vale is King's Bromley, once a home spot of Leofric, Earl of Mercia, husband of the celebrated naked lady of Coventry. The Trent glides past trees behind the fifteenth-century church tower and churchyard cross, and the prettiness of the village is emphasized with cottages, farmhouses, long barns and thatched roofs (176).

Past Alrewas the river turns north-east and sends along its gypsum waters to tickle up the beers at Burton-on-Trent. Without dwelling on blots added to landscapes through compounding beneficent products of hop-gardens and Trent water, it is better to contemplate an emblem of peace, the Dove, meeting the Trent, or to look across the broad vale to distant hills, visible from the Derbyshire soil at Newton Solney, centuries ago lived on by the de Solneys, now silent in stone and alabaster at the church. The characteristic scenes continue. There are the wide meadows, villages near the ever-winding stream, a charming group of church, rectory, and hall at Aston-on-Trent, a hall at Shardlow built of stone in 1684. Particular points for calling a halt include Repton, its medieval buildings at the school, the remarkable Saxon crypt in the church at this old capital of Mercia; the Georgian Cavendish Bridge put up in 1758, a gay spot in the coaching days on the route from London to the North; the medieval bridge at Swarkeston, a dismal spot in 1745 when the Young Pretender's advance petered out there, still a mile long, but a good deal altered since the thirteenth century and now without its chapel that used to stand at Stanton-by-Bridge; Melbourne, mentioned in Domesday Book, picturesque to-day, and noted for the Queen Anne gardens at the hall and the cruciform Norman church, one of the most interesting parish churches in England. Southward the woods and uplands rise from Ticknall, Calke and Hartshorne to the Leicestershire borders.

North of the Trent the sandstone plain is broken by patches of higher ground. Quiet villages, old-fashioned dreamy places like Findern, Etwall, and Sutton-on-the-Hill group round hilltops and hollows. Fine halls stand at Sudbury and Longford. Fame of the Middle Ages belongs to Chellaston and its hill. Alabaster from the quarries, artists, and the local craft workshops enriched the golden age of English handiwork. Particularly in the fourteenth and fifteenth centuries beauty spread from Chellaston to all parts of England, often abroad; it penetrated far and wide through the genius and skill of the men who created famous sculptured reredoses for altars, images, canopies, patterned tombs, and representations of armour and dress carefully rendered. Though many of these works met their doom from Cromwellians and other destroyers, numbers still remain fresh and vital to enthrall lovers of things stately and beautiful. In its prime years this busy centre, near medieval Derby and the ancient Trent crossing at Swarkeston, knew much coming and going while patrons and craftsmen flocked in and out; thus in 1414 the King's master mason of Rouen, de Berneval, visited Thomas Prentys "the alabasterman," the designer of the angel weepers with shields yet to be seen on a tomb in Lowick church, Northamptonshire.

To go across the stretches of productive land from Chellaston to Derby may seem like a jump of sorts from the golden age of English handiwork into the splendid epoch of genius for mechanical invention; a transition from carved alabaster that has lasted in beauty to locomotives with steam boilers, the finest petrol engines in the world, and other things for utility that eventually will end on Time's scrap-heap. If Derby is not one of my ideal towns for dreaming in, and is vitally remembered for platforms and sheds at a big railway centre, it has travelled through many stages and changes since Romans and Danes arrived and departed on roads and trackways now polished by motor cars. Normans built churches where five churches now stand. The chapel of St. Mary-on-the-Bridge, the timbered *Dolphin* in Queen Street, William Deusbury's Crown Derby porcelain, Joseph Wright the painter, and Samuel Johnson's marriage, all originated here in their various periods. Historical events happened, not to be detailed on these pages beyond a mention of the Young Pretender in and out of the town in December 1745, and whose whereabouts in that adventure we may find again on our way to Carlisle. Earlier years brought the Gothic church of All Saints with one of the finest Midland towers, completed in the sixteenth century shortly before the Reformation (195). The body of this church, demolished to the order of a turbulent parson, was replaced in 1723-25 by the graceful classic interior designed by James Gibbs. Splendid screens and gates, magnificently hand-wrought by Robert Bakewell, show this celebrated Derby smith's masterpiece, in its way and for its day quite comparable to the Derby mechanical feats in metal by Rolls-Royce in this present time o' day.

DERBYSHIRE HIGHLANDS AND THE CHESHIRE PLAIN

After Staffordshire, whose poor reputation for beauty I have endeavoured to raise a notch or two, northern Derbyshire presents me with an area of Dale and Peak country that still merits all the words of admiration showered by enthusiasts for many years past. Here are moors covered with heather, desolate heights, limestone cliffs, bold crags, ravines, rocky glens, caverns, waterfalls, luxuriant woods and verdure, fast clear streams, the Derwent, Wye, and Dove for rivers, deep gorges from Matlock and Dove Dales to Edale, Peak Forest leading up to the Peak at the end of the Pennines. Combinations of these natural features, the strong masses, varied groupings, the panoramas and distances where great clouds ride above untarnished glory offer exquisite landscape effects. Early natives left stone circles, many "lows," and Arbor Low, Derbyshire's competitor of Stonehenge. Romans used existing routes for conveying lead. At Castleton Peverel erected his Norman stronghold in a position most dramatic. Vernons settled down at Haddon Hall to create romantic picturesqueness that is hardly matched in all England. Dukes of Devonshire built the grand Renaissance mansion at Chatsworth (201) and the notable Crescent at Buxton. Stanton-in-the-Peak, Bakewell, Eyam, Sparrowpit, and more villages, remote hamlets, and towns made from the native stone, developed in wooded valleys and on hillsides. Dr. Johnson talked to Boswell of and in Dove Dale, declared that no one who had seen it need visit Scotland. John Ruskin remembered that in Monsal Dale,

> "You might have seen the gods there morning and evening, walking in fair procession on the lawns, and to and fro among the pinnacles of its crags."

The Derwent, a most beautiful river, bisects the county. Its course from south to north, which can be followed by road, gives the scenic transition complete. Pastoral landscapes of wide Trent–Derwent meadows extend at little more than 100 feet elevations around Cavendish Bridge and Wilne. Upward from Derby's railways and the Roman point of Little Chester the stream changes sandstone borderlands for the millstone grit and mountain limestone. From Duffield, prettily settled in its green hollow below slopes and the mound of Ferrers's huge Norman keep, banks and hills become higher and steeper. Belper and Ambergate passed, the characteristic and impressive groupings of limestone scenery mount up. Precipitous rocks, pinnacles, cliffs, and woods rise high from the waterside. Harmonies of cool stone tints and foliage colour bold shapes and varied arrangements. These fanciful designs piled by nature give effects of extraordinary beauty to which light, shade, and distance add brilliance and mystery. The vertical rifts of High Tor dominate the

Sparrowpit

KNUTSFORD, *1906. King Street in Mrs. Gaskell's "Cranford."*

MALPAS. *One of Cheshire's pleasant smaller towns in the pastoral countryside. Here are timbered buildings in black and white, a good church with sculptured monuments to the Cholmondeleys and Breretons, and the mound on the hill recalls a border castle.*

Bramhall
Hall

Gawsworth
Old Hall

Handforth
Hall 1562

Farmhouse
Prestbury

Heffner
Alderley

Farmhouse near
Sandbach

Sydney R.
Jones

CHESHIRE DETAILS *of patterns from the half-timber houses.*

setting of peculiar magnificence in Matlock Dale; from 800 feet high on Masson I have seen wonderful views of the river winding through the rocky gorge, with Tansley Knoll and Matlock Moor for backgrounds. At Oaker Hill —Wordsworth's "yon fair hill"—Darley Dale opens out in pastures and woods that continue to the old bridge of Rowsley. Here the Wye joins its parent stream after leaving Wye Dale and Topley Pike, circling round Chee Tor, shooting under the pointed arches of Bakewell Bridge, and passing Haddon Hall, one of the most romantic courses made by any river. It is an aristocratic Derwent in Chatsworth Park and looks so. The river, meeting the bridge ornamented with Cibber's carved figures, exactly fits the famed ducal scene of Talman's architecture (1687–1700) set in noble surroundings; whoever may have walked over the moor from Haddon to Chatsworth never will forget the first impression of the spectacle presented by "The Palace of the Peak," acres of lawns and gardens, parklands, continuous woods mounting to East Moor, the silver stream winding below, a perfect union of natural grouping enriched by man. Outside the park the three-arched bridge and stone cottages of Baslow have woods and steep hillsides to set them off, and the tree-clad slopes continue to Grindleford Bridge and Hathersage. The scenery rises higher and wilder, stretching up to the moors. The Hope valley opens out, directing to Castleton and Peverel's castle. Road and river traverse Derwent Dale between the Bamford Edge and Win Hill (1523 feet). The real Peakland heights are near. Years ago the Ashop river swept down from the solitudes of Kinderscout to its tryst with the Derwent under Crook Hill and Ladybower. The hills at present remain, but a spice of the romantic meeting has gone. Huge reservoirs have swamped most of Ashop Dale and extend for miles to the Slippery Stones on the Derwent at the Yorkshire border. They are dedicated to Sheffield and other centres of manufacture so that the inhabitants thereof can refresh and wash themselves.

Splendour of rocks, stream, foliage, and colouring are repeated along the course of the Dove at the western boundary of Derbyshire and obviously this river merits all the fame it owns; its paces and graces have been located in my previous Staffordshire notes. On and between the Dove, Wye, and Derwent are the dales, the Derbyshire Dales of Beresford and Dove, Ashwood, Miller's and Monsal on the Wye, Middleton (Eyam), Hope (Castleton) and others of renown, each abounding in exquisite pictures. One only do I particularize, the view of Monsal Dale and the sweep of the Wye seen from Little Longstone. On summer evenings I have watched the light flood this dale, trace patterns brilliant and dark over verdure and banks of trees, brighten exposed rocks and the tops of the heights, send lengthening shadows across the green floor and pick out the winding stream; there, and in other dales too, reality and suggestion can stimulate mental visions, gods in procession among the lawns, the pinnacles and crags such as Ruskin imagined, and much more than writer or artist ever set down on paper.

It is exhilarating to go from Ashford-in-the-Water up Kirk Dale, over Bole Hill, strike below the old marble quarries of Ricklow into Lathkill Dale, and thus sample specimens of the smaller wild dales that occur from Hartington and Winster up to the High Peak. The Lathkill stream hurries down through the steep and wooded glen, a true enchanted valley. Past picturesque banks the waters leap along to Conksbury bridge, Alport village and Alport Dale—enchanting waters all the way, pure and transparent as Charles Cotton saw them when he said they bred "the best trouts in England." Alport is one of my favourite villages, charmingly placed at the meeting of streams and dales. Stone cottages and gables stand high, low, and at quaint angles. Little waterfalls splash below rocks. Trout dart through pools by the bridge and round the mill. Natives welcome a stranger with the time o' day, and one kind soul used to tickle my appetite with strong tea and girdle cakes hot from her cottage hearth to help along my sketching—for here in Derbyshire, be it remembered, begins the north country famed throughout for girdle and tea-cakes. Apart from the joys of Lathkill Dale the surroundings are good. The stream joins the Wye near Haddon Hall. A big fifteenth-century tower at Youlgreave marks one of the best local churches. Stanton-in-the-Peak (207) is mounted high with its stone cottages, houses, and owns the three interesting halls of Stanton Old Hall, the eighteenth-century Hall in a deer park, and an Elizabethan Stanton Woodhouse facing Darley Dale. Searchers for fine views or reminders of prehistoric ancestors can find all they may wish from Stanton Moor to the stone circle at Arbor Low.

The above-mentioned places, with towns, villages, and hamlets up and down this district, introduce the native architecture developed with stone quarried from the hillsides, an expression in traditional building that is seen with local variations all along the northern stone belt, the great Pennine backbone of England directing through Lancashire and Yorkshire to the Border. In Derbyshire the characteristics begin to show. Homes and domestic buildings have a sturdy look, appear strong and workmanlike. Wall surfaces, heavy surrounds to doorways and windows, roofs of stone slates often large in size, exhibit the nature and texture of the millstone grit and limestone. Details are bold rather than finely wrought, made in simple and straightforward ways without any show of affectation. Masonry from foundations to chimneys and also the roofs illustrate traditional methods in construction and usage. Thus built up, this distinctive stonework is significant and suggestive. It reflects the spirit of locality and the life it served. Determined largely by physical and climatic conditions and based on practices accumulated by experience from generation to generation, these buildings of Derbyshire and further north do in a manner make known the way of life, the character, and temperament of the native people who looked no farther than near quarries for resources and used the stone to meet their needs of hearth and home. These stone houses in towns and villages, the cottages and the farmsteads group and combine well together, and boundary walls of stone carry the prevailing theme into the fields and over hillsides to the mountains. But the northern grey stone-work sinks into the landscapes rather than stands out from them; it takes a secondary and right place in the scenes, as it should do where nature reigns predominant and has worked in fine creative mood to mount grand sweeping lines and big effects.

Explorers with eyes now and again off the scenery will notice the most finished examples of the native architecture in the south and east parts of this stone district. Interesting features and pictures are visible at manor-houses, farms, village groups, and town streets in leading up from Ashbourne through Parwich, Bonsall, and Winster to Rowsley, Bakewell, Baslow, and Eyam. Gabled cottages with worked mullions to the windows in Alport might be mistaken for Cotswold examples by the unobservant. The *Peacock* inn at Rowsley is a capital specimen of developed 1652 stonework; being a place of delight for fishermen, you know the kind of fare to be expected inside behind the carved bird of the Manners family. An Elizabethan school-house with six gables, the *Green Man*, houses, and almshouses add distinction to Ashbourne. Perhaps Dr. Johnson did not notice how nice they looked on his frequent visits, after his mental reflection on the Staffordshire canal and " the great efforts of human labour and human contrivance," and not all people find lowly architecture much in their line. But for those that do, well worth exploration are the parts of Derbyshire beyond East Moor and Owler Bar in the direction of Holmesfield, Unthank, Dronfield Woodhouse (207), Dronfield town, and on again past Chesterfield's crooked leaden steeple to Barlborough and Whitwell near the county boundary. Here are houses built centuries ago in a local style very fitting for the local scene. A very good style it was, developed in stone throughout for walls, roofs, chimneys, doorways, and mullions, and not widely known to-day because coal-mining progressed after these buildings were made and George Stephenson arrived to bring that kind of prosperity concerned with making money, spoiling landscapes, and frightening searchers for beauty. Northward, under the flanks of the Peak where the scenery mounts up, observation proves that the finish of the rural architecture went down. Sparrowpit, for one instance, shows very rough rubble walling and heavy stone roofs (214); and through the Peak Forest and high lands round Castleton the cottages and farms generally, dotted here and there over the open expanses, are structures of extreme simplicity built to withstand the severities of climate. Nevertheless, they look right in their locations, accord with the natural backgrounds, seem to be growths of the moors and the mountains.

Hardy folk who were born and bred in these Derbyshire dales, uplands, and moors, set their stamp on the manor-houses and roomy homes which they built for themselves and their followers, particularly during the sixteenth, seventeenth, and eighteenth centuries. They constructed solidly, usually achieved the strong and severe individuality common to the traditional masonry. Nearly all the villages show one or more of these houses. Two are Unthank Hall and Hallows Hall on the hill at Dronfield; and Elizabethan Wolleys, Milwards, and Batemans built their halls at Riber, Snitterton, and Hartington. Often they stand in view, to be spied at beyond entrance gates and piers, lawns and gardens; fortunate wanderers may penetrate inside to see the panelling, oak staircases, the frequent plaster ceilings, adjuncts of a past day-to-day life lived comfortably by squires and country people who generally kept on good terms with their neighbours, looked after dependants, served their country well, and filled a social niche in the antiquated system developed before tax grabbers and land grabbers ruled the English roost. I illustrate two examples. Eyam Hall (210), built by the Wrights and their home ever since, dates from 1676, some years after the terrible visitation of the Plague had devastated the village, and the heroic devotion of the Mompessons and Thomas Stanley had given Derbyshire one of its most moving stories. Cartledge Hall (210) sits squat and four-square to the wind and the weather on the moor a few miles south of Sheffield. A home of the old Derbyshire family of Wolstenholme, it probably began early in the 1500's. From here in the reign of Edward VI John Wolstenholme went to London, and it was his son John (1562–1639) who became the rich merchant adventurer, and after whom Henry Hudson and William Baffin named Wolstenholme Cape (1610), Island, and Sound (1615) during their adventures in the North-west Passage and Hudson Strait. Long ago the Wolstenholmes left their home, but inside you can see how nicely they did for themselves with oak-panelled walls, deep-set windows, ceilings of ribbed and modelled plaster, a carved fireplace representing the temptation of Adam and Eve to serve for a warning, and a fret to show the hours on a clock-face cunningly contrived in the panelling.

At this house in my own years lived the author of *The Gentle Thespians*, Robert Murray Gilchrist, true artist in words, a humble student and storyteller of the lives, lore, and home places of the Derbyshire hill folk. Huge in build, his frame held a big heart and a nature lovable and humorous. By the wide fireplace do I remember him with his bosom crony, George Garfitt, and lecturing me with impish delight on the sins of extreme youth, a reflection on the success of my first book published at the time by *The Studio*.

"Jones is only sixteen," he said to George. "Dreadful. He ought to be

CHESTER CATHEDRAL *and St. Werburgh Street from Eastgate Street Row.
The Perpendicular tower crowns the former Benedictine abbey. It was converted
into a cathedral in 1541 and contains monastic features of great interest.*

RABY. *A characteristic village group on the levels of the Wirral Peninsula near to the sands of Dee.*

SMALLWOOD. *A black and white farmhouse of the type common in the Vale Royal.*

confined in a perambulator instead of cycling about to rob responsible workers of good bread and butter. And oh! the hairy butter he must consume for breakfasts at obscure pubs in prowling round out-of-the-way places! The thought makes me shudder. Much too young to be allowed off the lead."

"Have mercy, sir," I appealed. "I cannot help my looks and twenty-odd years. But what have you to say of your own efforts made in your teens?"

"That's the point," he gravely added. "You look on a warning, not an example."

Then he chuckled, ended leg-pulling, went to the old pianette by the window, played air after air charmingly and his tenor voice filled the room. Only a time or two more did I hear that voice or see those strong hands tinkling soft melodies. The gods winged the author away in his prime. The scenes that he loved and showed me in the High Peak to the west knew him no longer. His grave is in Holmesfield churchyard. Farewell.

Great families built the great houses. At Haddon and Chatsworth they gave to Derbyshire two of England's most famed and historic mansions. The manor-house at South Wingfield might have made a third if it had not come to grief in the Civil War. This home of Lord Treasurer Cromwell, dating from about 1440 and later a prison of Mary Queen of Scots in 1584, when the Babington plot was hatched, remains an extensive and interesting ruin of two courtyards, gatehouses, beautiful late Perpendicular windows, and one of the finest vaulted undercrofts in the country. Bess of Hardwick, proud collector of husbands, mansions, and vast wealth, made the immense windowed frontage of Hardwick Hall; the pierced parapets ornamented with the initials E S to flatter herself, and the Elizabethan showiness are retained unaltered to-day. Equally Elizabethan undiluted, but on a smaller scale, is Barlborough Hall, with its glassy bays and busy turrets erected to suit Judge Rodes in 1583. Where Peverel had ruled in Norman years at Bolsover, Cavendishs set up the early Renaissance walls, turrets, terraces, and long ranges of unfinished rooms, now grouped in dramatic skylines above the high rock on which, in 1634, courtiers performed Ben Jonson's masque of "Love's Welcome" before King Charles I. But for me Haddon is the prize. Occupying the slope above the Wye and banked in high trees of the upper ground, the setting is rare, perfect (202). The stonework blends, glints from the massed greenery in a fantasy of turrets, towers and chapel, bays and oriels, battlements of the upper and lower court-yards, gardens terraced towards the river. On outer walls and inside the great hall, state rooms, long gallery, and domestic apartments, the accumulations of craftsmanship in stone, wood, plaster, metals, and sixteenth-century leadwork tell the long story, adorn the tale of building, reconstruction, and enlargement successively advanced from the eleventh to the seventeenth centuries as Vernon followed Vernon and Manners followed Manners. Never a house for defence nor disturbed by wars, slowly developed during more than five hundred years and not altered since, it is an epitome of a way of thought and peaceful, cultivated life that gave lustre to a past England and beautified the scenes. That past is dead. Haddon expresses it, and nothing more captivating of the kind does any county show. The buildings continue lovely, cared for, rare and secluded. lived in by descendants of those who made them—for which, it seems to me, we ought to be thankful when the purpose, meaning, spirit, and charm of England's heritages are being shattered.

Up from Haddon and Bakewell through Taddington, Buxton, and Goyt's Moss to Macclesfield Forest, and there the Peakland heights soon drop to the levels. It is a bleak region, one in which travellers often have been glad to find the *Cat and Fiddle* at 1,690 feet above sea-level. The stone-built look is brought into Cheshire at Rainow and infrequent villages and hamlets. Stone field walls make sinuous lines over the slopes. Shuttlings Low (1,659 feet), Shining Tor (1,833 feet), and points all the way northward from Mow Cop (190) to Sponds Hill above Kettleshulme, well reward anybody in search of fine air and widespread views. You obtain overlooks swept from south, north, and westwards across the great plain of Cheshire. Distances blend with the outlines of Welsh mountains, where the River Dee winds from Llangollen bound for Chester and the sandy estuary at the Wirral Peninsula.

This Cheshire plain, widely viewed as stated above in remarkable prospects from the elevations above Lyme Park, Macclesfield and Congleton, also brings us to a gateway of the industrial North. Here the busy manufacturing centres of Merseyside face those in Lancashire. The tunnel connects Birkenhead with Liverpool. "People from Manchester and other big towns overflow into the country to grow bricks and mortar instead of crops," the agent of a large estate told me. Port Sunlight, the inspiration of its founder, William Lever, represents a splendid and pioneer effort in trying to make modern labour palatable to those who pursue it. Crewe, great and useful railway centre though it is, generally gives the impression of being dismal. Getting salt out of the earth from Nantwich to Northwich and Marston has produced peculiar streets and toppling houses settled out of the perpendicular; Boswell, bound for north Wales and evidently not interested in salt, summarily dismissed Middlewich as "a mean town, without any manufacture, but I think, a corporation"! Advantages and deficiencies such as these and the general flatness of the landscapes have caused observers now and again to dismiss Cheshire as being too busy and too level for real picturesqueness; it is not for me to direct my readers to the Vale Royal with the expectation of finding English scenery in its most exciting and spectacular mood.

But outside the industrial areas miles of real countryside spread far and wide.

There are many parks. Woodlands and meres denote a primeval character of forest and marsh. The rich agricultural land is coloured with pastoral greens and fertile surface textures. Prosperous farms and market gardens, the pastures, cattle, and cornfields make the rural scenes appear all the more friendly. A few isolated sandstone ridges break into the plain. The hill group at Alderley Edge, rocky and clad with fir trees, commands wide distances towards the Peak, Lancashire, and Wales; standing at the Armada beacon-stone in the evening I have seen fascinating effects of the lights twinkling five miles away at the hill town of Macclesfield. In the south another grouping is marked by Bickerton Hill, Harthill ridge, the Peckforton Hills, with a bold finish made at Beeston rock on which you can feel like a prophet viewing promised lands that seem to comprise half England. Strongholds of all ages on these wooded escarpments give a suspicion of romance, of "castles in the air." Though modern, the large castles of Peckforton and Bickerton stand out formidably from green backgrounds; poised on its cliff the thirteenth-century ruined walls and gatehouse of Beeston survive from Civil War batterings and Prince Rupert's escapades; far back in the Iron Age natives made the ramparts of Maiden Castle; and down below in Cholmondeley Park the towers and embattled walls would do very well for an excursion into the Middle Ages if they had not been erected in the eighteenth century by the ancient Cholmondeley family. The stretches of sandstone highlands from Tarporley to Frodsham are luxuriant with survivals of the great Forest of Delamere; here the British had their camp of Kelsborrow, and over the hills and through the forest Romans drove the route that still connects Chester and Manchester.

Across the plain are scattered attractive villages. The usual make-up is a good church built of the local sandstone, warm-coloured, often notable for a big tower finished with battlements and pinnacles; round about group old houses and cottages schemed in black timbers and white facings, a proportion of stonework, and eighteenth-century brick frontages. As likely as not the big house is one of the timbered manor halls for which the county is famous. Occasionally, as at Marton and Warburton, the timbered patterning is repeated by the ancient oak of the churches. Along the lanes and down in the fields the farmhouses add sparkle to the scenes with walls and gables of black and white; the effects they give are suggested by my examples sketched at Smallwood (222), Sandbach (216), Prestbury (216), and it is many years since I discovered the capital timbered cottages with overhanging dormers at Nether Alderley (216) and Artists' Lane, Alderley Edge. A number of the villages have particular interest and beauty to rank them as minor show-pieces; of these my space only permits a mention of Gawsworth, Lower Peover, Prestbury, Wybunbury, and Astbury completed at the corner of its green with a noble church and spire. Far afield in the deep rural country these pleasant places continue to Tushingham and Marbury near the Shropshire border and through the wide levels sloping down to the River Dee. Often a pretty out-of-the-way spot can bring to mind and fit a page out of *Cranford* :

"The aspect of the country was quiet and pastoral. Woodley stood among fields; and there was an old-fashioned garden where roses and currant-bushes touched each other, and where the feathery asparagus formed a pretty background to the pinks and gilly-flowers."

Cheshire's good examples of old English country towns resemble the villages for possessing sandstone churches and streets of black and white, brickwork, and stone buildings. Two worth finding are Audlem and Malpas in the country-side near Shropshire. Malpas, on a hillock facing Wales, and with a castle mound to recall the old border fighting, particularly attracted me for street pictures and Tudor details in the fine church containing the Cholmondeley and Brereton monuments (215). Progressing northward more pleasant town sights are offered in the long street of Tarporley; round the cross built on the rock at Lymm; at Parkgate and Neston on Wirral overlooking Dee sands and Welsh mountains; in the curious street with quaint houses and the stone gabled *Bear's Paw* inn at Frodsham, the home town and pastorate of Parson Gastrell, the scoundrel who pulled down Shakespeare's New Place at Stratford. Knutsford of course has literary and wide fame for being the original of *Cranford* and the place of Mrs. Gaskell's childhood (215). Popularity, modernism, and tea-shops have not dispelled all the qualities Miss Matty and Captain Brown knew; houses, streets, the seventeenth-century chapel, and little features help to add depths in the perspectives which still mirror a something of the fragrance and charm diffused by the gifted creator of the early Victorian ladies. My own and mundane reminiscences are liable to fix on the old *Angel* inn and the real Cheshire cheese it used to provide to aid me in my wanderings through this district.

Cheshire's most striking feats of architecture, the timbered buildings, are abundant in these small towns, in the larger towns among which Sandbach, Nantwich, Congleton, and Macclesfield may be cited, and throughout the countryside and the villages. Here, and in south Lancashire, we meet a culmina-tion of the native style in home construction that has shown brightly along our routes through Warwickshire, Worcestershire, Herefordshire, and Shropshire: the great domestic building style of the West, indigenous to and developed from the wooded and forest lands until it was superseded by the widespread use of brickwork in the seventeenth and eighteenth centuries. The timbering in Cheshire has ornate arrangements of black woodwork and white panels, storeys overhanging one above another, bays of extraordinary shapes, elaborate carv-ings on bargeboards, beams and brackets, combinations which border on the bizarre and fantastic. These may be thought either startling, masterpieces of late

RIBCHESTER, *at the site of the large Roman fortress on the River Ribble.* *The porch of the White Bull inn is supported on four Roman columns.*

HALL I' TH' WOOD, TONGE. *Tudor post and plaster in black and white. This fine example was presented to the Bolton Corporation by Lord Leverhulme. Here in 1779 Samuel Crompton invented and worked the Mule for spinning.*

TOWERED HALLS IN LANCASHIRE

Tudor, Elizabethan, and early seventeenth-century carpentry, or like nothing on earth; and indeed the manor-houses and halls, led by the incomparable Moreton, certainly are unique in England for their variety and exuberant patterning. They stand in all directions; in line from Little Moreton Hall towards Manchester at Brereton, Gawsworth (216), Chorley Hall (Alderley), Adlington, Woodford, Handforth (216), and Bramhall (216), at Moss Hall (Audlem), Holford, Tattenhall, Poole on Wirral, and village after village presents particular specimens. They are standing reminders of the old Cheshire families, the Warburtons, Fittons, Stanleys, Breretons, Leghs, Davenports, Mainwarings, and their like, many of whose monuments are to be found in the neighbouring churches.

The half-timbered style of these homes, one dear to the hearts of latter-day English people and sometimes sniffed at by innocents who see no more in it than antique combinations of the pretty-pretty, has suffered in repute from overmuch enthusiasm by admirers and because modern producers of fakes plastered town and country with cheap effects in black and white. Though the style is dead and could have no place in the life of to-day, it was true and real when it flourished, a logical expression of ideas in materials, construction, and workmanship. The inheritance from Gothic times dictated general principles and influenced the shapes of overhanging projections, gables, oriels, wood mullions, angle posts, and enrichments, all of which took new forms of detail as fashions moved with the impulses brought by the Renaissance. These Cheshire halls and houses, with those in south Lancashire, framed in timbers pegged together with oak pins and faced in panels of wattle and daub, reached their prime development and complexity in the 1500's and the early part of the following century, a period in which men's craniums and homes were not so exposed to summary cracks and dangers as in earlier years. Times had become more settled. Life could be lived comfortably, prosperously, even luxuriously. Provision might safely be made for generations to come. Scantlings of the timbers and the richness of effects show that the creators of these homes spared neither materials nor workmanship. They built with pride and in oak to last. Their work, tied with beam, mortise and tenon, became truly indicative of human character and an English way of life. Exteriors, and interiors now existing at Bramhall and elsewhere, with panelled walls, rich chimney-pieces, massive staircases, and carved fittings, illustrate the vivid domestic interlude of the sixteenth and seventeenth centuries. They show how and where men and women lived who saw the beacons on Overton Hill and Alderley Edge flash news of the Armada. Timbers and patterns call to mind adventurous days in which the wide world was sighted by Drake and Raleigh, days when the nation reached out to fuller expression in the flush of hope and expectation while poets and dramatists tuned exquisite numbers to the rhythm of brilliant years. In these present times, conspicuous for planning, controlling, and docketing inanimate things and human objects as economic units in a system notable for prefabricated miseries, it can be quite refreshing to ponder on such an old stalwart as Uryan Brereton contemplating with just pride the finishing touches on his fine entrance porch at Handforth, complete with uneconomic enrichment, arms, crest, and the inscription that still testifies,

"This haulle was buylded In the yeare of oure Lord God M. CCCCC. LXII by Uryan Breretoun Knight Whom maryed Margaret daughter and heyre of Wyllyam Handforth of Handforth Esquyer and had Issue VI sonnes and II daughters."

Original builders of timbered houses also knew a thing or two about prefabrication. It was customary to prepare the oak at "framing-places" before erecting on actual sites. Posts, vertical and horizontal timbers, beams and joists, were assembled together, the position of each piece being marked with a number, many of which are still visible lightly cut on the timbers. The structures then went to their sites for final erection. These mobile houses thus could be taken to pieces and fitted together elsewhere. One house I know of departed to Kent, where it now stands. In Shropshire, at Shrewsbury, the house at the castle gate originally stood in Castle Street, and a number of the Cheshire homes have been carefully pulled down, packed up, and exported to begin life anew in America. A good deal might be said in favour of these dwellings nowadays. Nasty neighbours or unpleasant conditions in general can be changed any time by moving house, bed, and hope for experiments in fresh directions. I live in a timber-framed house myself!

More timbered buildings attract us to Chester, the historic gateway to Wales for nearly 2,000 years, and also a pointer to the North, whither our tracks next lead. In this English show-town the large quantities of famous black-and-white decorate the streets in the gayest possible fashion and brightly animate scenes bustling with shoppers, tourists, traffic, antiques for sale, trippers in chars-à-bancs, and battalions from neighbouring industrial conglomerations invading to win the beaches, sea, and breezes of the Welsh resorts. It cannot be denied that Chester gives the impression of being a very lively and busy place, brilliant with high lights and the blackest of blacks when the sun shines. Jostled by crowds in the Rows, running up and down little stairways, and quizzing here and there, you find timberwork both genuinely ancient and obviously recent. It needs sorting out by those on the lookout for old patterns. Things have been erected in the newer antiquated manner that might make even the builders of Little Moreton Hall turn in their graves, and it is possible to enjoy tea and bread and butter under timbers hoary with stain and not age. But in this grand old city one need not carp overmuch on articles genuine and imitative standing in juxtaposition. They impel both admiration and amusement and can offer much for exhilaration. That is the right spirit for setting out to see and do Chester.

Centuries before the timbering arrived in bulk Chester began its crowded history which carries the English story far back and might fill volumes. Roman *Deva*, settled by the Twentieth Legion on the Dee estuary, successively fell to the Northumbrians, the Danes, and the Mercians. Before the Conquest it was important enough to have its own mint and royal palace. Conquering William made Chester one of the castled key-points for the dual purpose of defending the Welsh border and keeping his own turbulent companions in order. Here Hugh de Avranches spied out his chances, just as Roger de Montgomery did at Shrewsbury and William FitzOsborn at Hereford. When the last Norman earl died the earldom passed to the Crown and ever since has given the title of Earl of Chester to the eldest son of the King. An early church, by tradition founded in Roman times, developed into the powerful Benedictine Abbey of St. Werburgh. Kings arrived and departed both for warlike and peaceful deeds. One, Henry III, strengthened the castle with stone walls and towers; another, Richard II, mounted on a "nagge not worth 40 francs," got locked up there on his way to be deposed.

After early disturbances and unpleasant occasions Chester prospered and grew splendid. It did so in spite of fires, plagues, floods, and constant attacks by fierce Welshmen. The walls, first built by the Romans, were kept in order and further extended to the west and to the south in line with the river and the bridge. At various points towers rose above them. Strong gateways, replete with the contrivances of welcome for intruders usual in the Middle Ages, guarded entrances from the east and west, the north and the south. The port, outside the Watergate and defended by the Water Tower, brought wealth and prosperity with trade over the seas.

These walls, gates and towers enclosed the varied aspects of beauty, sparkle and gloom common to a medieval city of first rank. The castle made a base for war expeditions. Under the Norman earl, Hugh Lupus, Lord of the Welsh Marches, the Mercian church became the abbey of the Benedictines in 1093. It gained landed possessions far and wide and riches flowed in to the shrine of St. Werburgh. Black, Grey, and White Friars had their own establishments. Mansions served for town quarters of the county families. Sheriffs from Norman times, mayors onward from 1238, and the guilds all played their important and customary rôles. Groups of tradesmen and craftsmen banded together, kept to their own particular quarters mostly in sections of the curious Rows built on Roman foundations. Lines of buildings then newish, and here and there now remaining to show the old and worn faces of age, made backgrounds for movement and brave colouring as civic ceremonial, mystery plays, and pageants wound from street to street. These added liveliness to the regular scenes; a wonderful "Deluge" performed by the Water-leaders and Drawers of the Dee, "St. George and the Dragon," and the "Devil very boisterous" gained high favour. The mills near the end of the bridge ground corn for the whole population and at least one "jolly miller . . . sung from morn till night." The bridge itself, almost certainly first built by the Romans, mentioned in Domesday, rebuilt in the late 1200's, and arched to its present form in 1347, gave Chester particular importance by affording the strategic crossing into north Wales at the head of the Dee estuary. Unpleasant circumstances also developed behind the outward show. Raiding Welshmen, fires, plagues, and floods aforementioned did not add lustre to the city's most glorious years; and dungeons, one of them thirty feet deep in the rock, were only seen by certain people. But, all in all, medieval Chester with its walls and buildings, life, activities and diversions must have presented a shining example of a thriving centre in the old days, one very nice to think of and picture in bright trappings, especially if you prefer to forget, the smudges, the sanitation, and the dungeon chains.

Tangible reminders of the medieval brilliance, of the earlier phases, and of Tudor and succeeding centuries help to make Chester the great place it is for absorbing strong doses of historical suggestion and preserved beauty in circumstances that offer explorers no perils, and every comfort and discomfort of this age. Even the beams in the Rows, at *Ye Olde King's Head*, the *Grosvenor Hotel*, and the cafés do not administer bumps on the heads of the unwary, as sometimes happens in less sophisticated and more barbarous directions. The city's early beginnings in *Deva*, the fortress and Romano-British settlement with a port outside the Watergate, can be traced at many points and under the houses within the original rectangular area bounded by the north and east town walls. The crowded traffic in Eastgate Street, Northgate Street, Watergate Street, and Bridge Street follows the exact directions trodden by the Twentieth Legion. After the departure of the Romans and a gloomy period of which little is known, Chester brightened up and gained in status during late Saxon, Norman, and medieval years. Little of the once-important castle is visible. Embattled walls and the apparatus of war and chivalry were removed in 1789. A thirteenth-century tower with a chapel is the chief sustainer of glory and crime departed. A thriving port, source of great prosperity in the Middle Ages, is merely suggested by the landlocked Water Tower, built in 1322 for £100. In the fifteenth century the Dee decided to silt up. The port ran short of water. Consequently fame and fortune washed round to a lowly neighbour that eventually achieved celebrity under the name of Liverpool. Long ago, too, the monks ceased to chant over against the eastern town wall. But their abbey, converted into a cathedral of the new foundation by Henry VIII in 1541, is a perpetual and beautiful reminder of them. There are preserved the emblems of their faith, their times and life—the cloisters where they walked, meditated, and studied; the lavatory at which they washed; a noble refectory for meals below the

LANCASTER, *eighteenth-century and medieval. The Judge's lodgings below the castle built on the site of a Roman station.*

LANCASTER. *The ancient stone-built town on the River Lune is cap*
fortress, of which the great keep remains. The church interior is

…e castle and parish church. John of Gaunt restored the Norman
…urteenth-century stallwork of tracery patterns and foliage carving.

OLD LANCASHIRE COTTON MILL on the River Lune. The valley near this point below the Pennines made the subject for Turner's "Crook of Lune," and Ruskin described the view at Kirby Lonsdale as "one of the loveliest scenes in England—therefore in the world."

reader's rare stone pulpit; the great church of their praise and worship; remains of the fourteenth-century shrine of St. Werburgh that once was so gorgeous (and profitable); and most exquisite of all, the choir stalls and misericords of 1380 where Benedictines continuously performed acts of devotion amidst carved work and canopies, whose glory is hardly matched on earth nor probably in heaven.

In addition to the much-restored cathedral, old churches are well represented by St. Peter's, St. Mary-on-the-Hill, and St. John's. The last-named, probably founded under the Mercian rule, once a cathedral and now partly ruined, is an architectural prize, wonderfully impressive with Norman arcades and transitional upper work. In streets and byways the famed timbered houses and inns display the Cheshire black-and-white in its liveliest showing of contrasts and enrichment. Wide windows of many mullions extend across complete frontages. Elaboration reaches a climax at Bishop Lloyd's early seventeenth-century house in Watergate Street and at the *Bear and Billet*, dated 1664, in Lower Bridge Street, a former town house of the Earls of Shrewsbury. A good sprinkling of houses indicate late seventeenth- and eighteenth-century years. These make prim groups in Abbey Square, Bridge Place, and elsewhere; but their classical features and Georgian suggestiveness are not enhanced by the dull-coloured brickwork common in the north of England.

Of all Chester's weathered and still useful possessions the Rows and the walls are the oddest and most remarkable. No other English town retains a complete line of walled fortifications and nowhere else can be seen anything just like the Rows (208–209). How the Rows came into being nobody can say with certainty. Most likely the medieval builders did the obvious thing to do. Faced with extensive Roman ruins along the main streets, they made shops in front of the debris at street level, erected higher shops actually on the top of the ruins, and the flat roofs of the lower shops gave the walks, or rows, for access to the upper shops. This is certain. The Rows, which are first mentioned in early fourteenth-century records, only occur within the limits of the Roman settlement. Roman remains exist beneath them, Gothic crypts too, and fine old rooms are screened behind dark timbers. These strange ways, medieval leavings much touched up, permit one to look out over balusters to see how the world wags and keep dry when it rains (221). At any time you can walk or sit down on the top of the bits and pieces of centuries and centuries and wonder whether the shadows may shape into phantoms of Elizabethans, Plantagenets, or even Romans! Certainly the Rows of Chester, their curiosities and quantities of old curiosity shops, are unique.

Doubts and theories do not shroud the walls, their origin in Roman times and the subsequent extensions to the river frontage. Almost two thousand years meet at these walls. They have endured through wars, raids, sieges, bombardments, and fruitful times of peace bright with high hope, piety, and endeavour. What an excitement it is to walk round these walls! The footway leads for nearly two miles abreast of stone parapets. It goes by five towers from Thimbleby's to Bonewaldesthorne's, over seven gates, up and down steps, skirts the cathedral and the castle, and gives views of streets and buildings below, the river coursing over the weir to the bridge, and the distant mountains. Here, without twists of imagination, you really may feel like an Elizabethan, a Plantagenet, or a Roman, King Henry on the lookout for who might be coming from Wales, King Charles in the blues while seeing the defeat of his army from the Phœnix Tower in 1645; or you can just waddle along like an ancient duck stuck in the tracks of old time until roused into the day before yesterday at the recent Newgate, finely designed by Sir Walter Tapper.

Remembering all that the fortifications were made for and have been through, they may not be deemed especially economic, useful, or valuable to this age of paper currency. But since the walls were put up in stone they have accommodated all sorts of social and domestic incidents. In the early days no doubt other ranks of the Twentieth Legion chased British damsels round the parapets just as warriors off duty recently did flirting duties there with females. Miss Aldersey eloped down into the arms of her lover in 1573. Hopeful souls have been wishing while running up and down the Wishing Steps since 1785. George Borrow, out to conquer *Wild Wales*, met the ragged beggar, and the black man who lied, said work did not agree with him and "spat with considerable force in the direction of the river." This stonework, after maintaining an equilibrium for centuries and centuries, now keeps quite up to date by serving for pedestrian airings, lovers' meetings, somewhere to go for trippers off chars-à-bancs, and quite remarkably, for planned and unexpected encounters. Time and again I have been hailed and stopped with the exclamation, "Whoever would have thought of seeing you here!" and that is because people of all counties, nations, and languages go to see these unique fortifications of England. Of course all my readers have done so, will do so again; then perhaps—you never can tell—we all may meet, stand, look, admire the views and each other, and finally descend the steps to celebrate the occasion at somewhere or other in the treasured city gathered round the ancient walls of Chester.

5. NORTHWARD BOUND

LANCASHIRE, WEST YORKSHIRE BORDER, WESTMORLAND, CUMBERLAND

The scenery in this chapter's district is notable for mountains, moors, the Lakes, rivers of exceptional loveliness, signs of Border fighting, and England's greatest industrial concentrations. The Limestone heights of the Pennines strike northward to Cumberland; the dales run down into Yorkshire. Over the Lakes rise the peaks and dramatic outlines of the Cumbrian rocks. The Ribble, Lune, Eden, Irthing, and other rivers wind through beautiful valleys; their waters reach the low coastline broken by inlets and the tidal expanses of Morecambe Bay, Duddon Sands, and Solway Firth. Where nature's work predominates the stone-built efforts of man in villages and towns are not of much account, duly insignificant, and therefore appropriate. Elsewhere factories and smoking chimneys in Lancashire and Yorkshire tell their own tales of human enterprise and commercial prosperity. Scant relics of Hadrian's Wall, ancient towers at Skipton, Lancaster, Appleby, Carlisle, Naworth, castles in ruins, and many peel towers recall past strife in this land of ballad and story, the romantic ground in safer and later years for celebrated poets, novelists, and artists.

LANCASHIRE AND PENNINE COUNTRY

The obvious beginning for the next advance is to find or imagine ourselves just beyond the top ends of Cheshire and Derbyshire and prepared to face the best and the worst among a hundred manufactures in the greatest concentrations of industrial activity in England. These spread over south Lancashire and the West Riding of Yorkshire in the big and hilly area resembling a roughly-shaped parallelogram, with Runcorn and Sheffield, Leeds and Preston to mark the corners, and containing the emporium for cotton at Manchester, the centre for wool at Bradford, the home of steel at Sheffield. Just beyond this figure stands the great port of Liverpool, wonderfully placed at the end of the Mersey and facing the sea, a gateway to far countries and continents. Everybody knows of the English history made during the past century or two in this populous and busy region, and how the inhabitants set examples to the world in skilled manufacture, commercial enterprise, and speculation while they contributed to the country's material power, prosperity, wealth, and drabness. Things they thought of and did on certain days were only discovered by people elsewhere on the days following or some time afterwards, and qualities of foresight and shrewdness, highly developed locally and helped by nature's copious supplies of moist climate, soft water and bracing air, no doubt spurred onward John Kay, Hargreaves, Samuel Crompton, Arkwright, James Nasmyth, Benjamin Huntsman and a host of inventors, innovators, and astute men of business in the efforts and contributions they made to the evolution of England's commercial supremacy. The merchants of Manchester who began to run their own "Flying Coach" regularly to London as early as 1754 in order to take Time by the forelock, and the first main railway line in the country engineered by George Stephenson for much the same purpose from Liverpool to Manchester 76 years later, are but two instances of many schemes initiated for beating the clock, getting things done, and flowing on the tide that Shakespeare said leads to fortune in the affairs of men. Sightseers to-day in Warrington, Wigan, and Accrington, Huddersfield, Barnsley, Pudsey, and the crowded towns linked together for miles find ample evidence of the old progressive spirit furbished up and continuing in operation. It is still possible to learn and to realize that "You must wake up very early in the morning to get the better of a Lancastrian and to get the better of a Yorkshireman means not going to bed at all"—compliments recently told to me on the spot and which I understand are called chestnuts and also thought to be true.

If this book were in praise of commercial cities and districts, and of monuments to man's miracles in manufacture and production, I might say a good deal at this halt in our progress on the north side of the Mersey. But these present pages make no such claim; in that direction I consider my bit already

PENISTONE. *Kirkwood farmhouse with walls and roofs of local stone.
It stands between Sheffield and Huddersfield where high lands lead to the
moors and mountains of South Yorkshire.*

BOLTON ABBEY IN WHARFEDALE. *A lovely combination of ruins and parish church adjacent to the seat of the Dukes of Devonshire. Built in a setting of exceptional beauty, this priory of Austin Canons formed one in the chain of great monasteries notably developed in Yorkshire. It continued at this site from 1154 until the Dissolution in 1539.*

has been done with my sampling of the Black Country, Birmingham, the Industrial Revolution, and a matter of England's artistic heritage going bankrupt after Adam Smith made himself heard from Scotland. The well-known particulars, the towns, and the points of geography mentioned in the previous paragraph are given only because they relate to topography and caused re-arrangements in scenery. The area we now face offers curious contrasts for observation in the thickly populated spaces and strips of country sandwiched in between drab concentrations and smoke. Effects are varied, often unusual, sometimes impressive, yet the ground in general is not the kind that Thomas Cook would have selected for shepherding his tourists. But this cradle of industrial supremacy presents matter for meditation to inquisitive minds, and certainly has improved since Walpole considered Sheffield one of the foulest towns in a most charming situation, Blake sang of "dark satanic mills," the old saying announced, "From Hell, Hull, and Halifax, Good Lord, deliver us!", and the factory and chimney-stack system of progress proved that acceleration did not always achieve advance forward or enhance landscapes.

Writers on the English scene usually have not showered large bouquets of praise hereabout. Artists however, particularly recent ones, have found subject-matter awaiting to glorify, justify, apologize for, or present as it is the age of rationalism and scientific determination in which humanity latterly has struggled. From the back ages, too, relics have survived in the hurly-burly of making things new; they remain, grimy perhaps and strangely neighboured, yet mellow with suggestiveness of Middle Aged mysticism and of times that flourished before machinery conquered. Old houses stand, left over from the handicraft years. Hall i' th' Wood is one of them (227), a sixteenth-century home of the Brownlow family, once surrounded by great trees and facing woods as its name implies, and now facing Bolton. Inside this house, hand-made with oak framing, staircase, and carved fireplaces, it is curious to recall that Samuel Crompton lived frugal days and laborious nights in making and perfecting the "Hall i' th' Wood machine" for spinning, an innovation which hastened the change from handwork to mechanical production, brought great prosperity to the neighbourhood and England, and bestowed on the inventor little more than misfortune and poverty. This hall is but one of the examples conspicuous for timber construction and black-and-white patterns, a style of building formerly as prevalent in south Lancashire as in Cheshire. Led by Speke Hall near Liverpool, the most famous specimen completed in 1598, the timbered buildings in towns and their borderlands exist in greater numbers than is generally supposed and give Elizabethan flavours in directions where least expected. They are numerous, for instance, at and round Manchester, not infrequently hemmed in by mean surroundings. There the series includes Ordsall Hall with features of exceptional interest, and Clayton Hall, a home of

Humphrey Chetham who is ever remembered for the gracious medieval and cloistered Hospital that bears his name.

Other houses and halls show the northern type of masonry generally dating from the sixteenth and seventeenth centuries, the stone walls and heavy roofs, the low-pitched gables, the windows of many mullions. As might be expected, these are plentifully distributed in the Yorkshire section and particularly between Bradford, Wakefield, and Halifax, as at Hagstocks in Shibden Dale and Oakwell Hall, Birstall, built in 1583 and pictured by Charlotte Brontë in *Shirley*. Towns, too, preserve and care for their heirlooms—Bolling and Horton Halls at Bradford, Shibden Hall, Halifax, a splendid and historic Temple Newsam at Leeds, and more inheritances from the old families. Turton (228) introduces the peel tower, the form of defence peculiar to the northern counties and devised for the protection of hearth, home, and possessions when marauders from over the Border were almost as numerous as present-day raiders for taxes and spoliation of country. Solid and squat, Turton Tower stands near the Roman highway that led to Manchester from the great fortress now buried beneath Ribchester (227), a route used for centuries by plunderers in their descents on the Ribble valley and the fertile lands of south Lancashire. The massive tower, probably of early fifteenth-century date, with Elizabethan additions of timber and stone, came into the possession of Humphrey Chetham, the rich merchant, money-changer, and benefactor of Manchester.

Here and there old mills, in service or ruined, link with the early spinning and weaving; they modestly contrast with their successors, the giants of many windows, gaunt façades, and high chimneys. One of the older sort, though outside this big industrial area, is illustrated on page 236 to show the traditional stone architecture that served both for domestic and industrial buildings and made factories more pleasant to look at than those which followed in the nine-teenth century, some of the most deplorable objects ever produced by man. More ancient and nobler buildings, the churches, are obvious in various directions, as at Wakefield, Bradford, Halifax, Rochdale, and the fine fifteenth-century work at Manchester (now the cathedral) splendidly adorned with interior woodwork. These represented the good old custom of mixing religion with business. Medieval masters and men of the crafts combined pious observ-ance with daily labour, helped to make and support the Gothic churches inside which they went pretty often—for weavers already were settled in Wakefield in Conquest years, at Bolton in the twelfth century, and the workers in Man-chester had fame for cloth as early as the thirteenth century and for cottons and woollens in the sixteenth. Wakefield became famous for its remarkable miracle plays. Once, far away at Wilburton near Ely, I immediately thought of Brad-ford on discovering an ancient fresco depicting St. Blaise. This bishop of Sebaste in Asia Minor appears to have lost his head after being torn with iron combs by Roman persecutors more than sixteen hundred years ago, and then passed on to become the patron saint of the wool-combers. In Yorkshire, and particularly in Leeds and Bradford, he was highly venerated and his festivals, splendid occasions celebrated with joy and pageantry, included the pretty eulogy beginning with the lines,

> Hail to the day whose kind, auspicious rays
> Deigned first to smile on famous Bishop Blaise.

In fact, more numerous than is generally appreciated are the varieties of historical association, scene, beauty amongst ugliness, and stimulating experiences offered in this kingdom of industrialism, one strangely unfamiliar to most English people because they seldom explore there. Here are natural and man-made effects for enjoyment, praise or blame, instances of tremendous gains and tremendous losses, the pointers in the country's story common throughout England and which make the miles everywhere vivid with matter to see and something to think about. These afford memories. Out of past experiences I think of the pattern and character of Liverpool from sketching the shipping, banks, busy streets, the impressive Mersey frontage viewed across the water, the interior and tower of the Mersey Tunnel; from watching the animated life on land and water at the Landing Stage, seeing the great ships pass by and the sun setting in splendour at Waterloo where Turner looked out, dreamed and painted; from exhibiting at the Walker Art Gallery, and by recollections of two cathedrals in the making, to give to the city and posterity the great conceptions of Sir Giles Gilbert Scott and Sir Edwin Lutyens. Of Manchester, superior for gloom and damp, I recall depicting the array of begrimed chapels, the late-medieval carving on beautiful stalls and the parclose screens at the cathedral, and also on one occasion sketching towels, pillow cases, pants and their feminine equivalents, and almost the complete range comprised in the term, "Manchester goods." This collection of objects, with recent art represented by the notable design of the Central Library by Vincent Harris, the Anning Bell window inside it, the Ford Maddox Brown frescoes in the town hall, and literature's pages suggested by Mrs. Gaskell's associations with the old Cross Street Chapel and De Quincey running away from the school, seemed to me to express the purpose and the soul of the ancient and the great modern city. While engaged with the mundane articles above mentioned a shining light in the cotton constellation invited me to the Reform Club, a name that made me wonder if Peterloo and politics were much in my line.

"Is this really the holy of holies," I asked on arrival, "Free Trade, John Bright, and all that?"

"Yes, this is the spot," was the curt reply. "Come and have some lunch."

We sat down at one of the long tables lined with men eating hot stew to which they had applied cold pickled red cabbage. The combination, then new to me, suggested pains inside the human apparatus. Bravely I joined in, consumed the hot and cold mixture; to do so evidently was *comme il faut* in Manchester. Immediate impressions were good, after-effects harmless. "Thus is accumulated intimate knowledge of great peoples" I muttered as I sauntered across Piccadilly to my quarters at the *Queen's* hotel. Bolton, where my early morning slumbers were sadly rattled by the clatter of clogs on the stone pavings, gave me memories of Hall i' th' Wood here illustrated, Darcy Lever Hall going to ruin, and the black-and-white *Olde Man and Scythe* inn from which James Stanley, the Royalist Earl of Derby, went to his doom after being captured at the battle of Worcester in 1651. Chorley, not quite the place for summer holidays, presents its industrial character unashamed; but I found Astley Hall in the town's possession, weathered, lovely, containing the Elizabethan long gallery 72 feet in length, and the Astley bed of about 1590, enormous, a very king of beds, wonderfully carved and inlaid, the most remarkable specimen of its period in existence and fully justifying a pilgrimage. In all directions are the concentrations of mills, factories, and chimneys, grime, gloom and vapours, unlimited in supplies for those who like to seek the emblems of work and power that truly express the spirit and functions of the locality. Yet on these I have seen the veil of romance and poetry descend where little of either might be expected; remembered by massive purposeful compositions and gaunt shapes swathed in mist, entrancing evening light shimmering on wind-swept smoke and making drabness glow, and once, at Sowerby Bridge near Halifax, brazen beauty shining from woollen-mill windows lit up at night and defying the darkness.

The hills, always near, offer compensation enough for anything. Sweeping northward from the Peak, the Pennine heights divide industrial Lancashire from industrial Yorkshire. They send out moorland masses west and east, the wide and airy open spaces handy for those whose lives are cast amidst "the busie humm of men" (and machines) in the towns thickly planted on the lower slopes and along the valleys. The town workers certainly have good cause for thanks to God and nature for these high places of wild beauty so little distant from dingy streets and ugliness, large expanses as yet unspoiled, nor very likely to be knocked down or removed at present to satisfy the money-getting propensities of man. Within a few miles of the smoke of Bolton, Horwich, and Chorley anyone can be on Smithills Moor mounted at nearly 1,500 feet, on Rivington Pike commanding land and sea and where the beacon flamed in the Armada year. It's an easy and quick change from the unloveliness of Bacup, Accrington, and Burnley to the solitudes of Rossendale and over the hills and far away into Yorkshire. You can be high up among the mills of Queensbury, look over miles and miles of moors, choose any direction for exploration without fear of being much disturbed by human beings, and wander over the lonely

KEX GILL GORGE *between Blubberhouses Moor and Brandreth Crags.*

BUTTERTUBS PASS *from Wensleydale to Swaledale.*

CARTMEL. *A quiet and ancient town with this early fourteenth-century gateway and an exceptional church, remains of the priory of Austin Canons founded about 1189.*

DENT. *The narrow street high placed in Dentdale below the Yorkshire fells and Whernside. Made of stone throughout for walls, roofs, and street paving.*

spaces of Oxenhope and Haworth Moors to scenes of the Brontë drama, to Ponden and actual places pictured in *Wuthering Heights* and *Jane Eyre*. In no time I have been away from Sheffield, past Wharncliffe Crags, up the hill at Penistone to sketch the characteristic stonework of Kirkwood farmhouse (241), and on again through the stone-walled fields and the commons, where I met a farmer one day, stockily built and tanned, who told me that on these highlands not many really hot days are known, even in the best of summers—a chilly prospect for southerners, like Maria Brontë, born in more genial climates. Also there are the lookouts from the hills to the towns below, sometimes tuned in symphonies of smoke and sunshine, sometimes bright with industry's myriads of lights when night falls. Once, when going from Pendle Hill to the Ribble valley I spied Preston in the distance, a forest of chimneys all a-smoking and weaving changes and changes of pattern upward towards the azure, a sight wonderful enough to make a body think that after all a good deal might be said for industry's romantic moods in Lancashire.

Pendle Hill and the course of the Ribble below it, Keighley Moor above Airedale, and Rumbles Moor with the River Wharfe winding along the valley to Otley, indicate main lines of demarcation to divide landscape spoliations from scenery left much as nature intended it to be and wide acres improved by sons of the soil under clear and broad skies—that is to say, at this page we can forget all about industrialism and change over to works productive of less cash and higher standards in the real art of life, graciously presented beyond the barrier lines mentioned above in the forms of villages and country towns, farms and fields, dales and river valleys, rugged or wooded heights, untrodden ways over great silent moors, the infinite promise offered by England's best and highest mountains. These are just the places in which it is glorious to be alive, to look well around, do nothing in particular and, perched more than 2,000 feet towards heaven on Great Whernside or Ingleborough, say to hell with all politicians down at a few feet above sea-level in Westminster dictating welfare for everybody with very low standards of earthy living. It is amazing how brave and elevated you can feel, how satisfied with the world deficient in human planning when on the top of a really good mountain!

The Yorkshire Pennines can elevate our bodies and souls in remote and likely places for the purpose. They offer height and space very suitable for people fit in the legs, good with Ordnance one-inch maps, who are fond of seeing nobody about, and like unlimited draughts of bracing air coolish in temperature, for local upland dwellers have been reported to say the climate is wintry for three parts of the year and bad for the remainder—a weather depression I have found to be rather wide of the truth. Untrammelled by industry's encumbrances, this section of England's backbone is able to show off the real character and typical beauty of mountain limestone scenery, the spreading foothills, the long backs of moorlands, swelling upward curves, the outcrops and crags. The masses northward from Simon Seat, Burnsall Fell, Malham Lings and Gordale Scar, are punctuated by Great Whernside (2,245 feet), Ingleborough (2,373 feet), Whernside (2,414 feet), Baugh Fell (2,216 feet), Lovely Seat (2,213 feet), Great Shunner Fell (2,340 feet); the succession of fells, moors, and ridges mount up through Langstrothdale Chase, Abbotside, Angram and Birkdale Commons, and moors continuing to moors lead to Lune Forest and Mickle Fell (2,591 feet) at the top of Yorkshire's North Riding, a wild and solitary region that gave me the impression no human being was in residence for miles in this highest part of the county. In all these directions are the routes and no routes for discovering points and high places too good for words but true and good for the finding. They bring the feeling of being on the top of the grand world, of leaving that other spot of time and trouble far down on earth or in the bowels thereof while you see the unending panoramas, peak repeating peak, steep declivities leading to floors of valleys, the colours changing in brilliance and depth as clouds march along between the sun and mountain tops to variegate the lights and the shadows. There are the anticipated vistas you never find, those over the next hill, on the far side of that distant crag, always in the just-beyond, like the hidden treasures in the fairy tales. Here man and his works are duly insignificant; few, if any, stone buildings usually are visible among these big creations of the Master Architect.

From bleak sources—Ure Head at 2,186 feet on Lunds Fell is one good example—the becks and streams run down, growing from small beginnings to be the rivers sweeping along and ending in the River Ouse on the Plain of York. Flowing clear and fast, tumbling over rapids and waterfalls (as at Aysgarth), tuning waters' own songs against rocks, they hasten through the dales, the Yorkshire Dales loved by the dalesmen, adored by all Yorkshire folk and knowing people in every English county. Arkengarthdale, Swaledale, Wensleydate, Nidderdale, Wharfedale, and Airedale open out below the stretches of moor and fell set like the fingers of nature's hand extended from the great arm of the Pennines. Between the dales and connecting one to the other run the passes, gorges, and lesser dales, often prolific in bumps, steep gradients, twists and turns, "Paradise enow" for walkers strong on their feet but liable to be the very devil for adventurers mounted on internal-combustion engines. Typical specimens are Coverdale and Bishopdale between Wharfedale and Wensleydale; Garsdale directing west from Wensleydale below Baugh Fell to the remote market town and famous school of Sedbergh; West Stonesdale mounting to Tan Hill, to panoramas for making anybody speechless and breathless, and an inn for solace on the spot at 1,732 feet up; Stake Pass for a stiff method of progress from Buckden to Bainbridge. One way of going from Hawes and the upper reaches of the River Ure to Muker far up Swaledale is by the Buttertubs

tubs Pass (247), peculiar for limestone formations that give the pass its name; great distances show impressively, and if the route may seem forbidding and desolate in parts a certain grandeur is always piled below the upstanding peaks of Lovely Seat and Great Shunner Fell. More frequented is the way past the reservoirs, the trees, the stone farms at Blubberhouses and through Kex Gill Gorge (247). It leads to the glorious scenes of Wharfedale, and on again to Skipton commanding Airedale from its stronghold, still a great castle of massive walls, towers, fine gatehouse and Tudor buildings, a lurking-place in the good old Edwardian days for Robert Clifford who specialized in fighting the Scots and finally came to grief in the rout at Bannockburn.

Of its kind the dale scenery can give and does yield almost everything in landscape compositions and patterns schemed in nature's many moods, austere, grim, noble, buoyant, and smiling. A sombre dignity belongs to the wild places hemmed in by moors and mountains, such as you find in the upper fastnesses of Arkengarthdale, Swaledale, and Wensleydale above Langthwaite, Keld, and Hawes. Lower down the valleys open out wider, meet the slopes marked out with the stone byres and walls of fields. Variety is plentiful and well distributed. There are the cascades and waterfalls, dappled surfaces of streams running fast, ravines, wooded hollows, and distant green hills, the "rocks and crags" that Wordsworth saw, the "View of the Wharfe" painted by Girtin, the originals of dozens of subjects pictured by scores of artists. Churches, houses, and cottages harmoniously built of the native stone group in little grey towns and chains of riverside villages. Here and there particular features stand out—Grinton church, the earthworks of Maiden Castle, and Marrick priory ruins in Swaledale, the Scropes' gaunt fortress-mansion of Castle Bolton in which Mary Queen of Scots was a prisoner in Wensleydale, thick walls of the Nevilles' great stronghold and twelfth-century keep at Middleham, the old ruined church at Pateley Bridge in command of wonderful views over Nidderdale; and if it be possible to make the choice, I think best of all is Wharfedale with its wealth of natural and man-made beauty gathered at Bolton Bridge and Abbey (242), Barden Tower, Burnsall (11), Threshfield, Conistone with its bridge crossing to Kilnsey and Kilnsey Crag, and Kettlewell and Buckden crouched below the big shapes of Great Whernside, Buckden Pike, and the fells.

The Pennines face west towards Lancashire. Dominated by the long backs of Ingleborough and Whernside and cut by Dentdale, Kingsdale, and Ribblesdale, it is a part of the world full of good things. The steep heights, the streams and waterfalls, and all the features I have mentioned show the mountain scenery at its best. Typical stone villages and hamlets continue in a line from Dent (248) in its own dale to Thornton-in-Lonsdale, Ingleton, Newby, Clapham, Giggleswick, and Malham. Two in the number of family manorial homes are the Paleys' sixteenth-century hall at Langcliffe, and the Ingleby's seventeenth-

CLAPDALE
nr Ingleborough

century stone gables, mullions, and tower of Lawkland Hall. Others of the kind, and the farmhouses with rough stone or whitened walls and heavy roofs face wind and weather high up on the slopes.

The Pennines project the outlying moors and fells centred round Bowland Forest and spreading into Lancashire. The Ribble, down from the mountains, meets its lower borderlands. The lovely vale gradually widens. It gains in colour from woods, cultivated fields, parks, the lines of trees, and extends onward in broad green stretches between Harrop Fell and Pendle Hill, pointing for Whalley's splendid church and ruined abbey, and the horseshoe bend of the stream where Roman cavalry crossed the ford at Ribchester. Villages hereabout show prettily on and above the river, notably at East and West Marton, at Bolton-by-Bowland's cross on the green, Gisburn's street of stone houses, at a very attractive Downham. A picturesque landmark is made in the hilly town of Clitheroe with the castle on the rock, a battered ruin of de Lacy's Norman keep that fell to the Roundheads after their victory at Marston Moor.

One way out of Yorkshire into Lancashire is across the packhorse bridge over the River Hodder, a link between the two counties from Mitton Green to Stonyhurst College. Very graceful is the span of this bridge. It has a high central arch, smaller ones at each side, and gives a track of six feet wide as I measured it. A road bridge alongside serves for to-day now that packhorses are defunct. The country round is nicely wooded and charmingly watered by the Hodder and the Ribble flowing to and past their meeting-place. Stone buildings peep out from the greenery, seen at a restored Little Mitton Hall, New Hall of 1665, the tower and gables of Dutton Hall, and more old manor-houses and farms. Further north another and wilder connection between county and county

252

mounts from the River Hodder at Dunsop Bridge through the Trough of Bowland, lonely and impressive, between steep declivities of moors and marked in the defile at the top with the county boundary-stone. But whichever way you enter north Lancashire from the Pennine fells, ahead lies the plain, physically and geologically an extension of the Cheshire flats continued to Fleetwood and the Lune estuary. My notes made there indicate wide landscapes generally lying low at 15 to 50 feet above sea-level; open grass country with sheep, many streams, windmills in the Fylde, copses and orchards, a sprinkling of parks, grey stone villages; Greenalgh castle in ruins near Garstang, first built in 1490 by the Stanley who crowned King Henry on Bosworth Field; a quaint market-place at Poulton-le-Fylde; and for a coastal ending, miles of sands, parades, hotels, lodging-houses, peppermint rock and—Blackpool's Tower, democracy's monument made of 2,500 tons of steel and iron!

All roads next lead to Lancaster—and also to Morecambe for those in quest of proletarian Venuses who compete as bathing beauties on dry land for silver rose bowls and free holidays. My space is running too short for praise of feminine legs and accessories observed while celebrated connoisseurs judged them in the ozone of Morecambe, but Lancaster on the Lune, by contrast meekly attractive, ancient, and meriting pages, cannot be denied a word or two. This county capital stands well on its hills and in the valley between them. Castle, church, and town group picturesquely on one eminence above the river (234–235); the other height with the Ashton Memorial on it is a wonderful viewpoint for panoramas of walls, roofs, chimney-pots, churches, two town halls, shops, houses, and streets spread out and leading to open country in a manner right and typical for an English centre that thrives on agriculture, making things, and is pleasant to live in. Of course it is historic. Being so, you naturally think of John of Gaunt in winding up the steep cobbled ways to Castle Hill. But the great stronghold, first a Roman *castrum*, then a big Norman keep with walls ten feet thick to defy Scottish raiders, and later restored and enlarged by "time-honour'd Lancaster," has been so hemmed in with conveniences for lawyers, criminals, festivities, and modern uses that it disappoints for a reminder of Edward III's son, a figure so large on history's pages. For survivals of the gatehouse, keep, towers, and particularly the cells and dungeons we may be thankful and at the same time ungrateful at not finding more. The neighbouring church with the eighteenth-century tower has fared better. It shows the Perpendicular nave and choir, and the stallwork prodigal in tracery patterns, foliage carving, canopies, pinnacles and enriched misericords, the sumptuous finery of fourteenth-century carpentry. The town, coloured cool grey with stonework built in the solid northern style, also offered me the Judge's Lodging for a picture (233), the eighteenth-century quality of Queen Anne and Georgian houses round the castle and in the streets, comfort, food and sleep at a rejuvenated *Royal King's Arms*, and a shop's sign of "Clog Repairs" to denote a local fashion. Perhaps most exciting were my discoveries of numerous yards and narrow ways lined with houses and reached through small covered entrances from main streets. These reminders of the good old days, locally called "passages" or "ginnels," served to preserve human pates and household goods when marauders from the north paid frequent visits in search of booty. Inhabitants inside a ginnel could, and did, guard and hold the narrow entrance to keep invaders out. The example illustrated on page 259 was sketched in the Market Square at the side of the *Blue Anchor* inn. Similar defensive arrangements for domestic life are obvious in Penrith, Carlisle, and elsewhere. They influenced the planning of northern towns during the sixteenth and seventeenth centuries.

North of Lancaster more signs of turbulent years are given by the towered halls, usually built round a defensive peel tower as seen at Claughton Old Hall, Borwick Hall, and Thurland Castle, originally erected in the fourteenth century and mentioned in the old ballad of "Flodden Field" (228). These stand in the neighbourhood of the Lune, the lovely river in the loveliest of valleys, pictured by Turner and praised by Ruskin. The stream ripples over weirs and shallows, flows silently through deeper pools. Sweeping along in noble bends past Tunstall (Lowood in *Jane Eyre*) and Arkholme, it traces the Crook of Lune at Caton (Turner's subject), turns a V of rare beauty between wooded banks below Halton Green, and winds round the old cotton mill (236). Rocks here, rushy banks there, line the riversides in the sylvan vale stretching away to meet the moorland hills and Pennine mountains. Churches, houses and cottages in stone-built villages—Halton, Nether and Over Kellet are three—show prettily in the valley and among bumpy hills leading towards the coast. High places above flats and the shore yield shining visions; you look over miles of golden sands gleaming in Morecambe Bay, charming estuary scenery, the distant peaks beyond Coniston Water bounding the curiously detached piece of Lancashire that promises the sights of Cartmel priory church and gatehouse (248), Duddon Sands, and the great scene at Furness Abbey.

TO THE ROMAN WALL

Pennine and Lakeland mountains, England's biggest; valleys and rivers between them, very lovely; the undulating plain around Carlisle, green and pastoral; a seaward boundary of low coast—these mainly determine the landscapes in this final peregrination through Westmorland and Cumberland. The mountain masses predominate. Man, compared with them, appears small even when six feet odd in stature. Thus it is not surprising to find that his works are not very conspicuous or notable over wide areas; earlier dwellers, short of wireless, machinery, and other devices for bridging space and removing mountains, no doubt felt an inferiority complex in living amongst surroundings so much more elevated than themselves. For centuries the region was isolated, sparsely populated with a rude and self-contained civilization. Natives followed traditional methods of primitive agriculture and building, made homespun in spinning galleries from the wool of their sheep, spent a good deal of time in rows, scraps with marauders, bull-baiting, and cock-fighting (the bishops of Carlisle even had their own cockpit at Rose Castle). The few towns where industry managed to thrive supported weavers and other workers, tradesmen, merchants. Shakespeare must have known of this in 1597 when he clothed "three misbegotten knaves in Kendal green", and records prove the existence of Hamburg merchants in Carlisle to establish woollen manufacture soon after the Young Pretender's rebellion. In due course industry expanded at both these towns, along the coast with shipping, coal and iron, and lead-mining prospered around Alston. Walter Scott met Charlotte Carpenter at Gilsland, married her in Carlisle Cathedral; consequently, instead of emigrating to Jamaica he immortalized local scenes and characters in literature. Poets arrived in Lakeland, did just the same for daffodils, shepherd boys, Kirkstone Pass, Dungeon Ghyll, and other handy objects. Old Crome painted *Brathay Bridge*, Turner produced *Morning on Coniston Fells*, both for the National Gallery. The intelligentsia followed the poets, led the processions of tourists, coaches, and cars that ever since have headed for the same direction.

Through all the changes of Time the peaks, the fells, and the moors stood unmoved, consequential and supreme. They yet rule their dominion and are likely to go on doing so unless something very dreadful happens. They remain superior in authority, influence, and pictorial motive, the district's inspiration for poets, artists, novelists, and all mankind who scan the heights from far and near, scramble over them, crawl to the tops, and on lofty points learn nature's secrets and see visions from "the everlasting hills." Scafell, Skiddaw, Helvellyn, grand shapes of Saddleback and Langdale Pikes, sharp peaks and bold outlines command the dales and watery expanses of the Lake District. The one impression I give on page 258 might be amplified by a hundred variations of the mountains and lakes, passes and tarns. But this compact and popular area needs no further pictures or words from me to explain its features or enhance its great reputation; and a visit to the rebuilt Elizabethan *Oak* inn at Keswick (now the *Royal Oak*) serves to introduce names of the celebrated Lakeland forerunners who gathered there—the Wordsworths, Sir Walter Scott, Southey, Samuel and Hartley Coleridge, Shelley, de Quincey, Tennyson, R. L. Stevenson, and John Peel. The great Pennine fells, wild, lonely, and capped by Cross Fell, face the Lakeland peaks and continue northward. The ancient Maiden Way, leading from Lancashire to Bewcastle Cross and the Border, skirts Alston, England's highest

KILLHOPE PASS

market town (12). Eastward a road directs through Killhope Pass, also England's highest. Running fast from the mountains innumerable streams grow into rivers, the Lune, Eden, and Irthing, the Kent down from Kentmere, the Duddon, Derwent, and the streams of Lakeland—names which mean that Westmorland and Cumberland river scenery is rarely equalled and nowhere excelled in England.

The vernacular buildings in town and country modestly garnished their natural settings until England developed the bad mania for industrial expansion (dreary results thereof are visible in the southward approach to Carlisle) and Victorians left examples of their handiwork now fit to make beholders weep or shudder (painfully obvious in Windermere, Keswick, and other spoilt places). In this hilly, dale and vale district the old cottages, farms, churches, town quarters, and houses were sturdily made of the native stone, built straightforwardly, and without many fanciful or pretty bits added for the northern wet, blasts, and snows to weather off, the climate being an important influence in dictating appearance and style. Effects generally have a strong, plain, and serviceable look, and the homes of the statesmen and dalesmen particularly show a rugged quality in exact harmony with their surroundings. Original elements in this make-up of grey stone or whitewashed walls and slated roofs are retained in towns and villages by the score. Characteristic are Melmerby below its Pennine fell, little Whitbeck crouched facing the giant mass of Black Combe, and Troutbeck (257), with its cottages and statesmen's houses standing at the entrances to Kirkstone Pass and the Roman mountain road above Patterdale and Ullswater, in my choosing the most interesting of the Lakeland villages. Dalston, the home of the fighting cocks on the Caldew, and Temple Sowerby, once a home of the Knights Templars on the Eden, stand for two good samples of the valley villages beautifully settled along the rivers. Three other pleasant

·TROUTBECK. *One of the most characteristic stone villages in Lakeland, on the road from Kirkstone Pass.*

BOLTON-LE-SANDS. *Farmhouse, dated 1687, facing Morecambe Bay and distant Lakeland mountains.*

KESWICK, DERWENTWATER AND BORROWDALE. *Nature's architecture seen from the lower slopes of Skiddaw.*

PENRITH. One of the "yards" with houses. LANCASTER. Passage or "ginnel" at the Blue Anchor inn, formerly lined with houses. These characteristic features of the north country, reached from main streets only through narrow openings, were schemed for defence against marauders. Many of them date from the sixteenth century.

CARLISLE *keep and cathedral in the "Red City" of Border strife and ballad. The*
in 1745. Fire and war destroyed much of the cathedral and monastic buildings b

e a prison for Mary Queen of Scots and was captured by Bonnie Prince Charlie
eval choir remains with a masterpiece of Decorated tracery in the great east window.

YANWORTH, *built in the fourteenth century and subsequently altered. One of the defensive peel-towers peculiar to the counties where raids from over the Border constantly happened. It has very thick walls and look-out turrets at the top.*

CARLISLE. *Green Market and St. Alban's Row at the junction of English Street and Scotch Street. The Guildhall, dating from the fourteenth century, is on the left and at the right is the pretty Town Hall, built in 1673.*

BIRDOSWALD. *Wreckage of a lost empire. Relics of the fort at Ambloganna, the largest station on the Roman Wall. Here the track led Roman soldiers north to Bewcastle Fells and Scotland, and the Ninth Legion never came back.*

BROUGHAM CASTLE in *Westmorland. The gatehouse (c.1270) and the keep (c.1170) of the home of the Cliffords standing between the Pennine Range and the Lakeland mountains. A romantic story of Henry, the Shepherd Lord Clifford, inspired Wordsworth's poem, "Song at the Feast of Brougham Castle."*

and noteworthy places that I liked near Penrith are Greystoke with a collegiate church, Askham embowered in greenery, and Lowther, very remarkable for its classic air, Georgian formality, and a glorious backing of the lordly park. Market squares, High Streets and byways of the towns have dignified seventeenth- and eighteenth-century houses of a local quality. Poking about, I have discovered them in Kirkby Lonsdale, Kirkby Stephen, Appleby, Penrith, Carlisle, and at Wordsworth's birthplace, Cockermouth, a sedate and balanced frontage behind the forecourt wall and pillored gateway.

In this borderland of feuds and fighting, ballad, song, and story perhaps the most exciting days and moments quickly fly in tracking reminders of man's innate desire to break the Tenth Commandment. Here, there and everywhere stand the visible signs—town lanes and back yards, castles, peel towers, ruins, some romantically poised, others draughty or looking grim, and all of them at any time liable to make one recall a line or two from Scott,

> The frightened flocks and herds were pent
> Beneath the peel's rude battlement,

or another one by Canon Rawnsley,

> Here they heard the battle cry—when the Picts and Scots swept by.

Thrilling hours have I spent in finding these relics of strife at Lammerside and Pendragon high in the Pennines, at Kentmere and Sizergh near Kendal, at Yanworth (262), Brougham (263), Penrith castle and town yards (259), Norman keeps at Appleby and Brough, Naworth most impressive and beautifully situated, and north of the Roman Wall at Triermain, Askerton, Shank, and Bewcastle. Dozens more are there for the seeking, with stones erect or tumbled down to inspire new volumes of Border ballads.

Carlisle castle (260–261) brings the story of Border fighting to the "Red City" on the red sandstone of the fertile plain, historic ground trodden by successive invaders and where Romans settled behind Hadrian's Wall that stretched from the Solway to the Tyne. Alternatively held by the English and the Scots, besieged, burnt, successfully defended, and captured more times than anybody can count, you may stand in the city to-day by the pretty town hall, admire its dainty features of 1673 painted cream and green (262), look north along Scotch Street and south down English Street without noticing any bloodthirsty marauders or moss troopers on the rampage or even dogs fighting. With so many commotions going on in the old days the cathedral was not likely to remain unharmed for long periods. After being put up by the Normans, knocked down, and put up again in bits at various times it has emerged from the past like a fighting cock shorn of its tail, or nave, but complete in headpiece, or choir, adorned with a supreme east window, a most brilliant example of Decorated tracery. Names and initials roughly cut on the fifteenth-century choir stalls show that church made a prison for Jacobite captives in 1745; reading "Richard Spenglay" and "William Monk" on the woodwork may cause one to wonder if the poor devils met their doom on Gallows Hill and left wives and children sorrowing far away in Scotland.

Thoughts and excitements about the Roman Wall naturally come uppermost in Carlisle. These can be satisfied best by visiting the splendid Roman collection excellently displayed in Tullie House, a notable building of the seventeenth century with fine spout-heads dated 1689. Out in the open air this wall can be a disappointment for those who expect to see forts, mile-castles, turrets, and ramparts bristling all over the landscapes; owing to trouble with labour, materials, and perhaps trade unionists, the Romans could only erect their fortification with turf from the Solway to the River Irthing and confined the impressive stonework to Northumberland. After miles of tramping I did find Roman stone mixed with the beautiful masonry at Lanercost Priory, at farmhouses, in the chancel arch at Denton church, and stones to draw at Birdoswald (264), the place of *Amboglanna*, the largest of the forts dramatically situated above lovely wooded banks of the Irthing. Northward from there ran the track which led Romans to Scotland. It passed their isolated fort at Bewcastle, now to be traced near the ruined castle built of Roman stones, and the Bewcastle Cross of the eighth century, one of England's great art treasures. Early in the second century the men of the Ninth Legion went that way, vanished mysteriously; probably annihilated in battle over the Border, they faded from history. But while I sought these signs of distant times, pondered, and sketched here and there, the weather was mixed, wet and fine. The wind blew down from Bewcastle Fells. The Nine Nicks of Thirlwall frowned ominously in Northumberland. Clouds lowered and threatened over the loneliness. I began to realize why Roman soldiers considered it a kind of purgatory to do duties on the Wall, decided to hasten from it myself before being drenched or blown away. Soon I reached Carlisle. While looking at the perfect east window of the cathedral from outside, a man wearing a bowler hat and a blue suit (which may have concealed a gun) advanced from the iron gateway alongside and said,

"Ya canna get in. It's locked oop."

I fled, fearing that the ghosts of Kinmont Willie, Bold Buccleuch, and William of Cloudsley might rise up and grab me, sought refuge in the nearest peel tower, named the *Crown and Mitre*, fortified my spirits with grilled salmon (perhaps poached), roast duck (possibly decoyed), and something else (maybe smuggled), and thus completed my own raids on *England West*.

LIST OF ILLUSTRATIONS

INDEX